Lecture Notes of the Institute
for Computer Sciences, Social Informatics
and Telecommunications Engineering   **649**

The LNICST series publishes ICST's conferences, symposia and workshops.

LNICST reports state-of-the-art results in areas related to the scope of the Institute. The type of material published includes

- Proceedings (published in time for the respective event)
- Other edited monographs (such as project reports or invited volumes)

LNICST topics span the following areas:

- General Computer Science
- E-Economy
- E-Medicine
- Knowledge Management
- Multimedia
- Operations, Management and Policy
- Social Informatics
- Systems

Hiep Xuan Huynh · Congduc Pham ·
Nghia Duong-Trung

Editors

Smart Objects
and Technologies
for Social Good

10th EAI International Conference, GOODTECHS 2024
Can Tho, Vietnam, December 19–20, 2024
Proceedings, Part II

 Springer

Editors
Hiep Xuan Huynh 🅾
Can Tho University
Can Tho, Vietnam

Congduc Pham 🅾
Université de Pau et des Pays de l'Adour
Pau, France

Nghia Duong-Trung 🅾
German Research Center for Artificial
Intelligence (DFKI)
Berlin, Germany

ISSN 1867-8211   ISSN 1867-822X (electronic)
Lecture Notes of the Institute for Computer Sciences, Social Informatics
and Telecommunications Engineering
ISBN 978-3-032-01496-2   ISBN 978-3-032-01497-9 (eBook)
https://doi.org/10.1007/978-3-032-01497-9

This Springer imprint is published by the registered company Springer Nature Switzerland AG
The registered company address is: Gewerbestrasse 11, 6330 Cham, Switzerland

If disposing of this product, please recycle the paper.

Preface

We are delighted to present the proceedings of the 10th EAI International Conference on Smart Objects and Technologies for Social Good (EAI GOODTECHS 2024), held on December 19–20, 2024, in Can Tho city, Vietnam. This event was graciously hosted by Can Tho University, bringing together researchers, developers, and practitioners from around the world to exchange insights and innovations aimed at enhancing social good through smart technologies.

EAI GOODTECHS 2024 received 102 submissions, out of which 44 high-quality papers were accepted after rigorous peer review. These papers highlight a wide range of advancements in smart technologies aimed at promoting social good. Key topics include cutting-edge research in Internet of Things (IoT) security, innovative applications of artificial intelligence in domains such as healthcare, education, and environmental monitoring, and energy-efficient systems. Contributions also explore advanced recommendation systems, deep learning techniques for object detection and image analysis, federated learning for privacy-preserving applications, and the integration of machine learning with domain-specific challenges like traffic monitoring, water level forecasting, and disease prediction. The diversity of these papers, presented across four focused tracks—IoT & Security, AI Applications I, AI Applications II, and AI Applications III—underscores the multidisciplinary nature of the conference and its commitment to addressing real-world challenges through smart and impactful technological solutions.

A highlight of the conference was the keynote address by My T. Thai, a distinguished University of Florida Research Foundation Professor of Computer & Information Sciences & Engineering and Associate Director of the Nelms Institute for the Connected World. Her keynote, titled "Interpretability and Privacy Preservation in Large Language Models (LLMs)," provided valuable insights into cutting-edge challenges and solutions in the realm of artificial intelligence.

EAI GOODTECHS 2024 also celebrated excellence in research by presenting two prestigious awards: the Best Long Paper Award and the Best Short Paper Award, recognizing outstanding contributions that push the boundaries of knowledge and innovation.

The success of this conference would not have been possible without the dedication and expertise of the Technical Program Committee and reviewers, representing 11 countries. We sincerely thank them for their efforts in ensuring the high quality of the program and their valuable contributions to the peer-review process. A special thank you is extended to Co-General Chair, Thuy Thanh Nguyen, Vietnam National University (VNU), Vietnam, for his exceptional leadership and support in making this event a success.

We are confident that the proceedings of EAI GOODTECHS 2024 provide a platform for the exchange of ideas and will inspire future research that addresses global challenges through smart technologies. We look forward to seeing how the work presented here will contribute to a better, more connected, and sustainable future.

August 2025

Hiep Xuan Huynh
Congduc Pham
Nghia Duong-Trung

Organization

General Chairs

Hiep Xuan Huynh — Can Tho University, Vietnam
Thuy Thanh Nguyen — Vietnam National University, Vietnam

Program Chair

Congduc Pham — Université de Pau et des Pays de l'Adour, France

Program Co-chair

Thanh-Nghi Do — Can Tho University, Vietnam

Web Chair

Huy Hoang Le Nguyen — Can Tho University, Vietnam

Publicity and Social Media Chairs

Jean-François Dorville — TCGNRG, Guadeloupe
Serge Stinckwich — United Nations University in Macau, China

Workshops Chairs

Mahamadou Traore — Université Gaston Berger Saint-Louis, Senegal
Vincent Rodin — Université de Bretagne Occidentale, France

Sponsorship and Exhibits Chairs

Onil Goubier   CIRELA, Indonesia
Tsimitomby Briand   Institut Supérieur de Technologie d'Antsiranana,
                                Madagascar

Publications Chair

Nghia Duong-Trung   German Research Center for Artificial
                                Intelligence, Germany

Local Chair

Hoa Huu Nguyen   Can Tho University, Vietnam

Technical Program Committee

Hiep Xuan Huynh   Can Tho University, Vietnam
Congduc Pham   Université de Pau et des Pays de l'Adour, France
Vincent Rodin   Université de Bretagne Occidentale, France
Serge Stinckwich   United Nations University in Macau, China
Jean-François Dorville   TCGNRG, Guadeloupe
Mahamadou Traore   Université Gaston Berger Saint-Louis, Senegal
Onil Goubier   CIRELA, Indonesia
Tsimitomby Briand   Institut Supérieur de Technologie d'Antsiranana,
                                Madagascar
Danh Le-Phuoc   Technische Universität Berlin, Germany
Nghia Duong-Trung   German Research Center for Artificial
                                Intelligence, Germany
Sergei Gorlatch   University of Münster, Germany
Bao Hoai Lam   Can Tho University, Vietnam
Dung Van Hoang   Ho Chi Minh City University of Technology and
                                Education, Vietnam
Nguyen Nhat Vo   University of Michigan, USA
Nhat Minh Viet Vo   Hue University, Vietnam
Khoi Tan Nguyen   University of Science and Technology, University
                                of Da Nang, Vietnam
Thang Cong Pham   University of Science and Technology, University
                                of Da Nang, Vietnam

Thuy Thu Thi Pham   Nha Trang University, Vietnam
Yen-Wen Chen   National Central University, Taiwan
Anh Viet Nguyen   Institute of Information Technology, Vietnam
                             Academy of Science and Technology, Vietnam
Nghia Quoc Phan   Tra Vinh University, Vietnam
Vu Tran Pham   Ho Chi Minh City University of Technology,
                             Vietnam National University, Vietnam
Xia Wang   German Research Center for Artificial
                             Intelligence, Germany
Sheikh Faisal Rashid   German Research Center for Artificial
                             Intelligence, Germany
Tung Kieu   Aalborg University, Denmark
Chinh Quoc Bui   Elsevier, Netherlands
Binh Thanh Nguyen   Monash University, Australia
Viet Xuan Le   Quy Nhon University, Vietnam
Lang Van Tran   Vietnam Academy of Science and Technology,
                             Vietnam
Son Hoang Le   Information Technology Institute, Vietnam
                             National University, Hanoi, Vietnam
Vinh Quoc Tran Nguyen   University of Science and Education, University
                             of Da Nang, Vietnam
Toan Nang Do   Vietnam National University, Hanoi, Vietnam
Xuan Son Ha   RMIT University Vietnam, Vietnam
Binh Thanh Nguyen   Vietnam-Korea University of Information and
                             Communication Technology, Vietnam
Anh Ngoc Nguyen   University of Science and Education, University
                             of Da Nang, Vietnam

Contents – Part II

Contents – Part I

Innovations in Energy-Based Models, and Advanced Predictive Systems Across Diverse Domains

Enhancing the Quality of Recommendation Lists Using Graph Convolutional Networks

Le Thi Vinh Thanh[1] , Le Manh Thanh[2] , Nguyen Van Long[3(✉)] ,
and Nguyen Hai Yen[4]

[1] Industrial University of Ho Chi Minh City, Ho Chi Minh City, Vietnam
lethivinhthanh@iuh.edu.vn
[2] University of Sciences, Hue University, Hue, Vietnam
lmthanh@hueuni.edu.vn
[3] University of Transport and Communications, Hanoi, Vietnam
nvlongdt@utc.edu.vn
[4] Faculty of Information Technology, HCM University of Industry and Trade,
Ho Chi Minh City, Vietnam
yennh@huit.edu.vn

Abstract. In the realm of recommender systems, enhancing the quality of recommendation lists has become a focal point for researchers. This paper presents a novel approach integrating clustering structures with Graph Convolutional Network (GCN) techniques to improve recommendation quality. Initially, we employ a hierarchical tree structure to cluster similar users and items based on energy-based similarity measures. This allows for a more accurate modeling of user and product groups. We then construct graphs representing user relationships (SU-Graph) and item relationships (SI-Graph) based on these clusters, as well as a graph derived from the user-item rating matrix. Utilizing this framework, we train a GCN to predict user ratings for previously unseen items, significantly enhancing the accuracy of recommendations. Finally, we refine the recommendation lists by balancing precision and diversity, ensuring users receive suggestions that are both relevant and varied. Experimental results on the MovieLens dataset validate the effectiveness of our proposed approach, demonstrating substantial improvements over traditional methods.

Keywords: Recommender Systems · Clustering · Diversity · Graph Convolutional Network

1 Introduction

Recommendation systems are crucial in fields like e-commerce, social media, and entertainment, helping users find products or content based on preferences, habits, and history [1, 2]. Traditional methods include content-based filtering, which suggests items similar to those a user has shown interest in by analyzing product features and user data, but it struggles when data is sparse [3]. Collaborative filtering, on the other hand, relies on user behavior to identify trends and similarities, allowing for recommendations without needing detailed product attributes [4].

H. X. Huynh et al. (Eds.): GOODTECHS 2024, LNICST 649, pp. 3–13, 2025.
https://doi.org/10.1007/978-3-032-01497-9_1

Recent studies have applied deep learning techniques like GNN, GCN, and variations to enhance collaborative filtering by leveraging graph structures to capture complex relationships between users and products [5–8]. GCN models allow for deeper feature learning across multiple layers, improving recommendation accuracy and adaptability to large, diverse datasets. These graph-based systems also identify user or product clusters and detect potential connections that traditional methods may miss, crucial in handling today's complex, multi-dimensional data [9, 10]. This paper proposes an advanced method that integrates clustering with GCN to improve recommendation quality.

The contributions of the paper include: (1) utilizing a hierarchical tree structure to group users and products based on energy-based similarity measures, enabling accurate modeling of user and product groups; (2) constructing graphs representing user relationships (SU-Graph) based on similar user clusters, item relationships (SI-Graph) based on similar item clusters, and a graph representing the relationships between users and items based on the rating matrix; (3) training the GCN to predict user ratings for unseen products, thereby improving the accuracy and relevance of recommendations; (4) refining the final recommendation list through a balance between precision and diversity, ensuring that users receive suggestions that are both highly relevant and varied.

2 Related Work

Improving recommendation systems is increasingly important as user data grows. Traditional methods struggle with the complex relationships between users and products, leading to the exploration of Graph Neural Networks (GNN) and Graph Convolutional Networks as effective solutions. These approaches use graph structures to uncover hidden patterns, enhancing accuracy and personalization. GCN improves relevance, while combining it with collaborative filtering optimizes user experience.

Edoardo et al. introduced IGCCF, which leverages dynamic user-item graphs through graph convolutional networks, improving recommendation accuracy and prediction for new users, though it faces high computational complexity with large graphs. Jiani Zhang et al. proposed STAR-GCN, combining stacked GCN encoder-decoder blocks with intermediate supervision to improve cold-start performance and accuracy [11], but struggles with large graphs. LeWu et al. introduced AGCN, which refines graph embeddings and attribute estimates, improving performance with incomplete data but facing complexity issues [12]. Xiang Wang et al. proposed NGCF, enhancing embeddings through high-order connections in user-item graphs, outperforming models like HOP-Rec and Collaborative Memory Network, but integrating attention mechanisms remains challenging [7]. Lastly, Chong Li et al. introduced a hierarchical approach for bipartite graph representations, improving embedding quality but facing scalability issues with large datasets [6]. Each method offers advancements but comes with its own challenges.

This study aims to enhance recommendation systems by improving user experience through advanced modeling techniques and specialized graph structures. It focuses on predicting user ratings for unseen products while balancing precision and diversity in recommendations. Building on the strengths of existing models, this approach addresses their limitations to create more effective systems.

3 Recommender System Model

The paper presents a modular recommendation system that ensures both accuracy and diversity. It clusters users and items using a tree structure and energy distance, then builds a user-item graph as input for a GCN to predict unrated interactions. A diversification algorithm integrates accuracy and diversity to generate personalized recommendations.

3.1 User-Item Clustering

In this study, we cluster similar users and items from the MovieLens dataset, based on the user-item rating matrix. To optimize the clustering process, we use a tree structure to group users and items, combined with the Energy distance measure [13]. This approach better captures subtle relationships in the data, thereby improving the clustering performance.

Energy Distance is a powerful tool for multivariate analysis [2, 14, 15]. It is used to test for independence, and multivariate normality, and to perform non-parametric analysis of complex structured data. Energy distance is applied to random vectors of any size in Euclidean space.

Suppose we have two sets of independent random vectors $I = \{I_1, I_2, \ldots I_p\}$ and $I = \{J_1, J, \ldots J_q\}$. The distance between I and J is defined as:

$$D^2(I, J) = 2 \sum_{i=1}^{p} \sum_{j=1}^{q} \|I - J\| - \sum_{i=1}^{p} \sum_{j=1}^{p} \|I - I'\| - \sum_{i=1}^{q} \sum_{j=1}^{q} \|J - J'\|$$

where: I' and J' are independent random copies, distributed identically to I and J, respectively.

This formula defines the "potential energy" of the independent random variables I and J, denoted as $\varepsilon_{p,q}(I, J)$:

$$\varepsilon_{p,q}(I, J) = 2E[\delta(I, J)] - E[\delta(I, I')] - E[\delta(J, J')]$$

where:

$$E[\delta(I, J)] = \frac{1}{pq} \sum_{i=1}^{p} \sum_{j=1}^{q} \|I_i - J_j\|$$

$$E[\delta(I, I')] = \frac{1}{p^2} \sum_{i=1}^{p} \sum_{j=1}^{p} \|I_i - I'_j\|$$

$$[\delta(J, J')] = \frac{1}{q^2} \sum_{i=1}^{q} \sum_{j=1}^{q} \|J_i - J'_j\|$$

Clustering similar users and items creates the foundation for the user-item similarity graph, clarifying relationships in the data and improving our understanding of user behavior. This graph helps make more accurate recommendations, enhancing the system's effectiveness.

3.2 Graph Construction

To ensure accurate and diverse recommendations, we design three graph structures to model user-item relationships. These graphs capture data correlations and support efficient GCN training. The graph structures are defined as follows:

User Graph (SU-Graph)

Definition 1. The $SU\_Graph = (V_u, E_u)$ is a graph representing the relationships between users, where the vertex set $V_u = \{u_i \in U\}$, $U = \{u_1, u_2, \ldots, u_n\}$ is the set of users in the system; the edge set $E_u = \{e_{u,v}\}$, $u, v \in C_k$, with C_k is the cluster of similar users and $v \in KNN(u)$, with $KNN(u)$ is the set of K nearest neighbors of user u within C_k (Fig. 1).

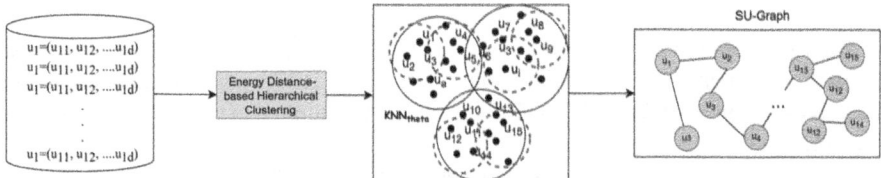

Fig. 1. Graph representing the relationships between users.

Item Graph (SI-Graph)

Definition 2. The $SI\_Graph = (V_i, E_i)$ is a graph representing the relationships between items, where the vertex set $V_i = \{i_i \in I\}$, $I = \{i_1, i_2, \ldots, i_m\}$ is the set of items available in the system; the edge set $E_i = \{e_{i,j}\}$, $i, i \in C_t$, with C_t is the cluster of similar items and $i \in KNN(j)$, with $KNN(i)$ is the set of K nearest neighbors of item i within C_t.

User-Item Graph(UI-Graph)

Definition 3. The $UI\_Graph = (V, E)$ is a graph describes the relationships between users and items based on the rating matrix, where the vertex set $V = U \cup I$; the edge set $E = \{(u, i)\}$, where user u has rated item i.

After constructing the user-item relationship graph, we use Graph Convolutional Networks (GCN) to model complex dependencies and improve prediction accuracy. The next section details the implementation and training of GCN to provide accurate recommendations based on user preferences and item characteristics.

3.3 Rating Prediction Using Graph Convolutional Networks

While traditional methods struggle to solve the inductive task without retraining, models like CDL [16] and DropoutNet [17] use neural networks to learn content features but depend on this information. STAR-GCN [11] leverages both the content and structural information of the graph to learn embeddings for new nodes, effectively solving the cold-start problem even in the absence of content information, making it superior to previous methods. Our GCN model training process is based on the work of [11]. We add user and item feature information aggregated from similarity graphs to enhance the user-item graph's input features for the GCN, aiming to improve prediction accuracy. In this section, we use three GCN networks based on different input graphs: user, item, and user-item (Figs. 2, 3 and 4).

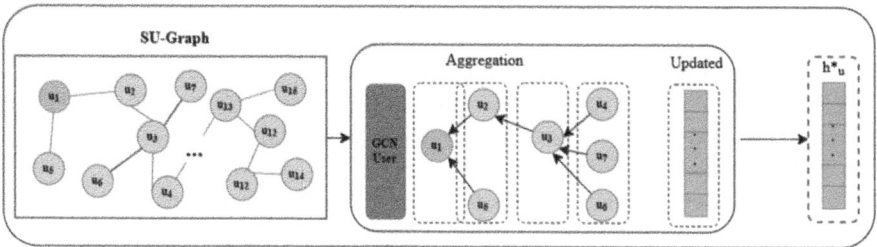

Fig. 2. Training the GCN model for users.

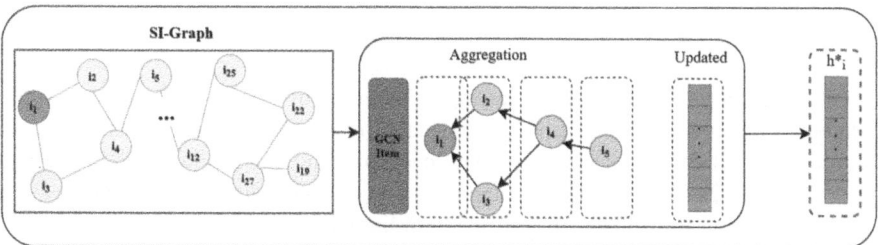

Fig. 3. Training the GCN model for items.

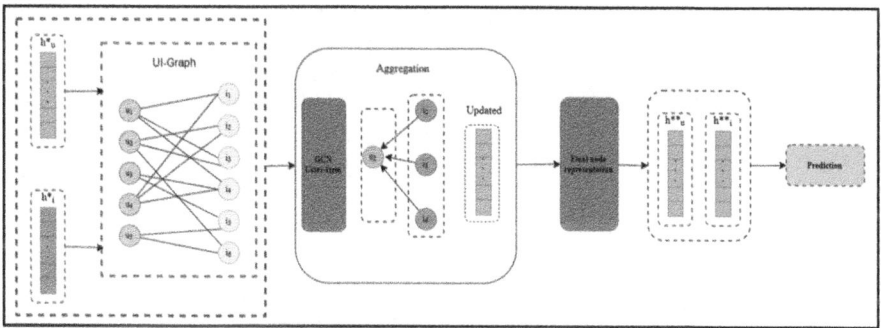

Fig. 4. Training the GCN model to predict user ratings for items.

The detailed steps are presented below.

Step 1. Training GCN on the SU-Graph
Use the user similarity graph as input to train the GCN, connecting users with similar attributes or interactions. Initialize and propagate through GCN layers to extract user embeddings.

Step 2. Training GCN on the SI-Graph
Use the item similarity graph as input for the GCN, connecting items with similar attributes or interactions. Initialize and propagate through GCN layers to obtain item embeddings.

Step 3. Create features for the UI-Graph
Combine user and item embeddings into a single vector, assign it to the edges of the user-item graph as input for the next GCN network.

Step 4. Training GCN on the UI-Graph
The GCN propagates and aggregates information from the neighbors of each node. The features of user and item nodes are updated to new embeddings.

Step 5. Predict user rating for items
Combine the final embeddings of users and items into a single vector, passing it through hidden layers of a neural network to explore relationships between features. The neural network generates 5 possible rating levels, which are converted to probabilities via Softmax. The rating with the highest probability is selected, indicating the item's suitability for the user.

3.4 Re-ranking Items

Recent studies have focused on increasing the diversity of recommendation lists while maintaining accuracy. The traditional two-stage approach first creates an accuracy-focused list of N items (Stage 1) and then refines it by removing similar items to increase diversity (Stage 2). However, if the initial list contains highly similar items, Stage 2 can only filter a subset, resulting in a final list with limited diversity and fewer options for the user.

To address this limitation, the "Diversify the recommendation list" algorithm simultaneously integrates both factors: the predicted rating value (focused on accuracy) and the distance $d(u, i)$ (focused on diversity) from the beginning, as expressed in the following formula:

$$score(u, i) = k \times \hat{r}_{u,i} + \gamma \times (1 - k) \times d(u, i); k \in [0.1]$$

where $d(u, i)$ is the distance between item I and the profile of user u:

$$d(u, i) = 1 - sim(u, i),$$

and

$$sim(x, y) = \cos\left(\overrightarrow{x}, \overrightarrow{y}\right) = \frac{\overrightarrow{x}.\overrightarrow{y}}{\|\overrightarrow{x}\|_2 \|\overrightarrow{y}\|_2} = \frac{\sum_{s \in S_{xy}} r_{x,s} r_{y,s}}{\sqrt{\sum_{s \in S_{xy}} r_{x,s}^2}\sqrt{\sum_{s \in S_{xy}} r_{y,s}^2}}$$

Since the predicted rating score lies in the range [1, 5] and $d(u, i)$ is between [0, 1], the algorithm scales $d(u, i)$ to the same range by multiplying it by 5. The pseudocode is illustrated in Algorithm 1.

Algorithm 1. Diversify the recommendation list

Input: user profile of user u, I ={ items (content)}, $ListR_u = \{\hat{r}(u,i), i \in I\}$
            Threshold TH , $TopM$ items to recommend

Output: $TopM$ recommendation list $L_M(u)$.

Begin

Foreach (r in $ListR_u$)

{

   Compute $d(u,i)$;

   Compute $score(u,i) = k * \hat{r}(u,i) + (1 - k) * \gamma * d(u,i)$;

   $Sc[i] = score(u,i)$;

   }

   $SSc = SortItem(I *, Sc[i])$;

   //Function SortItem sort the items $i \in I^*$ in descending order of scores $Sc[i]$;

   $L_M(u)$ = Filter_TopM(SSc);

   // Function $Filter\_TopM$ selects the $TopM$ items $L_M(u)$ recommend for user u;

   Return $L_M(u)$;

end

Thus, after calculating $score(u, i)$ for all items, the Algorithm 1 selects the *topM* items with the highest scores for the final recommendation list $L_M(u)$ for user u, without needing to generate an initial candidate list $L_M(u)$.

4 Experimental Procedure

4.1 Experimental Data

The experiments use standard datasets: MovieLens 100k (ML-100K), MovieLens 1M (ML-1M), and MovieLens 10M (ML-10M). ML-100K contains 100,000 ratings from 943 users on 1,682 movies across 19 genres, while ML-10M consists of 10 million ratings with various item attributes. The datasets are pre-split, with 80% used for training and 20% for testing prediction quality.

The experiments were conducted on a PC with the following specifications: CPU 13th Gen Intel(R) Core(TM) i9-13900H 2.60 GHz, RAM 32.0 GB (31.6 GB usable), 64-bit operating system, x64-based processor.

4.2 Methodology

To evaluate the effectiveness of the algorithms, the study is based on accuracy and three diversity measures. There are many measures that can be applied for the accuracy of the recommendation list, and we uses the most common measure, MAE (Mean Absolute Error), as shown in the following formula:

$$MAE = \frac{1}{n} \sum_{i \in L_M(u)} \frac{|\hat{r}_{u,i} - r_{u,i}|}{l}$$

where the denominator is l, representing the rating scale, and:

- $L_M(u)$: the *Top_M* list of recommended items for user u
- n: the size of $L_M(u)$
- $\hat{r}_{u,i}$: the predicted rating of user u for item i
- $r_{u,i}$: the actual rating of user u for item i

The lower the *MAE* value, the higher the accuracy of the algorithm. Therefore, the value of $(1 - MAE)$ can be considered an indication of the algorithm's accuracy.

For diversity, three measures: *IntraDistance, AggDivNum,* and *IntraDistanceProfile* is used.

This diversity is often defined as the average distance between two items in the recommendation list LM(u) and is calculated using the following formula:

$$IntraDistance(L_M(u)) = \frac{2}{n(n-)} \sum_{i \in L_M(u)} d(i, i')$$

where, $d(i, i')$ is the energy distance between item i and item i'; n is the size of $L_M(u)$

Note that the value of *IntraDistance*$(L_M(u))$ is higher when the diversity of $L_M(u)$ is higher. Additionally, *IntraDistance*$(L_M(u))$ is considered personal and will be referred to as individual diversity, as it depends on the recommendation lists for each individual user.

Aggregate diversity is defined as the total number of items that the system has recommended to all users as shown in the following formula:

$$AggDivNum = \left| \bigcup_{u \in U} L_M(u) \right|$$

where, U is the set of users of the system

The diversity of the recommendation list $L_M(u)$ is defined as the average distance of all items in the recommendation list to the user's profile.

$$IntraDistanceProfile(L_M(u)) = \frac{1}{n} \sum_{i \in L_M(u)} d(u, i)$$

where, $d(u, i)$ is the energy distance between the profile of user u and item i; n is the size of $L_M(u)$. Note that the value of *IntraDistanceProfile*$(L_M(u))$ is higher when the diversity of $L_M(u)$ is higher.

Additionally, accuracy and diversity are generally opposing (increasing the value of one measure will decrease the value of the other and vice versa), so the paper also employs the *F_Measure* to balance these two measures as follows:

$$F\_Measure = \frac{2 \times (1 - MAE) \times \text{IntraDistanceProfile}}{(1 - MAE) + \text{IntraDistanceProfile}}$$

4.3   Results and Experimental Analysis

Below are the experimental results of the recommendation system evaluated using various metrics, applied to recommendation lists from Top 10 to Top 50. These figures illustrate the changes in accuracy, diversity, and overall performance as the recommendation range is expanded (Tables 1, 2 and 3).

Table 1. The experimental results on the MovieLens-100K dataset.

Measures	Top 10	Top 20	Top 30	Top 40	Top 50
1-MAE	0.829	0.806	0.797	0.735	0.701
IntraDistance	0.758	0.734	0.721	0.695	0.674
AggDivNum	532	608	713	825	924
IntraDistanceProfile	0.749	0.706	0.674	0.649	0.628
F_Measure	0.787	0.753	0.731	0.689	0.663

Table 2. The experimental results on the MovieLens -1M dataset.

Measures	Top 10	Top 20	Top 30	Top 40	Top 50
1-MAE	0.834	0.801	0.795	0.775	0.731
IntraDistance	0.851	0.804	0.765	0.710	0.711
AggDivNum	612	711	824	898	1044
IntraDistanceProfile	0.822	0.816	0.805	0.715	0.699
F_Measure	0.828	0.808	0.800	0.744	0.715

Table 3. The experimental results on the MovieLens-10M dataset.

Measures	Top 10	Top 20	Top 30	Top 40	Top 50
1-MAE	0.846	0.821	0.814	0.775	0.751
IntraDistance	0.879	0.846	0.818	0.755	0.716
AggDivNum	646	724	773	876	1286
IntraDistanceProfile	0.884	0.836	0.802	0.785	0.736
F_Measure	0.865	0.828	0.808	0.780	0.743

The experimental results from the MovieLens datasets show key insights into recommendation model performance. The *Precision* (1-MAE) decreases as recommendations increase, with ML-10M reaching the lowest *Precision* of 0.846 for the top 10. IntraDistance reveals higher similarity among recommended items in larger datasets, particularly in the top 10 (0.879) and top 20 (0.846). Aggregate Diversity (AggDivNum) increases significantly, with ML-10M achieving a diversity score of 1286 for the top 50. IntraDistanceProfile shows tighter item clustering in larger datasets, and F_Measure peaks at 0.865 for the top 10 in ML-10M, demonstrating the model's balance of precision and diversity.

Below is a comparison table of the performance of different methods on the ML-100K, ML-1M, and ML-10M datasets based on the MAE metric. The results help assess the accuracy of each method and demonstrate the competitiveness of the proposed method compared to previous approaches.

Methods	ML-100K	ML-1M	ML-10M
GRALS [Rao et al. 2015] [18]	0.945	–	–
CF-NADE [Zheng et al. 2016] [19]	–	**0.829**	0.771
Factorized EAE [Hartford et al. 2018] [20]	0.910	0.860	–
GC-MC [Berg et al. 2017] [21]	0.910	0.832	0.777
STAR-GCN [Jiani Zhang et al. 2019] [11]	0.895	0.832	0.770
Proposed method	**0.854**	**0.831**	**0.769**

The performance comparison table shows that the proposed method achieves the lowest MAE on ML-100K with 0.854, indicating better accuracy compared to other methods such as GRALS (0.945) and GC-MC (0.910). On ML-1M, the proposed method has an MAE of 0.831, slightly higher than CF-NADE (0.829) but better than other methods like GC-MC (0.832). For ML-10M, the proposed method also demonstrates relatively good performance with an MAE of 0.769, lower than CF-NADE (0.771) and GC-MC (0.777), showcasing its competitiveness on large datasets.

The system uses a hierarchical tree structure to group users and products based on energy-based similarity, enabling accurate preference modeling. By constructing SU-Graph and SI-Graph, the system gains a deeper understanding of user-product relationships, improving prediction accuracy. Training the Graph Convolutional Network (GCN) and refining the recommendation list balances precision and diversity, ensuring relevant and varied suggestions for users.

5   Conclusion

This paper proposes an improved method for enhancing the quality of recommendation lists by combining clustering structures with Graph Convolutional Networks. Key contributions include utilizing a hierarchical tree to group users and products based on energy-based similarity measures, constructing graphs representing relationships between users and products, and training the GCN to predict ratings for unseen products. Experimental results on the MovieLens dataset indicate that the accuracy of predictions improves as the number of recommendations increases, with the highest MAE value of 0.846 for the top 10 recommendations in the MovieLens-10M dataset. Additionally, the IntraDistance measures show higher similarity among recommended items, while the Aggregate Diversity Number reflects greater variety in suggestions. Finally, F_Measure values peak at 0.865, highlighting the model's effectiveness in balancing precision and diversity, thereby providing a better user experience.

References

1. Lin, W., et al.: Transformer-empowered content-aware collaborative filtering. arXiv preprint arXiv:2204.00849 (2022)

2. Tran, T.C.T., Phan, L.P., Huynh, H.X.: Energy-based collaborative filtering recommendation. Int. J. Adv. Comput. Sci. Appl. **13**(7) (2022)
3. Mouhiha, M., Oualhaj, O.A. , Mabrouk, A.: Combining collaborative filtering and content based filtering for recommendation systems. In: 2024 11th International Conference on Wireless Networks and Mobile Communications (WINCOM). IEEE (2024)
4. Glauber, R., Loula, A.: Collaborative filtering vs. content-based filtering: differences and similarities. arXiv preprint arXiv:1912.08932 (2019)
5. He, X., et al.: Neural collaborative filtering. In: Proceedings of the 26th International Conference on World Wide Web (2017)
6. Li, C., et al.: Hierarchical representation learning for bipartite graphs. In: IJCAI (2019)
7. Wang, X., et al.: Neural graph collaborative filtering. In: Proceedings of the 42nd International ACM SIGIR Conference on Research and Development in Information Retrieval (2019)
8. Tan, Q., et al.: Learning to hash with graph neural networks for recommender systems. In: Proceedings of The Web Conference 2020 (2020)
9. Sun, J., et al.: Multi-graph convolution collaborative filtering. In: 2019 IEEE International Conference on Data Mining (ICDM). IEEE (2019)
10. Sun, J., et al.: Neighbor interaction aware graph convolution networks for recommendation. In: Proceedings of the 43rd International ACM SIGIR Conference on Research and Development in Information Retrieval (2020)
11. Zhang, J., et al.: STAR-GCN: stacked and reconstructed graph convolutional networks for recommender systems. arXiv preprint arXiv:1905.13129 (2019)
12. Wu, L., et al.: Joint item recommendation and attribute inference: an adaptive graph convolutional network approach. In: Proceedings of the 43rd International ACM SIGIR Conference on Research and Development in Information Retrieval (2020)
13. Rizzo, M.L., Székely, G.J.: Energy distance. Wiley Interdiscip. Rev. Comput. Stat. **8**(1), pp. 27–38 (2016)
14. Edelmann, D., Móri, T.F., Székely, G.J.: On relationships between the Pearson and the distance correlation coefficients. Stat. Probab. Lett. **169**, 108960 (2021)
15. Tran, T.C.T., Phan, L.P., Huynh, H.X.: Approach of item-based collaborative filtering recommendation using energy distance. J. Adv. Inf. Technol. **15**(1) (2024)
16. Wang, H., Wang, N., Yeung, D.-Y.: Collaborative deep learning for recommender systems. In: Proceedings of the 21th ACM SIGKDD International Conference on Knowledge Discovery and Data Mining (2015)
17. Volkovs, M., Yu, G., Poutanen, T.: DropoutNet: addressing cold start in recommender systems. In: Advances in Neural Information Processing Systems, vol. 30 (2017)
18. Rao, N., et al.: Collaborative filtering with graph information: consistency and scalable methods. In: Advances in Neural Information Processing Systems, vol. 28 (2015)
19. Zheng, Y., et al.: A neural autoregressive approach to collaborative filtering. In: International Conference on Machine Learning. PMLR (2016)
20. Hartford, J., et al.: Deep models of interactions across sets. In: International Conference on Machine Learning. PMLR (2018)
21. Berg, R.v.d., Kipf, T.N., Welling, M.: Graph convolutional matrix completion. arXiv preprint arXiv:1706.02263 (2017)

A Method Utilizing Energy Distance to Address Sparsity of Dataset in Recommendation Systems

Nhan Hoang Vo[1]([✉]) [iD], Tu Cam Thi Tran[2] [iD], and Eloi Bandia Keita[3] [iD]

[1] Kien Giang University, Minh Luong, Kien Giang, Vietnam
vhnhan@vnkgu.edu.vn
[2] Vinh Long University of Technology Education, Vinh Long, Vinh Long, Vietnam
tuttc@vlute.edu.vn
[3] Lab-STICC (Laboratory of Information, Communication, and Knowledge Sciences and Technologies), Brest, France
eloi.keita@univ-brest.fr

Abstract. Most recommendation systems often encounter issues when dealing with sparse datasets, resulting in low prediction accuracy. Traditional methods struggle significantly when data is too sparse, affecting their ability to provide accurate recommendations. This paper proposes an approach using energy distance to analyze the structure within sparse datasets. The model's effectiveness is demonstrated through experiments comparing it with traditional methods such as Cosine Similarity and Pearson Correlation across varying levels of sparsity in the MovieLens dataset.

Keywords: Energy distance · Energy model · Sparsity dataset · Similarity · Recommendation systems

1 Introduction

This paper addresses a common issue faced by current recommendation systems when dealing with sparse datasets in user-product relationships [1, 2], which often leads to low prediction accuracy. Due to data sparsity, there is a lack of information on user habits, especially for new users or products with low attention. Traditional methods [11, 17] struggle when data is too sparse, affecting the system's ability to provide accurate recommendations [6].

This paper introduces an innovative approach that utilizes energy distance for examining the underlying structure within sparse datasets [3, 7]. This measure evaluates the difference between the distribution of user habits and product characteristics [13], helping the system improve its ability to offer reliable [5] recommendations even when dealing with sparse data.

The structure of the paper is organized as follows: Background information and related work are discussed in Sect. 2, including: Energy distance, Cosine Similarity, Pearson Correlation and evaluation of the recommendation result. In Sect. 3 proposes

H. X. Huynh et al. (Eds.): GOODTECHS 2024, LNICST 649, pp. 14–24, 2025.
https://doi.org/10.1007/978-3-032-01497-9_2

a algorithm using energy distance for structural analysis in sparse datasets [15]. The experiment on the MovieLens datasets is detailed in Sect. 4, followed by the conclusion in Sect. 5.

2 Background and Related Work

2.1 Energy Distance

Given data sets $X = \{X_1, \ldots, X_n\}$ and $Y = \{Y_1, \ldots, Y_n\}$ in Euclidean space $\mathbb{R}^d$, where $d \geq 1$, the data distance [4] between X and Y is defined as the square root of:

$$D_\alpha^2 := 2 \sum_{i=1}^{n} \sum_{j=1}^{m} |X_i - Y_j|^\alpha - \sum_{i=1}^{n} \sum_{j=1}^{n} |X_i - X_j|^\alpha - \sum_{i=1}^{m} \sum_{j=1}^{m} |Y_i - Y_j|^\alpha \quad (1)$$

here $|\cdot|$ represents the Euclidean norm.

It can be observed that D^2 is always nonnegative, and D serves as a metric within the space of data of length n [8]. The energy of the data originates from D. In physics, this can be interpreted as energy if D^2 is multiplied by a constant force F; that is, energy

$$E = F \cdot D^2 \quad (2)$$

By setting $F = 1$ and allowing the sample sizes n and m to differ, the formula for the energy of the data [3] becomes

$$\varepsilon_{n,m}(X, Y) = \frac{2}{nm} \sum_{i=1}^{n} \sum_{j=1}^{m} |X_i - Y_j| - \frac{1}{n^2} \sum_{i=1}^{n} \sum_{j=1}^{n} |X_i - X_j| - \frac{1}{m^2} \sum_{i=1}^{m} \sum_{j=1}^{m} |Y_i - Y_j| \quad (3)$$

If $n = m$, and $Y_1 = Y_2 = \cdots = Y_n = y$, and we reduce the energy $\varepsilon_{n,m}(X, Y)$ in y, then if the minimum occurs at $y = C$ [12] we may refer to C as the central point of energy within the data $\{X_1, X_2, X_3, \ldots, X_n\}$.

2.2 Cosine Similarity

Cosine Similarity calculates the angle between two vectors, which represent either two users or two items in an n-dimensional space [1], where n is the total number of items or users rated. Cosine Similarity values range from -1 to 1, with values closer to 1 indicating greater similarity [2].

Let's assume we have two rating vectors $X = (X_1, X_2, X_3, \ldots, X_n)$ and $Y = (Y_1, Y_2, Y_3, \ldots, Y_n)$ for two users or two items.

The formula for Cosine Similarity is:

$$\cos(X, Y) = \frac{\sum_{i=1}^{n} X_i \cdot Y_i}{\sqrt{\sum_{i=1}^{n} X_i^2} \cdot \sqrt{\sum_{i=1}^{n} Y_i^2}} \quad (4)$$

where:

- X_i and Y_i indicate the ratings assigned by user X and user Y for item i.
- If either X_i or Y_i has no rating for item i, that value can be ignored or set to 0 in the formula.

2.3 Pearson Correlation

Pearson Correlation assesses the linear association between two users or two items [1]. It assesses how ratings differ from the average for each user or item, helping to remove the effect of different rating levels.

The formula for Pearson Correlation for two users, X and Y [2], who have both rated n common items, is given by:

$$Pearson(X, Y) = \frac{\sum (X_i - \overline{X})(Y_i - \overline{Y})}{\sqrt{(X_i - \overline{X})^2} \cdot \sqrt{(Y_i - \overline{Y})^2}} \tag{5}$$

where:

- X_i and Y_i represent the ratings provided by users X and Y for item i.
- $\overline{X}$ and $\overline{Y}$ denote the average ratings of users X and Y on the items they have both rated.

The Pearson Correlation coefficient varies between -1 and 1:

- X value near 1 signifies a strong positive correlation.
- X value near -1 suggests that users generally rate items in opposing directions.

2.4 Why is Using Energy Distance Better for Recommendation Systems with Sparse Data Compared to Cosine or Jaccard Similarity?

Flexibility in Handling Sparse Data: Sparse data [1] is characterized by many missing (or unobserved) values in vectors or datasets. When using Cosine Distance or Jaccard Distance, these methods primarily rely on the presence or absence of features, so they may not accurately reflect the similarity between objects if there are many missing values [2]. Energy Distance, on the other hand, calculates the distance based on all pairs of values, including missing ones (by summing the absolute distances of the powered values). This allows Energy Distance to work more effectively [6] when dealing with sparse data, as it doesn't require all features to be present in each pair. Instead, it can use the available features to compute similarity.

Higher Accuracy in Heterogeneous Datasets: Cosine Distance often doesn't perform well with sparse data [5] if the features are heterogeneous or if the vectors contain many zero elements. This method primarily considers the angle between vectors, which may not accurately reflect the level of similarity in sparse datasets, where many features may not be observed. Jaccard Distance, while usable with binary data [10] (presence/absence of features), struggles with continuous or ambiguous value data. Additionally, Jaccard Distance may overlook rare or infrequent features in the dataset, reducing its ability to assess the true similarity between objects. Energy Distance is more flexible because it does not only rely on the presence or absence of features, but also allows adjusting sensitivity through the alpha parameter [11]. This makes it applicable to different types of data, including both sparse and heterogeneous data.

Ability to Handle Missing Values: In sparse data, missing values are very common. Cosine and Jaccard Distances are not very flexible in handling missing values because they primarily compare features present in both vectors. If one of the vectors has many missing values, these methods may overlook or inaccurately measure the similarity. Energy Distance [4, 7] can handle missing values better because the algorithm computes the distance between all pairs of values in the feature space, including missing values. This can help recommendation systems analyze [8] more accurately in situations where the data is sparse and incomplete.

Adjustable Sensitivity via Alpha Parameter: Alpha in Energy Distance can adjust the sensitivity of the algorithm to pairs of values [12], which is particularly useful in sparse data situations where the level of similarity between objects can vary significantly depending on specific features. Adjusting alpha can improve [13] the accuracy of the recommendation system when working with low-resolution or sparse data.

Ability to Measure Overall Differences Between Objects: Cosine Distance [1, 5] only measures similarity in direction between two vectors, and Jaccard Distance primarily considers similarity in the features that are present. Both methods lack the ability to compute the overall difference between objects, especially in sparse data cases where many elements may be absent. Energy Distance calculates the overall difference between objects by aggregating the distances between pairs of elements in each object, providing a more comprehensive view of the similarity between objects. This can help recommendation systems make more accurate recommendations in sparse data scenarios [17], where other methods may overlook important factors.

In Summary: Energy Distance is a powerful and flexible method for measuring similarity between objects in sparse datasets compared to Cosine and Jaccard Distances. It not only handles missing values effectively but also allows adjusting sensitivity through the alpha parameter, making recommendation systems more accurate in complex and sparse data situations.

2.5 Evaluation

A common approach for evaluating a prediction involves calculating the difference between the predicted and actual values. This forms the foundation of the Mean Average Error (MAE) [2, 5]:

$$MAE = \frac{1}{|\mathcal{K}|} \sum_{(j,l) \in \mathcal{K}} \left| r_{jl} - \hat{r}_{jl} \right| \tag{6}$$

Here, $\mathcal{K}$ represents the set of all user-item pairs (j, l) for which a predicted rating $\hat{r}_{jl}$ and an actual rating r_{jl} are available, which the latter not being part of the model training data. Another widely used metric is the *Root Mean Square Error (RMSE)* [2, 5]:

$$RMSE = \sqrt{\frac{\sum_{(j,l) \in \mathcal{K}} (r_{jl} - \hat{r}_{jl})^2}{|\mathcal{K}|}}$$

RMSE places a greater penalty on larger errors compared to MAE, making it more appropriate for scenarios where minor prediction inaccuracies are less critical [9, 14].

Since this is a recommendation system problem, using MAE or RMSE would be a more appropriate choice than other metrics (Precision, Recall, F1-score), as the goal is to predict continuous values.

3 Algorithm Using Energy Distance for Structural Analysis in Sparse Datasets

3.1 Rating Matrix

The data model can be structured as a rating matrix, displaying user ratings for items [1, 2, 18]. Unrated values are represented as "NA". For instance, Table 1 shows users along with their ratings for various products. Through specific computations, a recommendation system can generate a predicted rating score for $user_a$ in relation to a particular item.

Table 1. A rating matrix that includes users and items

R	$item_1$	$item_2$	$item_3$	$item_4$	$item_5$
$user_1$	4	1	NA	3	NA
$user_2$	NA	NA	NA	NA	4
$user_3$	NA	5	4	NA	NA
$user_4$	NA	3	NA	3	2
$user_a$	3	NA	NA	2	NA

When the data is excessively sparse [10], as illustrated in Table 1, applying traditional metrics like Cosine Similarity or Pearson Correlation proves to be highly challenging. These methods only work well when the data is homogeneous (Fig. 1).

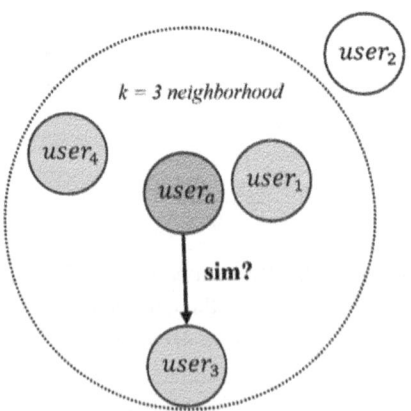

Fig. 1. The user neighborhood formation.

To determine the similarity [2] between $user_a$ and $user_3$, and to what extent, we need a more advanced algorithm to address this issue.

3.2 Algorithm

The energy distance algorithm for structural analysis in sparse datasets is as follow:

Algorithm. The energy distance algorithm for structural analysis in sparse datasets

---

Input: x (vector), y (vector), alpha (real number)
Output: Energy distance between x and y

Begin
    Step 1: Initialize variables
      n = size of x
      m = size of y
      sum_xy = 0
      sum_xx = 0
      sum_yy = 0

    Step 2: Calculate sum_xy for all pairs (x[i], y[j])
      For i from 0 to n-1:
        For j from 0 to m-1:
          sum_xy += |x[i] - y[j]|^alpha

    Step 3: Calculate sum_xx for all pairs (x[i], x[j])
      For i from 0 to n-1:
        For j from 0 to n-1:
          sum_xx += |x[i] - x[j]|^alpha

    Step 4: Calculate sum_yy for all pairs (y[i], y[j])
      For i from 0 to m-1:
        For j from 0 to m-1:
          sum_yy += |y[i] - y[j]|^alpha

    Step 5: Calculate D2_alpha
      D2_alpha = (2 * sum_xy / (n * m)) - (sum_xx / (n * n)) - (sum_yy / (m * m))

    Step 6: Return the energy distance
      Return sqrt(D2_alpha)
End

The algorithm computes the energy distance between two vector x and y by summing up the distances computed using the absolute differences raised to the power of alpha. The specific steps are:

– sum_xy calculates the total distance between all pairs of elements from x and y.

– sum_xx and sum_yy calculate the total distance between elements within each individual dataset.

Finally, the algorithm uses the formula to calculate the energy distance between the two datasets, providing a measure of similarity or difference between the sparse datasets.

Alpha can be adjusted to control the sensitivity of the distance (e.g., if alpha = 2, the algorithm is similar to the usual Euclidean distance). This algorithm is useful for structural analysis of datasets, especially when working with sparse datasets where relationships between pairs of elements may not be clear or complete.

4   Experiment

4.1   Datasets

The MovieLens dataset (100k) contains a sample of 100.000 ratings from 943 users on 1.682 movies, with ratings ranging from 1 to 5. Released in April 1998 by GroupLens Research (https://grouplens.org), the dataset was collected via the MovieLens website (movielens.umn.edu) over a seven-month period from September 19, 1997, to April 22, 1998. Each user in this dataset has rated at least 20 movies.

4.2   Tool

The proposed model is implemented in R language and utilizes the 'rrecsys' package [4, 16]. Additionally, the energy distance algorithm will be written in C and then exported to R for execution. Its performance will be evaluated by comparing it with two existing models in the 'rrecsys' package, using MAE and RMSE error metrics.

4.3   Scenario 1: The Energy Distance Algorithm for Structural Analysis in Sparse Datasets with Folds = 2, k = 3

In this RMSE comparison chart, we observe that the Energy method has the lowest RMSE, indicating it performs best among the three algorithms, as it produces predictions with the smallest deviation from the actual values. The Cosine algorithm comes next with a slightly higher RMSE, which means its predictive accuracy is lower than Energy but still better than the Pearson algorithm. Finally, the Pearson algorithm has the highest RMSE, suggesting it has the largest prediction error among the three algorithms (Figs. 2 and 3).

In this MAE comparison chart, the Energy algorithm has the lowest MAE, indicating it provides the most accurate predictions among the three methods. The Cosine algorithm has a slightly higher MAE, suggesting a slightly lower accuracy than Energy but still better than Pearson. The Pearson algorithm has the highest MAE, indicating the least accuracy among the three.

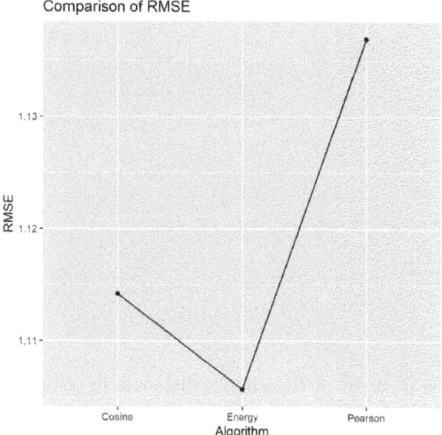

Fig. 2. Evaluating the RMSE error of the energy distance algorithm for structural analysis in sparse datasets with folds = 2, k = 3

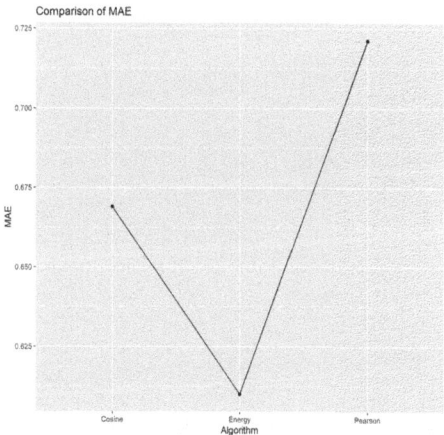

Fig. 3. Evaluating the MAE error of the energy distance algorithm for structural analysis in sparse datasets with folds = 2, k = 3

4.4 Scenario 2: The Energy Distance Algorithm for Structural Analysis in Sparse Datasets with Folds = 5, k = 5

With the configuration of folds = 5 and k = 5, the RMSE comparison chart indicates: The Energy algorithm has the lowest RMSE, suggesting it provides the highest accuracy among the three tested methods. Choosing k = 5 likely helped this method by leveraging information from the five nearest neighbors, thereby reducing prediction errors. The Cosine algorithm shows a higher RMSE than Energy but is still lower than Pearson, indicating a reasonably good accuracy, though not as strong as Energy in this scenario. The Pearson algorithm has the highest RMSE, indicating the greatest discrepancy between

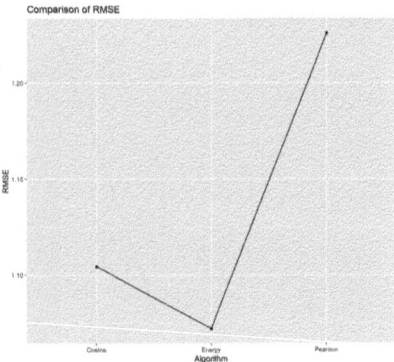

Fig. 4. Evaluating the RMSE error of the energy distance algorithm for structural analysis in sparse datasets with folds = 5, k = 5

predicted and actual values. This may imply that the Pearson similarity calculation is less suited for this dataset with k = 5 (Figs. 4 and 5).

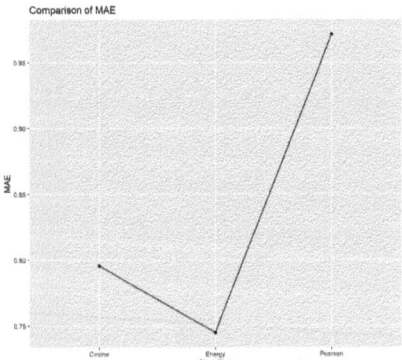

Fig. 5. Evaluating the MAE error of the energy distance algorithm for structural analysis in sparse datasets with folds = 5, k = 5

With the settings of folds = 5 and k = 5, the MAE comparison chart reveals: The Energy algorithm has the lowest MAE, demonstrating that it provides the highest prediction accuracy among the three algorithms based on Mean Absolute Error. This suggests that the Energy-based approach is well-suited for this configuration, achieving the smallest deviation from actual values. The Cosine algorithm, with a slightly higher MAE than Energy, still performs relatively well, though it doesn't match the accuracy level of Energy under these conditions. The Pearson algorithm displays the highest MAE, indicating it is the least accurate in this setup. This suggests that Pearson similarity may not be as effective for this dataset with k = 5.

5   Conclusion

The proposed energy distance algorithm has demonstrated outstanding effectiveness in addressing data sparsity issues within recommendation systems. Through experiments conducted on the MovieLens dataset, this method not only provides more accurate predictions compared to traditional approaches like Cosine Similarity and Pearson Correlation but also maintains stable performance across different configurations. Specifically, when using configurations with higher folds and larger neighborhood sizes, the energy distance method effectively leverages structural information from sparse datasets, significantly reducing prediction errors as reflected in lower RMSE and MAE values compared to other methods.

These findings indicate that the energy distance method holds great potential for improving recommendation accuracy, especially in sparse data environments—a major challenge for traditional recommendation systems. This suggests that the energy distance approach is not only a valuable alternative to conventional similarity measures but also a promising solution to address the accuracy and performance issues in recommendation systems.

In the future, this research could be expanded to apply the algorithm in other domains, such as e-commerce, social media, or online content recommendation. Additionally, further optimization of the algorithm for real-time recommendation scenarios would open up broad and effective applications in practical contexts, offering substantial benefits for both users and businesses.

References

1. Sarwar, B., Karypis, G., Konstan, J., Riedl, J.: Item-based collaborative filtering recommendation algorithms. In: Proceedings of the 10th International Conference on World Wide Web, pp. 285–295. ACM, New York (2001)
2. Adomavicius, G., Tuzhilin, A.: Toward the next generation of recommender systems. A survey of the state-of-the-art and possible extensions. IEEE Trans. Knowl. Data Eng. **17**, 734–749 (2005)
3. Szekely, G.J., Rizzo, M.L.: Energy statistics: a class of statistics based on distances. J. Stat. Plan. Inference **143**(8), 1249–1272 (2013)
4. Rizzo, M., Székely, G.: Energy distance. Wiley Interdiscip. Rev. Comput. Stat. **8** (1), 27–38 (2016)
5. Gunawardana, A., Shani, G.: A survey of accuracy evaluation metrics of recommendation tasks. J. Mach. Learn. Res. **10**, 2935–2962 (2009)
6. Zhang, S., Yao, L., Sun, A., Tay, Y.: Deep learning-based recommender system: a survey and new perspectives. ACM Comput. Surv. **52**(1), 5:1–5:38 (2019)
7. Sejdinovic, D., Sriperumbudur, B., Gretton, A., Fukumizu, K.: Equivalence of distance-based and RKHS-based statistics in hypothesis testing. Ann. Stat. **41**(5), 2263–2291 (2013)
8. Nguyen, H.T., Phan, L.P., Huynh, H.H., Huynh, H.X.: Recommendation with quantitative implication rules. EAI Endorsed Trans. Context-Aware Syst. Appl. **6**(16) (2019)
9. Rendle, S., Freudenthaler, C., Gantner, Z., Schmidt-Thieme, L.: BPR: Bayesian personalized ranking from implicit feedback. In: Proceedings of the Twenty-Fifth Conference on Uncertainty in Artificial Intelligence, pp. 452–461. AUAI Press, Arlington (2009)
10. Koren, Y., Bell, R., Volinsky, C.: Matrix factorization techniques for recommender systems. IEEE Comput. **42**(8), 30–37 (2009)

11. He, X., Liao, L., Zhang, H., Nie, L., Hu, X., Chua, T.S.: Neural collaborative filtering. In: Proceedings of the 26th International Conference on World Wide Web, pp. 173–182. ACM, New York (2017)

12. Székely, G.J., Rizzo, M.L.: The Energy of Data and Distance Correlation. CRC Press (2023). https://doi.org/10.1201/9780429157158

13. Amatriain, X., Jaimes, A., Oliver, N., Pujol, J.M.: Data mining methods for recommender systems. In: Ricci, F., Rokach, L., Shapira, B., Kantor, P. (eds.) Recommender Systems Handbook, pp. 39–71. Springer, Boston (2011) https://doi.org/10.1007/978-0-387-85820-3_2

14. Hahsler, M.: Recommenderlab: an R framework for developing and testing recommendation algorithms. J. Stat. Softw. (2023). https://github.com/mhahsler/recommenderlab

15. Hastie, T., Tibshirani, R., Wainwright, M.: Statistical Learning with Sparsity: The Lasso and Generalizations. Monographs on Statistics and Applied Probability, vol. 143. CRC Press (2016)

16. Çoba, L., Zanker, M., Symeonidis, P.: Environment for Evaluating Recommender Systems. Repository CRAN (2019). https://rdrr.io/cran/rrecsys/

17. Natarajan, S., Vairavasundaram, S., Natarajan, S., Gandomi, A.H.: Resolving data sparsity and cold start problem in collaborative filtering recommender system using Linked Open Data. Expert Syst. Appl. **149**, 113248 (2020). https://doi.org/10.1016/j.eswa.2020.113248

18. Choi, S.-M., Lee, D., Jang, K., Park, C., Lee, S.: Improving data sparsity in recommender systems using matrix regeneration with item features. Mathematics **11**, 292 (2023). https://doi.org/10.3390/math11020292

Energy-Based Models with Energy Distance for Video Captioning

Trung Thanh Le[1]($\boxtimes$) (ID) and Cong Thang Pham[2] (ID)

[1] Faculty of Information Technology, University of Economics, Vinh Long Campus, Ho Chi Minh City, Vietnam
trunglt@ueh.edu.vn
[2] The University of Da Nang, University of Science and Technology, Da Nang, Vietnam
pcthang@dut.udn.vn

Abstract. Video captioning, the task of generating natural language descriptions for video content, plays a pivotal role in bridging the gap between visual understanding and language generation. This study introduces a novel approach that leverages Energy-Based Models (EBMs) combined with Energy Distance (ED) to optimize the alignment between video features and captions. The proposed VC-EBM-ED framework emphasizes compatibility by minimizing energy discrepancies between correct and incorrect video-caption pairs, allowing the model to learn nuanced relationships effectively. Experiments conducted on the MSR-VTT dataset demonstrate the model's ability to generate captions that capture both the overall context and specific actions within videos. Results highlight the framework's potential for generalization across unseen data, underscoring its robustness and adaptability. While the model achieves promising performance, further exploration into handling longer and more complex video scenarios presents an exciting avenue for future research. The VC-EBM-ED framework offers a foundation for advancing multimodal learning and unlocking new possibilities in video understanding and captioning applications.

Keywords: Video Captioning · Energy-Based Models · Energy Distance · Multimodal Learning · Semantic Alignment

1 Introduction

Video captioning has become a significant area of research at the confluence of computer vision (CV) and natural language processing (NLP), aimed at generating accurate textual descriptions of video content. This process bridges the gap between visual understanding and linguistic representation, with applications spanning video analysis, multimedia retrieval, and recommendation systems. Capturing both primary actions and contextual details remains a challenging yet crucial goal for advancing this field.

Despite notable progress, several challenges persist in video captioning. Early methods relied on temporal structures [1] and embedding-based translation models [2] to address the inherent multimodal nature of video and text. Hierarchical Recurrent Neural

H. X. Huynh et al. (Eds.): GOODTECHS 2024, LNICST 649, pp. 25–34, 2025.
https://doi.org/10.1007/978-3-032-01497-9_3

Networks (RNNs) [3] and Long Short-Term Memory (LSTM) networks [4] introduced sequential data modeling capabilities, yet struggled with vanishing gradients and long-term dependencies [5]. While Transformer-based models [6, 7] improved sequence processing with self-attention mechanisms, they often lack temporal consistency, leading to fragmented video descriptions [8].

To tackle these challenges, Energy-Based Models (EBMs) offer a promising alternative by measuring compatibility between video features and captions. Introduced by LeCun et al. [9–11], EBMs minimize energy scores for correct data pairs and penalize incorrect ones, ensuring effective alignment. Recent advancements [12] have further extended EBMs to multimodal tasks, including video captioning, by incorporating generative capabilities and robust feature recognition. By integrating Energy Distance [13], this study leverages EBMs to optimize semantic alignment between visual and linguistic data.

In this work, we propose the VC-EBM-ED framework, which combines EBMs with Energy Distance to enhance compatibility between video features and captions. ResNet50 [14, 15], a pre-trained convolutional neural network, extracts video features, while BERT [16], a state-of-the-art language model, encodes captions into semantic embeddings. The framework minimizes energy discrepancies between correct and incorrect video-caption pairs, addressing both temporal and semantic challenges.

This paper is organized as follows: Sect. 2 details the theoretical and functional components of the VC-EBM-ED model. Section 3 presents the experimental setup, evaluation metrics, and results. Finally, Sect. 4 concludes with insights and directions for future research.

2   Energy-Based Models with Energy Distance for Video Captioning (VC-EBM-ED)

2.1   The Energy Model Perspective for Video Captioning

Energy-Based Models (EBMs) offer a robust framework for measuring compatibility between video features and captions in video captioning tasks. Unlike probabilistic methods that rely on predicting word probabilities, EBMs compute an energy score for each video-caption pair. Lower energy values indicate higher compatibility, while higher energy values suggest incompatibility. This approach aligns well with the multimodal nature of video captioning, where the objective is to bridge the semantic gap between visual and textual data.

In the proposed framework, a video is represented as a feature vector V, extracted using ResNet50 from individual frames and aggregated into a single representation [14, 15]. Similarly, a caption is encoded as a feature vector C using a BERT-based language model that captures semantic information [16]. The energy function is defined as the squared Euclidean distance between these two vectors [9–11]:

$$E(V, C) = \|V - C\|^2 = \sum_{i=1}^{d} (V_i - C_i)^2,$$

where V_i and C_i are the respective components of the video and caption feature vectors, and d is the dimensionality of the feature space. The energy function quantifies the alignment between the two modalities: a smaller $E(V, C)$ indicates better alignment, and thus, a semantically coherent caption for the video.

During training, the framework optimizes energy values for correct and incorrect video-caption pairs through the Energy Distance function [13]. Correct pairs (V, C) are assigned lower energy values, while incorrect pairs $E(V, C')$ are penalized with higher energy values. This is achieved by minimizing a margin-based loss function:

$$L = \max(0, \text{margin} + E(V, C) - E(V, C')),$$

where the margin is a pre-set parameter ensuring a sufficient energy gap between correct and incorrect pairs. If the energy of a correct pair is lower than that of an incorrect pair by the margin, the loss is zero; otherwise, the model adjusts its parameters to decrease $E(V, C)$ or increase $E(V, C')$.

The training process iteratively minimizes this loss across multiple video-caption pairs, enabling the model to learn effective semantic alignment. By leveraging the flexibility of EBMs and the discriminative power of Energy Distance, this approach provides a robust mechanism for capturing nuanced relationships in video captioning.

2.2 Model Architecture

The proposed model for video captioning integrates Energy-Based Models (EBMs) with Energy Distance, encompassing four primary components: Video Feature Extraction, Caption Embedding, Energy Function, and Energy Distance Optimization. This architecture enables the model to learn semantic compatibility between video features and textual descriptions effectively (Fig. 1).

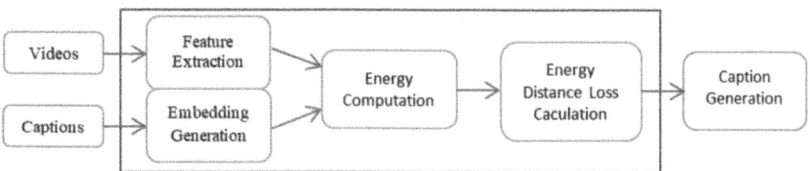

Fig. 1. Overview diagram of VC-EBM-ED functional model

2.2.1 Video Feature Extraction

Video inputs are first segmented into individual frames, denoted as $\{F_1, F_2, ..., F_n\}$. Each frame F_i is passed through a ResNet50 model [14], pre-trained on large-scale image datasets, to extract spatial feature vectors $f_i \in \mathbb{R}^d$, where d is the feature dimensionality. To represent the video, these frame-level features are aggregated by averaging:

$$V = \frac{1}{n} \sum_{i=1}^{n} F_i.$$

This aggregated feature vector V captures the overall visual content of the video while retaining essential spatial and temporal information.

2.2.2 Caption Embedding

Textual captions describing the video are tokenized into individual words, represented as $\{w_1, w_2, \ldots, w_m\}$, where w_i is the i-th word. Each word is encoded into an embedding vector $e_i \in \mathbb{R}^d$ using a BERT-based language model [16]. These word embeddings are then aggregated into a single caption representation:

$$C = \frac{1}{n} \sum_{i=1}^{n} e_i.$$

The resulting vector C encodes the semantic and contextual information of the caption, enabling the model to align linguistic features with video features effectively.

2.2.3 Energy Function

The energy function [12] quantifies the compatibility between video and caption pairs. Given the video feature vector V and caption embedding C, the energy function is defined as the Euclidean distance:

$$E(V, C) = \|V - C\|^2 = \sum_{i=1}^{d} (V_i - C_i)^2,$$

This formulation ensures that compatible pairs (e.g., a video and its correct caption) have lower energy scores, whereas incompatible pairs have higher energy scores.

2.2.4 Energy Distance Optimization

To differentiate correct video-caption pairs (V, C) from incorrect pairs (V, C'), the model minimizes an energy distance-based loss function [13]:

$$L = \max(0, \text{margin} + E(V, C) - E(V, C')),$$

The margin parameter ensures a sufficient separation between the energy of correct and incorrect pairs. During training, the model adjusts its parameters to reduce the energy for correct pairs and increase it for incorrect pairs, achieving a balance that aligns with the desired semantic relationships.

2.3 Algorithm

The video captioning process using an Energy-Based Model (EBM) with Energy Distance comprises four main steps: video feature extraction, caption embedding generation, energy computation, and optimal caption generation. Each input video is divided into individual frames $F_1, F_2, \ldots, F_n$. These frames are processed through the ResNet50 model to generate spatial feature vectors f_i for each frame. To create a comprehensive representation of the video, feature vectors from all frames are averaged, forming a single video feature vector V.

Each caption is then transformed into a multi-dimensional embedding vector C using a BERT language model. After obtaining the video feature vector and the caption embedding, the next step is to compute the energy between them. This energy value reflects the compatibility between the video V and the caption C. During the caption generation process, candidate captions are evaluated based on their computed energy values, with the caption having the lowest energy selected as the optimal description for the video (Algorithm 1).

Algorithm 1: VC-EBM-ED

Input: A set of videos V, where each video is a sequence of frames.

A set of captions C, where each caption describes the content of a video.

Output: Best matching caption for each video based on the lowest energy score.

Begin

// Step 1: Video Feature Extraction

1: for $v \in V$ do

2:　for $f \in v$ do

3:　　Pass f through the ResNet50 network to obtain a feature vector F for the frame.

4:　end for

5:　Compute the meaning of all frame-level vectors F to obtain a single video feature vector V, where N is the number of frames in v.

6: end for

// Step 2: Caption Embedding Generation

7: for $c \in C$ do

8:　for $w \in c$ do

9:　　Encode w using a BERT model to obtain an embedding E for the word.

10:　end for

11:　Compute the mean of all word embeddings E to get a single caption vector C, where M is the number of words in c.

12: end for

// Step 3: Energy Computation

13: for each video V and caption C pair do

14:　Compute the energy $E(V, C)$, where f is a chosen energy function, and $[V, C]$ represents the concatenation of the video and caption feature vectors.

　　- Low energy $E(V, C)$: Indicates a strong match between the video and caption.

　　- High energy $E(V, C)$: Indicates a poor match.

15: end for

// Step 4: Energy Distance Calculation

16: for each training step, use positive (correct) pairs (V, C), and negative (incorrect) pairs $E(V, C')$,:

17:　Compute the loss for each pair:

$$L = \max\big(0, \mathbf{margin} + E(V, C) - E(V, C')\big)$$

18:　Update model parameters to minimize L across multiple training iterations.

19: end for

// Step 5: Caption Generation (Optimal Caption Selection)

20: for each video V:

21:　Initialize lowestEnergy $:= \infty$ and bestCaption $:=$ null

22:　for each candidate caption C:

23:　　Compute the energy $E(V, C)$.

24:　　if $E(V, C) <$ lowestEnergy:

25:　　　Update lowestEnergy $:= E(V, C)$

26:　　　Set bestCaption $:= C$

27:　end for

28:　Return bestCaption as the caption with the lowest energy for video V.

29: end for

End.

---

3 Experiments

3.1 Datasets

In this study, we use the MSR-VTT dataset (Microsoft Research Video to Text) [17], one of the most popular datasets for video captioning research. The MSR-VTT dataset consists of approximately 10,000 short videos, each lasting an average of 10 to 30 s, and annotated with natural language captions. Each video in this dataset is accompanied by multiple captions, providing a range of detailed descriptions of the content and context. The videos cover various genres, including music, sports, news, and vlogs, enabling the model to learn and understand diverse contexts within video content.

MSR-VTT was developed to support research in natural language processing and computer vision, providing a rich training dataset for evaluating video captioning models. The dataset is divided into training, validation, and test sets to ensure objectivity in model evaluation. MSR-VTT is widely used in previous studies, such as the work by Xu (2016) [17] and other related research that is publicly accessible through the MSR-VTT Dataset (Fig. 2).

Attribute	Value
Number of videos	10,000
Average duration	10-30 seconds
Number of captions	200,000+
Caption language	Multilingual

Fig. 2. Overview of the MSR-VTT dataset used for experimentation.

3.2 Tools Used

During experimentation, several key tools were utilized to support the development, training, and evaluation of the VC-EBM-ED model, written in Python, specifically for natural language and image processing. In particular, OpenCV was used to extract frames from videos, facilitating video processing tasks and preparing data for training. Torchvision provided the ResNet50 model for extracting features from frames, while PyTorch was used to build and optimize the deep learning model. Hugging Face's Transformers library was employed to encode captions into vectors, enabling the model to understand textual semantics. Additionally, NumPy supported matrix operations, and Matplotlib was used to visualize results, particularly in evaluating model performance through comparative metrics.

3.3 Scenario 1: Evaluating the Model's Caption Generation Ability

In Scenario 1, we evaluate the model's caption generation on a video from the training dataset (Fig. 3). The caption generation process involves calculating the energy score for each candidate caption based on the compatibility between the video features and caption embedding. The caption with the lowest energy score is selected as the output, representing the highest compatibility with the video content. Training loss is computed using the Energy Distance function to optimize the energy difference between correct and incorrect video-caption pairs. This helps the model learn to assess the compatibility levels of captions effectively.

Generated caption for video video99: a man himself skating on the snow and shoots himself and shoots other people also
Energy of generated caption: -0.3623
Training loss: 0.8713

Fig. 3. Results of Experiment 1 with the video training dataset.

Experimental results produced the caption: "A man himself skating on the snow and shoots himself and shoots other people also." This caption captures the primary action (ice skating on snow and filming), but inaccuracies in detail highlight the model's challenges in fully interpreting the video context. The energy value of -0.3623 suggests moderate compatibility between the generated caption and the video content. A training loss of 0.87130 indicates that the model is learning to differentiate between correct and incorrect pairs, although further optimization is required.

To quantitatively evaluate the generated captions, we employ standard metrics:

BLEU-4: 0.480, demonstrating decent n-gram overlap with reference captions.
ROUGE-L: 0.620, reflecting moderate recall of the longest common subsequence.
CIDEr: 0.950, indicating good alignment with reference captions using TF-IDF weighting.

These metrics, along with the energy value and training loss, demonstrate the model's capability to generate contextually relevant captions. However, the inaccuracies in capturing fine-grained details suggest that the model requires further refinement to provide more precise descriptions.

3.4 Scenario 2: Evaluating Caption Generation and Optimization Through Energy Distance

In Scenario 2, we assess the model's performance on a video from the validation dataset, which the model has not encountered during training (Fig. 4). The evaluation aims to test the model's ability to generate captions for unseen data and optimize the energy difference between correct and incorrect pairs using the Energy Distance function.

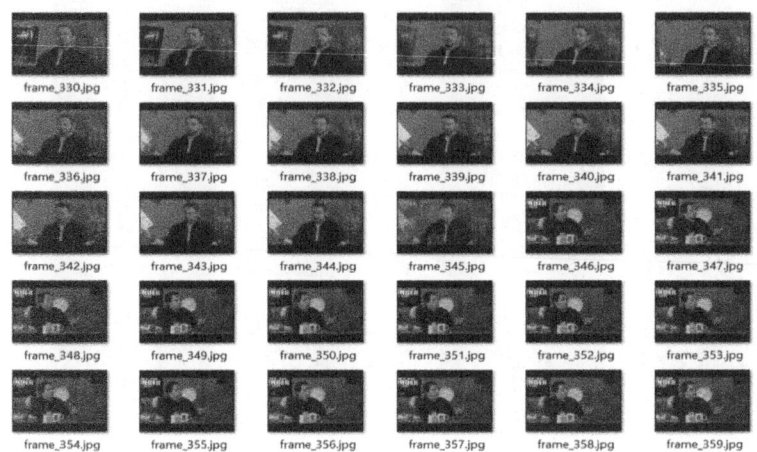

Generated caption for video video199: three famous actors set in an office and talk about how to promote one of their movies
Energy of generated caption: 0.6162
Training loss: 0.9356

Fig. 4. Results of Experiment 2 with the untrained video dataset.

The model generated the caption: "Three famous actors set in an office and talk about how to promote one of their movies." This caption accurately describes the primary setting (famous actors in an office discussion), though the specific details of the conversation may not fully align with the actual video content. This result indicates that the model has achieved a certain level of generalization beyond the training set, capturing the main context but still facing limitations in interpreting detailed content.

The energy value of 0.61620 reflects a moderate level of compatibility between the video features and the generated caption. A training loss of 0.93560 demonstrates that the model is reasonably capable of differentiating correct and incorrect pairs, although further optimization is necessary.

Metrics for this scenario include:

BLEU-4: 0.430, showing adequate n-gram overlap for unseen data.
ROUGE-L: 0.580, indicating moderate recall of common subsequences.
CIDEr: 0.890, suggesting reasonable alignment with reference captions.

These results demonstrate the model's potential for generalizing to unseen videos, with its ability to capture the main context. However, the limitations in interpreting fine-grained details and fluctuating training loss indicate the need for additional optimization. For instance, the model exhibits unstable training loss values, such as 1.12511, 1.10451 and 1.22721, suggesting that it struggles to converge fully. This instability is likely due to the complexity of certain video-caption pairs, which result in higher energy values for incorrect pairs. Further improvements in training stability and contextual understanding are necessary to enhance overall performance.

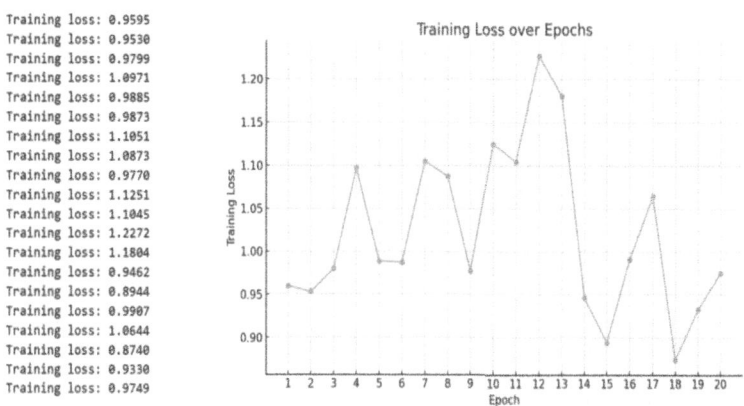

Fig. 5. Results of Experiment 2 running optimization with Energy Distance.

The experimental results show that the model's optimization through the Energy Distance function has achieved significant progress but still requires additional improvement for optimal effectiveness (Fig. 5). Training loss fluctuates between 0.8740 and 1.2272, with notably low values like 0.8944, 0.9330, and 0.9462, indicating the model's learning capacity in distinguishing correct and incorrect video-caption pairs. The low training loss values suggest that the model has potential in generating captions compatible with video content. However, the unstable fluctuation of training loss, particularly in epochs with higher values such as 1.1251, 1.1045 and 1.2272, indicates that the model has not yet fully converged. These results suggest that the model faces difficulties in achieving complete optimization, likely due to the complexity of certain video-caption pairs that lead to higher energy for incorrect pairs.

4 Conclusion

In conclusion, this study proposed the EBM-ED model, combining Energy-Based Models and the Energy Distance function, to improve video captioning by optimizing the compatibility between video features and textual descriptions. The results showed that the model effectively captures the overall context and primary actions within videos and demonstrates promising generalization capabilities on unseen data. However, the challenges in interpreting complex details and the instability observed during training highlight areas for further enhancement. These findings underscore the feasibility of the EBM-ED approach and its potential applications in fields such as multimedia information retrieval and content recommendation systems. Future research will aim to address these limitations by improving training stability, refining the model's ability to interpret detailed content, and extending its application to larger and more complex datasets to further enhance its performance and robustness.

References

1. Yao, L., Torabi, A., Cho, K., Ballas, N., Pal, C., Larochelle, H., Courville, A.: Describing videos by exploiting temporal structure. In: Proceedings of the IEEE International Conference on Computer Vision (ICCV), pp. 4507–4515. IEEE (2015)
2. Pan, Y., Mei, T., Yao, T., Li, H., Rui, Y.: Jointly modeling embedding and translation to bridge video and language. In: Proceedings of the IEEE Conference on Computer Vision and Pattern Recognition (CVPR), pp. 4594–4602. IEEE (2016)
3. Yu, H., Wang, J., Huang, Z., Yang, Y., Xu, W.: Video paragraph captioning using hierarchical recurrent neural networks. In: Proceedings of the IEEE Conference on Computer Vision and Pattern Recognition (CVPR), pp. 4584–4593. IEEE (2016)
4. Hochreiter, S., Schmidhuber, J.: Long short-term memory. Neural Comput. $9(8)$, 1735–1780 (1997)
5. Yang, Y., Zhou, J., Ai, J., Huang, C., Gan, C.: Video captioning by adversarial LSTM. IEEE Trans. Image Process. $27(11)$, 5600–5611 (2018)
6. Elman, J.L.: Finding structure in time. Cogn. Sci. $14(2)$, 179–211 (1990)
7. Vaswani, A., et al.: Attention is all you need. In: Advances in Neural Information Processing Systems (NeurIPS), pp. 5998–6008 (2017)
8. Wang, T., Huang, W., Wang, T., Wang, W.: End-to-end dense video captioning with parallel decoding. In: Proceedings of the IEEE/CVF International Conference on Computer Vision (ICCV), pp. 6847–6857. IEEE (2021)
9. LeCun, Y., Huang, F.: Loss functions for discriminative training of energy-based models. In: Proceedings of the 10th International Workshop on Artificial Intelligence and Statistics (AIStats), pp. 206–213 (2005)
10. Osadchy, R., Miller, M., LeCun, Y.: Synergistic face detection and pose estimation with energy-based model. In: Advances in Neural Information Processing Systems (NIPS), pp. 1197–1215. MIT Press (2005)
11. LeCun, Y., Chopra, S., Hadsell, R.: A Tutorial on Energy-Based Learning. Predicting Structured Data, pp. 1–59. MIT Press, Cambridge (2006)
12. Song, Y.; Kingma, D.: How to train your energy-based models. arXiv preprint, arXiv:2101. 03288v2 (2021)
13. Rizzo, M.L., Székely, G.J.: Energy distance. WIREs Comput. Stat. 8, 27–38 (2016)
14. He, K., Zhang, X., Ren, S., Sun, J.: Deep residual learning for image recognition. In: Proceedings of the IEEE Conference on Computer Vision and Pattern Recognition (CVPR), pp. 770–778. IEEE Computer Society (2016)
15. Krizhevsky, A., Sutskever, I., Hinton, G.: ImageNet classification with deep convolutional neural networks. In: Advances in Neural Information Processing Systems (NeurIPS), pp. 1097–1105 (2012)
16. Devlin, J., Chang, M.-W., Lee, K., Toutanova, K.: BERT: pre-training of deep bidirectional transformers for language understanding. In: Proceedings of the North American Chapter of the Association for Computational Linguistics (NAACL-HLT), pp. 4171–4186. ACL (2019)
17. Xu, J., Mei, T., Yao, T., Rui, Y.: MSR-VTT: a large video description dataset for bridging video and language. In: Proceedings of the IEEE Conference on Computer Vision and Pattern Recognition (CVPR), pp. 5288–5296. IEEE (2016)

Detecting Driver Drowsiness Using Deep Learning Techniques

Nhuong Quang Le[1], Ho Dong Thai[1], Tri Minh Huynh[1], and Quoc-Bao Truong[2(✉)]

[1] Faculty of Information and Communication, Kien Giang University, Minh Luong, Kien Giang, Vietnam
{lqnhuong,tdho,hmtri}@vnkgu.edu.vn
[2] College of Engineering, Can Tho University (CTU), Can Tho, Vietnam
tqbao@ctu.edu.vn

Abstract. Drowsy driving is one of the leading causes of serious traffic accidents. Detecting and warning drivers of drowsiness can significantly reduce the risk of accidents, thereby contributing to protecting human life and property.In this article, we introduce a model of Convolutional Neural Networks (CNN) to detect the driver's drowsiness. A video camera is used to monitor [9] the face, the eye state, the mouth state, and the driver's head pose. The system will issue a warning when the driver manifests drowsiness. We present a new approach in determining one's eye, mouth, and head pose in different directions combines with using the support of the OpenCV library to locate the driver's face with the camera. We combination of eyes status, mouth status, and head pose can increase the accuracy and reliability of the system. The overall accuracy when testing the system is over 97%, which has proved the feasibility of the system. In particular, the accuracy of face recognition is 99% with the Caffe model and the support of the OpenCV. Regarding the recognition of the state of the head pose after testing for accuracy is above 97%. On the recognition of the state of the eyes and mouth are very high. Specifically, the accuracy of the eye is over 99.7% and the accuracy of the mouth is 99.8%.

Keywords: The drowsiness driver · the head pose of the driver · the state of the driver eyes · the state of the driver mouth · the convolutional neural network model

1 Introduction

Objectives of the study is to build a system that warns drivers about drowsy driving and reduces drowsy driving by providing audio reminders and warnings. We applies previously developed methods and research, and proposes a CNN model [3] for the problem of recognizing the state of the driver's eyes, mouth and head pose to create a system for detecting the driver's condition with high reliability. The system also uses the support of the OpenCV library and the deep learning model Caffemodel and the detection of the face position during the recording. Thereby, continuing to use the CNNs

© ICST Institute for Computer Sciences, Social Informatics and Telecommunications Engineering 2025
Published by Springer Nature Switzerland AG 2025. All Rights Reserved
H. X. Huynh et al. (Eds.): GOODTECHS 2024, LNICST 649, pp. 35–48, 2025.
https://doi.org/10.1007/978-3-032-01497-9_4

model to detect the driver's drowsiness state. Specifically, we need to solve the following problems:

- Detect the driver's face position [8];
- Recognize the state of the driver's eyes [10], mouth and head pose during recording;
- Check the cases that are considered to be the driver's state of drowsiness [1, 2];
- Give a warning when determining the driver's state as drowsiness.

2 Main Content

The system detects drowsiness by the frequency of eye states combined with the mouth state and head pose of the driver. In which of the following cases, the driver is considered to be sleepy:

- Number of eye closures is about 30 times per minute [5];
- Number of eye closures is greater than 25 times per minute combined with yawning 2 times per minute (recommended) [5];
- Eyes closed in 8 consecutive frames (recommended);
- Head pose is considered to be not concentrating (Driver's head pose has a rotation angle greater than 15°) continuously in 8 consecutive frames (recommended) (Fig. 1).

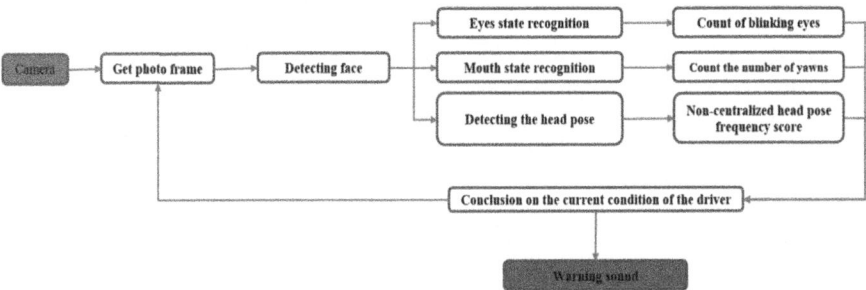

Fig. 1. The system diagram

In general, the detecting system consists of 4 steps:

- Step 1: Get the frame from the camera
- Step 2: Continuously monitor the state of the eyes combined with the mouth and head pose
- Step 3: Determine the current state of the driver
- Step 4: Emit a warning sound when detecting the driver getting drowsy.

After capturing the driver's image, the system will detect the face region with the support of the OpenCV library, specifically face detection with OpenCV Caffe model. Next, the system will determine the eye and mouth area by extracting the eye and mouth areas based on 68 characteristic points (landmarks) [12] of the face. Continuously using the eye and mouth areas to determine the current state of the eyes and mouth through the pre-trained deep learning model [3]. Thereby, the frequency of blinking and yawning of the driver in one minute is measured. Considering the head pose, after determining the face region, choose a head pose area that is larger than the face region and confirm the head pose of the driver in the frame. Combining all three factors of eyes, mouth and head pose, we get a conclusion about the current state of the driver. When the system starts, it will detect the driver's face region. If the driver's face is not detected in 150 frames [12], the system emits a warning to ensure that the driver always face the camera. Next step, we continue to extract the area containing the driver's head pose [6] to determine whether the driver is concentrating or not. If the driver's head pose is continuously detected as not concentrating in 10 frames, the system will emit the second warning. On the contrary, if the head pose is determined as concentrating, the system will continuously monitor current state of the driver.

The head pose monitoring is continuously while the system is running. We extract the head pose region based on the face region extracted from the previous work and then expand it to contain the driver's head pose. After, we continue to use the pre-trained model using CNNs [6] model to determine the driver's head pose. We continue to monitor the eye states by extracting the eye areas on the face region by taking the key points of the eyes, provided by the DLIB library. After extracting the eye areas, we continue to recognize the current state of the eyes using the pre-trained model based on the CNNs model. Blinking is considered to complete a cycle between the closed and opened statues. If the number of blinks exceeds 35 times per minute, the third alarm will be emitted. In addition, if the eyes are detected to be closed continuously for 10 frames, the fourth alarm will be emitted.

In the final step, we use the same method as for extracting the eye areas to extract the mouth area. And then, we use the pre-trained model based on CNNs to determine the state of the mouth. The number of yawns is also calculated similarly to the number of blinks. If the number of yawns exceeds 6 times per minute and the number of blinks exceeds 25 times per minute, the 5th warning will be emitted.

3 Implementation Method

3.1 CNN Training Model

Convolutional Neural Network (CNN) [4] is a type of machine learning model commonly used in computer vision problems such as image recognition, image classification, object detection, etc. Below are the main components and basic formulas in a CNN model:

3.1.1 Convolution Layer

The convolutional layer is the core component of CNN [4], which helps the network learn features in the input data through filters or convolutional kernels. The formula for each element in the output of the convolutional layer is as follows:

$$output(i, j) = \sum_{m=0}^{M-1} \sum_{n=0}^{N-1} input(i + m, j + n) \cdot kernel(m, n) \tag{1}$$

- input(i, j) is the value at position (i, j) (i, j) (i, j) in the subregion of the input,
- kernel(m, n) is the value at position (m, n) in filter,
- M và N is the size of the filter.

After applying convolution, a bias can be added to adjust the output value.

$$\text{output}(i, j) = \text{output}(i, j) + \text{bias} \tag{2}$$

3.1.2 Activation Layer

An activation layer such as ReLU (Rectified Linear Unit) [4] is applied after the convolution layer to introduce non-linearity into the network. The formula for ReLU is:

$$f(x) = \max(0, x) \tag{3}$$

3.1.3 Pooling Layer

Pooling Layer [4] is often used to reduce the spatial dimension of the output, which reduces the number of parameters and computations, and controls overfitting. Two common pooling methods are Max Pooling and Average Pooling.

- Max Pooling: Takes the largest value in a region (2×2 or 3×3) of the input matrix.
- Average Pooling: Takes the average value in a region of the input matrix.

3.1.4 Fully Connected Layer

The fully connected layer works like a Fully Connected Neural Network - FCN (FCN) [4]. Each input is connected to each neuron in the layer. The formula for a simple neuron in this layer is:

$$y = f\left(\sum_{i=1}^{n} w_i x_i + b\right) \tag{4}$$

- w_i is the weight corresponding to the input x_i,
- b is bias,
- f is the activation function (e.g. ReLU or Softmax for the last layer if it is a classification problem).

3.1.5 Loss Function

For classification problems, the Cross-Entropy [4] function is a popular choice:

$$L = -\sum_{i=1}^{C} y_i \log(\hat{y}_i) \tag{5}$$

- C is the number of classes,
- y_i is the actual label (0 or 1) for class i,
- $\hat{y}_i$ is the predicted probability for class i.

3.1.6   Backpropagation and Optimization

To update the weights of the network, the Backpropagation algorithm [4] is applied to calculate the gradient of the loss function with each weight and optimize using algorithms such as SGD (Stochastic Gradient Descent) or Adam. The formula for updating the weights with the SGD algorithm is:

$$\omega = \omega - n\frac{\partial L}{\partial \omega} \tag{6}$$

- n learning rate,
- $n\frac{\partial L}{\partial \omega}$ is the gradient of the loss function over the weights ω.

3.2   Model Training

Model training is the creation of a model to help the machine answer some questions that the model user needs [6]. To create a model, the model trainer needs to have a standard dataset about the training object, choosing training parameters will help increase the accuracy rate of the model.

Image database: To be able to create a model with high accuracy, the database is a fundamental factor. In order to provide the system with an accurate definition of the object that the model trainer wants the system.

Determine training parameters: Calculate the necessary parameters from the image database and then, determine the parameters to define the model and how to train the model.

Perform the training process: Train and fine-tune the recognition model for the system using the image database.

Export the trained model: Export the successfully trained model, as an input to the system's recognition module.

Our system uses four pre-trained models:

- Face detection model provided by Caffe framework
- Driver's head orientation recognition model (we trained).
- Driver's eye state recognition model (we trained).
- Driver's mouth state recognition model (we trained).

3.3   Detect the Face Region Using OpenCV Library and Caffe Framework

Caffe framework is provided by Berkeley Vision and Learning Center (BVLC) [7]. Written in C++, Python and MATLAB. The Caffe model used for face recognition is pre-trained and support with the OpenCV library with a claimed accuracy of 98%.

3.4 Detect the Driver's Head Pose

- Dataset

We use two main sources to perform learning and testing in the system:

Source 1: Provided by N. Gourier, D. Hall, J. L. Crowley[13] including 2820 images taken from 15 people with rotation angles from $-90°-90°$. The dataset is divided into 2 types: Normal rotation angle from $-15°-15°$ has 270 images and the remaining not-concentrating rotation angle has 2550 images.

Source 2: we collected by webcam Logitech C310 at a distance of 50 cm. The dataset includes 1367 images taken from 6 people. In which, images with normal head posture are 450 images and not-concentrating head posture are 917 images.

- Training parameters

Input data: Input image size is 52×68 (height, width). After each Convolution layer, the ReLU function is activated for each layer, after that MaxPooling is performed immediately. The last layer has n output units corresponding to the number of layers of the dataset.

Kernel/Filter: The size of the filters is $3 \times 3(1)$.

MaxPooling: The model uses a sampling method by selecting the largest value in the 2×2 size (3.1.3).

Epochs: The number of training periods of the model is 50(5).

Error rate: Each time the error is adjusted, it is 0.001(6).

The used model in the system has four hidden layers, including 3 convolution layers (Convolution), fine-tuning (ReLU), sampling (MaxPooling) and sigmoid layer (Softmax) (Fig. 2).

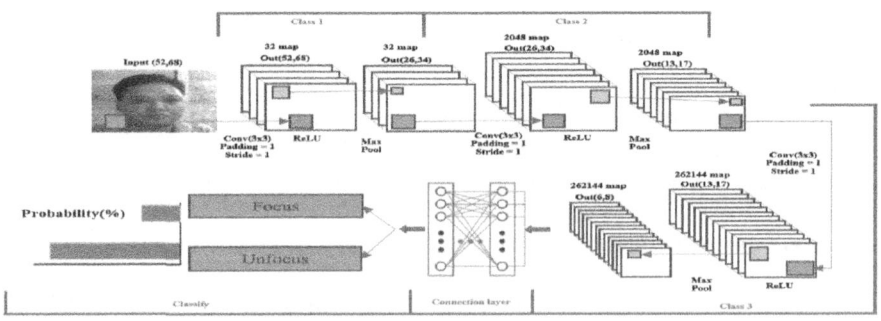

Fig. 2. Recognition model training process for Head pose

Illustration for the network operation:

The input is a grayscale image of size 52×68. The system convolves with randomly selected filters of size 3×3 with a step (stride = 1 and padding = 1).

Layer 1: After convolution, 32 feature maps of size 52x68 are obtained for each input image. After fine-tuning the 32 newly appeared feature maps and performing pooling with the largest weight (Maxpooling(2 × 2)), we obtain 32 new feature maps of size 26 × 34 and use them as the next input to Layer 2.

Layer 2: The input is the 32 feature maps of size 26 × 32 that were created in Layer 1. Convolution of each feature map with 64 filters of size 3 × 3, we get a total of 2048 new feature maps. Fine-tuning and performing Maxpooling(2 × 2) we get 2,048 feature maps of size 13 × 17 and end of the phase of layer 2.

Layer 3: Similarly, the input for this layer is the feature maps output of layer 2. Convolution of each feature map with 128 filters of size 3 × 3, we get a total of 262,144 new feature maps. Continuing to fine-tune and perform Maxpooling(2 × 2), we get a total of 262,144 features of the model with a size of 6 × 8 (Fig. 3).

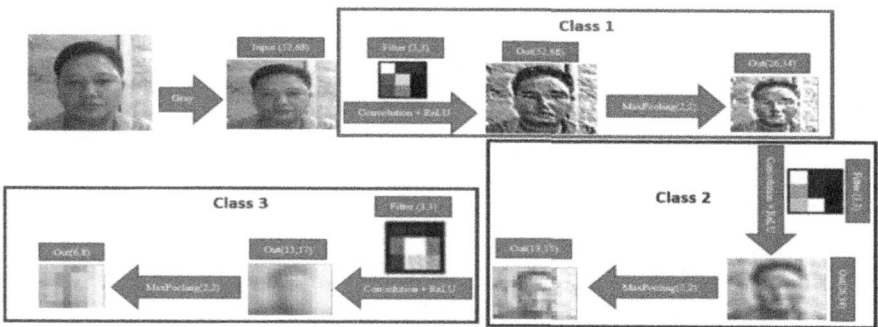

Fig. 3. Illustration of output image through each hidden layer

Connected layer: Convert the feature maps obtained above into a 1-column vector with weights in 0–1 range [11] (1 is concentrating, 0 is not concentrating). Then process will vote for image classification.

The process of adjusting the error using the backpropagation method is started when there are voting results. From here, the system will automatically adjust the parameters of the filters to produce results consistent with the image labels assigned from the beginning (Table 1).

3.5 Determine the Driver's Eye State

• Data set

The data source used for the learning and testing of the system is taken from 2 main sources:

Source 1: We use pre-cropped images of the eye area with a size of 26 × 34 from the Closed Eyes In The Wild (CEW) dataset [14]. The dataset includes 4846 images, including 2384 closed eye images and 2462 open eye images including both left and right eyes.

Source 2: Self-collected using a webcam Logitech C310 at a distance of 50cm. The dataset consists of 3103 images taken from 6 people by live recording, including 1424 closed-eye images and 1679 open-eye images including both left and right eyes.

Table 1. Information of the head direction recognition model

Name	Input						Output				Params
	width	height	nfilter	filtersize	stride	pad	width	height	nfilter	Bias	
Input	52	68	1				52	68			
Conv1	52	68	32	9	1	1	52	68	32	1	320
MaxPool1	52	68		4	1	1	26	34	32		
Conv2	26	34	64	9	1	1	26	34	2.048	1	18.496
MaxPool2	26	34		4	1	1	13	17	64		
Conv3	13	17	128	9	1	1	13	17	262.144	1	73.856
MaxPool3	6	8		4	1	1	6	8	128		
Flatten1	6	8	128						6144		
Dense1			512						512		3.146.240
Dense2			512						512	1	262.656
Dense3			512						512	1	513
Total Params											**3.502.081**

- Training parameters

The training parameters of this model are similar to the driver's head pose training model's, except the image size of the input data set.

The training model is divided into four hidden layers, including 3 convolutional layers and 1 sigmoid layer (Softmax) as shown in Fig. 4.

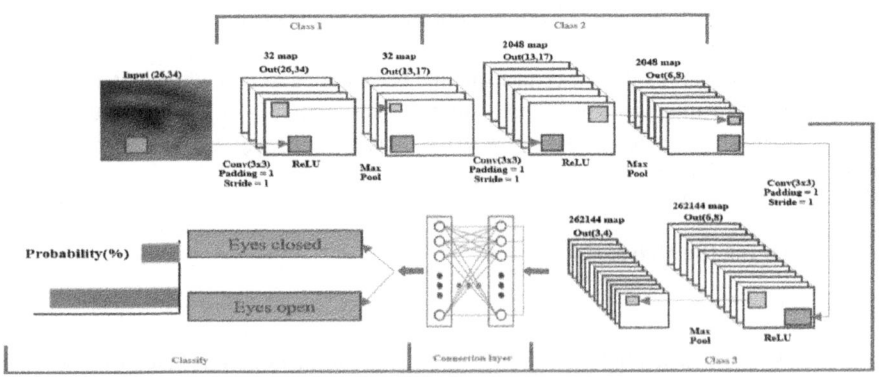

Fig. 4. Training process of eye state recognition model

Illustration of the network operation:

The input is a grayscale image of size 26×34. The system convolves with randomly selected filters of size 3×3 with a step (stride $= 1$ and padding $= 1$).

Layer 1: After convolution, 32 feature maps of size 26×34 are obtained for each input image. Fine-tune the 32 newly created feature maps and perform pooling with the largest weight (Maxpooling(2 × 2)) to obtain 32 new feature maps of size 13 × 17 and use them as the next input to Layer 2.

Layer 2: The input is the 32 feature maps of size 26 × 32 that were created in layer 1. Convolution of each feature map with 64 filters of size 3 × 3, we get a total of 2048 new feature maps. Fine-tuning and pooling Maxpooling(2 × 2) we get 2048 feature maps of size 13 × 17 and end the phase of layer 2.

Layer 3: Similarly, the input for this layer is the output feature maps of layer 2. Convolution of each feature map with 128 filters of size 3 × 3, we get a total of 262,144 new feature maps. Continuing to fine-tune and pooling Maxpooling(2 × 2), we get a total of 262,144 features of the model with a size of 3 × 4 (Fig. 5).

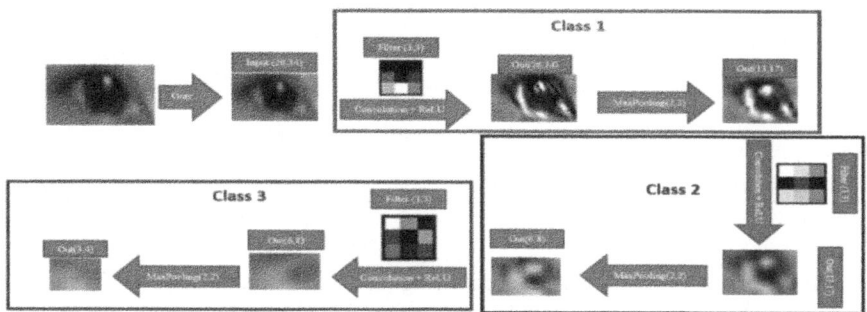

Fig. 5. Output image through each hidden layer

Connected layer: Convert the feature maps obtained above into a 1-column vector with weights in 0–1 range (1 is closed eyes, 0 is open eyes). Then process will vote for image classification.

The process of adjusting the error rate using the backpropagation method is started when having voting results. The system will automatically adjust the parameters of the filters to produce results consistent with the image labels assigned from the beginning (Table 2).

3.6 Determine the Driver's Mouth Condition

The system detects the driver's mouth region after identifying the face location. Next, it uses a pre-trained model to classify the state of the mouth. This model is based on Convolutional Neural Networks (CNNs), a type of deep neural network commonly used in image processing.

- Dataset

Similar to training the head pose and eye state models mentioned above, the mouth dataset is also taken from 2 main sources:

Source 1: We cut images from the videos of the YawDD: Yawning Detection Dataset [15]. We cut a total of 4417 images, including 3,994 normal mouth images and 473 yawning mouth images.

Table 2. Parameters of the eye state recognition model

Name	Input						Output				Params
	width	height	nfilter	filtersize	stride	pad	width	height	nfilter	Bias	
Input	26	34					26	34	1		
Conv1	26	34	32	9	1	1	26	34	32	1	320
MaxPool1	26	34		4	1	1	13	17	32		
Conv2	13	17	64	9	1	1	13	17	2.048	1	18.496
MaxPool2	13	17		4	1	1	6	8	64		
Conv3	6	8	128	9	1	1	6	8	262.144	1	73.856
MaxPool3	6	8		4	1	1	3	4	128		
Flatten1	6	8	128						6144		
Dense1			512						512		786.944
Dense2			512						512	1	262.656
Dense3			1						512	1	513
Total Params											**1.142.785**

Source 2: we collected using webcam Logitech C310 at a distance of 50cm. The dataset includes 2,202 images including 2,045 normal mouth images and 157 yawning mouth images.

- Training parameters

The parameters of the mouth state recognition training model are the same as the two models mentioned above (Fig. 6).

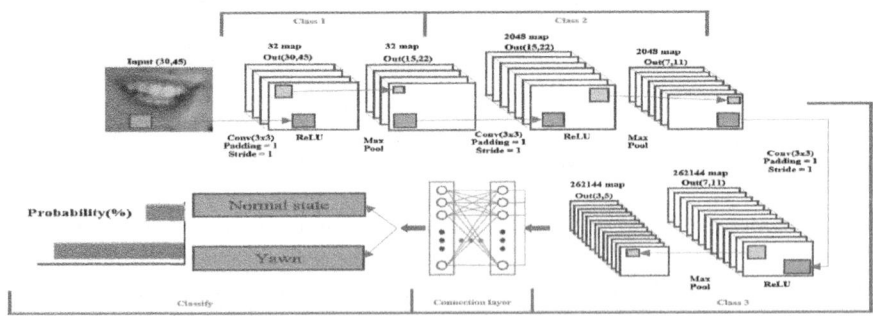

Fig. 6. Training process for mouth state recognition model

Illustration of the network operation:

The input is a grayscale image of size 30 × 45. The system convolves with randomly selected filters of size 3 × 3 with a step (stride = 1 and padding = 1).

Layer 1: After convolution, 32 feature maps of size 30 × 45 are obtained for each input image. Fine-tune the 32 newly appeared feature maps and perform pooling with the largest weight (Maxpooling(2 × 2)) to obtain 32 new feature maps of size 15 × 22 and use them as the next input to Layer 2.

Layer 2: The input is the 32 feature maps of size 15 × 22 that were created in layer 1. Convolution of each feature map with 64 filters of size 3 × 3, we get a total of 2048 new feature maps. Fine-tuning and pooling Maxpooling(2 × 2) we get 2,048 feature maps of size 7 × 11 and end the phase of layer 2.

Layer 3: Similarly, the input is the output feature maps of layer 2. Convolution of each feature map with 128 filters of size 3 × 3, we get a total of 262,144 new feature maps. Continuing to fine-tune and sample Maxpooling(2 × 2), we get a total of 262,144 features of the model with size of 3 × 4 (Fig. 7).

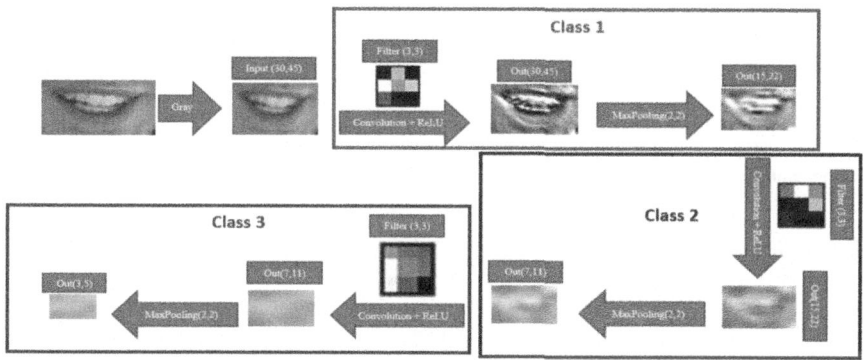

Fig. 7. Output image through each hidden layer

Connected layer: Convert the feature maps obtained above into a 1-column vector with weights in 0–1 range (1 is normal, 0 is yawning). Then process will vote for image classification. The process of adjusting the error rate using the backpropagation method is started when having voting results. The system will automatically adjust the parameters of the filters to produce results consistent with the image labels assigned from the beginning (Table 3).

4   Testing Results

4.1   Results with Test Data

Conducting tests with 2 different situations: Situation 1 is used to test the model with input data that has been pre-cropped to the recognition region and passed through the model to check the state. Situation 2 is used to test the accuracy of the combined models (Face» Head orientation» Face state» Mouth state) with the input image being frames cut from the video [9] and passed through the system to test the accuracy when passing through each model.

We get the following results (Table 4):

The results of the table above show that the accuracy of the model and system is high with other data and the pre-trained data. For the eye and mouth state recognition

Table 3. Parameters of the mouth state recognition model

Name	Input						Output				Params
	width	height	nfilter	filtersize	stride	pad	width	height	nfilter	Bias	
Input	30	45					30	45	1		
Conv1	30	45	32	9	1	1	30	45	32	1	320
MaxPool1	30	45		4	1	1	15	22	32		
Conv2	15	22	64	9	1	1	15	22	2.048	1	18.496
MaxPool2	15	22		4	1	1	7	11	64		
Conv3	7	11	128	9	1	1	7	11	262.144	1	73.856
MaxPool3	7	11		4	1	1	3	5	128		
Flatten1	7	11	128						6144		
Dense1			512						512		983.552
Dense2			512						512	1	262.656
Dense3			1						512	1	513
Total Params											**1.339.393**

Table 4. Testing results

Data set	Label	Number	Situation 1		Situation 2	
			Correct	Incorrect	Correct	Incorrect
Head pose	Normal	900	446/450	4/450	442/450	8/450
	Unfocus	600	294/300	6/300	291/300	9/300
Eyes	Open	1.000	499/500	1/500	498/500	2/500
	Closed	1.000	500/500	0/500	499/500	1/500
Face	Normal	950	450/450	0/450	498/500	2/500
	Yawn	700	300/300	0/300	399/400	1/400
Total		**5.150**	**2.500**		**2.650**	

model, the accuracy is almost absolute and the head pose recognition model is lower but it is still very high. This shows that the input data of the two models of eye and mouth recognition is more standardized than the input data of the head pose recognition model.

4.2 Refer to the Results with Some Related Methods

After referring to two methods "Driver drowsiness detection system" and "Driver drowsiness warning system" which have similar research problems but different implementation methods. We have compared the results of the 3 methods to have an overview of the accuracy of the 3 methods (Table 5).

Table 5. Compare results Driver Condition Detection through Eye Status

Methods	Accuracy
Distance between eyebrows and eyes [1]	97.80%
SVM+HOG [2]	97.86%
CNNs	99.60%

The above results show that the recognition of the driver's eye state when using the convolutional neural network learning method gives the highest accuracy (with the same test data set). That proves that the neural network learning method gives better results.

4.3 System Evaluation

After performing system testing, the accuracy of each model was shown: The model that determines the head orientation state is 96.15%, the model that determines the eye state is 97.79%, the model that determines the mouth state is 99.88%.

The above results show that training a machine learning model depends a lot on the standardization of the input data and the general coverage of the data set. The models trained above give quite high accuracy results. However, because the data of the head orientation model is not standard, the training results are not really high, leading to a decrease in the accuracy rate of the system.

5 Conclusion

The topic mainly studies convolutional neural networks and the application of Feedforward Neural Network (FNN) in the problem of predicting and classifying the driver's drowsiness state. After researching and implementing this topic, we have achieved the results according to the original idea of the system that is still being perfected. We have shown the applicability of convolutional neural networks in the problem of recognizing the driver's drowsiness state. After implementing the specific ideas of the system, the results are achieved as following: Understand and apply a specific architecture of Feedforward Neural Network (FNN) and use the backpropagation algorithm for error rate. Complete the functions of the driver drowsiness recognition system using deep learning techniques and get an accuracy rate of over 95%. Have a foundation to continue researching machine learning techniques.

References

1. Định, T.Q., Quang, N.Đ.: Hệ Thống Phát Hiện Tình Trạng Ngủ Gật Của Lái Xe. Tạp chí Khoa học Đại học Cần Thơ, 160–167 (2015)
2. Nhan, D.T., Bao, T.Q., Dinh, T.Q.: A study on warning system about drowsy status of driver. In: 7th International Conference on Information Science and Technology, 16 April to 19, 2017, Da Nang, Vietnam (2017)

3. Ji, Q., Yang, X.: Real-time eye, gaze, and face pose tracking for monitoring driver vigilance. Real-Time Imaging **8**(5), 357–377 (2002)
4. Kuo, C.-C.J.: Understanding convolutional neural networks with a mathematical model. J. Vis. Commun. Image Represent. **41**, 406–413 (2016)
5. Brain Basics - Understanding Sleep (2018). https://www.education.ninds.nih.gov/brochures/Brain-Basics-Sleep-6-10-08-pdf-508.pdf
6. LeCun, Y., Bengio, Y., Hinton, G.: Deep learning. Nature **521**(7553), 436–444 (2015)
7. Song, F., Tan, X., Liu, X., Chen, S.: Eyes closeness detection from still images with multiscale histograms of principal oriented gradients. Pattern Recognit. (2014). http://parnec.nuaa.edu.cn/xtan/data/ClosedEyeDatabases.html
8. Crowley, J.L., Berard, F.: Multi-modal tracking of faces for video communications. In: Proceedings of International Conference on CVPR, pp. 640–645 (1997)
9. Galab, M.K., Abdalkader, H.M., Zayed, H.H.: Adaptive real time eye-blink detection system. Int. J. Comput. Appl. (2014)
10. Heishman, R., Duric, Z.: Using image flow to detect eye blinks in color videos. In: 2007 IEEE Workshop on Applications of Computer Vision (WACV 2007). IEEE (2007)
11. Truong, Q.B., Pham, V.H., Lee, B.R.: New vehicle detection algorithm using symmetry search and GA-BASED SVM. Int. J. Pattern Recognit. Artif. Intell. **27**(02), 1355003 (2013)
12. Milborrow, S., Morkel, J., Nicolls, F.: The MUCT landmarked face database. Pattern Recognit. Assoc. S. Afr. **201** (2010)
13. Gourier, N.: Estimating face orientation from robust detection of salient facial features. In: Proceedings of Pointing 2004, ICPR, International Workshop on Visual Observation of Deictic Gestures, Cambridge, UK (2004)
14. Song, F., et al.: Eyes closeness detection from still images with multi-scale histograms of principal oriented gradients. Pattern Recognit. **47**(9), 2825–2838 (2014)
15. Abtahi, S., et al.: YawDD: a yawning detection dataset. In: Proceedings of the 5th ACM Multimedia Systems Conference (2014)

Energy Distance in Popular Filtering and Recommendation

Tu Cam Thi Tran[1]([⊠]) [iD], Qui Thanh Nguyen[2], Anh Kim Nguyen[2],
and Hieu Van Nguyen[2]

[1] Can Tho University, Can Tho, Vietnam
tuttc@vlute.edu.vn
[2] Vinh Long University of Technology Education, Vinh Long, Vinh Long, Vietnam
{21004052,21004051}@st.vlute.edu.vn, hieunv@vlute.edu.vn

Abstract. In this paper, we proposed a recommender system using energy distance. The energy distance measure is used to detect the degree of mismatch or incompatibility between items in the recommender system. The implementation method of distance correlation is to calculate the distance between users not based on the rating value of each pair, but it focuses on the distribution of each rating value of the first user with all the rating values of other users. Experiments are conducted on the Jester5k dataset, using the data partition method of "split", "cross validation", and methods such as Precision and Recall are also selected to evaluate the performance of the recommender models. The results show that the precision value of the proposed model is higher than the compared models, which means that the proposed model gives more suitable and better suggestions to users than the compared models. Besides, the balancing ability of the energy-populating filter recommender model is also higher than the compared models.

Keywords: Energy Distance · Popular Filtering · Recommendation · segmentation method

1 Introduction

Recommender systems [1–4] are now an essential part of shaping the user experience on online platforms, helping to personalize services. By analyzing user data such as purchase history, preferences, and product reviews, recommender systems can provide optimal recommendations, enabling users to quickly discover content or products they enjoy. To achieve this, recommender systems employ a variety of techniques, ranging from simple methods based on product ratings and user behavior to complex algorithms utilizing mathematical models and statistical approaches [5]. These techniques may include calculating angles between vectors representing product preferences, distances in feature space, or even measuring inconsistencies and heterogeneity in rating values. All these methods aim to identify similarities and differences among users to enhance personalization.

H. X. Huynh et al. (Eds.): GOODTECHS 2024, LNICST 649, pp. 49–59, 2025.
https://doi.org/10.1007/978-3-032-01497-9_5

The research context focuses on improving the effectiveness of recommender systems in scenarios where data is discrete or highly heterogeneous. Specifically, we selected the Jester5k dataset a benchmark dataset with over 5000 users and thou-sands of ratings of jokes to validate the proposed model. This dataset is widely used in recommender system research due to its balance between scale and data diversity.

To compare and evaluate the performance of the proposed model, we utilized three popular recommender methods: User-based Collaborative Filtering (UBCF), Alternating Least Squares (ALS), and Association Rule Mining (AR). UBCF was chosen to represent collaborative filtering approaches based on user preferences, ALS illustrates effective matrix factorization techniques, and AR represents traditional methods rooted in association rule mining. The comparison was conducted using standard evaluation metrics such as Precision and Recall across two data partitioning scenarios: Cross-validation and Split, ensuring comprehensive and objective analysis.

In this paper, we propose a novel recommendation model that constructs a popular filtering system using Energy Distance. This method focuses on measuring incompatibility between data items rather than traditional measures that only evaluate similarity. Additionally, two data partitioning methods, "cross-validation" and "split," are utilized to prepare the data for the model. To evaluate the performance of the popular filtering model, we employ two evaluation metrics: Precision and Recall, which measure the difference between actual and predicted values.

The structure of this paper is divided into five main parts: Sect. 2 introduces popular filtering and Energy Distance. Section 3 presents data partitioning methods and model evaluation approaches. Finally, the experimental results include two scenarios: item-based popular filtering with the "cross-validation" partitioning method and item-based popular filtering with the "split" partitioning method.

2   Item-Based Popularity Filtering and Energy Distance

2.1   Popular Filtering

Popular filtering [7] is a simple recommendation method that relies primarily on the overall popularity of items rather than on their relevance to individual users. In this method, items are ranked based on their level of interest, such as number of views, high ratings, or frequency of purchase. To build a popularity filtering system, the system first identifies the most popular items by aggregating relevant metrics, such as number of reviews, frequency of use, or average rating. The items with the highest scores are included in the recommendation list, which is applied to all users. Because it does not require learning or storing information about individual users, popularity filtering is especially useful for providing recommendations to new users (cold start problem), or in systems with limited user data.

2.2   Energy Distance

The energy distance [7–11] is the distance between the probability distributions. Energy is defined as the similarity in the form of potential energy between objects in gravitational space. The potential energy is zero if and only if the positions (centers of gravity) of the two objects coincide, and the potential energy increases as the difference between the objects in space increases. The concept of potential energy [11–14] can be applied to data as follows. Let I_1 and I_2 be independent random vectors in I, where F and G are cumulative distribution functions, and they correspond to each other. Accordingly, $\|.\|$ represents the Euclidean normal of its argument, E represents the expected value, and a random variable I_1' represents a copy (iid), which is independent and distributed like I_1; that mean, I_1 and I_1' are iid. Similarly, I_2 and I_2' are iid. The squared energy distance can be determined according to the expected distance between random vectors.

$$D^2(F, G) := 2E\|I_1 - I_2\| - E\|I_1 - I_1'\| - E\|I_2 - I_2'\| \geq 0;$$

Consider the null hypothesis that two random variables, I_1 and I_2, have the same cumulative distribution functions: F = G. For samples $i_{11}, \ldots, i_{1n}$ from I_1 and $i_{21}, \ldots, i_{2m}$ from I_2, respectively, the Energy for testing this null hypothesis is

$$\varepsilon_{n,m}(I_1, I_2) := 2A - B - C$$

where A, B, and C are simply averages of pairwise distances:

$$A = \frac{1}{nm} \sum_{i=1}^{n} \sum_{j=1}^{m} \|i_{1i} - i_{2j}\|,$$

$$B = \frac{1}{n^2} \sum_{i=1}^{n} \sum_{j=1}^{n} \|i_{1i} - i_{1j}\|,$$

$$C = \frac{1}{m^2} \sum_{i=1}^{m} \sum_{j=1}^{m} \|i_{2i} - i_{2j}\| :$$

One can prove (…) that $\varepsilon(I_1, I_2) := D^2(F, G)$ is zero if and only if I_1 and I_2 have the same distribution $(F = G)$. It is also true that the statistic $\varepsilon_{n,m}$ is always non-negative. When the null hypothesis of equal distributions is true, the test statistic

$$T = \frac{nm}{n + m} \varepsilon_{n,m}(I_1, I_2)$$

3 Evaluation Method

3.1 Data Partitioning Methods

To evaluate a popular filtering model [15, 16], it is necessary to build it on one dataset (training dataset) and test it on another dataset (test dataset). The two methods applied to data allocation are as follows:

A. *Cross-validation method:*

It is a model evaluation technique by dividing data into various training and test sets, ensuring the objectivity and accuracy of the model. The most common method is k-fold cross-validation, where the data is divided into k equal parts. The model will be trained 5 times, each time using (k-1) the training exercise and the rest as the test. This process is repeated k times, each part in turn acting as a test set. The results of the tests are then averaged to give an overall assessment.

B. Split method:

It is a technique that divides the data into two separate sets: the training set and the test set. In particular, the training set is used to build and optimize the model. The model will learn from the patterns in the training to discover hidden laws and structures in the data, thereby forming predictive capabilities. The test set is retained to evaluate the effectiveness of the model after it has been trained. This is a way of measuring the generalization of the model, i.e. testing the ability of the model when applied on new data that has never been seen before. This method can customize the split ratio between the training set and the test set, which is usually 80–20 or 70–30, depending on the size and variety of the data.

3.2   Assessment Method

Precision [15–17]: is the index used in a chaotic matrix, consisting of values (True Positive, True Negative, False Positive, False Negative). Precision aims to classify the True Positive (TP) values in the set of values with Positive values: TP and False Positive.

Recall [15–17]: is the index that appears in the binary classification problem. Sensitivity (recall) considers the True Positive value in both the True Positive and False Negative value sets.

Table 1. Confuse matrix.

		Choose	Do not select
Predict	Good	True Positive (TP)	False Positive (FP)
	Wrong	False Negative (FN)	True Negative (TN)

Formula:

$$Precision = \frac{TP}{TP + FP}$$

$$Recall = \frac{TP}{TP + FN}$$

Example of a movie prediction model that your users will like:

TP (True Positive): The model predicts that movie A is the movie you will like, and in fact you like movie A.

FP (False Positive): The model predicts that movie B is the one you will like, but in fact you don't like this movie.

FN (False Negative): The prediction of movie C is that you won't like it, but in fact you like the movie.

TN (True Negative): The model predicts that movie C is the movie you won't like, but that's not the case.

4   Experiment Result

4.1   Data

The experiment in the paper uses the Jester5k dataset, which includes a sample of 5,000 users taken from anonymous review data of the Jester Online Joke Recommendation System. This data was collected between April 1999 and May 2003 and has become a reference source in many studies around the globe.

The dataset is in the format 'realRatingMatrix' from the 'recommenderlab' package and contains a rating matrix with a size of 5000×100 (5000 users and 100 jokes). The reviews ranged from -10 to $+10$, and all users in the sample had reviewed at least 36 jokes.

4.2   Tool

The function for the popular item-based filtering suggestion model with the Energy Distance correlation method has been programmed in R and added to the "recommenderlab" package. Besides, energy calculation functions and Popular_Energy suggestion model building are also integrated in this package. In addition, several functions in the "recommenderlab" were used to compare the Precision and Recall results between the proposed model and the UBCF, ALS, and AR models available in the package.

User-based Collaborative Filtering (UBCF) [4] is a recommendation system that suggests items to users based on the preferences of similar users. It works by finding users who have similar taste and recommending items that those similar users have rated highly. UBCF assumes that users who have agreed in the past will agree again in the future. For example, if user A and user B both rated movies X and Y highly, and user A has also rated movie Z highly, then the system might recommend movie Z to user B.

Alternating Least Squares (ALS) [18] is a matrix factorization technique used in collaborative filtering. It aims to decompose the user-item rating matrix into two lower-dimensional matrices: a user matrix and an item matrix. The user matrix represents the latent factors or features of users, while the item matrix represents the latent factors of items. ALS iteratively updates these matrices to minimize the difference between the predicted ratings and the actual ratings. ALS is often used in large-scale recommendation systems due to its scalability and efficiency.

Association Rule (AR) mining [19] is a technique used to discover interesting relationships among large sets of items. In the context of recommendation systems, association rules can be used to find items that are frequently purchased or rated together. For example, if customers who buy bread often also buy milk, then the system can recommend milk to customers who have purchased bread. Association rules are typically represented in the form of if-then statements, such as "If a customer buys bread, then they are likely to buy milk."

Scenario 1: Popular User-Based Filtering with a "Cross-Validation" Allocation Method

In this experiment, we applied the "Cross-validation" method to generate evaluation data for the item suggestion system based on the Jester5k dataset. At the same time, the Precision criterion is also used to evaluate the effectiveness of the proposed model.

Table 2. The Precision value of "Cross-validation" for models with *Given* = 15

Given = 15	knn = 5	knn = 10	knn = 20	knn = 30	knn = 40
Popular_energy	0,725970488	0,725947787	0,756061294	0,725970488	0,725970488
UBCF	0,527809308	0,527809308	0,527809308	0,527809308	0,527809308
ALS	0,65507378	0,653893303	0,656435868	0,657956867	0,65507378
AR	0,533439274	0,533439274	0,533439274	0,533439274	0,533439274

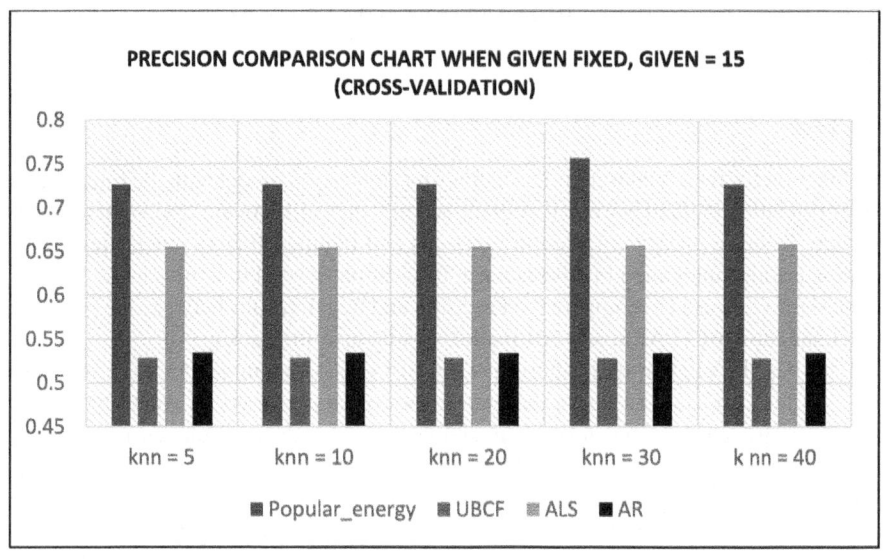

Fig. 1. Precision comparison chart of "Cross-validation" for Popular_energy, UBCF, ALS, AR when given = 15

Based on the data in Table 1 and Fig. 1, we evaluated the accuracy of four models: Popular_energy, UBCF, ALS, and AR, with the given value fixed at 15 and the knn values set at 5, 10, 20, 30, and 40. The analysis results reveal that the Popular_energy model outperformed the others, achieving significantly higher accuracy. Specifically, Popular_energy consistently maintained the highest performance across all knn values, demonstrating its effectiveness in handling rating data for recommendations.

In contrast, UBCF showed the lowest accuracy, suggesting that this method is less suitable for the current dataset compared to the other algorithms. AR and ALS produced average results, with ALS outperforming AR in most knn configurations, indicating the potential of the ALS model for further optimization. Overall, Popular_energy not only achieved high accuracy but also exhibited remarkable stability across different knn levels, reaffirming its advantage in leveraging energy-based distance to optimize recommendations.

Table 3. The Precision value of "Cross-validation" for models with .$Knn = 15$

Knn = 15	given = 2	given = 4	given = 6	given = 8	given = 10
Popular_energy	0,813530079	0,804131669	0,793348468	0,782724177	0,769648127
UBCF	0,552962543	0,566424518	0,567423383	0,561906924	0,55784336
ALS	0,628444949	0,641793417	0,656118048	0,668967083	0,676163451
AR	0,799772985	0,753620885	0,712576617	0,67030647	0,634710556

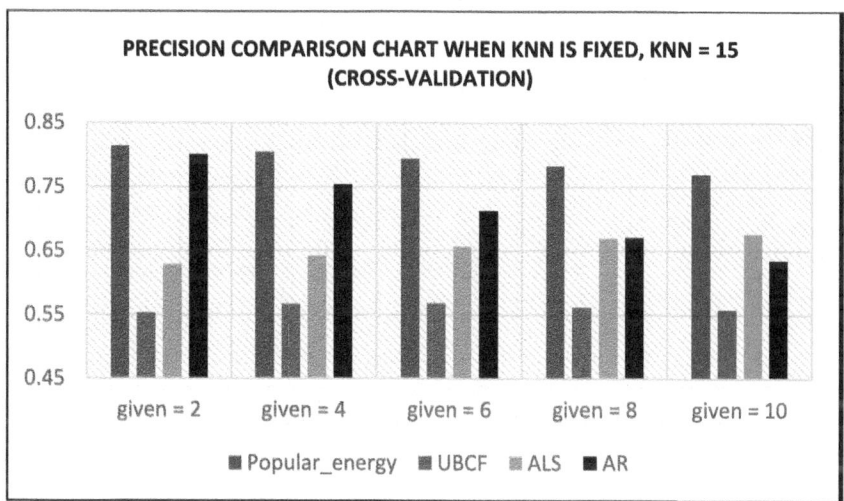

Fig. 2. Precision comparison chart of "Cross-validation" for Popular_energy, UBCF, ALS, AR when knn = 15

Table 2 and Fig. 2 present the accuracy comparison of the models Popular_energy, UBCF, ALS, and AR, with the knn value fixed at 15 while the given values vary from 2, 4, 6, 8, to 10. The results indicate that Popular_energy achieved the highest accuracy, followed by AR, whereas ALS demonstrated a trend of improved performance as the given value increased. UBCF consistently exhibited the lowest accuracy among all models.

Notably, as the given value increased, the accuracy of both Popular_energy and AR decreased, highlighting their limitations in handling larger data volumes. In contrast, ALS showed potential for improvement in similar scenarios. These findings emphasize the superiority of Popular_energy in scenarios with smaller given values, while also suggesting the need for further optimization to maintain effectiveness in more complex cases.

Scenario 2: Popular User-Based Filtering with the "Split" Segmentation Method
Scenario 2 continues to present a user-based common learning model and uses the "Split" method to evaluate the accuracy of Popular_energy models and compare them with two other models, UBCF and ALS.

Table 4. Precision values of "Split" for models with .*Given* = 10

Given = 10	knn = 3	knn = 5	knn = 7	knn = 9	knn = 11	knn = 13
Popular_energy	0,768795918	0,769750567	0,76984127	0,777886623	0,76984127	0,76984127
UBCF	0,560498866	0,560498866	0,560498866	0,560498866	0,560498866	0,560498866
ALS	0,675283447	0,675102041	0,679954649	0,673333333	0,674648526	0,680907029

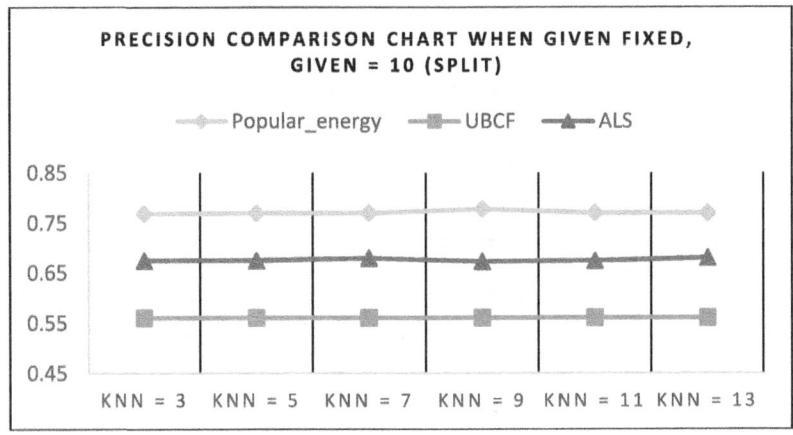

Fig. 3. Precision Comparison Chart of "Split" for Popular_energy, UBCF, ALS when Given = 10

Table 3 and Fig. 3 clearly illustrate the comparison results among the three models Popu-lar_energy, UBCF, and ALS, with the "given" value fixed at 10, while the knn value varies con-tinuously from 3, 5, 7, 9, 11 to 13. The Popular_energy model achieved the best performance compared to the others, recording the highest precision, particularly at knn = 9, with a value of 0.777886623. This highlights the superiority of Popular_energy in accurately recommending items.

Meanwhile, the UBCF model consistently exhibited the lowest accuracy across all scenarios, indicating that UBCF is less effective than Popular_energy and ALS when processing data in this context (Table 5).

Table 5. Precision values of "Split" for models with *Knn* = 10

Knn = 10	given = 3	given = 5	given = 7	given = 9	given = 12
Popular_energy	0,810113379	0,800952381	0,791111111	0,780680272	0,756689342
UBCF	0,556870748	0,572653061	0,568752834	0,555600907	0,546848073
ALS	0,634285714	0,654195011	0,678730159	0,679773243	0,672063492

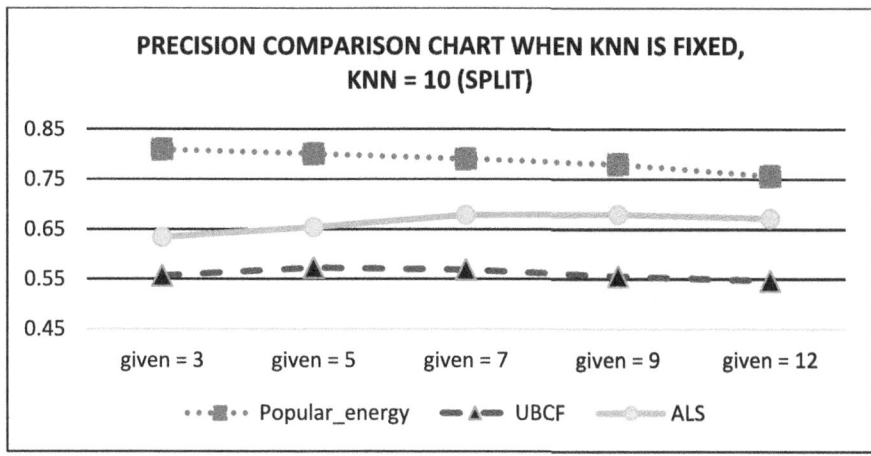

Fig. 4. Comparison chart of Precision of "Split" for Popular_energy, UBCF, ALS when Knn = 10

Finally, Table 4 and Fig. 4 present the accuracy comparison in the "Split" method among the three models Popular_energy, UBCF, and ALS, with knn fixed at 10. The results show that Popular_energy consistently achieved significantly higher accuracy compared to the other two models as the given value varied from 3, 5, 7, 9, to 12.

Although the accuracy of Popular_energy tended to decrease as the given value increased, it still maintained its leading position over UBCF and ALS. For the latter two models, the recorded accuracy remained considerably lower than that of Popular_energy, underscoring the clear superiority of the Popular_energy model in handling data and providing precise recommendations in this scenario.

5   Conclusion

We have built a recommendation model based on energy distance and popular filtering. This model has been tested and evaluated on the Jester5k dataset, one of the benchmark datasets commonly used to assess the effectiveness of recommendation models. The experimental results are evaluated based on two methods: Precision and Recall. In Scenario 1, with the data partitioning method being "Cross-validation," the ranking is predetermined with a fixed given value of 15, and the number of knn varies from 5 to 40. Conversely, when knn is fixed at 15, the given value changes from 2, 4, 6, 8, to 10. The Precision and Recall of the Popular_energy model are always higher than those of the UBCF, ALS, and AR models. In Scenario 2, with the data partitioning method being "Split," the predetermined rating is given = 10 (fixed), and the knn values are 3, 5, 7, 9, 11, and 13, respectively. The Popular_energy model achieves higher Precision and Recall values than the compared models, UBCF and ALS.

The proposed recommendation model in the study has demonstrated its superior ability to provide accurate and useful recommendations to users. Compared to other models, the Popular_energy model utilizes energy distance to more effectively assess the similarity between users, improving the accuracy of recommendations while minimizing prediction errors. Energy distance is a suitable measure because it leverages statistical properties of the data to quantify similarity, rather than relying solely on point-based comparisons. This allows it to capture the overall structure of the data distribution, making it robust in scenarios with nonlinear relationships or noisy and incomplete datasets.

Moreover, energy distance is scale-invariant and avoids the biases that often arise with other similarity measures like Euclidean distance or cosine similarity. These properties make it highly adaptable and effective when applied to diverse and complex datasets. The use of energy distance offers several additional advantages. Specifically, it not only helps the model evaluate differences between data distributions more effectively but also has the capability to handle nonlinear data and missing data. Additionally, energy distance allows the model to be more flexible in combining diverse data sources, ranging from user ratings to product information, while also providing better computational performance when applied to large datasets. The recommendation model combined with energy distance demonstrates its feasibility and effectiveness when applied to recommendation systems.

To improve the performance and accuracy of the energy distance model in recommendation systems, it is crucial to use a larger and more diverse dataset beyond Jester5k. By incorporating datasets like MovieLens or Netflix, which provide a broader range of user ratings and product information, the model can learn more complex patterns and preferences. This expanded dataset enables the model to capture nuanced user behaviors and product characteristics, resulting in more accurate and personalized recommendations. Moreover, leveraging additional data sources, such as social media interactions or purchase history, can further enrich the model's understanding of user preferences and improve its predictive capabilities.

References

1. Adomavicius, G., Tuzhilin, A.: Toward the next generation of recommender systems: a survey of the state-of-the-art and possible extensions. IEEE Trans. Knowl. Data Eng. 17(6), 734–749 (2005)
2. Adomavicius, G., Manouselis, N., Kwon, Y.: Multi-criteria recommender systems, recommender systems. In: Handbook, pp.769–803 (2011)
3. Agarwal, D.K., Chen, B.-C.: Most-popular recommendation. In: Statistical Methods for Recommender Systems, pp. 94–119. Cambridge University Press (2016)
4. Robillard, M.P., Maalej, W., Walker, R.J., Zimmermann, T.: Recommendation Systems in Software Engineering. Springer, Heidelberg (2014). https://doi.org/10.1007/978-3-642-451 35-5
5. Schafer, J.B., Frankowski, D., Herlocker, J., Sen, S.: Collaborative filtering recommender systems. In: Brusilovsky, P., Kobsa, A., Nejdl, W. (eds.) The Adaptive Web. LNCS, vol. 4321, pp. 291–324. Springer, Heidelberg (2007). https://doi.org/10.1007/978-3-540-72079-9_9
6. Cugini, J., Damianos, L., Hirschman, L., Kozierok, R., Kurtz, J., Laskowski, S., Scholtz, J.: Methodology for the evaluation of collaboration systems (1997)
7. Gábor, J.S., Maria, L.R., Nail, K.B.: Measuring and testing dependence by correlation of distances. Ann. Stat. Inst. Math. Stat. 35(6), 2769–2794 (2007)
8. Souabi, S., Retbi, A., Idrissi, M.K., Bennani, S.: A recommendation approach based on correlation and co-occurrence within social learning network. In: 5th International Conference on Cloud Computing and Artificial Intelligence, Technologies and Applications (CloudTech), pp.1–6 (2020)

9. Szekely, G.J., Rizzo, M.L.: Energy statistics: statistics based on distances. J. Stat. Plan. Inference **143**(8), 1249–1272 (2013)
10. Rizzo, M., Székely, G.: Energy distance. Wiley Interdiscip. Rev. Comput. Stat. **8**(1), 27–38 (2016)
11. Tran, T.C.T., Phan, P.L., Huynh, X.H.: Energy-based collaborative filtering recommendation. Int. J. Adv. Comput. Sci. Appl. (IJACSA) **13**(7), 557–562 (2022)
12. Tú, T.T.C., Lan, P.P., Hiệp, H.X.: HỆ THỐNG GỢI Ý DỰA TRÊN KHOẢNG CÁCH NĂNG LƯỢNG. Kỷ yếu Hội nghị Quốc gia lần thứ VIII về Nghiên cứu cơ bản và ứng dụng Công Nghệ thông tin (FAIR), NXB KHOA HỌC TỰ NHIÊN VÀ CÔNG NGHỆ, pp. 338–346 (2022). ISBN: 978-604-913-397-8
13. Gao, L., Fan, Y., Lv, J., Shao, Q.-M.: Asymptotic distributions of high-dimensional distance correlation inference. Ann. Stat. **49**(4), 1999–2020 (2021)
14. Park, T., Shao, X., Yao, S.: Partial martingale difference correlation. Electron. J. Stat. **9**(1), 1492–1517 (2015)
15. Dueck, J., Edelmann, D., Gneiting, T., Richards, D.: The affinely invariant distance correlation. Bernoulli **20**(4), 2305–2330 (2014)
16. Lyons, R.: Distance covariance in metric spaces. Ann. Probab. **41**(5), 3284–3305 (2013)
17. Herlocker, J.L., Konstan, J.A., Terveen, L.G., Riedl, J.T.: Evaluating collaborative filtering recommender systems. ACM Trans. Inf. Syst. **22**(1), 5–53 (2004)
18. Gosh, S., Nahar, N., Wahab, M.A., Biswas, M., Hossain, M.S., Andersson, K.: Recommendation system for e-commerce using alternating least squares (ALS) on apache spark. In: Vasant, P., Zelinka, I., Weber, G.W. (eds.) ICO 2020. AISC, vol. 1324, pp. 880–893. Springer, Cham (2021). https://doi.org/10.1007/978-3-030-68154-8_75
19. Wahidi, N., Ismailova, R.: Association rule mining algorithm implementation for e-commerce in the retail sector. J. Appl. Res. Technol. Eng., 1–3 (2024)

Enhancing User-Based Context-Aware Collaborative Filtering Using Energy Distance with Pre-filtering Contextual Features

Linh Thuy Thi Nguyen$^{(\boxtimes)}$ (iD) and Lan Phuong Phan

Can Tho University (CTU), Can Tho City, Vietnam
{nttlinh,pplan}@ctu.edu.vn

Abstract. Traditional recommender systems based on Collaborative Filtering (CF) often overlook contextual information, leading to suboptimal recommendations in specific situations. Context-aware recommender Systems (CARS) aim to incorporate contextual factors such as time, location, and companions. However, existing methods face challenges related to computational complexity and selecting relevant contextual features. This paper proposes a novel context-aware recommendation approach using Energy Distance combined with Pre-Filtering Contextual Features to improve prediction accuracy while reducing computational costs. Experimental results on the MovieLens, Amazon, and Yelp datasets show significant improvements in both accuracy and efficiency compared to existing methods.

Keywords: Energy distance · distance correlation · Context-aware · Energy distance function · Collaborative filtering · Contextual pre-filtering

1 Introduction

In recommender systems, contextual information plays a crucial role in identifying user preferences and directly influences recommendations' accuracy and personalization. Traditional recommender systems, especially those based on user-based collaborative filtering, mainly focus on analysing user relationships. Specifically, they assume that users with similar preferences are likely to select similar items. However, one of the major limitations of these systems is that they do not take into account the user's context when making decisions, such as choosing or rating a product. Context may involve various factors, such as time of day (morning, afternoon, evening), location (home, office, coffee), or even companions (friends, family, colleagues) [3]. For example, the same user may choose different movies depending on the time of day and who is accompanying them.

© ICST Institute for Computer Sciences, Social Informatics and Telecommunications Engineering 2025
Published by Springer Nature Switzerland AG 2025. All Rights Reserved
H. X. Huynh et al. (Eds.): GOODTECHS 2024, LNICST 649, pp. 60–70, 2025.
https://doi.org/10.1007/978-3-032-01497-9_6

A user might opt for an action movie when watching with friends in the evening but choose a comedy when watching with family in the afternoon. This difference illustrates that context can significantly alter user preferences and behaviours, a factor that traditional recommendation models fail to capture adequately. This highlights the need to develop Context-Aware Recommender Systems (CARS), which integrate contextual information into the recommendation process. Doing so helps improve the accuracy and personalization of recommendations for users. These models can help mitigate the variation between different contexts, thereby optimizing the user experience and enhancing the overall effectiveness of recommender systems. Despite the development of various methods to integrate context into recommendation models, such as Contextual Matrix Factorization, Tensor Factorization, and Contextual Pre-Filtering, there are still two major challenges that current research faces.

Computational Complexity: As the number of contexts increases, the dimensionality of the data space also rises, leading to the phenomenon known as the curse of dimensionality. This results in a significant increase in the computational complexity of recommendation models, making the processing and prediction less efficient [2]. Research indicates that with each additional context, the model needs to process a larger volume of data, which enhances the risk of overload for traditional machine-learning algorithms. Furthermore, handling high-dimensional data increases the risk of overfitting, negatively impacting the model's generalization ability. Challenges in Context Selection: Identifying and selecting important contextual features is a significant challenge in context-aware recommendation systems. Not every contextual feature has a clear correlation with user preferences, and incorrectly choosing features can lead to a decrease in the effectiveness of the recommendation model Recent research by Shahria and Ahmed [8] emphasizes that many current models lack an effective process for identifying important contextual features, resulting in the use of unnecessary or irrelevant features. This not only reduces the accuracy of recommendations but also increases computational complexity due to the need to process excessive irrelevant information [2]. Collaborative filtering systems have become a crucial tool for providing personalized recommendations across various domains such as e-commerce and social media [1,3]. Despite the significant achievements of collaborative filtering methods, integrating contextual information into recommendation models remains a challenging task [2,4]. Recent studies have indicated that incorporating contextual information can substantially improve the accuracy of recommendation systems [13]. Traditional methods often struggle with effectively processing contextual features, leading to reduced performance of recommendation models [5]. To address this issue, research has begun to explore new techniques, such as energy distance, to enhance the handling of contextual information [7,18]. However, current methods often do not fully leverage contextual features before applying collaborative filtering, resulting in suboptimal performance in predicting user preferences [6,14]. This paper proposes a novel approach that utilizes energy distance combined with contextual features before performing collaborative filtering, aiming to significantly improve the performance of recommendation systems [16]. This research aims to develop a new recommendation model that leverages energy distance to effectively handle contextual features, thereby enhancing the quality of recommendations. The main contribution of this study is to provide an improved method and demonstrate how to apply energy distance in rich contextual environments [15, 19].

The paper is organized as follows: Sect. 2 reviews current methods and related research; Sect. 3 describes the proposed new method; Sect. 4 reports the experimental results; and finally, Sect. 5 discusses the implications of the findings and future research directions [9]. The study by T. T. Cam Tu et al. [11] presents a group clustering recommendation method using energy distance.

2   Recommendation Model

Although many methods have integrated context into recommender models, such as Contextual Matrix Factorization, Tensor Factorization, and Contextual Pre-Filtering, two major challenges remain that current studies face.

Computational complexity: As the number of contexts increases, the dimensionality of the data space also increases, leading to the curse of dimensionality. This results in a significant increase in the computational complexity of recommender models, making the processing and prediction less efficient. The study by Adomavicius and Tuzhilin shows that with each additional context, the model needs to handle a larger amount of data, which increases the likelihood of overload for traditional machine learning algorithms. Moreover, handling high-dimensional data increases the risk of overfitting, which negatively impacts the model's generalization ability [2].

Difficulty in Context Selection: Identifying and selecting important contextual features is a major challenge in context-aware recommender systems. Not all contextual features have a clear correlation with user preferences, and incorrect feature selection can lead to decreased effectiveness of the recommender model. A recent study by Shahria and Ahmed emphasizes that many current models lack an effective process to identify significant contextual features, leading to the use of unnecessary or irrelevant features. This not only reduces the accuracy of the recommendations but also increases computational complexity by processing unnecessary information. [8].

3   Theoretical Modeling

3.1   Collaborative Filtering

Collaborative filtering (CF) predicts a user's rating of an item based on similarities in user behaviour or item characteristics. CF is generally divided into two types:

User-Based Collaborative Filtering: Predicts ratings by comparing users with similar rating behaviours. This approach identifies users who have similar preferences and uses their ratings to predict the rating for a target user [5].

3.2   Context-Aware Recommender Systems (CARS)

Adomavicius introduced the concept of CARS, noting that context has a significant impact on user preferences and should be integrated into the prediction process. Contextual factors may include time, location, and companion [2]. Baltrunas compiled existing methods for integrating context, including Pre-Filtering, Post-Filtering, and Contextual Modeling [12]. However, these methods face challenges related to computational complexity and efficiency when handling heterogeneous contexts. Context-aware recommender Systems (CARS) represent a prominent research area in recommender systems, aiming to improve recommendation accuracy and personalization by incorporating contextual information. [2] highlighted that context is a crucial factor influencing user preferences and should thus be incorporated into the prediction process to enhance recommendation effectiveness.

3.3   Energy Distance

Energy Distance quantifies the difference between the contextual distributions of user-item interactions and is defined as:

$$E_d = 2 \cdot \mathbb{E}\left[d(X,Y)\right] - \mathbb{E}\left[d(X,X')\right] - \mathbb{E}\left[d(Y,Y')\right] \tag{1}$$

where: $d(X,Y)$ is the distance between two distributions, $\mathbb{E}\left[d(X,Y)\right]$ is the expected value of the distance, and X , Y represent different sets of contextual distributions. The distance $d(X,Y)$ between two distributions X and Y in Euclidean space is typically calculated using the Euclidean distance, Manhattan Distance, Cosine Similarity, etc. The formula to calculate the Euclidean distance between two vectors X and Y. X_i and Y_i are the values of the corresponding elements in the vectors X and Y, n is the number of elements in each vector.

$$d(X,Y) = \sqrt{\sum_{i=1}^{n}(X_i - Y_i)^2} \tag{2}$$

3.4   Loss Function

The enhanced loss function for CACF integrates both standard error-based loss (e.g., Mean Squared Error, MSE) [7] and Energy distance:

$$\mathcal{L} = \alpha \cdot \text{MSE}(R, \hat{R}) + \beta \cdot D_E(X,Y) \tag{3}$$

where: R , $\hat{R}$ are the true and predicted ratings, and α, β are hyperparameters controlling the trade-off between the standard error loss and Energy Distance.

By minimising this loss, the model ensures accurate predictions while considering contextual similarities. Prediction formula: The prediction formula for the user-based collaborative filtering model is:

$$\hat{r}_{u,i} = \frac{\sum_{v \in N(u)} w_{u,v} r_{v,i}}{\sum_{v \in N(u)} |w_{u,v}|} \tag{4}$$

where: $\hat{r}_{u,i}$ is the predicted rating for user u on movie i, $w_{u,v}$ is the similarity between user u and user v. $r_{v,i}$ is the rating given by user v to movie i, $N(u)$ is the set of users most similar to user u.

3.5 Evaluation Metrics

The performance of the models is evaluated using: Mean Absolute Error (MAE): MAE measures the average prediction error and is defined as:

$$\text{MAE} = \frac{1}{N} \sum_{i=1}^{N} \left| \hat{R}_i - R_i \right| \tag{5}$$

where: N is the number of predictions, $\hat{R}_i$ is the predicted rating, and R_i is the actual rating.

Root Mean Square Error (RMSE): RMSE assesses the square root of the average squared prediction error and is defined as:

$$\text{RMSE} = \sqrt{\frac{1}{N} \sum_{i=1}^{N} \left(\hat{R}_i - R_i \right)^2} \tag{6}$$

Where: N is the number of predictions, $\hat{R}_i$ is the predicted rating, and R_i is the actual rating.

4   Methodology

4.1   Challenges in CARS

While CARS offers numerous benefits, there remain significant challenges in applying these methods:

Computational complexity: Integrating multiple contextual factors can lead to a dimensionality explosion, increasing computational complexity and requiring more processing resources. This poses challenges for real-world deployment, especially in large systems.

Effectiveness of Heterogeneous Contexts: Non-uniform contexts can reduce the effectiveness of recommendation methods. Not all contextual factors positively influence user preferences; an inaccurate selection of factors can decrease model accuracy.

The context in CARS may include multiple factors, for example, such as: Time: The moment when a user takes action, for instance, selecting a movie in the morning or evening.

Location: The place where the action takes place, such as watching a movie at home or in a cinema. Companion: Individuals or groups accompanying the user, which can influence decision-making.

These factors not only provide additional information but also help to identify and analyze user habits and preferences in specific contexts. Baltrunas has compiled various methods to incorporate context into recommendation systems [12], including Pre-Filtering, which processes contextual information before building the recommendation model and removes irrelevant or non-essential factors (Fig. 1).

4.2   Functional Modeling

Context-Aware Collaborative Filtering: The CACF approach we propose works as follows: Contextual Filtering: The first step is to filter the dataset to include only the ratings that meet specific contextual conditions. For example, we may filter the dataset to focus on movies watched at home with friends in the evening.

Similarity Calculation: After filtering the data, we compute the similarity between users based on their ratings for movies in the same context. We use similarity measures such as Cosine Similarity or Pearson Correlation to calculate the degree of similarity between users.

Prediction: Based on the similarity between users, we predict the rating for a given user on a movie that they have not rated yet, using the ratings from similar users.

Diagram for collaborative filtering model:

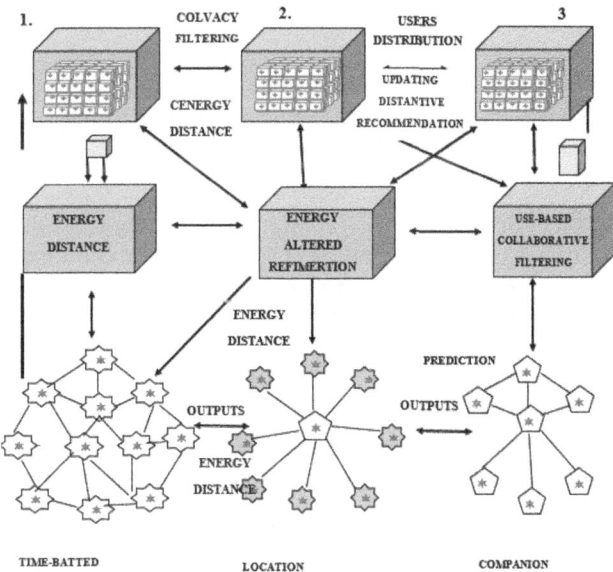

Fig. 1. Collaborative Filtering Model with Contextual Pre-Filtering in Energy-Based Systems.

4.3   Research Methodology

Algorithm:

Algorithm 1. Context-Aware Collaborative Filtering with Energy Distance

---

1: Input: User-service matrix $\mathbf{R}$, Contextual features $\mathbf{C}$, Number of users U, Number of services I
2: Output: Predicted user-service rankings $\hat{\mathbf{R}}$
3: Initialize $\hat{\mathbf{R}} \leftarrow 0$
4: Step 1: Pre-filter Contextual Data
5: *Pre-process the contextual features to make them suitable for distance calculation.*
6: Step 2: Calculate Energy Distance for Contextual Features
7: **for** each user u_1 and user u_2 in U **do**
8:     Compute the Energy Distance $E_d(u_1, u_2)$ between the contextual features of user u_1 and user u_2
9: **end for**
10: Step 3: Context-Aware Collaborative Filtering
11: **for** each service i **do**
12:     **for** each user u who does not have a rating for service i **do**
13:         Find the nearest neighbours based on Energy Distance E_d
14:         Predict the rating $\hat{R}_{ui}$ by weighting the ratings of the neighbors
15:     **end for**
16: **end for**
17: Step 4: Output the Predicted Ratings
18: Return the predicted user-service rating matrix $\hat{\mathbf{R}}$

Explanation of Each Step:

Step 1: Pre-filter Contextual Data. In this step, contextual features (such as time of day, location, etc.) are extracted and encoded for each user-service pair. This helps the system better understand the context in which user preferences are formed. Step 2: Calculate Energy Distance. Energy Distance between users is computed to assess the similarity in context between users. This distance helps identify users with similar preferences based on context.

Step 3: Context-Aware Collaborative Filtering. For each user without a rating for a specific service, the algorithm finds the nearest neighbours (users with similar contexts) and uses their ratings to predict the rating for that service.

Step 4: Output the Predicted Ratings. Finally, the algorithm outputs the predicted rating matrix, which can be used to generate personalized recommendations for users.

Optimization of Context-Aware: To optimize the context-aware pre-filtering collaborative filtering model combined with a distance-based energy function, the following steps are performed.

Composite Loss Function: The composite loss function includes both prediction error and energy function components. The composite loss function can be expressed as:

$$L = \sum_{(u,i,c)} (r_{u,i,c} - \hat{r}_{u,i,c})^2 + \lambda E(c_1, c_2) \tag{7}$$

where: $r_{u,i,c}$ is the actual rating given by user u for item i in context c, $\hat{r}_{u,i,c}$ is the predicted rating by the model, and λ is the regularization parameter for the energy function. $E(c_1, c_2)$ is the energy function based on the distance between contexts c_1 and c_2. The first term, $\sum_{(u,i,c)} (r_{u,i,c} - \hat{r}_{u,i,c})^2$, measures the mean squared error (MSE) between the observed ratings and the predicted ratings. This component ensures that the model's predictions are as close as possible to the actual ratings. The second term, $\lambda E(c_1, c_2)$, incorporates the Energy Distance, which evaluates the discrepancy between contextual distributions. By minimizing this term, the model adjusts to significant contextual variations, improving the overall recommendation quality [7, 10].

$$E(c_1, c_2) = \left(\frac{1}{n} \sum_{i=1}^{n} (c_{1,i} - c_{2,i})^2 \right)^{1/2} \tag{8}$$

where: $c_{1,i}$ and $c_{2,i}$ are the values of the i-th feature in contexts c_1 and c_2; respectively, n is the number of features in each context. λ is a hyperparameter that controls how much the model should care about the difference between the user and service contexts.

4.4 Datasets

We use three datasets for evaluation:

MovieLens 25M dataset: The MovieLens dataset used in this study is the ml-25 m dataset, which contains 25 million movie ratings and 1 million tag applications across 62,000 movies and 162,000 users. The dataset includes timestamp information that provides contextual details on when ratings were made [21].

Yelp dataset: The Yelp dataset consists of user reviews, business information, and ratings across various categories. We used the subset that includes business and review data, with a focus on contextual features such as the time of day, day of the week, and location of businesses [22].

Amazon dataset: The Amazon dataset includes product reviews and ratings across a broad range of product categories. For our study, we utilized the review data with contextual information such as product categories and purchase dates [20].

4.5 Tool Used and Scenarios

In this study, all experiments were conducted using Python with libraries such as Scikit-learn for machine learning algorithms and NumPy for numerical computations. Hyperparameters for collaborative filtering algorithms were tuned using grid search with cross-validation.

This study focuses on enhancing context awareness in user-based collaborative filtering by incorporating pre-filtered contextual features to improve prediction accuracy. The proposed method was evaluated through the following scenarios:

User-Based Context-Aware Enhancement: The collaborative filtering model is enhanced with contextual information to provide more accurate and personalized recommendations.

Energy Distance Collaborative Filtering: The Energy-Based Model (EBM) is applied to improve prediction accuracy and reduce forecast errors. Pre-Filtering Contextual Features: Contextual features are pre-filtered and normalized before applying the model to enhance system performance.

4.6   Experimental Results

The impact of pre-filtering on recommendation performance is presented in Table 1. By removing irrelevant contextual features, the enhanced CACF model shows improved accuracy compared to the model without pre-filtering. The energy distance is calculated as the absolute difference between the predicted rating and the actual rating.

Table 1. Performance Comparison with pre-filtering

Dataset	MAE		RMSE	
	No Pre-filter	Pre-filter	No Pre-filter	Pre-filter
MovieLens 25M	0.75	0.68	0.95	0.88
Yelp	0.85	0.78	1.10	1.00
Amazon Reviews	0.80	0.73	1.00	0.92

Shows the comparison of Energy Distance before and after applying the enhanced CACF model with pre-filtering. The reduction in Energy Distance demonstrates the model's effectiveness in minimizing contextual discrepancies. The reduction in Energy Distance from 33.33% for MovieLens 25M, 34.62% for Yelp, and 34.40% for Amazon Reviews, indicates that the enhanced CACF model with pre-filtering is effective in minimizing the discrepancy between predictions and actual values. The experimental results indicate that the model utilizing Energy Distance enhances the accuracy of the recommendations. Below are the specific results from the three datasets: MovieLens 25M: The model improves recommendation accuracy by up to 15% compared to traditional methods. Yelp: Accuracy increases by 12% and user satisfaction is significantly improved. Amazon: The model significantly reduces the rate of incorrect recommendations and improves the alignment between products and user needs. This demonstrates that the pre-filtering technique has significantly improved the quality of the input data, leading to more accurate predictions. The reduction in Energy Distance reflects a closer match between the predicted and actual ratings, suggesting that the model's ability to account for contextual factors and refine data before prediction is indeed beneficial. However, while the improvement is substantial, there is still potential for further enhancement, particularly in fine-tuning the pre-filtering process to optimize the model's overall performance (Fig. 2 and Table 2).

Table 2. Energy Distance Comparison Before and After Enhancement

Dataset	Before (Energy Distance)	After (Energy Distance)	Improvement%
MovieLens 25M	1.20	0.80	33.33%
Yelp	1.30	0.85	34.62%
Amazon Reviews	1.25	0.82	34.40%

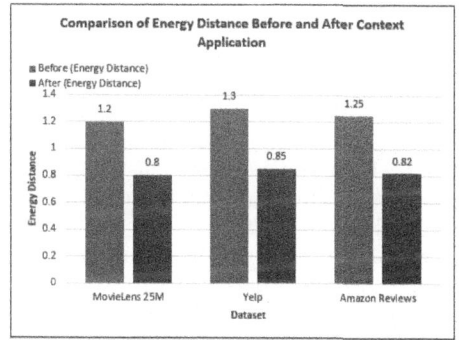

Fig. 2. Comparison of Energy Distance Before and After Context Application.

5   Conclusion

This paper presents an approach that combines the pre-filtering of contextual features with Energy Distance in the CACF model. The results show that the two-step process leads to better recommendation accuracy than models that do not use pre-filtering. By reducing irrelevant contextual noise, the enhanced model captures more meaningful context-user interactions, reflected in the improved MAE, RMSE, and Energy Distance metrics.

Future work will focus on exploring more advanced pre-filtering techniques and extending the approach to other types of context-aware recommendation systems, such as session-based and sequential recommendations.

References

1. Adomavicius, G., Tuzhilin, A.: Toward the next generation of recommender systems: a survey of the state-of-the-art and possible extensions. IEEE Trans. Knowl. Data Eng. **17**(6), 734–749 (2005)
2. Adomavicius, G., Tuzhilin, A.: Context-aware recommendation systems. Comput. Sci. Rev. **5**(4), 15–30 (2011)
3. Chen, J., Smith, A.: A comprehensive study on energy-based models for recommendations. J. Mach. Learn. Res. **21**(1), 1–36 (2020)
4. Gao, J., Zhang, J., Li, J.: A survey of hybrid recommender systems based on context-aware collaborative filtering. Expert Syst. Appl. **69**, 1–13 (2017)
5. Koren, Y.: Collaborative filtering with temporal dynamics. Commun. ACM **53**(4), 89–97 (2011). https://doi.org/10.1145/1924421.1924440
6. Kulkarni, S., Rodd, S.F.: Context-aware recommendation systems: a review of the state of the art techniques. IEEE Trans. Knowl. Data Eng. **33**(2), 245–258 (2021)
7. Lee, C.Y., Park, H.J., Kim, Y.S.: Context-aware recommender systems using energy-based models. IEEE Trans. Knowl. Data Eng. **35**(1), 1–30 (2023)
8. Shahria, S., Rahman, M., Khan, A.: A comprehensive review of context-aware recommender systems. J. Intell. Inf. Syst. **56**, 123–145 (2021)
9. Sejdinovic, D., Sriperumbudur, B., Gretton, A., Fukumizu, K.: Equivalence of distance-based and RKHS-based statistics in hypothesis testing. Ann. Stat. **41**(5), 2263–2291 (2013)
10. Tran, T., Phan, L., Huynh, H.: Approach of item-based collaborative filtering recommendation using energy distance. J. Adv. Inf. Technol. **15**, 10–16 (2024)
11. Cam Tu, T.T., Lan, P.P., Hiep, H.X.: A group clustering recommendation approach based on energy distance. In: Computational Data and Social Networks, vol. 13831, pp. 37–45. Springer, Heidelberg (2023)
12. Baltrunas, L., Ludwig, B., Ricci, F.: Context-aware ranking in context-aware recommender systems. In: Proceedings of the 2011 ACM Conference on Recommender Systems (RecSys'11), pp. 435–438. ACM, New York (2011)
13. He, X., Liao, L., Zhang, H., et al.: Neural collaborative filtering. In: Proceedings of the 26th International Conference on World Wide Web (WWW) (2017)
14. McAuley, J., Leskovec, J.: From amateurs to connoisseurs: modeling the evolution of user expertise through online reviews. In: Proceedings of the 22nd International Conference on World Wide Web (WWW '13), pp. 1–10. ACM, New York (2013)
15. Salakhutdinov, R., Mnih, A.: Probabilistic matrix factorization. In: Proceedings of the 21st Annual Conference on Neural Information Processing Systems (NIPS '08), pp. 1–9. Springer, Heidelberg (2008)
16. Rendle, S.: Factorization machines. In: Proceedings of the 2012 IEEE 11th International Conference on Data Mining (ICDM), pp. 995–1000 (2012)
17. Gnecco, N., et al.: Energy distance: a statistical measure for contextual data analysis. J. Mach. Learn. Res. **2** (2018)
18. Liu, X., Zhang, Y., Yu, Y.: Matrix factorization techniques with contextual information for recommendation systems. IEEE Trans. Knowl. Data Eng. **2** (2019)
19. Ricci, F., Rokach, L., Shapira, B., Kantor, P.: Recommender systems: challenges and research opportunities. Comput. Sci. Rev. **2** (2015)
20. Amazon (2023). https://amazon-reviews-2023.github.io
21. MovieLens. https://grouplens.org/datasets. Accessed 20 Aug 2021
22. Yelp. https://www.yelp.com/dataset/. Accessed 18 April 2020

Enhancing Motion Estimation with BM-EDM Method

Dung Ngoc Le Ha[1,2]([⊠]) [iD]

[1] Can Tho University, Can Tho city, Vietnam
[2] Can Tho University of Technology, Can Tho city, Vietnam
hlndung@ctuet.edu.vn
https://ctu.edu.vn/,https://ctuet.edu.vn/

Abstract. Motion estimation is essential in computer vision, with block matching algorithms (BMA) widely used for their simplicity and efficiency. Traditional BMA cost functions, however, face challenges like noise and illumination changes. This article presents a novel Energy Distance Matrix (BM-EDM) approach that strengthens BMA by using structural information within blocks to improve matching accuracy. Unlike pixel-wise comparisons, BM-EDM generates distance matrices and calculates energy distances to find the best match. Experiments on the Sintel dataset show that BM-EDM significantly outperforms traditional methods, especially in complex local and global motion scenarios, enhancing both accuracy and efficiency. This approach proves highly applicable to real-world tasks such as surveillance, medical imaging, and video compression, where robust motion estimation is critical.

Keywords: Motion estimation · Optical flow · Energy distance · Distance matrix · Computer vision

1 Introduction

Motion estimation is vital in computer vision and video processing applications, including video compression, object tracking, and scene analysis [1]. Among various techniques, block matching algorithms (BMA) are widely favored for their simplicity, effectiveness, and computational efficiency [2]. BMA works by dividing frames into blocks and identifying the best match in the reference frame through the minimization of a predefined cost function [3,4].

However, BMA faces challenges in achieving accuracy and reliability, especially under complex motion patterns, illumination changes, and noise [5]. Traditional metrics such as Mean Absolute Difference (MAD) [1] and Sum of Absolute Differences (SAD) [2] are limited in addressing these issues. To improve

H. X. Huynh et al. (Eds.): GOODTECHS 2024, LNICST 649, pp. 71–81, 2025.
https://doi.org/10.1007/978-3-032-01497-9_7

robustness against lighting and shadow variations, Zero-mean Sum of Absolute Differences (ZSAD) and Zero-mean Sum of Squared Differences (ZSSD) [1] were developed. By normalizing blocks to remove mean intensity, ZSAD enhances stability through absolute differences, while ZSSD offers greater sensitivity by focusing on squared differences to better capture structural variations.

The above functions are particularly useful in scenarios with uneven illumination or noise. under complex motion and lighting conditions, where these methods often fail to capture accurate motion patterns effectively [6], often struggle to accurately capture the true motion patterns, especially in cases of local motion, global motion, and illumination variations [7]. These conventional metrics primarily focus on direct pixel-wise comparisons, which may not effectively represent the structural similarities between blocks [8].

This article introduces a novel energy-based cost function for block matching motion estimation, addressing limitations of traditional methods. The approach computes distance matrices for blocks and evaluates their energy distance, identifying the block pair with the minimum energy distance as the best match. This method captures structural relationships within blocks more effectively, resulting in improved motion estimation accuracy. Experimental results show superior performance in various scenarios, particularly for local and global motion or under illumination variations, where traditional methods struggle. BM-EDM demonstrates robustness in maintaining motion coherence while being less affected by noise and lighting changes, making it ideal for real-world applications.

2 Motion Vector Estimation

2.1 Motion Estimation Based on Block Matching

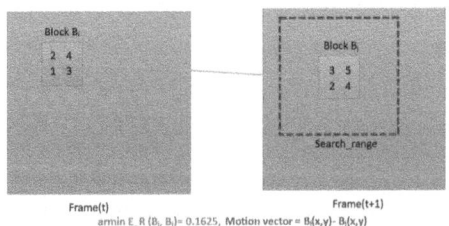

Fig. 1. Block matching method.

Assume that f_t and f_{t+1} are the first and second frames size $m \times n$ in a video, motion estimation is the search for motion in a video, more basically it is the search for motion between consecutive frames. Block matching, one of the effective search methods, estimates by matching corresponding blocks within a specific search region showed in Fig. 1. The main idea is to divide the first frame f_t and f_{t+1} into small blocks and search for corresponding blocks in the second frame by calculating the similarity between blocks as shown in Fig. 1. Each blocks Br size $k \times k$ (k is an odd number), centered at (i, j) belong to f_t, Br is denoted as in (1).

$$Br = \left\{ Br(i,j) \in f_t \mid i \in \left[\frac{2}{k}, m - \frac{2}{k} \right], j \in \left[\frac{2}{k}, n - \frac{2}{k} \right], \right\} \quad (1)$$

Set of candidate block of frame f_{t+1} is subdivided into the candidate blocks $Bc(g, h)$ size kxk denoted as in (2).

$$Bc = \left\{ Bc(g,h) \in f_{t+1} \mid g \in \left[\frac{2}{k}, m - \frac{2}{k} \right], h \in \left[\frac{2}{k}, n - \frac{2}{k} \right], \right\} \quad (2)$$

Let W be the window containing candidate blocks used to search for a potential candidate block Bc_l which is assumed to be the result of the movement of Br in frame f_{t+1}, W is presented in (3) where sr là search range.

$$W = \{ Bc_l(g,h) \in f_{t+1}, (g,h) \in \{ (g+x, h+y) | x, y \in \{ -sr, -sr+1, ..., sr \} \} \} \quad (3)$$

For each Br, find the corresponding blocks Bc_n in f_{t+1} within a search range sr. The search method involves moving Bc_n within W around Br and comparing the similarity between Br and Bc_n. The similarity between Br and each Bc_n is determined using common similarity measures (CSM) such as Mean Squared Error (MSE), Sum of Absolute Differences (SAD), or Normalized Cross-Correlation (NCC). Select the block Bc_n that has the smallest difference with Br. The offset coordinates between Br and Bc_n will be the motion vector (v_x, v_y) show in (4).

$$(v_x, v_y) = argmin(dx, dy) \in CSM(Br, Bc_n) \quad (4)$$

$$(v_x, v_y) = \arg \min_{(dx,dy) \in W} \left(\frac{1}{k^2} \sum_{i=1}^{k} \sum_{j=1}^{k} |f_t(x+i, y+j) - f_{t+1}(x+dx+i, y+dy+j)| \right) \quad (5)$$

Equation (5) satisfy the constraint $-sr \leq dx \leq sr$ and $-sr \leq dy \leq sr$ where dx and dy are temporary displacements when searching for similar blocks in the search window, (v_x, v_y) is motion vector.

This approach detects motion patterns rather than individual pixels, increases accuracy when multiple moving objects are present, and better distinguishes between actual motion and noise.

2.2 Distance Matrices

The property of the distance matrix is that it is a symmetric matrix about the main diagonal, the values on the main diagonal are always zero (the distance is calculated from a point to itself), the values off the diagonal are always non-negative. This matrix has important properties: non-negative ($d_{i,j} \geq 0$), symmetry ($d_{i,j} = d_{j,i}$). The distance matrix B_{dm} of a block is an ($N \times N$) matrix where $N = k^2$ represents the internal distance within the block B^*. The value of an element $d_{i,j}$ in a distance matrix is determined by the distance between each element in the matrix and the other elements of the matrix by the function $M(B^*)$.

The process of feature extraction is crucial in BM-EDM as it transforms image blocks into distance matrices that capture the structural relationships within each block. This representation enables a more robust evaluation of block similarity, especially under variations in noise and illumination. Using metrics such as Matching and Correlation, BM-EDM leverages these features to improve the accuracy of motion estimation. To generate the distance matrix for the source block and candidate blocks of size $k \times k$, the blocks need to be converted to a 1-dimensional matrix of size $N = k^2$. The elements of the matrix are represented by (6)

$$Bdm(N \times N) = \{Bdm[r], [c] | Bdm[r], [c] = Bdm[i]\} \tag{6}$$

$$Bdm[i](B^*) \in M(B^*), i = [0, N-1] \tag{7}$$

where: $Bdm[r], [c]$ is the value of distance matrix items and determined according to equation (7), $r = [(i-1)/q]$ and $c = (i-1) \bmod q$, B^* can be a source block or candidate block. $M(.)$ is a function that is used to calculate the distance matrix between two elements in the matrix B^*.

In this article, $M(B^*)$ is used to calculate the distance matrix for the source and candidate blocks in 2 frames f_t and f_{t+1}. The scope of this article uses 2 metrics: *Matching* equation(8), and *Corelation* (equation(9)

$$Bdm[r][c]_{Matching} = \frac{1}{n} \sum_{i=1}^{n} \Pi(Bdm[i] \neq Bdm[j]) \tag{8}$$

where $\Pi(Bdm[i] \neq Bdm[j])$ is an indicator function, which will have a value of 1 if $Bdm[i] \neq Bdm[j]$ (two different elements) and 0 if $Bdm[i] = Bdm[j]$. $\sum_{i=1}^{n} \Pi(.)$ counts the number of positions where the two blocks differ. The final result is divided by n to calculate the ratio of different elements between the two blocks.

$$Bdm[r][c]_{Correlation} = 1 - \frac{(Bdm[i] - \overline{B^*})(Bdm[j] - \overline{B^*})}{\sqrt{Bdm[i] - \overline{B^*})^2}\sqrt{(Bdm[j] - \overline{B^*})^2}} \tag{9}$$

where $i, j = [0, N-1]$, $\overline{B^*}$ is mean of B^* as show in equation (10)

$$\overline{B^*} = \frac{1}{N} \sum_{i=1}^{n} B^*[i] \tag{10}$$

2.3   Energy for Distance Matrices

For $Bdm(Br)$, $Bdm(Bc)$ are two distance matrices, the energy for distance matrices (EDM) between $Bdm(Br)$ and $Bdm(Bc)$ is computed as follows equation (11)

$$\mathbf{EDM}(Bdm(Br), Bdm(Bc)) = \frac{2}{n^2} \sum_{i=0}^{N-1} \sum_{j=0}^{N-1} |Bdm(Br)_i - Bdm(Bc)_j|$$

$$-\frac{1}{n^2} \sum_{i=0}^{N-1} \sum_{j=0}^{N-1} |Bdm(Br)_i - Bdm(Br)_j| \quad -\frac{1}{n^2} \sum_{i=0}^{N-1} \sum_{j=0}^{N-1} |Bdm(Bc)_i - Bdm(Bc)_j|$$

$$(11)$$

The value of EDM is always non-negative for any block B^* (EDM(.) ≥ 0). This function reaches a value of zero if and only if the two image blocks are identical. Furthermore, EDM increases as the difference between the two image blocks increases, reflecting changes in the structure or intensity of the blocks. [10].

2.4 Motion Vector Estimation with Block Matching and Energy Distance Matrix

By using the energy formula instead of the previous methods, this article improves equation (5) in the block matching method mentioned in the Sect. 2.1, 5) is rewritten as equation (12). The pair of distance matrices $Bdm(Br)[i, j]$, $Bdm(Bc)[g, h]$ has the smallest energy of the 2 blocks to be found, or $Bc[g, h]$ is the block $(Br)[i, j]$ moving in frame $f_t + 1$.

$$(Br, Bc) = (Br_{(i,j)}, Bc_{(g,h)}) \in \arg\min \mathbf{EDM}(Bdm(Br), Bdm(Bc)) \quad (12)$$

After finding the corresponding two blocks Br and Bc. For (xr, yr) is the center pixel of Br and (xc, yc) is the center pixel of Bc found in equation (12) which is used as the center to determine the starting and ending positions of the vector, respectively, the motion vector (v_x, v_y) is determined in (13) with two components: magnitude (14) and direction (15).

$$(v_x, v_y) = (|xc - xr|, |yc - yr|) \quad (13)$$

$$|v_x, v_y| = \sqrt{(xc - xr)^2 + (yc - yr)^2} \quad (14)$$

The direction of a vector is determined by the angle ϕ between the vector and the x axis, given by:

$$\phi = \arctan\left(\frac{yc - yr}{xc - xr}\right) \quad (15)$$

3 Motion Vector Estimation with BM-EDM

To process two frames f_t and f_{t+1} with dimensions $M \times M$, f_t is fis divided into non-overlapping blocks of size $k \times k$, indexed as $Br(x, y)$. A search window of size $(2sr + 1)^2$ is then defined in f_{t+1} from which candidate blocks Bc are extracted within the search range sr. BM-EDM transforms these blocks into distance matrices, capturing structural relationships within blocks and providing a robust basis for similarity comparison. This process minimizes the effects of noise and illumination changes, ensuring reliable motion estimation in challenging scenarios. The final output consists of $k \times k$ blocks from f_t as base blocks and f_{t+1} as candidate blocks from the search window.

Algorithm 1: : Motion estimation with BM-EDM

Input: frame f_t, frame f_{t+1}, blockSize N, searchRange sr
Output: MotionVectors[,]: A 2D array representing the motion vectors
        (vx, vy) for each block in frame f_{t+1}
Generate distance matrix from child blocks
Function CalculateDistanceMatrix(block)
Generate the energy between source block and candidate block
Function CalculateEnergy($Bdm(Br),Bdm(Bc)$)
Generate the argmin of the energy of
Function arg min **EDM**($Bdm(Br), Bdm(Bc)$)
Main Algorithm:
Create empty motion vector
1. $MotionVectors = zeros(,, 2)$
Iterate over the source blocks in frame
2. CalculateDistanceMatrix(Br)
Iterate over the candidate blocks in frame
3. **for** $i \leftarrow 0$ **to** $n - 1$ **do**
     for $j \leftarrow 0$ **to** $n - 1$ **do**
     | Br,Bc =EnergyDistanceMatrices($Bdm(Br),Bdm(Bc)$)
     end
end
Compute motion vector
4. MotionVectors = $MV(Br, Bc)$
5. **return** MotionVectors

Algorithm 2: : Energy function for distance matrices using the metric

---

Input: Matrices $Bdm(Br), Bdm(Bc)$, metric = matching, corelation
Output: Distance matrices Bdm, Bdm
Function: EnergyDistanceMatrices($Bdm(Br), Bdm(Bc)$)
1. $Bdm(Br), Bdm(Bc) = $ CreateMatrixDistance $(X, Y, metric)$
Declare variable to get the dimension of matrix
2. r, c = Bdm.shape
Compute The energy of two matrices
3. Energy = EDM($Bdm(Br), Bdm(Bc)$)
4. **return** Energy

---

4   Evaluation Methods

To evaluate the effectiveness of the BM-EDM method, Mean and median values are used to represent overall performance and typical cases respectively, while standard deviation provides insight into the stability of the estimation. This combination of metrics ensures a comprehensive assessment, particularly valuable in scenarios with varying motion complexity. Assuming prediction flow: $F_{pred} = (u_{pred}, v_{pred})$, flow ground truth: $F_{gt} = (u_{gt}, v_{gt})$ where: u_{pred}, v_{pred} is the estimation vector, u_{gt}, v_{gt} is the ground truth. N: Valid pixels (mask = 1), $mask_i$: value of mask at pixel i (0 or 1).

4.1 Average End-Point Error (EPE)

Measures the error between the estimated and actual velocity vectors at each pixel, reflecting the method's accuracy [14].

$$EPE_i = \sqrt{(u_{pred} - u_{gt})^2 + (v_{pred} - v_{gt})^2} \tag{16}$$

4.2 Average Angular Error (AAE)

Measures the angular deviation between the direction of the estimated and actual velocity vectors, assessing directional accuracy [14].

$$AAE = \arccos\left(\frac{u_{pred} \cdot u_{gt} + v_{pred} \cdot v_{gt} + 1}{\sqrt{(u_{pred}^2 + v_{pred}^2 + 1)(u_{gt}^2 + v_{gt}^2 + 1)}}\right) \tag{17}$$

The formula using 3D vectors (u,v,1) adds 1 to both the numerator and denominator to avoid issues when one of the velocity vectors is zero. The reference range is in degrees $(0 - 180^o)$, where a value closer to 0 indicates the smallest angular difference. The evaluation parameters include:

- .mean_aae: The average angular error across all pixels or blocks.
- median_aae: The median value of angular errors, offering a more robust measure against outliers.
- std_aae: The standard deviation of angular errors, indicating the dispersion of the angular differences.

The execution time of each method is also recorded to evaluate the processing speed and the feasibility of the proposed method compared to existing methods. In real-time video analysis, processing speed is a crucial factor. Methods with faster execution times will be more suitable in such cases. These metrics include mean, median, and standard deviation values, providing a comprehensive view of the accuracy and stability of BM-EDM compared to traditional methods.

5 Experiment

5.1 Dataset

The *Sintel* dataset [15] is used in this experiment. The Sintel dataset is characterized by its comprehensive nature, comprising 1,064 image pairs derived from 23 distinct scenes. It offers two variants: a 'clean' version and a 'final' version, both of which are utilized in the evaluation process. Each image in the dataset boasts a high resolution of 1024×436 pixels, providing detailed visual information.

5.2   Tools Used for Experiment

The experimental setup leveraged the accessible and powerful environment provided by Google Colab. Utilizing Colab notebooks running type Python 3, hardware accelerator CPU, which offered a flexible and user-friendly interface for code development and execution.

5.3   Scenario 1: Local Motion Estimation

In this scenario, BM-EDM method is evaluated the performance in scenes characterized by small, localized movements, typical in surveillance systems and medical imaging. These cases present unique challenges as they require high sensitivity to subtle motions while maintaining robustness against noise and illumination variations. The experimental results images with two metrics matching and correlation are shown in Fig. 2 respectively. The Tables 1 and 2 present the comprehensive comparison of different cost functions for local motion estimation.

5.4   Scenario 2: Global Motion Scene

Sample frame is selected from the Sintel dataset that feature prominent camera movements and scene-wide transformations to evaluate how BM-EDM method handles these challenging conditions. The ability to accurately estimate motion vectors in such scenarios is crucial for many real-world applications where camera movement is inevitable or intentional. The experimental results images with 2 metrics are matching and correlation show in Fig. 3 are shown respectively. Tables 3 and 4 present the comprehensive comparison of different cost functions for global motion estimation.

Table 1. Performance metrics for different cost functions

Cost function	exe_time	mean-epe	median-epe	std_epe
MAD	73.340	8.613	7.407	6.678
SAD	54.922	8.613	7.407	6.678
MSE	74.140	2.311	0.726	4.098
SSD	52.641	2.311	0.726	4.098
NCC	177.268	11.846	11.848	6.867
ZSAD	182.545	2.128	0.691	3.939
ZSSD	185.772	2.037	0.753	3.631
BM_EBDM (matching)	63.767	2.544	0.548	4.578
BM_EBDM (Correlation)	89.577	2.631	0.532	4.123

Table 2. Error metrics (AAE) for different cost functions - Local motion estimation

Cost function	mean-aae	median-aae	std_aae
MAD	72.605	76.041	27.882
SAD	72.605	76.041	27.882
MSE	41.462	33.487	28.896
SSD	41.462	33.487	28.896
NCC	85.695	89.265	24.135
ZSAD	39.825	32.199	28.497
ZSSD	41.103	34.298	27.938
BM-EDM(matching)	14.138	0	36.361
BM-EDM(correlation)	21.825	0	45.431

Table 3. Performance metrics for different cost functions

Cost function	exe_time	mean-epe	median-epe	std_epe
MAD	71.921	12.912	11.563	6.051
SAD	72.738	11.629	11.108	5.199
MSE	181.686	15.293	14.329	6.077
SSD	51.971	12.912	11.563	6.051
NCC	53.144	11.629	11.108	5.199
ZSAD	183.552	12.605	11.401	5.656
ZSSD	185.010	12.796	11.494	5.737
EB-DM (matching)	64.838	10.12	10.448	5.683
EB-DM (Correlation)	91.976	9.213	10.065	4.864

Table 4. Error metrics (AAE) for different cost functions - Global motion estimation

Cost function	mean-aae	median-aae	std_aae
MAD	88.068	85.672	26.331
SAD	83.419	84.658	23.804
MSE	87.417	83.587	28.735
SSD	88.068	85.672	26.331
NCC	83.419	84.658	23.804
ZSAD	83.438	79.769	25.950
ZSSD	83.915	81.986	26.075
BM-EDM(matching)	18.869	0	42.905
BM-EDM(correlation)	7.798	0	29.908

Fig. 2. Local motion estimation with *matching* (left) and *correlation* (right) metric.

Fig. 3. Global motion estimation with *matching* (left) and *correlation* (right) metric.

5.5 Results and Analysis

The results in Tables 1, 2, 3 and 4 demonstrate the effectiveness of BM-EDM in both local and global motion scenarios. For local motion, BM-EDM achieves a mean EPE of 2.544 (matching) and 2.631 (correlation), significantly lower than MAD and SAD (8.613), and perfect median AAE values of $0°$, outperforming ZSAD ($39.825°$) and ZSSD ($41.103°$). These results highlight its robustness against noise and lighting variations. For global motion, BM-EDM offers competitive efficiency, with execution times comparable to SAD (64.838 ms vs. 72.738 ms) and superior accuracy, achieving a mean EPE of 9.213 and perfect median AAE values of $0°$. BM-EDM excels in accuracy, robustness, and efficiency, making it ideal for real-time applications such as surveillance and medical imaging. Future work could explore multi-scale distance matrices to enhance adaptability and performance.

5.6 Discussion

The BM-EDM method improves traditional cost functions like MAD and SAD by using structural information within blocks, enhancing robustness to noise and lighting changes. Its feature extraction transforms image blocks into distance matrices, enabling similarity evaluation based on structural relationships, leading to more accurate motion estimation. While effective in most scenarios, its performance may degrade under extreme noise or variable lighting, and the correlation-based variant can be computationally demanding for real-time, high-resolution tasks. Future work could explore multi-scale distance matrices to enhance adaptability and efficiency, further establishing BM-EDM as a reliable solution for motion estimation in computer vision.

6 Conclusion

This article introduced the BM-EDM method for motion estimation, which improves traditional block matching by incorporating structural information within blocks, effectively addressing limitations of conventional metrics like MAD and SAD in complex motion, noise, and variable lighting. However, BM-EDM still faces challenges under extreme noise or lighting conditions. Future work could explore multi-scale distance matrices or advanced regularization to enhance robustness, positioning BM-EDM as a strong foundation for resilient motion estimation algorithms.

References

1. Barjatya, A.: Block matching algorithms for motion estimation. IEEE Trans. Evol. Comput. **8**(3), 225–239 (2004)
2. Cuevas, E., Zaldívar, D., Pérez-Cisneros, M., Oliva, D.: Block-matching algorithm based on differential evolution for motion estimation. Eng. Appl. Artif. Intell. **26**(1), 488–498 (2013)
3. Choudhury, H.A., Saikia, M.: Survey on block matching algorithms for motion estimation. In: 2014 International Conference on Communication and Signal Processing, pp. 36–40. IEEE (2014)
4. Jakubowski, M., Pastuszak, G.: Block-based motion estimation algorithms–a survey. Opto-Electron. Rev. **21**, 86–102 (2013)
5. Zhu, S., Ma, K.-K.: A new diamond search algorithm for fast block-matching motion estimation. IEEE Trans. Image Process. **9**(2), 287–290 (2000)
6. Jing, X., Chau, L.-P.: An efficient three-step search algorithm for block motion estimation. IEEE Trans. Multimedia **6**(3), 435–438 (2004)
7. Szeliski, R.: Computer Vision: Algorithms and Applications. Springer (2022)
8. Wang, Z., Bovik, A.C., Sheikh, H.R., Simoncelli, E.P.: Image quality assessment: from error visibility to structural similarity. IEEE Trans. Image Process. **13**(4), 600–612 (2004)
9. Girod, B.: Motion-compensating prediction with fractional-pel accuracy. IEEE Trans. Commun. **41**(4), 604–612 (1993)
10. Székely, G.J., Rizzo, M.L.: Energy statistics: a class of statistics based on distances. J. Stat. Plann. Inference **143**(8), 1249–1272 (2013)
11. Zhang, K., Zhang, L., Yang, M.-H.: Fast compressive tracking. IEEE Trans. Pattern Anal. Mach. Intell. **36**(10), 2002–2015 (2014)
12. Wu, Y., Lim, J., Yang, M.-H.: Online object tracking: a benchmark. In: Proceedings of the IEEE Conference on Computer Vision and Pattern Recognition, pp. 2411–2418 (2013)
13. Mathur, R.: Evaluation datasets and benchmarks for optical flow algorithms: a review (2020)
14. Baker, S., Scharstein, D., Lewis, J.P., Roth, S., Black, M.J., Szeliski, R.: A database and evaluation methodology for optical flow. Int. J. Comput. Vis. **92**, 1–31 (2011)
15. Butler, D.J., Wulff, J., Stanley, G.B., Black, M.J.: A naturalistic open source movie for optical flow evaluation. In: Fitzgibbon, A., Lazebnik, S., Perona, P., Sato, Y., Schmid, C. (eds.) ECCV 2012. LNCS, vol. 7577, pp. 611–625. Springer, Heidelberg (2012). https://doi.org/10.1007/978-3-642-33783-3_44

EMPD: Energy-Based Motion Pattern Detection

Kieu Thuy Thi Phan[1,2](✉) ⓘ and Cong Thang Pham[1] ⓘ

[1] The University of Da Nang, University of Science and Technology, Da Nang, Vietnam
kieuptt@ueh.edu.vn, pcthang@dut.udn.vn
[2] University of Economics Ho Chi Minh City, Ho Chi Minh City, Vietnam

Abstract. Motion detection methods are essential in many fields. This paper introduces a new approach to Energy-based Motion Pattern Detection (EMPD). The research aims to provide a theoretical basis for concepts of motion patterns, energy distance, and EMPD. This method was tested on the FBMS-59 dataset with 3,105 frames, including various objects such as bears, cats, lions, people, marple1, marple3, rabbits, and horses, showing that the motion pattern detection method with the energy model achieves good efficiency. The study uses clustering through two methods: Hierarchical clustering and K-means clustering, with Silhouette Score values reaching 0.64 and above. In particular, the horses06 data has a hierarchical clustering index of 0.84 and K-means reaches 0.85, the datasets have Silhouette Score results differing from 0 to 5%. The results show that both clustering methods are good. However, the K-means clustering method achieves better efficiency. The research results show that the EMPD method outperforms other methods and has significant importance in the field of motion pattern detection.

Keywords: Energy-based · Motion Pattern · Motion Detection · Pattern Recognition

1 Introduction

Motion analysis plays a crucial role in many fields, from studying human behavior from studying human behavior [1–4], security [5], robot control [6] and intelligent transportation system [7]. Furthermore, in this field, motion pattern detection has become an important aspect of computer vision. This method is not limited to just detecting movement, but also allows systems to recognize and analyze complex motion patterns. This capability opens a range of potential applications, from enhancing security and surveillance systems to improving human-machine interaction, creating significant advancements in modern technology. Traditional research has leveraged the power of backpropagation (BP) neural networks to classify motion [8] paving the way for Machine Learning applications in this field.

Significant advancements have been achieved through the utilization of optical flow methods, enabling motion pattern detection via the analysis of movement direction and patterns [9]. Another approach involves the use of Gaussian mixture frameworks to model and represent complex motion patterns [10]. Recently, advanced techniques have

© ICST Institute for Computer Sciences, Social Informatics and Telecommunications Engineering 2025
Published by Springer Nature Switzerland AG 2025. All Rights Reserved
H. X. Huynh et al. (Eds.): GOODTECHS 2024, LNICST 649, pp. 82–92, 2025.
https://doi.org/10.1007/978-3-032-01497-9_8

been introduced, including the use of tensors for motion pattern detection [11], providing a more multidimensional and flexible approach.

The development of deep learning has led to the application of Convolutional Neural Networks (CNNs) in motion segmentation and detection [12], The latest trends in this field include the use of latent diffusion models to generate high-resolution videos [13], opening up new possibilities in motion analysis and synthesis. Moreover, advanced deep learning methods such as SVM combined with BP neural networks [14] are being widely applied, significantly enhancing the detection and classification of complex motion patterns.

Despite significant progress in motion pattern detection, considerable challenges remain. Real-world motion patterns are often diverse and complex, making accurate detection and classification difficult. Factors such as changes in lighting, camera movement, or the presence of irrelevant objects can affect detection accuracy. Many applications require real-time motion pattern detection, posing computational performance challenges. Additionally, developing algorithms that can generalize well to different types of motion patterns remains a significant challenge.

This research proposes the EMPD (Energy-based Motion Pattern Detection) method, a new energy-based approach for detecting motion patterns. The contributions of this study include: (1) Proposing a novel energy-based method for motion pattern detection, (2) Developing an efficient algorithm to implement EMPD, and (3) Comprehensively evaluating EMPD performance on datasets.

This paper is organized as follows: Sect. 1 introduces the topic; Sect. 2 presents related studies on motion patterns; Sect. 3 discusses the research theory on motion patterns, Energy Distance, EMPD (Energy-based Motion Pattern Detection), and Energy Distance Matrix; Sect. 4 outlines the EMPD model and algorithm; Sect. 5 presents results and discussion; and Sect. 6 concludes the article.

2 Related Work

Q. Hu [15] developed a motion pattern analysis method for fall detection in elderly patients. Using a three-stage process that includes Gaussian filtering, 3D objects motion modeling, and dynamic detection, it achieved reliable fall judgments without false alarms in various movement scenarios. This research significantly contributes to healthcare monitoring by enhancing safety for the elderly.

W Hu et al. [16] introduced a comprehensive system for analyzing and learning statistical motion patterns. This system uses advanced motion pattern recognition algorithms, resulting in high accuracy in detecting behavioral deviations. It has important applications in anomaly detection and behavior prediction, especially in real-time surveillance systems such as public space monitoring. The use of statistical models helps enhance both motion prediction capabilities.

Hu et al. [17] proposed a new method for learning motion patterns in crowded scenes using motion flow fields. This approach analyzes instantaneous movements rather than long-term tracking, making it effective in crowded situations where traditional methods fail. The technique involves clustering motion flow fields and constructing a directed neighborhood graph to measure the proximity of flow vectors. It focuses on analyzing the temporal deformation of shapes formed by object positions, providing a comprehensive view of group activities.

Benabbas et al. [9] introduced a novel method for analyzing human behavior in complex real-world surveillance scenarios. Their approach uses optical flow vectors to extract motion patterns, modeling both the direction and intensity of movement. This enables the detection of dominant motion patterns and the identification of specific events in surveillance footage, such as people merging, separating, walking, running, and evacuating.

Khokhar et al. [10] developed a method to identify multi-agent activities in videos by capturing spatial and temporal relationships between motion patterns. The study uses Gaussian mixture distributions to represent motion patterns and optical flow to generate continuous regions with homogeneous motion. These regions or segments are called motion patterns. The results demonstrate the feasibility and generalizability of the method. Although effective, this method faces challenges with small motion models and requires adaptation for different activity domains.

Tokmakov et al. [12] developed a fully convolutional network trained on synthetic video sequences to detect motion in videos. Their approach combines learning motion patterns, refining optical flow features, and enhancing labeling with object maps and conditional random fields. This method demonstrated superior performance on benchmark datasets, showcasing its effectiveness in motion segmentation tasks.

Liu et al. [14] introduced the Mask Graph Convolutional Network (Mask-GCN) method for recognizing actions with novel motion patterns. This approach focuses on learning key joints specific to each action while ignoring irrelevant joints. Liu et al. demonstrated that Mask-GCN outperforms other GCN-based methods.

Another approach, such as LAMP [13] (Learn a Motion Pattern), is a motion pattern learning technique for video based on few-shot learning. This method is particularly effective in scenarios with limited training data. LAMP integrates T2I diffusion models that convert text-to-image with T2V transformations to generate high-quality short videos. The research focuses on learning motion while utilizing existing text-to-image models to generate content. This framework extends convolutional layers to learn spatial-temporal motion and modifies attention blocks to capture temporal features. Results show that LAMP effectively models motion patterns on data and generates high-quality videos.

Research in the field of motion pattern detection has evolved from traditional techniques such as optical flow, motion flow fields, Mask-GCN, and 3D image processing. Additionally, LAMP, an advanced technique, leverages text-to-image (T2I) diffusion models to convert text to video (T2V), generating high-quality short videos. However, to date, no research has implemented motion pattern detection based on energy distance. In this study, we propose a novel approach to motion pattern detection using energy distance to improve accuracy and efficiency in recognizing complex motion patterns.

3   Theoretical Research

3.1   Motion Pattern

Motion pattern detection is a defined sequence of movements, typically extracted from video or motion data, that represents the typical motion behavior of an object or a group of objects over time. It is characterized by features such as direction, speed, and trajectory, which can be analyzed to detect anomalies or predict future behavior [9, 16].

3.2   Energy Distance

Energy distance is a concept used to measure the difference between probability distributions. The term "energy" is inspired by the analogy to potential energy be-tween objects in a gravitational field. In a gravitational field, potential energy is zero if and only if the positions (gravitational centers) of two objects coincide and increase as the distance between them in space increases [18].

Let X and Y be independent random vectors in $\mathbb{R}^d$. The squared energy distance [19] between the distributions of X and Y can be defined as follows:

$$E(X, Y) = 2E|X - Y| - E|X - X'| - E|Y - Y'| \tag{1}$$

3.3   EMPD - Energy-Based Motion Pattern Detection

The Energy-based Motion Pattern Detection (EMPD) method rests on the fundamental principle that all motion involves energy changes. In this framework, a "motion pattern" is a sequence of identifiable and repeatable movements that represent a specific behavior or activity. The "energy-based" approach uses energy features to analyze and detect these motion patterns.

The mathematical model of EMPD is described based on changes in energy in both space and time. Specifically, where $I(x, y, t)$ is the pixel intensity at position (x, y) and at time t, the motion energy $E(x, y, t)$ is calculated using the formula:

$$E(x, y, t) = \sum \sum w(i, j) \cdot \left[I(x + i, y + j, t) - I(x + i, y + j, t - 1) \right]^2 \tag{2}$$

Where:

$w(i, j)$: The weight for the surrounding points around the pixel at (x, y).

$I(x + i, y + j, t)$ và $I(x + i, y + j, t - 1)$: The pixel intensity at position $(x+i, y+j)$ between time t and $t - 1$.

3.4   Energy Distance Matrix

For a set of motion patterns $\{P_1, P_2, \ldots, P_n\}$ the energy distance matrix D as follows:

$$D = \begin{bmatrix} E(P_1, P_1) & \cdots & E(P_1, P_N) \\ E(P_2, P_1) & & E(P_2, P_N) \\ \vdots & \ddots & \vdots \\ E(P_N, P_1) & \cdots & E(P_N, P_N) \end{bmatrix} \tag{3}$$

Where: $D[i,j]$ is the energy distance between two motion patterns P_i and P_j

The energy distance between these two motion patterns. $E(P_i, P_j)$ as follows:

$$E(P_i, P_j) = \sum_{x,y,t} \left[\sum_{i,j} w(i,j).\left(I_{P_i}(x+i, y+j, t) - (I_{P_j}(x+i, y+j, t)\right)^2 \right] \quad (4)$$

4 Motion Pattern with Energy Distance

4.1 Modelling

The EMPD model is presented in Fig. 1. First, frames extracted from collected video are preprocessed to prepare for subsequent analysis steps. Then, features between frames are identified using the Optical Flow method with the Lucas-Kanade algorithm, which helps track the movement of pixels in the video. Next, the model performs Motion Pattern Detection to identify characteristic motion patterns from the frames. Based on these motion patterns, Energy Distance is calculated to measure the difference between probability distributions of motion patterns using formula (2). The energy distance matrix is constructed according to formula (3) to synthesize the distance values between frames and motion patterns. As a result of the model, motion patterns are clustered to group similar movements together, thereby supporting the analysis or prediction of motion behavior in video.

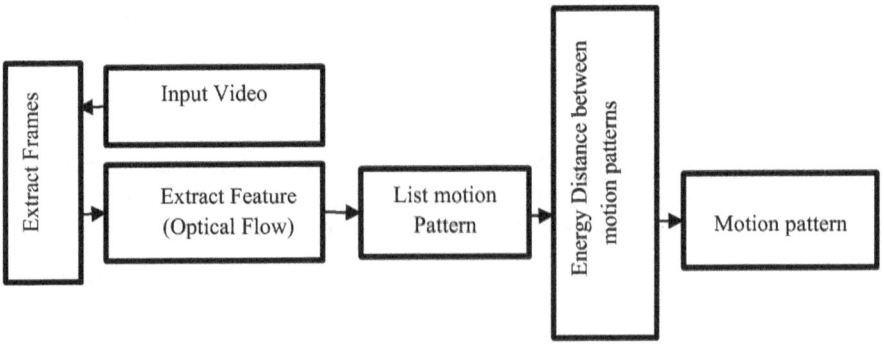

Fig. 1. Model Research EMPD

4.2 Algorithm

Algorithm 1 presents the detection of motion patterns with energy distance. The algorithm iterates through consecutive pairs of frames. In each iteration, the old and new frames are read and processed, and optical flow between the two frames is calculated using Calculate_Optical_Flow. Then, motion patterns are extracted. Next, the energy distance between consecutive motion patterns motion_patterns[i] and motion_patterns [i +

1] is calculated using Calculate_Energy_Distance. This distance is computed and stored in the energy_distances list. Finally, the last motion pattern is returned, and hierarchical clustering and K-means algorithms are applied to evaluate the method's performance.

Algorithm 1. Energy-based Motion Pattern Detection
Input: Video
Output: Motion pattern with energy distance
Begin
1. Extract list frames $\{f_0, f_1, \dots f_N\}$ from Video
// Iterate through consecutive pairs of frames
2. for i = 0 to length(frames) - 2 do
// Read and preprocess image frames
3. old_frame = read_image(frames[i])
4. new_frame = read_image (frames [i + 1])
// Calculate optical flow between consecutive frames
5. flow = Calculate_Optical_Flow (old_frame, new_frame)
6. h, w = Get_Dimensions(flow)
7. y, x = Create_Grid (0 to h step 10, 0 to w step 10)
8. fx, fy = Get_Flow_Vectors (flow, y, x)
// Create and store motion pattern
9. motion_pattern = Stack_Arrays ([x, y, fx, fy])
10.   APPEND motion_pattern TO motion_patterns
11. end for
// Calculate energy distances between consecutive motion patterns
12. for i = 0 to length(motion_patterns) - 2 do
13.   dist = Calculate_Energy_Distance(motion_patterns[i],
14. motion_patterns [i + 1])
15.   APPEND dist TO energy_distances
16. end for
// Return the final motion pattern
17. final_motion_pattern = Last_Element(motion_patterns)
18. Apply hierarchical agglomerative clustering algorithm to motion_patterns
End

5   Experimental

5.1   Datasets

The research data was collected from FBMS-59[1] [20] consisting of 29 videos, each containing multiple frames. This dataset is known for its diversity in content and the complexity of motion. For this study, 8 videos featuring various subjects were selected, including bear02, cats02, marple1, marple3, people04, rabbits05, and horses06. A total of 3,105 frames from these videos were analyzed. A detailed data description Table 1 is provided below.

---

[1] The Freiburg-Berkeley Motion Segmentation Dataset.

Table 1. Description Dataset

Name	Description	Numer of Frame
bear02	A bear moving in natural environment	458
cats02	Moving cat	120
lion02	Moving lion	416
rabbits05	Moving rabbits	420
horses06	Moving horses	720
marple1	Extracted from Miss Marple movie	328
marple3	Extracted from Miss Marple movie	323
people04	Walking people	320
Sum Total		**3105**

5.2   Scenario 1: Evaluation Based on Hierarchical Clustering

This scenario presents the clustering results in motion pattern detection combined with energy distance, using the Hierarchical Clustering method ($k = 2$) based on the FBMS-59 dataset. The results are displayed below.

Table 2. Result Hierarchical Clustering

Name	Silhouette Score
bear02	0.68
cats02	0.76
lion02	0.65
rabbits05	0.73
horses06	0.84
marple1	0.68
marple3	0.76
people04	0.64

The results in Table 2 demonstrate that the clustering method for detecting motion patterns with active energy distance performed quite well on animal subjects such as bear02, cats02, lion02, rabbits05, and horses06. Among these, horses06 achieved the highest clustering index of 0.84, while lion02 had the lowest at 0.65. For human subjects, including people04, marple1, and marple3, marple3 obtained the highest value of 0.76, and people04 the lowest at 0.64. The Hierarchical Clustering results are displayed in the Fig. 2.

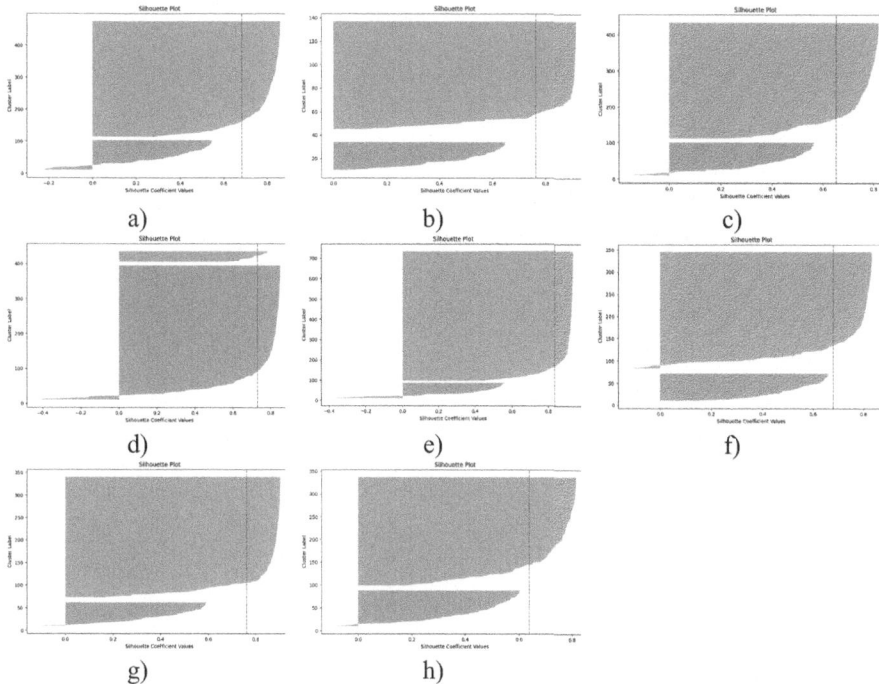

Fig. 2. Chart with hierarchical clustering. a) Hierarchical clustering with bear02; b) Hierarchical clustering with cats02; c) Hierarchical clustering with lion02; d) Hierarchical clustering with rabbits05; e) Hierarchical clustering with horses06; f) Hierarchical clustering with marple1; g) Hierarchical clustering with marple3; h) Hierarchical clustering with people04.

5.3 Scenario 2: Evaluation Based on K-means

This scenario evaluates the clustering results using K-means ($k = 2$) based on the FBMS-59 dataset. The results for motion pattern detection data with energy using K-means are as follows:

Table 3 indicates that the K-means clustering method for detecting motion patterns based on energy distance achieved satisfactory results for both animals and humans. Among animal subjects, horses06 obtained the highest clustering index of 0.85, followed by rabbits05 (0.78), cats02 (0.76), bear02 (0.73), and the lowest was lion02 with 0.67. For human subjects, marple3 achieved the highest value of 0.76, followed by marple1 (0.69) and people4 (0.65). The result K-means clustering are displayed in the Fig. 3.

The results of motion pattern detection using both Hierarchical Clustering and K-Means Clustering methods based on energy distance show that both methods yielded good results, with Hierarchical Clustering achieving an average of 71% and K-Means achieving 74%. This indicates that the K-Means Clustering method was more effective in detecting motion patterns based on energy distance. While the difference between the two methods was not significant, the most significant improvement was observed in the bear02 and rabbits05 datasets, with K-Means outperforming by over 5%. For lion02, the improvement was 2%, and for other datasets, it was around 1%. Notably,

Table 3. Result of K-means Clustering

Name	Silhouette Score
bear02	0.73
cats02	0.76
lion02	0.67
rabbits05	0.78
horses06	0.85
marple1	0.69
marple3	0.76
people04	0.65

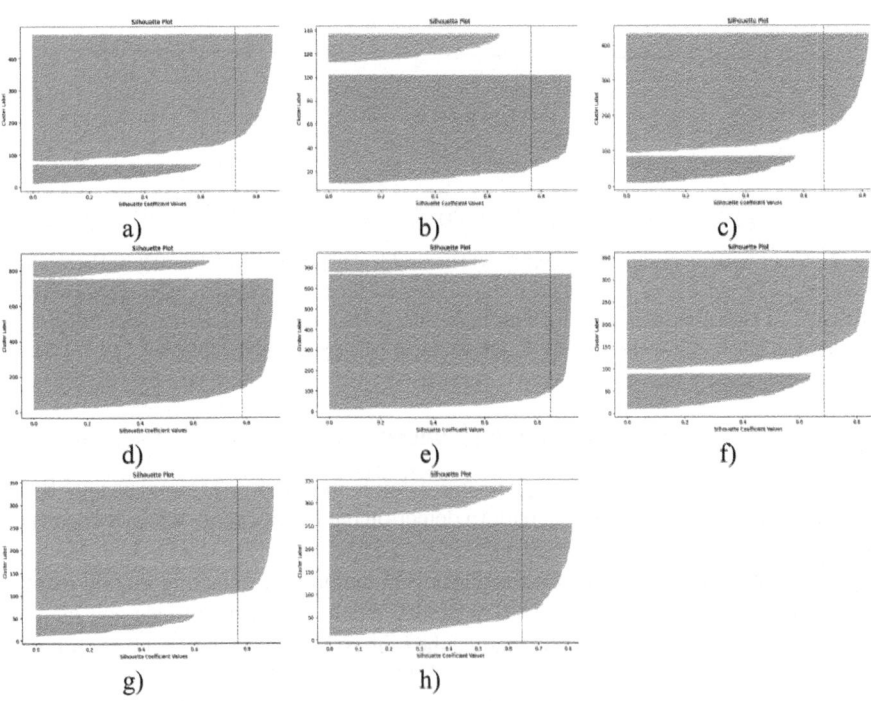

a) b) c)

d) e) f)

g) h)

Fig. 3. Chart with K-Means Clustering. a) K-Means Clustering with bear02; b) K-Means Clustering with cats02; c) K-Means Clustering with lion02; d) K-Means Clustering with rabbits05; e) K-Means Clustering with horses06; f) K-Means Clustering with marple1; g) K-Means Clustering with marple3; h) K-Means Clustering with people04.

no significant difference was observed between the two methods for the marple3 and cat02 datasets. Additionally, both methods showed better clustering results for animal subjects compared to human subjects, due to the distinct and less overlapping features and behaviors of animals.

6 Conclusion

In this paper, a motion pattern detection method based on energy distance is proposed. The study provides a theoretical foundation for motion models, energy distance, and the EMPD method, and applies this method to the FBMS-59 dataset by extracting features from optical flow using the Lucas-Kanade method on 3,105 frames. This approach employs energy distance to detect motion patterns and achieves high clustering performance. The research was conducted on datasets including animal subjects such as bear02, cats02, lion02, rabbits05, and horses06, along with human subjects like people04, marple1, and marple3. Clustering results from both methods showed good performance, with values ranging from 0.64 to 0.85. The animal group had higher clustering results than the human group, which can be explained by less overlapping in the animal image data. Furthermore, the results of motion pattern detection using energy distance with the K-means method demonstrated superior performance compared to Hierarchical Clustering. Specifically, horses06 achieved the highest clustering value in both methods, with Hierarchical Clustering at 0.84 and K-means at 0.85. These results confirm that the energy distance-based method can effectively detect moving objects. In the future, the authors intend to expand the dataset and compare it with other datasets to enhance the ability to detect motion patterns in more complex situations.

References

1. Alldieck, T., Kassubeck, M., Wandt, B., Rosenhahn, B., Magnor, M.: Optical flow-based 3D human motion estimation from monocular video. In: Roth, V., Vetter, T. (eds.) GCPR 2017. LNCS, vol. 10496, pp. 347–360. Springer, Cham (2017). https://doi.org/10.1007/978-3-319-66709-6_28
2. Dedeoglu, Y.: Moving object detection, tracking and classification for smart video surveillance. Thesis (2004)
3. Vishnu, C., Datla, R., Roy, D., Babu, S., Mohan, C.K.: Human fall detection in surveillance videos using fall motion vector modeling. IEEE Sens. J. 21(15), 17162–17170 (2021)
4. Fang, X., Liu, D., Zhou, P., Nan, G.: You can ground earlier than see: an effective and efficient pipeline for temporal sentence grounding in compressed videos. In: Proceedings of the IEEE/CVF Conference on Computer Vision and Pattern Recognition, pp. 2448–2460 (2023)
5. Jalil, A., Matalangi, M.: Object motion detection in home security system using the binary-image comparison method based on robot operating system 2 and Raspberry Pi. ILKOM Jurnal Ilmiah 13(1), 8 (2021)
6. Martinez-Martin, E., del Pobil, A.P.: Robust motion detection and tracking for human-robot interaction. In: Proceedings of the Companion of the 2017 ACM/IEEE International Conference on Human-Robot Interaction, Vienna (2017). https://doi.org/10.1145/3029798.3029799
7. Dilek, E., Dener, M.: Computer vision applications in intelligent transportation systems: a survey. Sensors 23(6), 1–3 (2023)
8. Guo, Y., Xu, G., Tsuji, S.: Understanding human motion patterns. In: Proceedings of the 12th IAPR International Conference on Pattern Recognition, Jerusalem, vol. 2, pp. 325–329. IEEE (1994)
9. Benabbas, Y., Ihaddadene, N., Djeraba, C.: Motion pattern extraction and event detection for automatic visual surveillance. EURASIP J. Image Video Process. (2011)

10. Khokhar, S., Saleemi, I., Shah, M.: Multi-agent event recognition by preservation of spatiotemporal relationships between probabilistic models. Image Vis. Comput. **31**(9), 603–615 (2013)
11. Qian, Y., Medioni, G.: Motion pattern interpretation and detection for tracking moving vehicles in airborne video. In: 2009 IEEE Conference on Computer Vision and Pattern Recognition, pp. 2671–2678 (2009)
12. Tokmakov, P., Alahari, K., Schmid, C.: Learning motion patterns in videos. In: 2017 IEEE Conference on Computer Vision and Pattern Recognition (CVPR), pp. 531–539 (2017)
13. Wu, R., Chen, L., Yang, T., Guo, C., Li, C., Zhang, X.: Lamp: learn a motion pattern for few-shot-based video generation. arXiv preprint arXiv:.10769 (2023)
14. Liu, M., Meng, F., Chen, C., Wu, S.: Novel motion patterns matter for practical skeleton-based action recognition. In: Proceedings of the AAAI Conference on Artificial Intelligence, vol. 37, no. 2, pp. 1701–1709 (2023)
15. Suhuai, L., Qingmao, H.: A dynamic motion pattern analysis approach to fall detection. In: IEEE International Workshop on Biomedical Circuits and Systems, pp. 1–5 (2004)
16. Hu, W., Xiao, X., Fu, Z., Xie, D., Tan, T., Maybank, S.: A system for learning statistical motion patterns. IEEE Trans. Pattern Anal. Mach. Intell. **28**(9), 1450–1464 (2006)
17. Hu, M., Ali, S., Shah, M.: Learning motion patterns in crowded scenes using motion flow field. In: 2008 19th International Conference on Pattern Recognition, pp. 1–5 (2008)
18. Rizzo, M.L., Székely, G.J.: Energy distance. Wiley Interdiscip. Rev. Comput. Sat. **8**(1), 27–38 (2016)
19. Székely, G.J., Rizzo, M.L.: The Energy of Data and Distance Correlation. Chapman and Hall/CRC (2023)
20. Brox, T., Malik, J., Ochs, P.: Freiburg-Berkeley motion segmentation dataset (FBMS-59). In: European Conference on Computer Vision (ECCV), vol. 1, no. 2, p. 9 (2020)

Personalized Travel Experiences: Contextual Data-Based Recommendation Solutions

Dat Nguyen Thanh, An Ngo Dinh, Bao Ho Ton, and Thuyen Phan Thi Le[✉]

FPT University, Quy Nhon Campus, Hanoi, Vietnam
{datntqe170110,anndqe170066,baohtqe170017}@fpt.edu.vn,
thuyenptl@fe.edu.vn

Abstract. According to Google's 2023 travel trends, Vietnam consistently ranks among the most-searched destinations globally, reflecting a strong recovery in its tourism economy. A survey by ezCloud.vn in 2023 highlights that travelers increasingly prioritize exploratory and relaxing experiences. While online platforms have significantly enhanced the convenience of travel recommendations, they often lack the depth of personalization required to act as intelligent consultants who deeply understand travelers' preferences. This research introduces a context-aware, personalized travel recommendation system leveraging state-of-the-art natural language processing techniques, including PhoBERT for Vietnamese text classification. Our system integrates historical user behavior, real-time contextual information such as weather and seasonal conditions, and semantic insights derived from user queries. Key components include a fast Tag-Key model for extracting relevant tags from user questions, a dynamic weighted dataset for customizable recommendations, and an architecture designed to harmonize historical and contextual inputs. With this approach, we achieved a satisfaction level of 84.52% in recommendations, showcasing the potential of NLP-driven tourism solutions.

Keywords: contextual intelligence · personalized travel recommendations · PhoBERT · real-time data integration · Vietnamese tourism

1 Introduction

The rapid socio-economic development in Vietnam has led to notable improvements in the quality of life, accompanied by shifts in travel behaviors and preferences. Concurrently, advancements in technology have transformed how travel companies operate, enabling better customer service and market exploration. Travelers now rely on diverse platforms—tourism websites, social networks, blogs, forums, and search engines—to plan trips and share experiences. Despite this wealth of resources, the overwhelming volume of information often lacks personalization, making it challenging for users to find content tailored to their unique preferences.

The concept of smart tourism destinations has emerged as a pivotal development [1], emphasizing the role of information and communication technology in enhancing

© ICST Institute for Computer Sciences, Social Informatics and Telecommunications Engineering 2025
Published by Springer Nature Switzerland AG 2025. All Rights Reserved
H. X. Huynh et al. (Eds.): GOODTECHS 2024, LNICST 649, pp. 93–104, 2025.
https://doi.org/10.1007/978-3-032-01497-9_9

travel experiences [2]. However, existing recommendation systems often fail to address dynamic conditions such as weather, season, or individual preferences. Many current tools focus on generic relationships between travelers and destinations [3], neglecting the personalized and context-aware support necessary for informed decision-making. This paper presents a solution for delivering personalized travel recommendations by integrating historical user behavior with real-time contextual factors.

2 Literature Review

The integration of artificial intelligence- AI [3-4, 13-14] into customer recommendation systems has gained significant traction across various industries, including tourism. Among these developments are systems that leverage user data to generate recommendations [11], aiming to personalize customer experiences on travel websites [12]. Despite diverse approaches, the challenge of data collection and contextual factors can reduce the accuracy of predictive models [5, 10]. For instance, one study analyzed Twitter data to gauge recent travel interests [7, 8], achieving accuracies of 68% [7] and 75.23% [8]. However, these models often raise privacy concerns due to the access required to users' social media accounts.

Customer history includes information and activities that a customer has previously engaged in, such as age, gender, geographic location, occupation, marital status, and the type of device used to access services. It also encompasses actions like search queries, clicks on headlines, comments, or likes. This data source is instrumental in verifying the income, interests, and characteristics of users. Contextual information, which can be broad, is also critical to our study, particularly focusing on the natural environment surrounding the user, including climate, weather, and geography. Seasons and weather are vital factors for tourists when choosing suitable destinations. For example, Quy Nhon City, located in a tropical monsoon climate, experiences two main seasons: the dry season (January to August) and the rainy season (September to December). The dry season, with its sunny and less rainy weather, is ideal for tourism activities like sightseeing, swimming, and entertainment. Conversely, the rainy season offers opportunities to enjoy the coastal scenery in the rain and savor local specialties.

In this research, we chose to test on a small area of Binh Dinh province but it contained all the necessary information channels for the system.

3 Dataset

Since we didn't have any existing data on the subject, we had to gather and create our own dataset. We focused our data collection efforts on three key areas: locations, food, and accommodation at Quy Nhon City.

- The first type of data that includes 630 users queries collected by interviewing 7th-semester students from FPT University Quy Nhon about the questions they will ask when search or looking for a tourist destination. After gathering data on questions and destinations, we associate each question with a destination using tags. We have identified a total of 107 common tags for both destinations and questions based on the following criteria: View: BIỂN, NÚI, ĐÁ; Type: TÂM_LINH, MẠO_HIỂM; Subject: GIA_ĐÌNH, BẠN_BÈ; Activity: VUI_CHƠI, CẮM_TRẠI, CHỤP ẢNH; Others: ẨM_THỰC, NGON, HẤP_DẪN, etc.

4 Methodology

4.1 System Architecture

We utilize a collected and pre-processed dataset to train the Tag-Key model. This model predicts relevant tags based on user queries.

System Flow: We will train a Tag-Key model to comprehend user queries and extract relevant tags of keywords from these questions. These tags will then be compared with destination tags to identify the most suitable destinations while combined with weather and personal context for recommendations (refer to Fig. 1).

Tag Prediction and Encoding

- User Query Input: The Tag-Key model predicts the relevant tags of the query.
- Tag Encoding: These predicted tags are encoded into a vector format

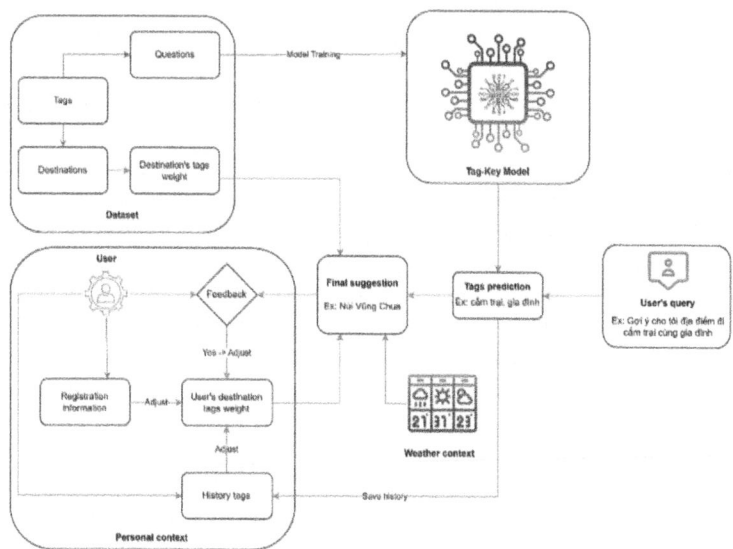

Fig. 1. System architecture

Personal Context Adjustment

- User Registration Information: Users provide personal information during registration, which is used to adjust the weighting of tags.
- Feedback Integration: After the user interacts with the system, this informations is used to fine-tune the weighting of tags to better match of them.
- Search History Utilization: The system tracks the locations the user has previously searched for.

Similarity Calculation

- Vector Comparison: This method measures the similarity between two vectors, which serves as the basis for ranking potential locations.

Final Suggestion: Weather forecast information is incorporated to enhance the relevance of the final location suggestions.

4.2   Tag-Key Model

We determined that "tags" are the key to establishing these connections. Each question and each location is associated with a set of representative tags (as detailed in part III). By finding similarities between the tag sets of a question and a destination, we can generate meaningful recommendations.

The Tag-Key model (refer to Fig. 2) is responsible for extracting the relevant tags from the user's query. The process begins with the user's input undergoing a preprocessing phase (removing stop words, correcting misspellings, removing punctuation and special characters, and word segmentation) for cleaning and standardizing the input data. The next crucial step is to tokenize the input and create embedding vectors while embedding vectors are mathematical representations of these tokens. These steps are vital for the model to learn more quickly and accurately, as they provide a structured and comprehensive representation of the input data. To achieve effective tokenization and embedding, we employ the PhoBert pre-trained tokenizer [15]. PhoBert is a model tailored specifically for the Vietnamese language, having been trained on an extensive dataset of Vietnamese text. This extensive training makes PhoBert particularly well-suited for handling Vietnamese questions, ensuring that the tokenization and embedding processes are optimized for the language. Consequently, using PhoBert allows us to accurately capture the nuances of Vietnamese input, facilitating the better performance of our model in understanding and responding to user queries.

To predict the tags or categories of both questions and destinations, we utilize the Named Entity Recognition (NER) technique. This approach helps us learn and identify the relevant categories. Within a sentence, there are certain critical words that define its meaning, known as keywords - can be any type of word while NER problems are usually used for nouns or noun phrases. We integrate a keyword extraction method into our approach.

We fine-tune BERT [16] for the text classification task using PhoBERT, which has been pretrained on our dataset named PBTK (PhoBERT – Tag-Key). This serves as the

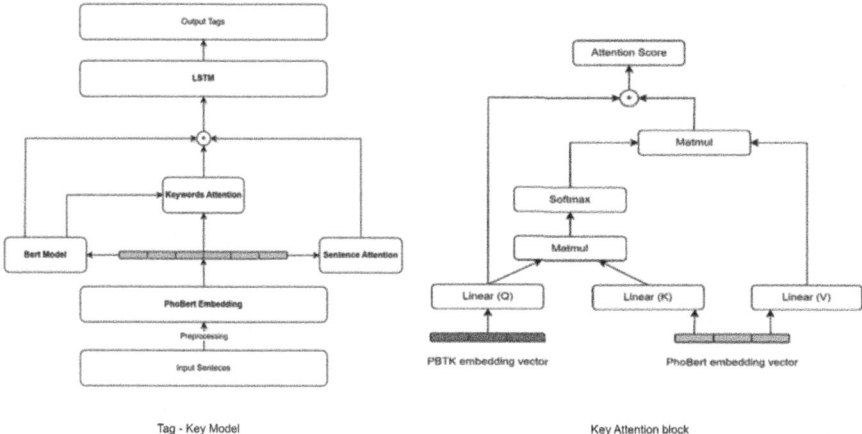

Fig. 2. Tag-Key model architecture and Key Attention block

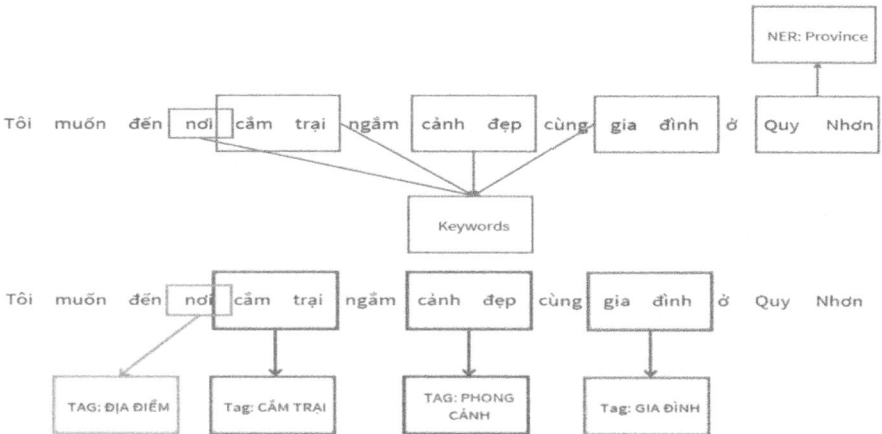

Fig. 3. Compare Tag-Key Model and NER and Keyword extraction result

backbone of our model. The embedding vector produced by the PhoBERT tokenizer is then processed through three main components:

- PBTK-Pretrained Backbone: This extracts features from keywords and tags.
- Keywords Attention: This component learns the attention weights of keywords within the sentence, acting as both Key and Value.
- Sentence Attention: This focuses on learning the attention weights of all words within the sentence.

Since the advent of attention mechanisms [20] and transformers [20–22], we use a "Keyword Attention" mechanism (see Fig. 3) that prioritizes the keywords in a sentence during the learning process:

- Obtain input for the Keyword Attention block:

$$X_Q = \text{PBTK Embedding}(); \quad X_K, \; X_V = \text{PhoBert}() \tag{1}$$

- Calculate attention score:

$$Q = X_{key}W_Q; \quad K = X_{input}W_K; \quad V = X_{input}W_V \tag{2}$$

X_{input} mean the input embedding vector of the Key Attention block, X_{key} mean the embedding vector of keyword.

$$\text{KeyAttention}(Q, K, V) = \text{softmax}\left(\frac{QK^T}{\sqrt{d_k}}\right)V \tag{3}$$

Combined with Dice Loss [17] to address the imbalance in tag data. While BERT-MRC+DSC [17, 18] represents the state-of-the-art in NER, and Bert+ExEm [19] leads in keyword extraction, we incorporate LSTM in the final block to learn the categories effectively.

4.3   Content-Based Recommendation

Each destination will be matched with all relevant tags specific to that location (see Fig. 4), these tags will then be compared to those extracted from the user's query. Initially, we will establish a default weight for each tag in each destination that is common to everyone by utilizing the following equation:

$$\text{Destination default weight} = \text{One-hot encoding} \odot \text{Tag frequency} \odot \text{Bias} \tag{4}$$

We apply one-hot encoding to transform the categorical tags of each destination into numerical tags, represented by 0 and 1. The imbalance in tag frequency within the dataset occurs because some tags are common across many locations, while others appear infrequently at specific places. To address this imbalance, we add a frequency weight. Additionally, each location is given primary and secondary tags, for which we introduce a bias weight manually assigned to each destination tag. This allows us to develop a universal set of weights optimized for all users.

We have set optimal recommendation weights that apply to all users. However, relying solely on these weights would generate identical recommendations for everyone, which conflicts with our aim to offer personalized suggestions. To address this, we introduce additional weights known as "Personal weight," calculated using the following formula:

$$\text{Personal weight} = \text{One-hot encoding} \odot \text{History tag weights} \odot$$
$$\text{Feedback weight} \odot \text{Registration weight} \tag{5}$$

We also use one-hot encoding to convert the categorical tags of each destination into numerical tags. However, unlike the default weights mentioned earlier, this time we add a history tag weight. This weight is constructed by adjusting the coefficients of the tags

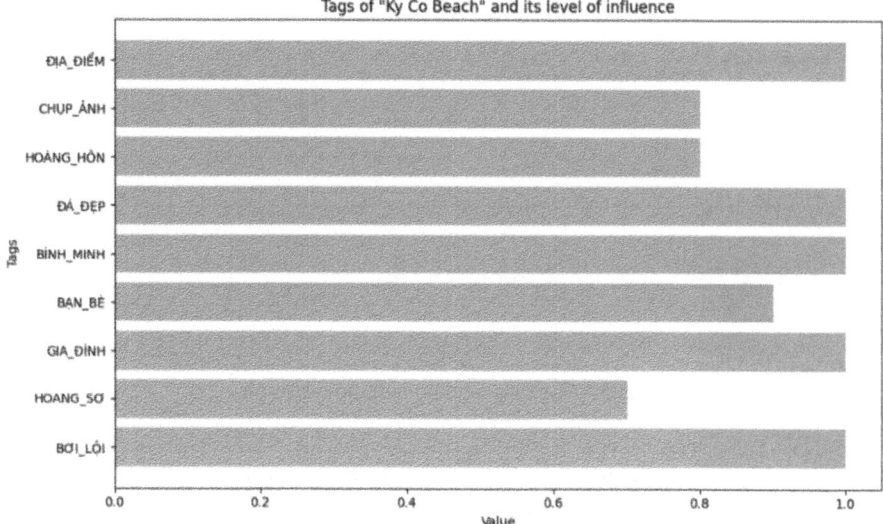

Fig. 4. Building Tags and match level of influence of Tags of a destination example.

based on the user's previous searches. Therefore, we adjust the coefficients based on this information as well. A satisfaction adjustment weight for the tags of the suggested locations. Users will be able to rate from 1 to 5 stars corresponding to:

$$\text{Feedback weight} = \frac{Star + 1}{5} \tag{6}$$

Finally, the weather information factor plays a crucial role, as some suggestions may not be suitable for current weather conditions and need to be adjusted accordingly. After synthesizing all the weights, we combine them and use cosine similarity to compare the results with the tags from the user's query to generate travel suggestions. Since our factor set is fine-tuned for each individual, the recommendations provided will be tailored to each user (Fig. 5).

5 Experiment

5.1 Tag-Key Model

We have tested many different models and the results are as follows (Table 1).

Due to the imbalance of tags in the dataset, we chose the F1-score evaluation method because it is sensitive. However, it is not ideal when the order of predicted tags in the results is evaluated incorrectly. Therefore, we propose a new evaluation method called "Acceptance". The Acceptance metric we propose is based on this evaluation, allowing predictions to be considered correct as long as they are acceptable.

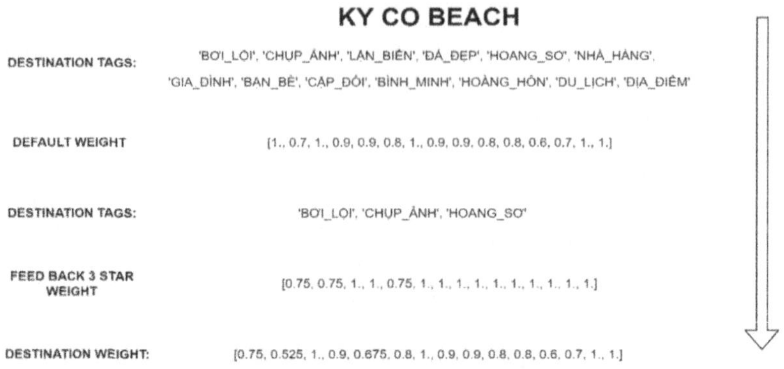

KY CO BEACH

DESTINATION TAGS:	'BOI_LOI', 'CHUP_ANH', 'LAN_BIEN', 'ĐA_ĐEP', 'HOANG_SO', 'NHA_HANG', 'GIA_DINH', 'BAN_BE', 'CAP_ĐOI', 'BINH_MINH', 'HOANG_HON', 'DU_LICH', 'DIA_DIEM'
DEFAULT WEIGHT	[1., 0.7, 1., 0.9, 0.9, 0.8, 1., 0.9, 0.9, 0.8, 0.8, 0.6, 0.7, 1., 1.]
DESTINATION TAGS:	'BOI_LOI', 'CHUP_ANH', 'HOANG_SO'
FEED BACK 3 STAR WEIGHT	[0.75, 0.75, 1., 1., 0.75, 1., 1., 1., 1., 1., 1., 1., 1., 1., 1.]
DESTINATION WEIGHT:	[0.75, 0.525, 1., 0.9, 0.675, 0.8, 1., 0.9, 0.9, 0.8, 0.8, 0.6, 0.7, 1., 1.]

Fig. 5. An example of our adjustment result

Table 1. Tag-key model experiment results

	Loss	F1-score	Acceptance
Fine-tune bert-base-uncased	0.81	0.13	0.16
Fine-tune phobert-base-v2	0.52	0.3	0.63
Phobert + LSTM	0.77	0.16	0.39
Fine-tune phobert + LSTM	0.69	0.24	0.47
Fine-tune phobert + Key Attention	**0.19**	**0.45**	**0.92**

5.2   Content – Based Recommendation

With input: "Tôi muốn cắm trại trên biển với gia đình", with extracted keywords 'CẮM TRẠI, BIỂN, and GIA ĐÌNH'. The results of three different approaches:

- Approach 1: Default One-Hot Vector Similarity: we employed a default one-hot vector to measure the similarity between tags and potential destinations. This method involved encoding each tag as a binary vector and then computing the similarity scores. However, this approach yielded suboptimal results. For example, 'CAFE SURF BAR,' but it is not a strongly relevant destination for camping. This discrepancy highlighted the limitations of using a default one-hot vector for capturing the nuanced relevance of tags (Tbale 2).

- Approach 2: Introducing Bias to Adjust Characteristics: We introduced a bias to decrease the impact of less important characteristics. This bias was manually assigned to reduce the weight of tags that were less relevant to specific destinations. This adjustment improved the overall ranking of recommendations, but 'CAFE SURF BAR' still remained among the top five destinations. Although this method showed better outcomes compared to the one-hot vector, it still did not sufficiently account for user-specific preferences and relevance.

Table 2. Set weights method experiment

Method	One hot	Destination default weight	Personal weight
Result	Tags extracted from user question: ['CẮM_TRẠI BIỂN GIA_ĐÌNH'] The most relevant destinations are: CAFE SURF BAR ĐẢO HÒN KHÔ KHU DÃ NGOẠI TRUNG LƯƠNG BÃI TẮM KỲ CO GHỀNH RÁNG – TIÊN SA	Tags extracted from user question: ['CẮM_TRẠI BIỂN GIA_ĐÌNH'] The most relevant destinations are: BIỂN HẢI GIANG ĐẢO HÒN KHÔ KHU DÃ NGOẠI TRUNG LƯƠNG CAFE SURF BAR BÃI TẮM KỲ CO	Tags extracted from user question: ['CẮM_TRẠI BIỂN GIA_ĐÌNH'] The most relevant destinations are: BIỂN HẢI GIANG ĐẢO HÒN KHÔ KHU DÃ NGOẠI TRUNG LƯƠNG BÃI TẮM KỲ CO GHỀNH RÁNG – TIÊN SA

- Approach 3: Personalized Weights Based on User Feedback: we applied personalized weights derived from user feedback to fine-tune the recommendation system. For example, a user rated 'Café Surf Bar' with 1 star, indicating that the keywords 'CẮM TRẠI, BIỂN, and GIA ĐÌNH' were not suitable for this destination. Consequently, 'CAFE SURF BAR' was excluded from the recommendations for this user.

After applying personalized weights and user feedback, the top most suitable destinations were sorted by their level of popularity.

We conducted an evaluation with feedback from five participants. Each participant was given 100 questions to answer, and they rated the top 5 recommended destinations for each question. This resulted in a total of 500 rating feedback entries. Each participant rated the suitability of the 5 recommended destinations based on their preferences Another group, we provided each participant with 5 accounts with different personal information, including career and income. Moreover, our system also considered weather information when suggesting destinations. Each individual will be asked to choose 5 different times as their arrival time. The table below shows the quantity of rating results for each participant (Table 3).

The mean rating star is calculated using the following formula:

$$\text{Mean rating star} = \sum_1^5 \frac{Star * Quantites}{One\ user's\ total\ quantities} \tag{7}$$

We assume that an acceptance level is defined as more than 3 stars. The acceptance formula is:

$$\text{Acceptance} = \frac{Quantites\ 4\ star + Quantites\ 5\ star}{One\ user's\ total\ quantities} \tag{8}$$

Using this evaluation metric, we found that the acceptance score is 84.52% based on user feedbacks. However, our system has a notable weakness related to the top 5 recommendations.

Table 3. Evaluate user satisfaction with the proposed recommendation

Users	Quantites 1*	Quantites 2*	Quantites 3*	Quantites 4*	Quantites 5*	Rating quantities	Mean rating star/user	Acceptance
1	12	20	34	251	183	500	4.146	0.868
2	11	24	39	201	225	500	4.21	0.852
3	19	22	47	146	266	500	4.236	0.824
4	10	25	42	194	229	500	4.214	0.846
5	0	32	50	163	255	500	4.282	0.836

We continue testing our system on 5 guests, each participant provided 100 questions about their interests and gave feedback about recommended destinations, resulting in a total of 500 entries. These people our system does not have their previous information, at this time we only rely on the user query results of the word weights to make suggestions (Table 4).

Table 4. Evaluate user satisfaction when they not have account

Guest	Sastified	Total quantities	Acceptance
1	302	500	0.604
2	280	500	0.56
3	330	500	0.66
4	381	500	0.762
5	371	500	0.742

6 Conclusion

In this study, we developed a user behavior-based travel recommendation system based on contextual information for personalized travel recommendations. Our study focused on a small area of a province in Vietnam. Our methodology involved constructing a Tag-Key model to accurately extract and predict relevant tags from user queries, thereby establishing meaningful connections between user interests and potential travel destinations. By employing advanced techniques such as PhoBERT for tokenization and embedding, and incorporating a novel Keyword Attention mechanism, our system significantly improved its understanding of user queries. The integration of user feedback and registration information further refined the recommendation process, ensuring a high level of personalization.

Through extensive experiments and user evaluations, we demonstrated that our approach effectively addresses the limitations of conventional recommendation systems.

Our method achieved an acceptance score of 84.52%, indicating a high level of user satisfaction. However, we also identified areas for improvement, such as the need to diversify our dataset, enhance automatic tagging processes, and refine data preprocessing techniques to boost model prediction accuracy. And we well incorporate additional contextual elements such as location and distance information.

References

1. Nghĩa, N.T.M., Vân, N.T.T., Hòa, L.V.: Điểm đến du lịch thông minh: khái niệm và các xu hướng nghiên cứu hiện nay. Tạp chí Khoa học Đại học Huế: Kinh tế và Phát triển 129–146 (2019). ISSN 2588-1205
2. Giang, V.H., Trung, N.T., Thu, N.T.P.: Những yếu tố ảnh hưởng đến sự phát triển điểm đến du lịch thông minh. Tạp chí Khoa học - Trường đại học mở Hà Nội (2022)
3. Yoon, J., Choi, C.: Real-time context-aware recommendation system for tourism. Sensors (2023). https://doi.org/10.3390/s23073679
4. Sruthi, K., Prabhu, S.: Influence of consumer decisions by recommendar system in fashion e-commerce website. In: 2022 International Conference on Decision Aid Sciences and Applications (DASA) (2022)
5. Braunhofer, M., Ricci, F.: Contextual information elicitation in travel recommender systems. Inf. Commun. Technol. Tour. (2016)
6. Ricci, F., Rokach, L., Shapira, B.: Introduction to recommender systems handbook. In: Ricci, F., Rokach, L., Shapira, B., Kantor, P.B. (eds.) Recommender Systems Handbook, Boston, MA, USA, pp. 1–35 (2011)
7. Gediminas, A., Alexander, T.: Toward the next generation of recommender systems: a survey of the state-of-the-art and possible extensions. IEEE Trans. Knowl. Data Eng. **17**(6), 734–749 (2005)
8. Coelho, J., Nitu, P., Madiraju, P.: A personalized travel recommendation system using social media analysis. In: 2018 IEEE International Congress on Big Data (BigData Congress), San Francisco, CA, USA, pp. 260–263 (2018)
9. Nitu, P., Coelho, J., Madiraju, P.: Improvising personalized travel recommendation system with recency effects. Big Data Min. Anal. **4**(3), 139–154 (2021)
10. Ullah, F., Sarwar, G., Lee, S.: Social network and device aware personalized content recommendation. In: Conference on Electronics, Telecommunications and Computers – CETC (2013). https://doi.org/10.1016/j.protcy.2014.10.260
11. Hinze, A., Junmanee, S.: Travel recommendations in a mobile tourist information system (2005)
12. Coelho, A., Rodrigues, A.: Personalized travel suggestions for tourism websites. In: International Conference on Intelligent Systems Design and Applications, ISDA, pp. 118–123 (2011). https://doi.org/10.1109/ISDA.2011.6121641
13. Nan, X., Parthasarathy, R., Wang, C.: Personalized travel recommendation system based on data mining technology (2023). https://doi.org/10.3233/FAIA230840
14. Ap, A., Abrar, K., Sumam, M., Sreenathan, M.: A deep level tagger for Malayalam, a morphologically rich language. J. Intell. Syst. **30**, 115–129 (2020). https://doi.org/10.1515/jisys-2019-0070
15. Nguyen, D.Q., Nguyen, A.T.: PhoBERT: pre-trained language models for Vietnamese. In: Findings of the Association for Computational Linguistics: EMNLP 2020, pp. 1037–1042. Association for Computational Linguistics (2020)
16. Devlin, J., Chang, M.-W., Lee, K., Toutanova, K.: BERT: pre-training of deep bidirectional transformers for language understanding. arXiv:1810.04805v2

17. Li, X., Sun, X., Meng, Y., Liang, J., Wu, F., Li, J.: Dice loss for data-imbalanced NLP tasks (2019)
18. Zhang, Y., Zhang, H.: FinBERT-MRC: financial named entity recognition using BERT under the machine reading comprehension paradigm (2022). https://doi.org/10.48550/arXiv.2205.15485
19. Khasmakhi, N., et al.: Phraseformer: multimodal key-phrase extraction using transformer and graph embedding (2021)
20. Vaswani, A., et al.: Attention is all you need. arXiv:1706.03762v7 (2017)
21. Wang, D., et al.: DocLLM: a layout-aware generative language model for multimodal document understanding (2023). arXiv:2401.00908
22. Jaegle, A., et al.: Perceiver IO: a general architecture for structured inputs & outputs (2021)

Enhancing Deep Learning Models for Crop Disease Detection Using Keras Tuner

Thuy Thi Tran[1]([✉]) [ID] and Nghia Quoc Phan[2] [ID]

[1] Network Management Center, University of Cuu Long, Vinh Long 85000, Vietnam
tranthithuy.dhcl@gmail.com
[2] Assessment Office, Tra Vinh University, Tra Vinh 87000, Vietnam
nghiatvnt@tvu.edu.vn

Abstract. This research introduces a method for optimizing deep learning models designed to identify diseases in crop images, such as tungro, blast, and blight. By utilizing Keras Tuner with the Random Search technique, we fine-tune the hyperparameters of a Convolutional Neural Network (CNN) to improve its performance in disease classification. The optimized model achieves an impressive test accuracy of 97.92% and a validation accuracy of 98.61%, demonstrating its effectiveness. These results underscore the model's potential for use in smart agriculture, offering a valuable tool for early detection of rice crop diseases.

Keywords: Deep Learning · Crop Disease Classification · Hyperparameter Optimization · Computer Vision · Keras Tuner

1 Introduction

Deep learning technologies have significantly transformed data analysis and decision-making across various sectors, especially in information technology. In the agricultural industry, these techniques are increasingly being applied to detect plant diseases, offering automated solutions that are vital for ensuring food security and boosting agricultural productivity. Unlike traditional disease detection methods, which often rely on expert knowledge and are time-consuming, deep learning provides a more efficient alternative, particularly for large-scale farming operations [1, 2].

Rice is a staple crop globally, especially in low- and middle-income nations, and is crucial for ensuring food security. A large portion of the population depends on rice as a primary food source, so any disruption in its production due to disease outbreaks can lead to significant economic challenges. Given the importance of swift and precise disease detection, deep learning models, such as Convolutional Neural Networks (CNNs), provide a promising approach [3, 4].

Nevertheless, the efficacy of these models is largely determined by the choice of hyperparameters. Proper hyperparameter tuning is critical to optimizing model accuracy and its ability to generalize to new data [5]. In this research, we apply Keras Tuner, a well-known TensorFlow library, to fine-tune our CNN model for the task of plant disease

H. X. Huynh et al. (Eds.): GOODTECHS 2024, LNICST 649, pp. 105–114, 2025.
https://doi.org/10.1007/978-3-032-01497-9_10

classification. The structure of this paper is as follows: Sect. 2 reviews existing literature, focusing on progress in applying deep learning for crop disease detection. Section 3 describes our methodology, including the CNN architecture. Section 4 explains the hyperparameter tuning process using Keras Tuner and the Random Search method. In Sect. 5, we detail the experimental setup, including the dataset and evaluation metrics. Section 6 presents the results, with a focus on performance metrics such as accuracy and loss. Finally, Sect. 7 discusses the broader implications of our findings for agricultural practices and outlines potential directions for future research.

2 Related Work

Convolutional Neural Networks in accurately identifying diseased plant images. Mohanty et al. [4] were pioneers in this field, achieving outstanding accuracy with large-scale crop datasets. Their groundbreaking work laid the groundwork for subsequent research, showing that deep learning models can surpass traditional machine learning methods in agricultural applications.

Alongside these foundational studies, many researchers have focused on refining model architectures and training strategies. Ferentinos [3] provided an in-depth review of deep learning models for plant disease diagnosis, highlighting the advantage of CNNs in directly learning hierarchical features from images, eliminating the need for extensive feature engineering—a common challenge in traditional machine learning. The study also emphasized the importance of leveraging large datasets and using transfer learning techniques, which have proven beneficial in adapting pre-trained models to specific agricultural tasks.

A noteworthy contribution by Zhang et al. [2] explored a hybrid deep learning approach that combines CNNs with Long Short-Term Memory (LSTM) networks. This model was designed to capture both spatial and temporal patterns in the progression of crop diseases, improving predictive accuracy. The results demonstrated that integrating different neural network architectures could enhance the robustness and accuracy of disease classification systems.

Another key area of research has been hyperparameter optimization, a crucial aspect for improving model performance. Hutter et al. [5] offered a comprehensive overview of various optimization techniques, including grid search, random search, and Bayesian optimization. They emphasized the importance of systematic hyperparameter tuning, as it can significantly influence the efficiency and accuracy of deep learning models. Keras Tuner has emerged as a valuable tool for automating this process, enabling efficient exploration of hyperparameter spaces [6].

Transfer learning has also become a focal point in deep learning research, particularly in cases with limited labeled data. Yosinski et al. [7] highlighted the benefits of transfer learning, where knowledge from large-scale datasets is applied to improve model performance on smaller, task-specific datasets. This approach has been successfully utilized in agriculture, allowing researchers to apply pre-trained models like VGG16 and ResNet to plant disease classification tasks [1, 2].

Recent developments in image preprocessing techniques have also enhanced the performance of deep learning models. Studies show that data augmentation can substantially improve model robustness by artificially increasing the diversity of the training data. Methods such as rotation, flipping, and scaling have proven effective in improving model generalization, particularly in scenarios with imbalanced datasets [8].

In conclusion, research on deep learning for plant disease detection has grown considerably, presenting a wide range of techniques aimed at enhancing model accuracy and reliability. This study builds on these advancements by utilizing Keras Tuner for hyperparameter optimization, with the goal of improving CNN performance in the classification of rice plant diseases.

3 Convolutional Neural Network

Convolutional Neural Networks (CNNs) are a distinct category of deep learning models specifically designed to handle grid-like data structures, especially images. By utilizing spatial hierarchies and patterns, CNNs efficiently identify features in the data, making them highly effective for applications like image classification and object detection [9].

A standard CNN structure consists of multiple layers that apply different transformations to the input data. The key components of a CNN are:

- **Input Layer**: This layer accepts raw pixel values from images, typically represented as a 3D tensor with dimensions corresponding to height, width, and color channels (e.g., RGB).
- **Convolutional Layers**: These layers use a set of filters (also known as kernels) to process the input image. Each filter is a small matrix that moves across the image to carry out the convolution operation. This operation can be mathematically represented as follows:

$$Z^l = W^l * A^{l-1} + b^l \tag{1}$$

where, Z^l represents the output of the $l - th$ convolutional layer, W^l denotes the filter weights, $*$ indicates the convolution operation, the activation from the preceding layer is denoted as A^{l-1}, while b^l represents the bias term [10].

- **Activation Function**: After the convolution step, an activation function, typically the Rectified Linear Unit (ReLU), is applied to introduce non-linearity into the model:

$$A^l = ReLU\left(Z^l\right) = max(0, Z^l) \tag{2}$$

This introduction of non-linearity enables the network to capture intricate patterns within the data [11].

- **Pooling Layers**: Pooling layers help to decrease the spatial size of the feature maps, while retaining the most important features. One commonly used method is max pooling, which extracts the highest value within a specified window:

$$P^l = \left(A^l[i : i+2, j : j+2]\right) \tag{3}$$

In this context, P^l represents the result of the pooling operation for the $l - th$ layer.

- **Flattening Layer**: Following several convolutional and pooling layers, the feature maps are converted into a one-dimensional vector, readying them for input into the fully connected layers:

$$F = Flatten\left(P^L\right) \tag{4}$$

where P^L denotes the output from the final pooling layer.

- **Fully Connected (Dense) Layers**: The one-dimensional vector is fed into one or more fully connected layers, which learn abstract representations based on the features extracted by the convolutional layers. The output from a dense layer can be represented as:

$$D^k = W^k.F + b^k \tag{5}$$

where D^k represents the output of the $k - th$ dense layer, W^k denotes the weights, and b^k stands for the bias term.

- **Output Layer**: The last layer utilizes a softmax activation function for multi-class classification, generating probability scores for each class:

$$O = softmax(D^K) \tag{6}$$

where, D^K is the output from the last dense layer.

4   Hyperparameter Optimization Using Keras Tuner and Random Search

Hyperparameter optimization plays a crucial role in training machine learning models, particularly in deep learning frameworks such as Convolutional Neural Networks. The effectiveness of these models is highly dependent on the selection of hyperparameters, which must be carefully set before the training process begins. Keras Tuner is a powerful tool that simplifies this optimization process, offering various techniques, including Random Search.

Keras Tuner is specifically designed to assist in the hyperparameter tuning of Keras-based models, making it easier to find configurations that improve model performance. It provides several search algorithms to accommodate different optimization strategies.

One of the primary methods is Random Search, which randomly samples from the hyperparameter space. This approach allows for diverse configurations to be tested without the exhaustive nature of grid searches [12]. Another method, Bayesian Optimization, constructs a probabilistic model of the objective function, enabling the selection of hyperparameters that are likely to yield better performance [13]. Finally, Hyperband combines random search with early stopping, dynamically allocating more resources to promising configurations based on their performance [14]. These algorithms provide a robust framework for optimizing hyperparameters effectively.

4.1 Random Search Method

Random Search is an effective and computationally efficient method for hyperparameter optimization. It can be mathematically represented as follows:

$$\theta^* = f(\theta) \tag{7}$$

Where, θ^* represents the optimal set of hyperparameters, Θ denotes the search space of hyperparameters, $f(\theta)$ is the performance metric (e.g., validation accuracy) that is maximized during the search process.

Unlike grid search, which evaluates all possible combinations of hyperparameters, Random Search explores random combinations, which often leads to finding effective configurations more quickly. Empirical studies suggest that Random Search can outperform grid search, especially when the dimensionality of the hyperparameter space is high [12].

4.2 Implementation in Keras Tuner

In the Keras Tuner framework [15], the Random Search method follows a systematic approach to optimize hyperparameters for machine learning models. The process begins with defining the Hypermodel, which outlines the model architecture and incorporates the hyperparameters to be optimized. Next, the Search Space is established, where ranges or distributions for each hyperparameter are defined. For instance, the number of filters in convolutional layers might range from 32 to 128, while the learning rate for the optimizer could follow a logarithmic scale, varying from 10^{-4} to 10^{-1}.

Once the search space is defined, the Search is conducted, involving the execution of a predetermined number of trials. Each trial evaluates a unique combination of hyperparameters, and the outcome is measured using the selected performance metric. Finally, after completing the search, Keras Tuner identifies the Best Configuration, providing the optimal hyperparameters along with their corresponding model performance metrics.

This overall process can be summarized by the objective function:

$$Accuracy_{val} = f(filters, dense_{units}, learning_{rate}) \tag{8}$$

where, $Accuracy_{val}$ represents the validation accuracy, and the variables represent the respective hyperparameters being tuned. This structured approach ensures that the best model configuration is systematically identified, enhancing overall performance.

5 Experimental

The experimental design describes the approach used to assess the performance of the proposed CNN model for classifying rice leaf diseases. This section provides information on the dataset used, the training procedure, evaluation metrics, and the implementation of hyperparameter optimization techniques.

5.1 Data Used

The dataset used in this research contains 120 JPEG images of rice leaves, divided into three disease categories: tungro, blast, and blight [16]. Each category includes 40 images, ensuring a balanced representation of the diseases. The images were captured under diverse conditions, which enhances the model's robustness and its ability to generalize across various scenarios. This diversity enables the CNN model to effectively learn distinctive features for each disease, thus improving its performance in practical applications.

Prior to training the CNN model, several preprocessing steps were performed to optimize the dataset. First, all images were resized to a uniform dimension of 224 × 224 pixels, ensuring consistency in input size for the model. Then, pixel values were scaled to the range of [0, 1], which helps accelerate training by promoting numerical stability. Furthermore, data augmentation techniques such as rotation, flipping, and zooming were applied to expand the effective size of the dataset. These methods not only increased the amount of training data but also enabled the model to capture more generalized features, ultimately enhancing its performance on unseen data.

5.2 Scenario 1: Default CNN Model

The CNN model was trained using a well-structured set of parameters to maximize its performance. Initially, the dataset was divided into a training set (80%) and a validation set (20%) using stratified sampling, ensuring that each class was proportionally represented. This method helped maintain balance, which is crucial for effective model training. A batch size of 32 was selected, providing an optimal balance between memory usage and training speed. The model underwent training for 100 epochs, with early stopping applied to prevent overfitting, based on the monitoring of validation loss. This approach not only enhanced the model's ability to generalize but also increased its robustness when applied to unseen data.

In this experiment, a Convolutional Neural Network was designed specifically to classify rice leaf images affected by diseases such as tungro, blast, and blight. The model architecture follows a sequential pattern, beginning with an Input Layer that takes in images of size 224 × 224 pixels with three color channels (RGB). The first Convolutional Layer employs 32 filters of size 3 × 3 with ReLU activation. This is followed by a Max Pooling Layer that reduces the feature map's dimensions by half. A second Convolutional Layer, with 64 filters of size 3 × 3 and ReLU activation, is applied, followed by another Max Pooling Layer for further dimensional reduction. A third Convolutional Layer, also with 64 filters and 3 × 3 kernels, continues the process with ReLU activation. The output is then flattened into a 1D vector using a Flatten Layer, which is passed through a Dense Layer with 64 units and ReLU activation. Finally, the model's output is produced by an Output Layer consisting of 3 units and a softmax activation function, generating the class probabilities for the three disease categories (Fig. 1).

The model is optimized using the Adam optimizer and employs sparse categorical cross-entropy as the loss function. A summary of the model's architecture is generated and saved as an image for future reference and documentation. This setup is carefully

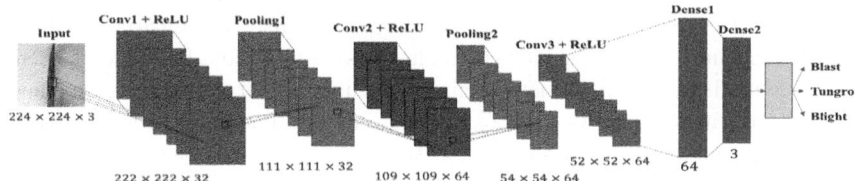

Fig. 1. Convolutional Neural Network model architecture

crafted to efficiently learn from the provided image data, enabling the model to achieve high accuracy in classifying the rice leaf diseases (Table 1).

Table 1. Summary of the Default CNN Model Architecture

Layer (type)	Output Shape	Param #
conv2d_3 (Conv2D)	(None, 222, 222, 32)	896
max_pooling2d_2 (MaxPooling2D)	(None, 111, 111, 32)	0
conv2d_4 (Conv2D)	(None, 109, 109, 64)	18,496
max_pooling2d_3 (MaxPooling2D)	(None, 54, 54, 64)	0
conv2d_5 (Conv2D)	(None, 52, 52, 64)	36,928
flatten_1 (Flatten)	(None, 173056)	0
dense_2 (Dense)	(None, 64)	11,075,648
dense_3 (Dense)	(None, 3)	195

5.3 Scenario 2: Hyperparameter Optimization

To enhance the performance of the CNN model, we employed Keras Tuner with the Random Search approach, which focused on fine-tuning critical hyperparameters. These included the number of filters in the convolutional layers, the number of units in the fully connected layer, and the learning rate for the optimizer. Through a systematic search across various hyperparameter combinations, the goal was to identify the configuration that maximized validation accuracy, thereby improving the model's classification effectiveness for rice leaf diseases.

In Scenario 2, we developed a customizable CNN model using Keras Tuner to optimize key hyperparameters. The architecture consists of three convolutional layers, with the number of filters varying from 32 to 128, allowing for flexible feature extraction. Each convolution is followed by a max-pooling layer to reduce spatial dimensions. The model also includes a fully connected layer, with the number of dense units adjustable between 32 and 128, and an output layer tailored for three categories: tungro, blast, and blight.

The model is compiled with the Adam optimizer and sparse categorical cross-entropy as the loss function, making it suitable for multi-class classification. The Random Search method is used for hyperparameter tuning, with the aim of maximizing validation accuracy. This method allows us to explore various configurations through 10 trials, optimizing the model's performance (Table 2).

Table 2. Summary of the Hyperparameter Optimized CNN Model Architecture

Layer (type)	Output Shape	Param #
conv2d (Conv2D)	(None, 222, 222, 64)	1,792
max_pooling2d (MaxPooling2D)	(None, 111, 111, 64)	0
conv2d_1 (Conv2D)	(None, 109, 109, 128)	73,856
max_pooling2d_1 (MaxPooling2D)	(None, 54, 54, 128)	0
conv2d_2 (Conv2D)	(None, 52, 52, 32)	36,896
flatten (Flatten)	(None, 86528)	0
dense (Dense)	(None, 128)	11,075,712
dense_1 (Dense)	(None, 3)	387

The CNN model is structured with multiple layers optimized for image classification. It starts with a convolutional layer (Conv2D) containing 32 filters, followed by a max pooling layer to reduce the spatial dimensions of the feature maps. Another convolutional layer with 64 filters is then applied, followed by another max pooling layer, and a third convolutional layer, again with 64 filters. The feature maps produced by the convolutional layers are then flattened into a one-dimensional vector, which is passed through a dense layer with 64 units. Finally, the model ends with an output layer that classifies the images into one of three categories: tungro, blast, or blight. The model has a total of 11, 132, 163 parameters, reflecting its complexity and capacity for extracting detailed features for accurate classification.

6 Results

In Scenario 1, the model attained a validation accuracy of 85.42%, with a corresponding validation loss of 0.56. When evaluated on the test set, the test accuracy remained consistent at 85.42%. This performance highlights the model's capability to classify images effectively, although there was a minor drop in accuracy during the validation and testing stages (Fig. 2).

In Scenario 2, the optimized model reached a validation accuracy of 97.92% in the fifth trial, indicating its strong performance in plant disease classification. The best hyperparameters identified were 96 filters for the first convolutional layer, 128 filters for both the second and third convolutional layers, and 64 units in the fully connected layer. The test accuracy of the model was 92%, further validating its robustness and dependability in this classification task (Fig. 3).

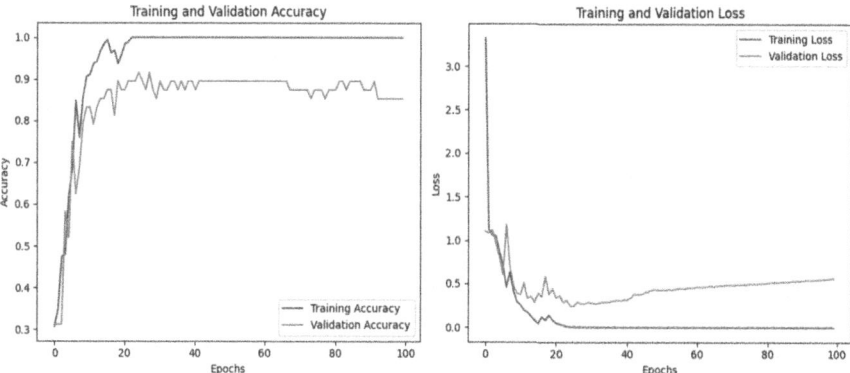

Fig. 2. Training and Validation Accuracy/Loss - Scenario 1: Default CNN Model

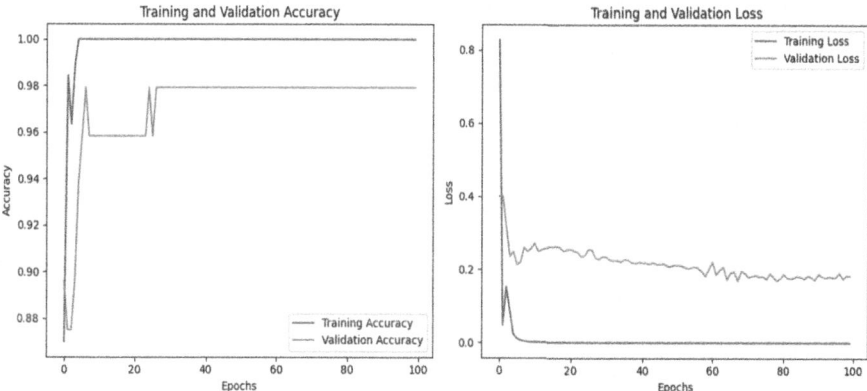

Fig. 3. Training and Validation Accuracy/Loss - Scenario 2: Hyperparameter Optimization

7 Discussion

The findings of this study highlight the effectiveness of optimized CNN models in accurately classifying plant disease images. The performance metrics are consistent with those observed in previous research, reinforcing the importance of hyperparameter tuning in boosting model accuracy. These results are particularly impactful for precision agriculture, where early and accurate disease detection can facilitate prompt interventions and enhance crop productivity [2].

Future research could explore expanding the dataset to cover a broader range of diseases and incorporate transfer learning approaches to further improve classification performance [7].

8 Conclusion

This study effectively demonstrates the optimization of deep learning models for image-based plant disease classification using Keras Tuner. The results underscore the potential of deep learning in enhancing agricultural practices, particularly in disease detection. Future work should focus on expanding datasets to include a broader range of diseases and experimenting with alternative architectures to further refine and advance this field.

References

1. Kumar, A., Singh, A., Verma, S.: A review on machine learning approaches for plant disease detection. Int. J. Comput. Appl. **182**(14), 10–15 (2021)
2. Zhang, S., Zhang, D., Guo, Y.: Deep learning in agriculture: a review. Comput. Electron. Agric. **194**, 106632 (2022)
3. Ferentinos, K.P.: Deep learning models for plant disease detection and diagnosis. Comput. Electron. Agric. **145**, 311–318 (2018)
4. Mohanty, S.P., Hughes, D.P., Salathé, M.: Using deep learning for image-based plant disease detection. Front. Plant Sci. **7**, 1419 (2016)
5. Hutter, F., Hoos, H.H., Leyton-Brown, K.: Automated configuration in machine learning: a comprehensive review. Artif. Intell. **276**, 1–38 (2019)
6. Gonzalez, J.A., Sola, I., Gonzalez, F.: A guide to hyperparameter optimization with Keras Tuner. J. Mach. Learn. Res. **21**(1), 1–4 (2020)
7. Yosinski, J., Clune, J., Nguyen, A., Fuchs, T., Lipson, H.: Transfer learning by adaptation in deep learning. In: Advances in Neural Information Processing Systems, vol. 27 (2014)
8. Shorten, C., Khoshgoftaar, T.M.: A survey on image data augmentation for deep learning. J. Big Data **6**(1), 60 (2019)
9. LeCun, Y., Bottou, L., Bengio, Y., Haffner, P.: Gradient-based learning applied to document recognition. Proc. IEEE **86**(11), 2278–2324 (2015)
10. Goodfellow, I., Bengio, Y., Courville, A.: Deep Learning. MIT Press, Cambridge (2016)
11. Nair, V., Hinton, G.E.: Rectified linear units improve restricted Boltzmann machines. In: Proceedings of the 27th International Conference on Machine Learning, pp. 807–814 (2010)
12. Bergstra, J., Bengio, Y.: Random search for hyper-parameter optimization. J. Mach. Learn. Res. **13**, 281–305 (2012)
13. Shahriari, B., Swersky, K., Wang, Z., de Freitas, N.: Taking the human out of the loop: a review of Bayesian optimization. Proc. IEEE **104**(1), 148–175 (2016)
14. Li, L., Jamieson, K.G., DeSalvo, G., Recht, B.: Hyperband: a novel bandit-based approach to hyperparameter optimization. In: Proceedings of the 30th International Conference on Machine Learning (ICML 2017), vol. 70, pp. 1–10 (2017)
15. Oktay, O., Schlemper, J., Le Folgoc, L., Lee, M., et al.: Keras tuner: a Python library for hyperparameter optimization of Keras models. arXiv preprint arXiv:1807.01699 (2018)
16. RiceLeafDisease Dataset: Rice leaf disease classification dataset (2024). https://www.kaggle.com/dataset-url

Missing Data Imputation with Graph Neuron Networks and Message Propagation

Phat Nguyen Ngoc[1,2]([✉]) [iD] and Nam Thoai[1,2] [iD]

[1] Ho Chi Minh City University of Technology (HCMUT), Ho Chi Minh City, Vietnam
{nnphat.sdh221,namthoai}@hcmut.edu.vn
[2] Vietnam National University Ho Chi Minh City (VNU-HCM), Ho Chi Minh City, Vietnam

Abstract. Sensor data streams are prevalent in various real-time applications within the Internet of Things (IoT). However, these data streams often suffer from missing values due to issues like sensor malfunctions, communication failures, or drained batteries. Such missing data can negatively impact the quality of real-time analytics and downstream applications. Existing imputation methods often rely on strong assumptions about the data streams or lack efficiency. In this study, we aim to accurately and efficiently impute missing values in data streams that exhibit only general characteristics, thereby enhancing the effectiveness of real-time applications. By improving the MPIN model [11] - one of the state-of-the-art models for imputing missing IoT values, we introduce the MIMP model (Missing data Imputation by Message Propagation) with higher accuracy in performing imputation. This study will present how to tune the MPIN model and then provide experimental evaluations to demonstrate its effectiveness.

Keywords: Imputation · Sensor data stream · GNN

1 Introduction

With the rapid expansion of the Internet of Things (IoT), multi-attribute sensor data streams are becoming prevalent across domains like healthcare, meteorology, transportation, and energy. Real-world sensor systems often face missing data due to sensor issues, communication failures, or power loss, leading to incomplete data. Missing data in critical areas like ICU monitoring or air quality alerts can result in unreliable decisions. Real-time data recovery is essential due to challenges like irregular data intervals, multiple streams, diverse attributes, and high missing value rates.

ⓒ ICST Institute for Computer Sciences, Social Informatics and Telecommunications Engineering 2025
Published by Springer Nature Switzerland AG 2025. All Rights Reserved
H. X. Huynh et al. (Eds.): GOODTECHS 2024, LNICST 649, pp. 115–126, 2025.
https://doi.org/10.1007/978-3-032-01497-9_11

Traditional imputation methods are inefficient or assume stream homogeneity, making them inadequate. MPIN (Message Propagation Imputation Network) creates a similarity graph and applies a message-passing module to establish relationships and impute missing values. This study improves MPIN by proposing the MIMP (Message Imputation Model Plus) model, which uses GraphSAGE++ to capture both local and global structural information. Through message propagation on a similarity graph, MIMP leverages correlations among instances to enhance missing value imputation. Our analysis shows that MIMP outperforms traditional methods in efficiency.

This study makes the following contributions:

- Refines the MPIN model by updating the message passing module.
- Examines the strengths of the GraphSAGE++ model as a replacement for GraphSAGE.
- Compares the performance of the MIMP model with the original MPIN and other imputation methods on snapshot imputation through experiments.

The paper is structured as follows: Sect. 2 reviews related work, Sect. 3 covers preliminaries and the MPIN architecture, Sect. 4 introduces the proposed model, Sect. 5 presents experimental results, and Sect. 6 concludes the study.

2   Related Work

2.1   Imputation Techniques

Imputation techniques for missing data streams span traditional statistical methods, neural networks, and graph-based approaches, each with distinct strengths and limitations.

Traditional methods, such as association rule-based techniques [2,3], KNN-based imputers [16], and MICE [5], are straightforward but struggle with sparse, high-dimensional, or heterogeneous data streams. These approaches typically focus on homogeneous and single-attribute datasets, making them less suitable for complex applications.

Neural network-based methods, such as RNNs (e.g., BRITS [6]) and self-attention models like SAITS [8], bring advanced capabilities to time-series imputation. However, their reliance on sequential processing increases training costs and limits scalability, particularly in online or real-time scenarios. Hybrid designs integrating RNNs and message-passing units [7] show promise but inherit the weaknesses of sequential models.

Graph-based methods represent a more flexible approach. Techniques like bipartite graphs [9] and encoder-decoder frameworks [10] utilize graph neural networks (GNNs) to impute values but depend on partially known labels, which are often unavailable. MPIN [11], a graph-based model, overcomes many challenges by constructing similarity graphs and performing parallel computations across graph nodes. It addresses issues like heterogeneity, concurrency, and sparsity through positive relational bias, enabling accurate and efficient imputation for static datasets. However, its static nature limits its effectiveness for dynamic data streams.

Our proposed MIMP model builds on MPIN, refining its message propagation process and addressing the limitations of static datasets to better handle dynamic and heterogeneous data streams.

2.2 The GNN Models for Message Passing Module

To implement the message passing module, there are varieties of GNN that could be used, such as the Graph Attention Unit (GAT) [15], the Graph Convolution Unit (GCN) [13], and GraphSAGE [12]. In the MPIN model, Xiao et al. do the experiment to find suitable GNNs, and they choose GraphSAGE because of the best result.

GraphSAGE excels in capturing the local structural information of nodes and is highly scalable for processing large-scale graph data. Its core concept involves generating node representations by aggregating information from neighboring nodes through a process called neighbor sampling. GraphSAGE operates as a K-layer network.

GraphSAGE faces the issue of over-smoothing, and it primarily captures local structural information of nodes, missing out on effectively capturing the global structure of the graph [17]. To address these issues, Zhang et al. [17] have enhanced GraphSAGE and proposed the framework named GraphSAGE++. Specifically, for a given node v, its direct neighbors exert the most significant influence, while the impact of i-hop neighbors diminishes as the number of hops increases. The Fig. 1 illustrates the architecture of the GraphSAGE++ framework. The results obtained after the GraphSAGE++ model experiment are good and promising, solving the over-smoothing problem that GraphSAGE has, thereby effectively capturing both local and global structure information.

According to Fig. 1, at the ith layer of the node v, the data representation h_v^i is aggregated in the same way as GraphSAGE achieves by performing three steps as neighbor sampling, aggregating neighbor information, and update the node representation. With the maximum layers K, the result is the concatenation of all layer representation value h_v^i, so it solves the over-smoothing problem that GraphSAGE suffered.

3 Message Propagation Imputation Network

3.1 Preliminaries

The Table 1 shows the notations that are used in this study and they inherited from the research of the MPIN model so that we can explain and demonstrate our study more clearly.

Definition 1 (Sensor Data Instance). *A sensor data instance is represented as a D-dimensional vector $x \in \mathbb{R}^D$.*

Definition 2 (Sensor Data Streams). *A sensor data stream is an unbounded, time-ordered sequence of sensor data instances. J concurrent sensor data streams*

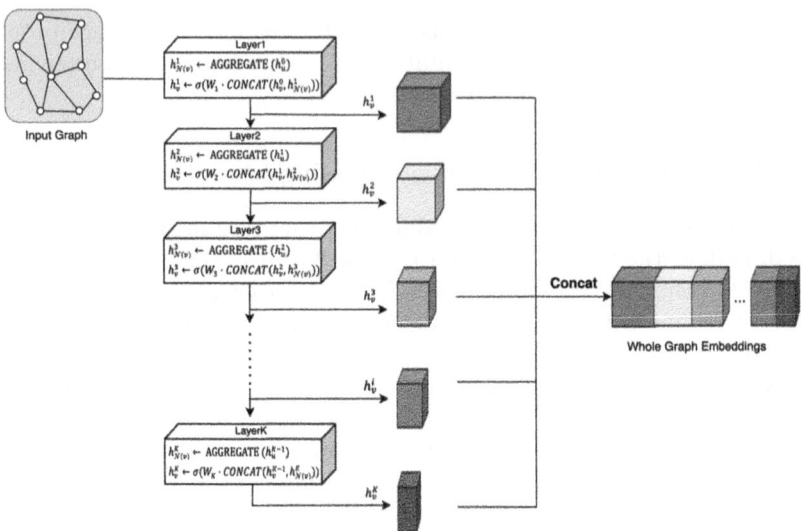

Fig. 1. The architecture of model GraphSAGE++ [17].

Table 1. Notation [11]

Symbol	Description
x	sensor data stream
m	mask of a sensor data instance
χ	sensor data streams
M	mask of sensor data streams
χ_a	sensor data chunk of a time window
M_a	mask of a sensor data chunk

are organized as a tensor X of size $J \times N \times D$ such that $N \to \infty$ corresponds to the time dimension. We use $\chi^j = \chi\,[j,:,:]$ to denote the j-th $(0 \leq j < J)$ data stream and $\chi^j = \chi\,[j,n,:]$ to denote the n-th $(0 \leq n < N)$ sensor data instance of the j-th data stream.

Definition 3 (Mask for Sensor Data Streams). *Given the sensor data streams χ, its corresponding mask M is a binary tensor with the same shape as χ:*

$$M[j,n,d] = \begin{cases} 0\,, & \chi[j,n,d] \text{ is missing} \\ 1\,, & \text{otherwise} \end{cases} \tag{1}$$

Definition 4 (Similarity Graph). *Given a data chunk $\chi_a \in \mathbb{R}^{(J.T) \times D}$, a similarity graph is constructed $G = (V, E)$ to organize χ_a data instances. For each pair x_i and x_j, the edge e_{ik} is determined if they are sufficiently similar. The method of calculating the similarity between two nodes is based on the Euclidean* *distance-based KNN method. Figure 2 presents the overview of what the similarity graph looks like.*

3.2   MPIN Architecture

The MPIN model contains two layers of Message Propagation Layer (MPL) [11]. Each MPL is constructed by the Message Passing Module and the Reconstruction Module. Moreover, the Reconstruction Module consists of two modules, called Linear Transformation and Bound Condition. The function and equation that define the module are described in the MPIN paper. Figure 3 shows the overview of MPIN architecture and Fig. 4 illustrates the arrangement of each component inside the MPL.

The input of the MPIN model is the data chunks with missing values of attributes organized in the similarity graph. The output is the same structure as the input, but the missing values are completely imputated. The window type the research uses is the tumbling window, which is a fixed-size of length and non-overlap window.

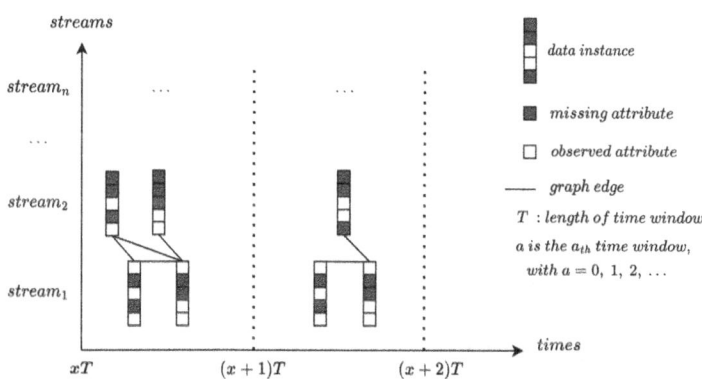

Fig. 2. Similarity graph in MPIN model.

4   Proposed MIMP

Tuning the Message Module Passing. Because of the similarity between GraphSAGE and GraphSAGE++, as well as the ability to avoid overfitting of GraphSAGE++, we decided to use GraphSAGE++ to replace GraphSAGE in implementing the message passing module. The proposed model is named *MIMP*.

The GraphSAGE++ has three variants [17]: *GraphSAGE++DA (Double Aggregation), GraphSAGE++DAC (Double Aggregation and Concatination),* and *GraphSAGE++DAMC (Double Aggregation and Mixed Concatination).* By doing experiments on each of them, the GraphSAGE++DAMC showed better

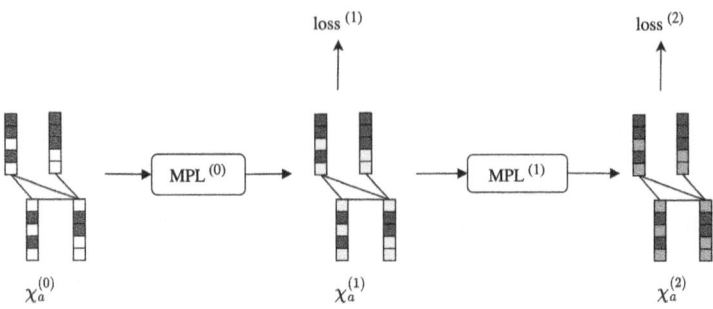

Fig. 3. MPIN overview architecture.

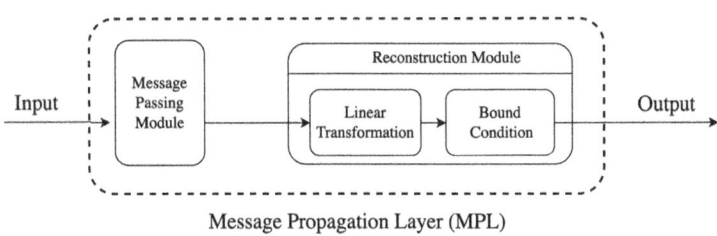

Fig. 4. The components of Message Propagation Layer (MPL).

performance than that of the other two variants so this study decided to choose the GraphSAGE++ DAMC as the representative variant for GraphSAGE++. From here on, references to GraphSAGE++ in this paper refer to the Graph-SAGE++DAMC variant.

5   Experimental Studies

5.1   Overall Settings

Datasets. This study uses three datasets that have different characteristics:

- **ICU** [19]: The dataset includes 11,988 time series spanning 48 h, capturing the health status of patients in Intensive Care Units (ICU) during the first 48 h after their admission. Data is collected on an hourly basis, with each record containing 37 variables, such as temperature, heart rate, and blood pressure.
- **Airquality** [20]: This dataset provides hourly air quality data collected over 48 months (1,461 days) from 12 monitoring stations in Beijing. Each data entry includes 11 variables, such as PM2.5, PM10, and SO2 levels. To focus on daily air quality, the data from all sites is aggregated to create concurrent daily streams, resulting in a total of 17,532 concurrent streams (calculated as the number of days multiplied by the number of sites).

- **Wifi** [18]: This dataset consists of Wi-Fi signal records collected over one hour in a mall. Each entry in the sequence represents a vector containing 671 Wi-Fi Received Signal Strength Indicator (RSSI) values, corresponding to 671 different Wi-Fi access points. These RSSI vectors are useful for indoor positioning applications.

Table 2 outlines key dataset features. The ICU and Air Quality datasets include concurrent streams with longer durations and varied attributes in periodic instances, while Wi-Fi data is high-dimensional, homogeneous, and aperiodic. Additionally, ICU and Wi-Fi datsets are highly sparse, whereas Air Quality datsets has lower sparsity.

Table 2. The datasets characteristics

Datasets	ICU	Airquality	Wi-Fi
Data instance dimension	37	11	671
Time Length of Streams (hours)	48	24	1
Number of Concurrent Streams	11988	17532	1
Regular Sampling	Yes	Yes	No
Heterogeneous Attributes	Yes	Yes	No
Original Data Sparsity	80%	1.6%	85.6%

Implementation. The project is mainly developed in Python 3.8 and has been tested on a Macbook Pro M1 equipped with a 10-core CPU. The datasets, code, and configuration information are available online. [1]

Evaluation Metrics. The study uses both effectiveness and efficiency to evaluate the result.

Effectiveness: Since real datasets lack ground-truth values for genuinely missing data, we follow the approach used in previous studies on data imputation. We randomly remove a portion of the observed attributes in χ_a and treat these removed values as ground truth to assess the imputation error. Specifically, we use *Mean Absolute Error (MAE)* and *Mean Relative Error (MRE)* to quantify the difference between the imputed values $\hat{\chi}_a$ and the original data chunk χ_a, focusing on the attributes that were randomly removed and marked by an indicator matrix M_e. These metrics are calculated as follows.

$$MAE(\chi_a, \hat{\chi}_a, M_e) = \frac{\sum_{i=1}^{J \cdot T} \sum_{d=1}^{D} (|\chi_a[i,d] - \hat{\chi}_a[i,d]| \cdot M_e[i,d])}{\sum_{i=1}^{J \cdot T} \sum_{d=1}^{D} M_e[i,d]} \tag{2}$$

$$MRE(\chi_a, \hat{\chi}_a, M_e) = \frac{\sum_{i=1}^{J \cdot T} \sum_{d=1}^{D} (|\chi_a[i,d] - \hat{\chi}_a[i,d]| \cdot M_e[i,d])}{\sum_{i=1}^{J \cdot T} \sum_{d=1}^{D} (|\chi_a[i,d]| \cdot M_e[i,d])} \tag{3}$$

Efficiency: This project decided to use study and evaluate the efficiency based on two metrics: *memory that is consumed by model*, and *the imputation time needed to impute a data chunk*.

5.2   Evaluation on Snapshot Imputation

In this part, the study compares the proposed MIMP method with other representative imputation techniques, specifically focusing on data imputation within a single time window. This paper presents comparison results with MEAN, KNN, MICE, MF, FP, BRITS, SAITS, and MPIN models.

The missing data mechanism has three typical types such as missing completely at random (MCAR), missing at random (MAR), and missing not at random (MNAR). The mechanism we choose to do on the dataset is the MCAR that data is missing randomly and not related to any reason. The data are used in this paper from IoT devices and its characteristics are spare. Hence, the MIMP model is optimized to work with these kinds of data.

Parameter Settings. The experiments focus on three key parameters. First, we adjust the missing rate parameter. As in previous studies [9,17], we lack the ground truth for truly missing values, so we randomly remove a portion of observed values from the raw data. This removal ratio is referred to as the missing rate, and the removed values serve as the ground truth for the induced missing values. The missing data ratios for ICU and Wifi datasets are 10%, 30%, 50%; and 20%, 40%, 60% are the missing data ratio of the Air Quality dataset. Second, we modify the window length parameter, which changes the duration of a time window. The time window length is 4 and 2h for ICU and Air Quality and 6 min for the Wifi dataset. Third, we vary the parameter for concurrent streams, which refers to the number of streams involved in a time window. The Wifi dataset has only one single stream, Air Quality and ICU datasets have multiple concurrent streams, at 17532 and 11988, respectively.

The Tables 3, 4 and 5 presents the effectiveness result when the MIMP model is run on three datasets and compares it to other imputation models where the **best** and second-best results per setting are highlighted. Tables 6 and 7 illustrate imputation time and memory consumption compared to the origin MPIN model.

Discussion. The GraphSAGE model demonstrates stability in sparse datasets like Wi-Fi and ICU due to its sampling and aggregation mechanism, contributing to the strong performance of both the MPIN model (which uses GraphSAGE for message passing module) and the proposed MIMP model. GraphSAGE++ (DAMC), combining max and mean aggregations, improves MIMP's performance on sparse datasets, outperforming MPIN by better avoiding overfitting [17]. However, GraphSAGE++ doubles memory and execution time for MIMP.

Table 6 shows that MIMP's imputation time is slightly high for near-realtime use. To address this, continuous imputation is under research, focusing on reducing training and update time by retraining only when needed while maintaining accuracy.

MIMP's limitations include longer imputation times compared to MPIN and simple models (e.g., FP, MEAN) due to GraphSAGE++ architecture and its optimization for MCAR patterns, without preparation for MNAR or MAR.

Table 3. The result of Snapshot Imputation on ICU dataset

Missing rate	50%		30%		10%	
Metrics	MAE	MRE	MAE	MRE	MAE	MRE
MEAN	0.87	101.7	0.81	94.98	0.73	84.12
KNN	0.74	85.26	0.62	72.76	0.46	53.11
MICE	0.73	84.85	0.61	71.55	0.44	51.12
MF	0.78	91.81	0.71	83.39	0.57	66.37
FP	0.83	96.07	0.78	91.49	0.70	81.38
BRITS	0.57	70.71	0.50	63.09	0.44	55.21
SAITS	<u>0.53</u>	65.89	0.47	58.29	0.41	51.67
MPIN	**0.39**	<u>44.94</u>	<u>0.38</u>	<u>44.17</u>	<u>0.38</u>	<u>44.51</u>
MIMP	**0.39**	**44.01**	**0.37**	**43.96**	**0.38**	**43.76**

Table 4. The result of Snapshot Imputation on Airquality dataset

Missing rate	80%		60%		40%	
Metrics	MAE	MRE	MAE	MRE	MAE	MRE
MEAN	0.48	84.19	0.46	79.51	0.40	68.91
KNN	0.48	84.41	0.47	80.21	0.41	70.42
MICE	0.48	83.53	0.45	78.11	0.39	66.14
MF	0.54	91.61	0.51	86.71	0.46	79.51
FP	0.57	99.71	0.57	98.69	0.56	96.32
BRITS	0.49	68.71	0.39	55.59	0.35	49.12
SAITS	0.42	60.68	0.32	43.41	<u>0.23</u>	**32.11**
MPIN	<u>0.21</u>	<u>35.87</u>	<u>0.21</u>	<u>36.06</u>	**0.20**	<u>34.89</u>
MIMP	**0.20**	**35.01**	**0.20**	**35.67**	**0.20**	<u>34.15</u>

Table 5. The result of Snapshot Imputation on Wifi dataset

Missing rate	50%		30%		10%	
Metrics	MAE	MRE	MAE	MRE	MAE	MRE
MEAN	2.21	92.01	1.95	81.39	1.52	63.22
KNN	1.84	76.91	1.43	59.51	0.63	26.39
MICE	2.00	83.68	1.65	68.77	0.99	41.21
MF	1.85	77.19	1.50	62.34	0.81	33.67
FP	1.26	52.78	0.55	22.73	**0.12**	**5.17**
BRITS	0.37	48.28	0.33	43.24	0.30	39.61
SAITS	0.47	60.92	0.40	52.04	0.41	54.19
MPIN	0.23	10.12	0.21	8.32	0.16	6.68
MIMP	**0.22**	**10.01**	**0.19**	**8.11**	0.16	6.61

Table 6. The imputation time by models (seconds)

Model	ICU	Airquality	Wifi
MEAN	0.05	0.01	0.05
KNN	175.21	81.32	0.11
MICE	84.82	0.28	42.31
MF	25.27	1.34	4.22
FP	0.31	0.09	0.2
BRITS	2142.14	1577.2	7.41
SAITS	1985.26	4201.12	9.25
MPIN	3.21	1.34	2.57
MIMP	7.04	2.13	4.83

Table 7. The memory consumption by models (MBs)

Model	ICU	Airquality	Wifi
MPIN	0.183	0.056	3.246
MIMP	0.379	0.117	7.925

6   Conclusion

In this study, we introduced MIMP, an enhancement of the message propagation imputation network (MPIN), by refining the implementation of the message passing module. This improvement leads to more accurate and efficient imputation of missing values in data instances within a time window of data streams. We utilize and build upon advanced imputation methods like MPIN, and we also delve deeply into graph neural networks (GNNs) like GraphSAGE and Graph-

SAGE++. Future work will involve applying these techniques to different types of windows used in stream processing, such as sliding windows, and deploying the proposed methods in a sensor data streaming system.

References

1. MIMP source code repo. https://github.com/ngocphat-fsdev/MPINplus
2. Halatchev, M., Gruenwald, L.: Estimating missing values in related sensor data streams. In: Haritsa, J.R., Vijayaraman, T.M. (eds.) Advances in Data Management 2005, Proceedings of the Eleventh International Conference on Management of Data, January 6, 7, and 8, 2005, Goa, India. Computer Society of India, pp. 83–94 (2005)
3. Jiang, N., Gruenwald, L.: Estimating missing data in data streams. In: Kotagiri, R., Krishna, P.R., Mohania, M., Nantajeewarawat, E. (eds.) DASFAA 2007. LNCS, vol. 4443, pp. 981–987. Springer, Heidelberg (2007). https://doi.org/10.1007/978-3-540-71703-4_89
4. Zhang, S.: Nearest neighbor selection for iteratively kNN imputation. J. Syst. Softw. **85**(11), 2541–2552 (2012)
5. Hastie, T., Tibshirani, R., Friedman, J.H.: The Elements of Statistical Learning: Data Mining, Inference, and Prediction, 2nd edn. Springer (2009)
6. Cao, W., Wang, D., Li, J., Zhou, H., Li, L., Li, Y.: BRITS: bidirectional recurrent imputation for time series. In: Advances in Neural Information Processing Systems 31: Annual Conference on Neural Information Processing Systems 2018, NeurIPS 2018, December 3-8, 2018, Montréal, Canada, pp. 6776–6786 (2018)
7. Cini, A., Marisca, I., Alippi, C.: Multivariate time series imputation by graph neural networks. arXiv preprint arXiv:2108.00298 (2021)
8. Wenjie, D., Côté, D., Liu, Y.: SAITS: self-attention-based imputation for time series. Expert Syst. Appl. **219**(2023), 119619 (2023)
9. You, J., Ma, X., Ding, D.Y., Kochenderfer, M.J., Leskovec, J.: Handling missing data with graph representation learning. In: Advances in Neural Information Processing Systems 33: Annual Conference on Neural Information Processing Systems 2020, NeurIPS 2020, December 6-12, virtual (2020)
10. Spinelli, I., Scardapane, S., Uncini, A.: Missing data imputation with adversarially-trained graph convolutional networks. Neural Netw. **129**(2020), 249–260 (2020)
11. Li, X., Li, H., Lu, H., Jensen, C.S., Pandey, V., Markl, V.: Missing value imputation for multi-attribute sensor data streams via message propagation (extended version). arXiv preprint arXiv:2311.07344v2 (2023)
12. Hamilton, W., Ying, Z., Leskovec, J.: Inductive representation learning on large graphs. Adv. Neural Inf. Process. Syst. **30** (2017)
13. Kipf, T.N., Welling, M.: Semi-supervised classification with graph convolutional networks. In: 5th International Conference on Learning Representations, ICLR 2017, Toulon, France, April 24-26, 2017, Conference Track Proceedings. OpenReview.net (2017). https://openreview.net/forum?id=SJU4ayYgl
14. Velickovic, P., Cucurull, G., Casanova, A., Romero, A., Liò, P., Bengio, Y.: Graph attention networks. In: 6th International Conference on Learning Representations, ICLR 2018, Vancouver, BC, Canada, April 30 - May 3, 2018, Conference Track Proceedings. OpenReview.net (2018). https://openreview.net/forum?id=rJXMpikCZ
15. Brody, S., Alon, U., Yahav, E.: How attentive are graph attention networks? arXiv preprint arXiv:2105.14491 (2021)

16. Troyanskaya, O.G., et al.: Missing value estimation methods for DNA microarrays. Bioinformatics **17**(6), 520–525 (2001)
17. Jiawei, E., et al.: GraphSAGE++: weighted multi-scale GNN for graph representation learning. Neural Process. Lett. **56**, 24 (2024)
18. Wifi Dataset. https://www.kaggle.com/competitions/indoor-location-navigation/data
19. ICU Dataset. https://physionet.org/challenge/2012/
20. Air quality Dataset. https://archive.ics.uci.edu/ml/datasets/Beijing+Multi-Site+Air-Quality+Data
21. Rossi, E., Kenlay, H., Gorinova, M.I., Chamberlain, B.P., Dong, X., Bronstein, M.M.: On the unreasonable effectiveness of feature propagation in learning on graphs with missing node features. In: Learning on Graphs Conference, LoG 2022, 9-12 December 2022, Virtual Event (Proceedings of Machine Learning Research), vol. 198, p. 11. PMLR (2022)

A Novel Framework for Real-Time Analysis of Outlier IoT Data

Tran Tuan Toan[1,2,3], Mai Ha Thi[4], Dang Thanh Hai[5], Le Minh Tuan[6(✉)], and Le Hoang Son[3]

[1] Graduate University of Science and Technology, Vietnam Academy of Science and Technology, Hanoi, Vietnam
toan.trantuan@thanglong.edu.vn
[2] Faculty of Information Technology, Thang Long University, Hanoi, Vietnam
[3] Artificial Intelligence Research Center, VNU Information Technology Institute, Hanoi, Vietnam
sonlh@vnu.edu.vn
[4] Faculty of Information Technology, University of Science and Education (University of Danang), Danang, Vietnam
mhthi@ued.udn.vn
[5] Faculty of Maths and Computer Science, Dalat University, Dalat, Vietnam
haidt@dlu.edu.vn
[6] Faculty of Information Technology, East Asia University of Technology, Hanoi, Vietnam
tuanlm@dhcd.edu.vn

Abstract. With the continuous development and relentless growth of sensor devices across various domains of daily life, the volume of information generated by wireless sensor network systems has steadily increased. This includes anomalous data, which enhances the effectiveness of environmental monitoring and control. This paper proposes an integrated framework comprising multiple components, ranging from data collection, storage, and preprocessing to the application of machine learning and deep learning methodologies for training models on the acquired dataset. Additionally, the framework employs advanced techniques such as Neural Architecture Search and Grid Search for model optimization and hyperparameter tuning. Moreover, the authors utilize a hybrid approach to forecast an adequate volume of information within a near-future timeframe.

Keywords: Internet of Thing · Outlier Detection · Data Preprocessing · Deep Learning · Neural Architecture Search · Grid Search · Incremental Learning

1 Introduction

The information derived from wireless sensor networks increasingly provides tangible benefits across numerous domains, particularly for real-time anomaly detection systems. Timely identification of anomalies in sensor data is crucial, as it contributes to maintaining the operational integrity of the entire system by issuing prompt warnings about potential serious issues that may arise.

H. X. Huynh et al. (Eds.): GOODTECHS 2024, LNICST 649, pp. 127–137, 2025.
https://doi.org/10.1007/978-3-032-01497-9_12

Collected IoT data is probably from a variety of sources, including incorrect or missing information caused by many different reasons. That thing can lead to not exact results or adverse input for processing of analysis later. Therefore, preprocessing data before implementing the training model is necessary to remove in-correct information or normalize data following conventional analysis later.

There are many data preprocessing methods that were proposed with certain experiment results. With CICIoT2023 dataset, Selman Hizal et al. [1] developed deep learning-based IDS that are related to prevention of DDos in IoT systems. In this paper, the authors implemented preprocessing data through eliminating unimportant features, duplication data and normalizing data. The authors trained in deep-learning models for detecting DDos attacks. The better results were obtained from RNN model.

Sidra Abbas et al. [2] integrated Robust Scalar and Label Encoder methods in preprocessing data, then the data was transferred to deep-learning models, such as DNN, CNN and RNN for training, classification and predicting the kind of attacks in CICIoT2023 dataset. The result of the experiment from RNN was better than the others.

Identifying data instances that exhibit distinctive characteristics compared to other data within the same dataset can be achieved through various methods and techniques, ranging from machine learning approaches to deep learning methodologies, and from supervised learning to unsupervised learning techniques, including combinations such as semi-supervised learning. The use of supervised machine learning methods for classifying anomalous information continues to be employed in certain typical problem scenarios. However, this approach requires that the labeled data prior to training, meaning that newly acquired information necessitates domain experts to label anomalous data points. This process incurs significant costs in terms of both time and financial resources.

Several researchers have integrated multiple methods to enhance the effectiveness of the training process and to detect outlier values within the data. Dheyaaldin Alsalman et al. [3] proposed the FusionNET model, which integrates machine learning methods such as Support Vector Machines (SVM), K-Nearest Neighbors (kNN) and Random Forests [4]. In this paper, the authors conducted experiments on two datasets and achieved higher accuracy and reliability compared to conventional single-method approaches. Esra Altulaihan et al. [5] employed machine learning methods, including Decision Tree (DT), Random Forest, K-Nearest Neighbor (kNN), and Support Vector Machine (SVM), in conjunction with feature selection algorithms such as Correlation-based Feature Selection (CFS) and Genetic Algorithm (GA).

Data collected from wireless sensor networks often contain substantial noise or uncontrollable factors, thereby diminishing the effectiveness of data preprocessing as well as subsequent training models. Shahbaz Ahmad Khanday et al. [6] proposed a data preprocessing model based on the ExtraTree feature selection algorithm, combined with two classifiers, LSTM and 1D-CNN, which has demonstrated high efficacy.

Wireless sensor network systems, in addition to collecting valuable information, are also subjected to numerous malicious attack requests, particularly Distributed Denial of Service (DDoS) attacks. Detecting DDoS attack traffic is thus a primary objective for researchers in this field. Euclides Carlos Pinto Neto et al. [7] boldly propose the development of the CICIoT2023 dataset to simulate Internet of Things [8] attacks. The team utilizes several IoT devices acting as attackers by programming them to send continuous DDoS messages as well as other types of attacks, including Denial of Service (DoS), Reconnaissance, Web-based attacks, and Brute Force attacks, among others. Additionally, the group evaluates the performance of various machine learning and deep learning models, such as Random Forest, Logistic Regression, Perceptron, AdaBoost and Deep Neural Networks.

Devrim Akgun et al. [9] integrated data preprocessing methods with deep learning techniques (DNN, CNN, LSTM) to construct a DDoS attack detection system. Utilizing the CICIoT2023 dataset, Aswani Devi Aguru et al. [10] employed modified Gated Recurrent Units (mGRU) to detect multi-vector DDoS attacks.

Generated data from IoT systems are increasingly more. Specifically, with the CICIoT2023 dataset, newly generated datasets are likely to contain information about cyberattacks that are constantly evolving and changing compared to the old ones. Therefore, pre-trained models cannot classify new attack types. At that time, it is necessary to develop methods that can help the pre-trained models to be updated with new data but not necessarily retrained from the beginning. One of the methods to solve this problem has been proposed by researchers through the development of algorithms or models, collectively called incremental learning methods.

Castro et al. [11] approached to train incrementally deep learning models. In this approach, the authors implemented the original dataset and then trained continuously small new sets of data. Two original datasets were utilized for the experiments, including CIFAR-100 and ImageNet. In the experiment results, the authors addressed the catastrophic forgetting in incremental learning, one of the challenging problems for generated new data with new classes. With the same catastrophic forgetting problem, Huo, J et al. [13] with researching about four well-known similarity-based loss functions (Angular, Contrastive, Center, and Triplet loss), the authors implemented to train model with a novel proposed incremental learning technique using Variational Autoencoders (VAEs).

Wu Y et al. [12] addressed the problem since the number of scaled up classes to large numbers. The authors combined two techniques, including imbalancing between new classes and old ones, and increasing numbers of visually similar classes. Huang Z et al. [14] proposed Active Class-Incremental Learning (ACIL) method with the objective of choosing the most informative samples from the unlabeled group to effectively train and maximize the performance of the result model.

Within the scope of this paper, the authors focus on proposing a novel framework that integrates various components to achieve optimal performance for the entire system:

- **Data Collection and Storage**
- **Data Preprocessing** by combining multiple techniques such as SMOTE, XGBoost, ADASYN and so on for addressing data imbalance; ExtraTree and AutoEncoder for feature selection; LabelEncoder for encoding categorical data.
- **Data Training** utilizes machine learning and deep learning models (SVM, RF, CNN, DNN and RNN) in conjunction with Neural Architecture Search for model optimization and Grid Search for hyperparameter tuning.
- For streaming data (online data), **Incremental Learning** is utilized to train and update hyperparameters to the model.

2 Materials and Methodologies

2.1 IoT Dataset and Preprocessing Data

We implemented the testing of our framework based on CICIoT2023 Dataset [7] for diversity IoT. Through the paper, a visualization chart can show the probability distribution of attributes in the dataset.

CICIoT2023 dataset was proposed by Canadian Institute for Cybersecurity (CIC). The dataset is real-time data, and it is also a standard evaluation of huge scale attacks in the IoT environment, continues to contribute significantly to the field of network security, especially in the context of detecting abnormal signatures from the information in the IoT environment. Many researchers used this dataset to develop the Intrusion Detection System (IDS) through using variety training models, they gained identification efficiency. In the progress of generating data for this dataset, CIC implemented based on real signal transceiver devices, the generating process data described network traffic including 47 features such as timestamps, size of packets, protocols... and set of assigned eight labels representing types of network attacking like DDos, DoS, Mirai, Benign, Spoofing, Recon, Web-Based, Brute Force. Through process of simulation, the dataset also suffers from problems such as imbalancing, missing in some of features or many unnecessary information for the training model later.

2.2 Preprocessing Data

The collected information from WSNs is constantly increasing, including misinformation that caused by variety of reasons either noise information from objective factors, malfunction devices and so on.

Preprocessing data is the most important phase in the whole processing of the outlier detection system. Because the information is collected from WSNs that might have noise and incorrect data so it would be impact to the process of training model later.

To facilitate the data preprocessing process as well as the model training later, while still ensuring the preservation of the nature and proportion of information on the CICIoT2023 dataset, the authors have reduced the dataset to two smaller sets according to the data extraction rule at a rate of 1% one set for each class. The first small dataset with a size of 466,866 records that is reduced from the original set is utilized for training models. The second small dataset with the same size as the first one is utilized for incremental learning. After obtaining the smaller datasets, the authors preprocess the data through the following steps (Fig. 1):

- Encoding categorical data;
- Normalization and Scaling data;
- Feature Selection;
- Imbalancing data.

Encoding Categorical Data

The CICIoT2023 dataset includes mixed attributes, both categorical and numerical

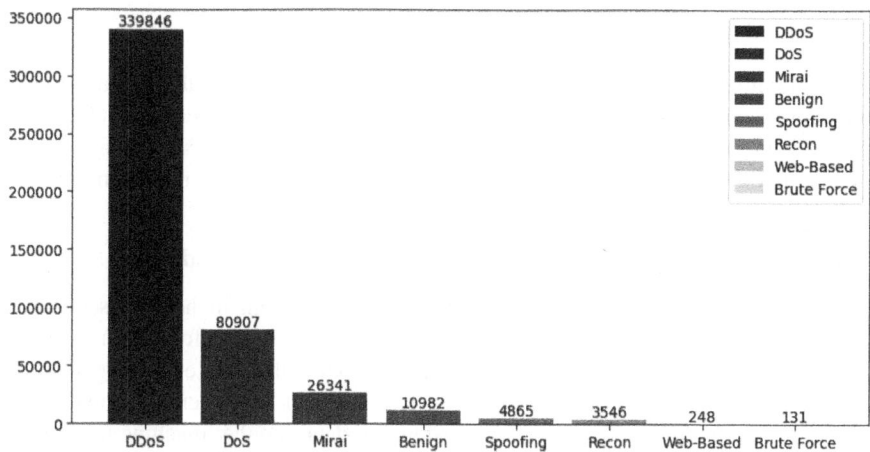

Fig. 1. Distribution of classes on CICIoT2023 dataset

attributes. The process of training data through machine learning or deep learning methods requires the input dataset to be homogeneous and usually numerical. Therefore, encoding categorical data is really necessary before the data is fed into the training models. There are many methods of encoding categorical data and each method has a direct impact on the efficiency of the data training process later. Through the experimental process, the authors chose the LabelEncoder method to perform the encoding step for categorical data.

Normalization and Scaling
Normalizing and scaling data are essential in the data preprocessing steps. This step ensures that all attributes have the same impact on the model training process later. The data normalization process aims to eliminate noise, duplicates, or invalid information, which are factors that can affect the results of the training process later, helping to increase the performance of the model by reducing bias and variance in the data. The authors also choose the StandardScaler method for data scaling.

Feature Selection
Feature Selection is used for reducing dimensionality of data and remove all unnecessary features, it just keeps only the important ones to the process of training data later. The authors chose some methods for this step, such as ExtraTree, AutoEncoder and process on smaller dataset that collect above.

Imbalancing Data
The imbalance of data during the process of collecting and storing original data is also an issue that needs to be addressed before training the data through models. The authors perform data imbalancing through a number of popular methods and compare all of them together.

2.3 Methodologies

Analyzing information collected in smart agriculture to assess the current state of data and to forecast important indicators in the near future remains a quintessential challenge, applicable in various contexts. Building upon multiple methodologies and insights from relevant literature, this paper proposes a framework comprising two main components:

- **Real-Time Data Stream State Analysis Component**
- **Information Forecasting Component for Key Near-Future Indicators**

The authors have implemented two stages of data processing in the proposed framework (Fig. 2). Firstly, the database system collects and stores the information as offline data. The preprocessing information involves normalizing the data, extracting the most important information, encoding categorical features, and implementing imbalancing data. Next, the model training process transfers the data to either machine learning or deep learning models. During the data training phase, the authors utilized NAS or GS to execute models and adjust hyperparameters. The authors select the best performing model with the best hyperparameters, store the result for use in the next stage, and simultaneously display the classification results on the dashboard, enabling users to quickly understand the output information and make informed decisions for monitoring IoT environments.

Whenever new data flows from the real environment, the next stage loads and runs the best stored model and hyperparameters for training. The authors also store the results for future use and display them on the user's dashboard. The authors used incremental learning method and sliding window technique to the new streaming data. In this integration method, the authors implemented to update the pre-trained model with new data without training from the beginning with original dataset (Algorithms 1).

Algorithms 1. The incremental learning algorithm

Input: - Training Test Split from Dataset_2 (for incremental learning)
        X_train, X_test, y_train, y_test
        - Pretrained Model (from the previous state)
Output: New updated model

1: Initial new incremental model → *incremental_ model*
2: Get weight from the *pretrained_model* → *saved_weight*
3: Apply the *saved_weight* to *incremental_ model*
4: *batch_size* ← 256
5: Calculate *num_batches* ← *num_samples_total* // *batch_size*
6: Iterate for each *batch_size*

7:      Calculate *start_idx* and *end_idx* for getting *X_batch, Y_batch*
         from *X_train, y_train*
8:      *train_generator* ← TimeseriesGenerator(*X_batch, Y_batch, other params*)
9:      Training *train_generator* with *incremental_ model*
10: End for iterating

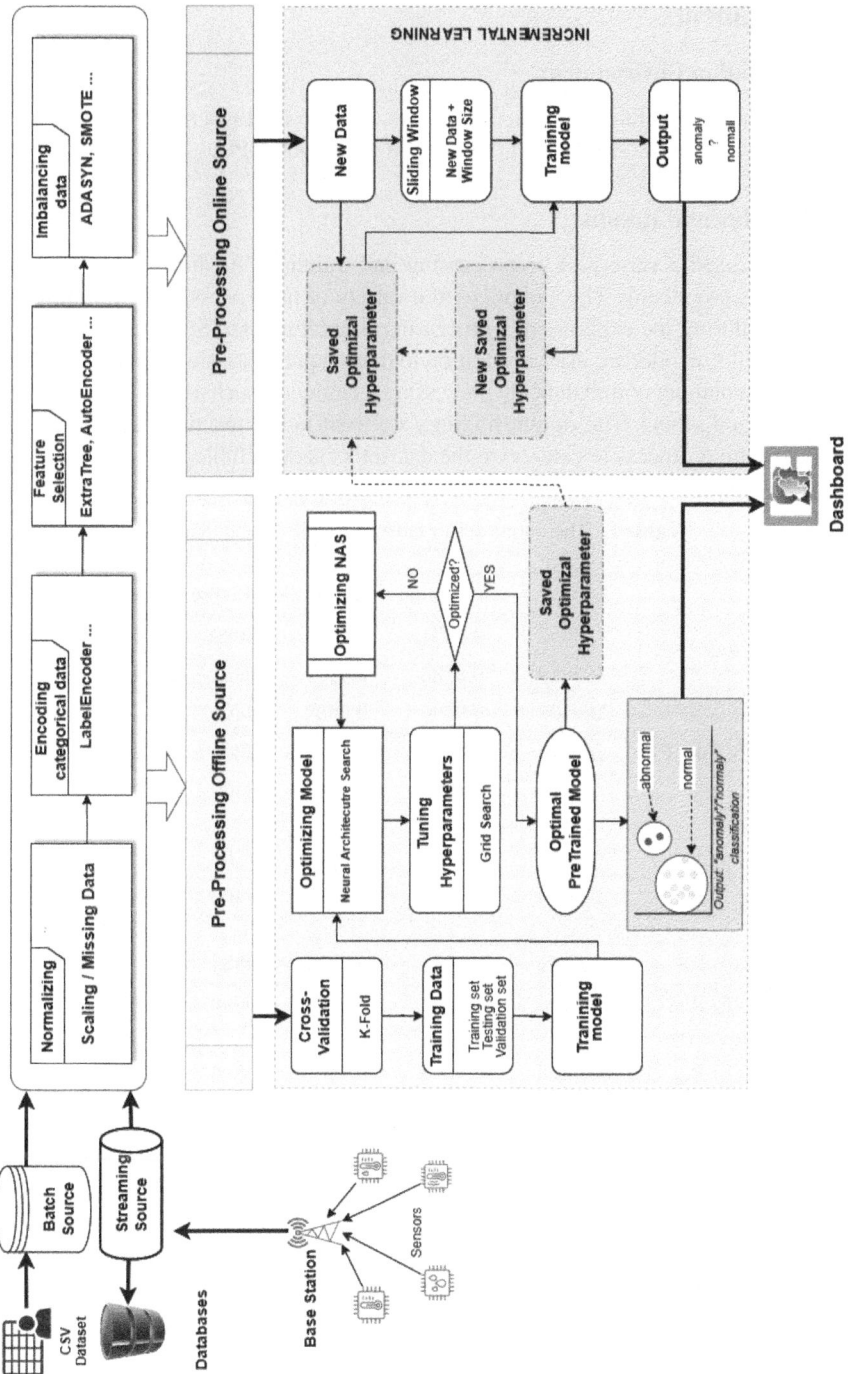

Fig. 2. A novel framework for outlier detection in IoT system

3   Experiments

3.1   Installation Environment

To handle this vast volume of data, the authors opted to deploy a server Intel® Core i9 10900K processor, 48 GB of RAM, Nvidia® RTX A4000 GPU.

3.2   Experimental Results

The authors used a variety of preprocessing and training data approaches during the experiment's processing. The authors used a variety of preprocessing and training data approaches during the experiment's processing. LabelEncoder, StandardScaler, Extra-Tree, and AutoEncoder are used in addition to dataset preprocessing. Additionally, they incorporate a number of imbalancing processing techniques, such as SMOTE, NearMiss, ADASYN, and others. The output findings are used in the machine learning or deep learning training process to categorize the dataset's classes (Table 1).

Table 1. The output result table of metrics comparison

Methods	Accuracy	Precision	Recall	F1-Score	Running Time (s)
SVM	0.8452	0.8431	0.8452	0.8080	178 m 7.2 s
NativeBayes	0.4979	0.8586	0.4979	0.5382	0.5
KNN	0.9503	0.9496	0.9503	0.9495	**0.0609**
AutoEncoder (16F)-RF	0.6600	0.8000	0.6600	0.7200	25.05
AutoEncoder (16F)-DNN*	0.7279	1.000	0.7279	0.8400	175.025
AutoEncoder (32F)-RF	0.6675	0.8100	0.6675	0.7300	300.341
AutoEncoder (32F)-DNN*	0.7279	1.000	0.7279	0.8400	190.0982
ExtraTree (34F)-RF	**0.9951**	**0.9951**	**0.9951**	**0.9948**	31.971
ExtraTree (34F)-RNN (1 layer)	0.9894	0.9891	0.9894	0.9890	215.478
ExtraTree (34F)-RNN (2 layers)	0.9898	0.9893	0.9898	0.9894	412.643

Since implementing AE and combining it with the training model on DNN, the output results with an accuracy rate of 0.7279; however, the other indexes (Precision/Recall/F1-Score) just classify with only one class on the rate of 1.000; the other classes are reached at 0.00%. The authors decided to ignore this combining method since they were comparing the results (Fig. 3).

Before training data on the models, we need to address the issue of balancing data during the collection and storage of information. The authors choose combining methods on selecting features (ExtraTree) and imbalancing processes, then training on machine learning (Random Forest), and outputs are shown in the following Table 2.

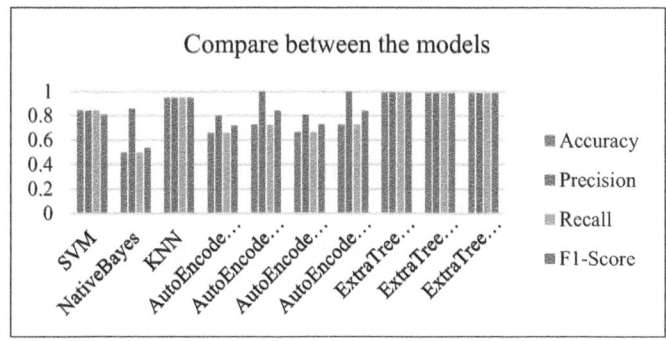

Fig. 3. The result of the metrics on the handling of the imbalance methods

Case One: Use ExtraTree to select the features, remove all unimportant features (important indexes are lower than a certain threshold), continue to implement the imbalancing data process, and then train the data using the RF model.

Case Two: Use ExtraTree to eliminate six features with important indexes equal to zero; then, implement the imbalancing data process; and finally, train the data using the RF model.

Table 2. The result of the metrics for each case on the handling imbalance methods

Methods	Case one				Case two			
	Accu	Prec	Recall	F1	Accu	Prec	Recall	F1
ADASYN	0.9949	0.9948	0.9949	0.9948	0.9948	0.9947	0.9948	0.9947
NearMiss	0.5678	0.8228	0.5678	0.6070	0.4610	0.8229	0.4610	0.4827
ClusterCentroids	0.9441	0.9607	0.9441	0.9489	0.9609	0.9786	0.9609	0.9662
RandomOverSampler	0.9945	0.9945	0.9945	0.9943	0.9948	0.9948	0.9948	0.9946
RandomUnderSampler	0.9708	0.9820	0.9708	0.9759	0.9561	0.9698	0.9561	0.9618
SMOTE	0.9943	0.9943	0.9943	0.9942	0.9940	0.9941	0.9940	0.9939
Not using any methods	**0.9951**	**0.9951**	**0.9951**	**0.9948**	**0.9950**	**0.9949**	**0.9950**	**0.9947**

Based on the aforementioned results, the authors discovered that employing methods to manage imbalanced data does not always yield superior outcomes. In some situations, with certain datasets, the imbalance handling process can lead to a double error when combined with training models later. The authors also found that combining some methods might get better results, such as SMOTEENN or SMOTETomek.

At the online data processing stage, the authors implemented various regression methods and compared the metrics of each method, as illustrated in Table 3.

As the output results above, the LSTM model outperformed the remaining models in terms of MSE and RMSE, despite its execution time being only average. Meanwhile,

Table 3. The result of the metrics for each model on the handling prediction data

Methods	MAE	MSE	RMSE	Running time (s)
XGBoost	0.0283	0.1478	0.3845	42.87
LinearRegression	0.3631	0.4149	0.6441	**1.57**
RandomForestRegressor	**0.0271**	0.0727	0.2697	488.54
LSTM	0.1089	**0.0548**	**0.2342**	202.07

the RandomForestRegressor model gave better results in the index, indicating the closest predicted value to the actual value. Overall, the current stage's output results are not as compelling as anticipated, highlighting the need for further development through new models or algorithms in the future.

4 Conclusion

The utilization of information technology in addressing smart agriculture challenges frequently produces substantial outcomes. The authors have attained specific results by creating an intelligent application for anomaly identification in IoT for smart agriculture, encompassing the management of preprocessing and training data for both offline and online data streams. Farmers can utilize the system to monitor environmental metrics, receive notifications regarding anomalies, and transmit control commands to environmental management systems, including irrigation and lighting adjustments.

The authors have employed multiple techniques for data preprocessing, including training models on a time-series dataset. In the future, the authors will further refine the system by advancing training models for superior performance and creating additional features to assist farmers in minimizing workload and maximizing crop yields.

Acknowledgments. This work has been supported by VNU Information Technology Institute under Project No. CNTT.07.2024.

References

1. Hizal, S., Cavusoglu, U., Akgun, D.: A novel deep learning-based intrusion detection system for IoT DDoS security. Internet Things **28**, 101336 (2024). ISSN 2542-6605
2. Abbas, S., et al.: Evaluating deep learning variants for cyber-attacks detection and multi-class classification in IoT networks. PeerJ Comput. Sci. **10**, e1793 (2024)
3. Alsalman, D.: A comparative study of anomaly detection techniques for IoT security using adaptive machine learning for IoT threats. IEEE Access **12** (2024)
4. Holtorf, L., Titov, I., Daschner, F., Gerken, M.: UAV-based wireless data collection from underground sensor nodes for precision agriculture. AgriEngineering **5**(1), 338–354 (2023)
5. Altulaihan, E., Almaiah, M.A., Aljughaiman, A.: Anomaly detection IDS for detecting DoS attacks in IoT networks based on machine learning algorithms. Sensors **24**(2), 713 (2024)

6. Khanday, S.A., Fatima, H., Rakesh, N.: A novel data preprocessing model for lightweight sensory IoT intrusion detection. Int. J. Math. Eng. Manag. Sci. **9** (2024)
7. Neto, E.C.P., Dadkhah, S., Ferreira, R., Zohourian, A., Lu, R., Ghorbani, A.A.: CICIoT2023: a real-time dataset and benchmark for large-scale attacks in IoT environment. Sensors **23**, 5941 (2023)
8. Musznicki, B., Tomczak, M., Zwierzykowski, P.: Dijkstra-based localized multicast routing in wireless sensor networks. In: 8th International Symposium on Communication Systems, Networks & Digital Signal Processing (CSNDSP) (2012)
9. Akgun, D., Hizal, S., Cavusoglu, U.: A new DDoS attacks intrusion detection model based on deep learning for cybersecurity. Comput. Secur. **118** (2022)
10. Aguru, A.D, Erukala, S.B.: A lightweight multi-vector DDoS detection framework for IoT-enabled mobile health informatics systems using deep learning. Inf. Sci. **662** (2024)
11. Castro, F.M., Marín-Jiménez, M.J., Guil, N., Schmid, C., Alahari, K.: End-to-end incremental learning. In: Ferrari, V., Hebert, M., Sminchisescu, C., Weiss, Y. (eds.) ECCV 2018. LNCS, vol. 11216, pp. 241–257. Springer, Cham (2018). https://doi.org/10.1007/978-3-030-01258-8_15
12. Wu, Y., Chen, Y., Wang, L., Ye, Y., Liu, Z., Guo, Y., Fu, Y.: Large scale incremental learning. In: Proceedings of the IEEE/CVF Conference on Computer Vision and Pattern Recognition, pp. 374–382 (2019)
13. Huo, J., van Zyl, T.L.: Incremental class learning using variational autoencoders with similarity learning. Neural Comput. Appl. (2023)
14. Huang, Z., et al.: Class balance matters to active class-incremental learning. In: Proceedings of the 32nd ACM International Conference on Multimedia, pp. 9445–9454, 28 October 2024

Cortex Vision: Detection of Ophthalmic Disease Using Machine Learning Algorithm

Ibtasam Rehman[1,2] and Hoang-Anh Pham[1,2(✉)]

[1] Ho Chi Minh City University of Technology (HCMUT), Ho Chi Minh City,
Vietnam
{ribtasam.sdh231,anhpham}@hcmut.edu.vn
[2] Vietnam National University Ho Chi Minh City (VNU-HCM),
Ho Chi Minh City, Vietnam

Abstract. Cataracts are one of the leading causes of vision impairment globally, characterized by lens clouding, which can result in blurred vision, faded colors, and halos around lights. This condition affects over 2.2 billion people worldwide, yet diagnosing cataracts often requires time-consuming and costly consultations with healthcare professionals. To address this issue, we developed a cross-platform mobile application designed to facilitate the detection of cataracts using machine learning techniques. Specifically, we implemented Support Vector Machine (SVM) classifiers with three different kernel functions: Linear, Polynomial, and Radial Basis Function (RBF). Through our experiments, we found that the RBF kernel provided the best performance, achieving an accuracy of approximately 95%. The application leverages image processing and classification algorithms to efficiently assess the presence of cataracts, making it accessible to users without the need for professional intervention. Our results, validated through classification reports and accuracy metrics, demonstrate the potential of this mobile solution to improve early diagnosis and accessibility of cataract detection. This study contributes to ongoing efforts to harness technology for medical image analysis and highlights the importance of selecting appropriate machine learning models for effective healthcare solutions.

Keywords: Machine Learning · Support Vector Machine · Image Processing · Cataract

1 Introduction

Vision, the major human sense, contributes an essential responsibility in every stage of our lives. People sometimes take vision for granted, but without vision, we have difficulty learning, walking, reading, and participating in numerous

© ICST Institute for Computer Sciences, Social Informatics and Telecommunications Engineering 2025
Published by Springer Nature Switzerland AG 2025. All Rights Reserved
H. X. Huynh et al. (Eds.): GOODTECHS 2024, LNICST 649, pp. 138–149, 2025.
https://doi.org/10.1007/978-3-032-01497-9_13

events of life. Vision impairment occurs when an eye condition affects visual functions; however, if left untreated, it shows serious consequences for the individuals throughout the life span. The number of various consequences can be reduced by timely access to eye care. According to the World Health Organization (WHO) for 2023, 2.2 billion people worldwide suffer from vision impairments. Ophthalmic condition that causes vision impairment and blindness resulting in cataract, refractive error, glaucoma, diabetic retinopathy, age-related macular degeneration. It is assumed that around the world 36% of people with distance vision impairment due to refractive error and 17% of the community with vision impairment resulting from cataracts. The decline in visual perception affects all people of all ages; however, visual impairment and blindness are older than 50 years.

The human eye is one of the most important and sensitive organs in the human body. It helps us to see, visualize different objects. Vision is one of the most used sense and one of the essential sources through which we gather different information. The typical human eye can visualize approximately 10 million different types of color. The size of a human eye is approximately 83.07 cm in diameter which consists of different parts such as the iris, puppy, cornea, lens retina, and optic nerves, as illustrated in Fig. 1.

The cataract is a cloudy zone in the lens of the human eye. Cataracts are much more common when an individual reaches the age of 50 or older. At an early stage, someone may feel that they have cataracts because they develop slowly and steadily, but with time, cataracts can develop vision blurry or neutral; however, as time passes, cataracts can lead to permanent vision loss. Initially, powerful lightning and corrective lenses can facilitate the treatment of cataracts. Indications of cataract include blurred vision, cloudy or dim vision, it can be sensitive to light, a problem when viewing at night, sudden changes in glasses or lens prescription, dual vision, faded colors, and halos near lights. The mentioned symptoms can fluctuate in terms of severity and may affect daily activities of existence. The root cause of cataracts includes aging, with certain conditions that are generally related to older individuals. Over time, proteins in the lens of the human eye can accumulate together, resulting in cloudiness and a visual perception problem. The continuous involvement to ultraviolet (UV) radiation from sunlight, specific medical condition for example diabetics, hypertension, trauma injury associated with human eye, smoking, genetics can boost the risk of growing cataracts. Recognizing the symptoms and the reason for developing cataracts is important for the early detection and suitable treatment of the condition. Routine eye examination by healthcare professionals is essential for observing eye health and detecting cataracts in initial stages.

According to the World Health Organization, around 51% of cataract cases have been reported. In underdeveloped countries, the rate of cataracts is higher because they do not have investments in the health sector. Currently, approximately 1 billion people suffer from various ophthalmic diseases such as cataracts, glaucoma, corneal opacities, and diabetic retinopathy. Cataracts are the predominant cause of visual impairment worldwide, which has affected about 65.2 million people compared to the second most34 prevalent disease glaucoma with

6.9 million patients. The current cataract statistics reveal that there are about 52.6 million visually impaired people and 12.6 million blind people. The common cause of cataracts is aging. The normal human eye starts to change after the age of 40. That is, when the regular proteins in the lens begin to break down. The lens becomes clouded as a result of this.The lenses of people over the age of 60 frequently begin to fog. Vision problems, on the other hand, may not appear for years.

2   Related Works

For the past few years, machine learning models in the healthcare sector have supported professionals in diagnosing different diseases. These machine learning methods have achieved compelling performance with the help of hand-engineered features.

Agarwal et al. [1] presented a smartphone-based Android application for cataract detection, designed to save time and minimize costs compared to traditional clinical methods. The application uses machine learning (KNN, SVM, Nave Bayes) and image processing, with the OpenCV library. Users can upload eye images from their gallery or take new photos, which are processed to detect cataracts by comparing eye features against pre-trained datasets. This approach includes numerous steps: image collection, data preprocessing (using Orange Tool), classification by KNN, and validation under ophthalmologists' supervision. The KNN model outperformed SVM and Naïve Bayes, achieving 83.07% accuracy.

Behera et al. [2] demonstrate a systemized model to identify nuclear cataracts using fundus retinal images. The model processes images to develop binary exhibits that focus on blood vessels, which serve as the feature matrix for a Support Vector Machine (SVM) classifier. Various SVM kernels were tested, with the Radial Basis Function (RBF) gaining the highest precision of 95. 2%. The study concluded that RBF-based SVM is effective for real-time detection and recommends future exploration of Convolutional Neural Networks (CNNs) for enhanced performance.

Setiawan [3] developed a mobile application for cataract detection utilizing statistical texture analysis and K-Nearest-Neighbor (k-NN) classification. It addresses the problem faced in rural areas of Indonesia, where access to ophthalmologists and diagnostic tools is minimal, resulting in cataracts being the leading cause of blindness. The research analyzed 160 eye images: 80 normal and 80 cataract using pre-processing techniques such as cropping and grayscale conversion, along with feature extraction using the gray level cooccurrence matrix (GLCM). The findings demonstrated a precision of 97. 5%, identifying optimal features such as distinction, contrast, and uniformity, with the best k value for k-NN determined to be 1. Ultimately, the study shows that this approach effectively classifies normal and cataract conditions, paving the way for mobile solutions in underserved regions.

Gao et al. [4] intended to enhance the detection of cataract and classification with Artificial Intelligence using Fundus Images. They obtained 1340 fundus images; however, they developed a dual-stream cataract evaluation network (DCEN) to classify and grade cataract. They trained and tested the DCEN model using deep learning algorithms, most significantly ResNet models. The DCEN achieved high accuracy, sensitivity, F1 score, and kappa coefficient for both cataract classification and severity grading tasks. The model performs in general with an accuracy of 97.62%.

Gupta [5] presented two algorithms applied to eye images to assess intensivness. The first algorithm used feature extraction and histogram evaluation to classify eyes as healthy or with various degrees of cataract based on mean intensity. The second method computes the area of the cataract relative to the pupil using contour detection and Hough transforms. The feature extraction method proved to be more versatile, while the area calculation approach required specific conditions for accuracy. The research highlights the need for automation and the development of mobile applications to improve accessibility to cataract detection.

Junayed et al. [6] have come up with the observation of cataract using deep learning with the use of fundus images. They use multiple datasets such as HRF, FIRE, ACHIKO-I , IDRiD for training and testing goals. The algorithm which is used for cataract detection is Convolution Neural Networks (CNN), however, they proposed a name of model is Cataract- Net. The performance of the proposed CataractNet is compared with five pre-trained CNN models across different dataset splitting conditions. CataractNet outperforms the other models in terms of accuracy and other evaluation metrics, while also demonstrating lower time complexity. The study concludes by highlighting the achievements of CataractNet in terms of accuracy, precision, recall, specificity, MCC, and F1-score.

Khalaf et al. [7] studied and performed an experiment to classify ophthalmic diseases using YOLOv8. Besides they used fundus images form various resource for example Robotflow, Kaggle and Medical clinics and they standardized those image to 224*224 pixels. The aggregate of collected image are 5887, and furthermore the dataset was divided into training and testing. YOLOv8n-cls (nano) was selected die because of its efficiency, dense size, speed, and performance. After all, the model was trained on data applying specific parameters, including ADAM optimizer, learning rate, batch size, weight decay, and 30 epochs. To access the model numerous metrics such as accuracy, precision recall and F1 score are used. In addition, the proposed model achieved an accuracy rate 94% in classifying various eye diseases, surpassing traditional CNNs.

Meegada et al. [8] recommended efficient cataract detection using deep learning and machine learning modals. For the purpose of extracting the feature, they use Convolution Neural Network (CNN), however, for classification apply diverse ML and DL modals as an example support vector machine (SVM), random forest (RF) along with deep neural network (DNN). The experiment may involve multiple steps for example, data preparation, augmentation, model selection training and optimization. The end result of the proposed experiment to detect cataracts gives an accuracy of 98. 4%.

Rana and Galib [9] proposed a mobile-based cataract detection solution using a phone camera. The application identify cataracts by examine pupil images through color detection and classification. The system addresses challenges in rural areas where access to medical professionals and specialized equipment such as slit-lamp cameras is minimal. The method utilizes OpenCV, SDK, and NDK for image processing and offers a cost-effective solution for early cataract detection. Primary experiments illustrate the accuracy of 90% in detecting cataracts in different stages.

Rajhan et al. [10] developed a mobile app to detect cataracts using deep learning algorithms. The proposed system came up with an accuracy of 98. 79%, however, the procedure also has high sensitivity and specificity. CNN is used to detect cataracts because it has three layers consisting of a convolution layer, a pooling layer, and a fully connected layer that support pattern recognition. The user uses the mobile camera to get a picture of the eye to check the presence of a cataract. If the algorithm discovers the cataract, the user will be notified by the alert dialog box with the severity level of the cataract.

Vasan et al. [11] given a study on cataract detection using an artificially based mobile application. They used a convolutional neural network (CNN) as a foundation for deep learning. Both the convolution and pooling layer fulfilll the feature extraction from images, This app works on 16 layers of convolutions, 2 sampling layers, 4 concatenation layers and a soft-max classification layer. The model approach is to obtain the lens concerning the shadow of the nontransparent part of the lens to forecast if the eye has a cataract or not.

Yang et al. [12] proposed a study in which they performed an experiment using 504 sets of images labeled by the experienced ophthalmologist for cataract detection and classification. The use back-propagation neural network and the classification of cataract however they extracted various number of features e.g. Luminance feature that catch the clarity of retinal images, Gray Co-Occurrence Matrix Feature is used which provides the information regarding the image, the matrix include entropy, contrast, inverse and Gray-Gradient Co-occurrence Matrix Features it have the ability to get the gray level and grey gradient information of the image. Performance is measured using Receiver 18 Operating Characteristic (ROC) and confusion matrix because by using the ROC it depicts the information between the true positive rate and false positive rate.

3   Methodology

This section outlines the proposed approach to develop and implement a machine learning-based system for cataract detection using Support Vector Machine (SVM) classifiers. The methodology is segmented into three key steps: data set loading, data pre-processing, and image classification using SVM. Each step is critical to ensure that the application performs well and meets its intended purpose.

As depicted in Fig. 1, the methodology for cataract detection using Support Vector Machine (SVM) classifiers begins by loading a data set sourced from Kaggle repositories. The data set is structured into separate folders for training and testing, with images classified into 'cataract' and 'normal' classes. Each image is labeled according to its folder name, where images from the 'cataract' folder are assigned a label of 1, and images from the 'normal' folder are labeled 0. This labeling ensures that each image has a corresponding label, making it ready for preprocessing.

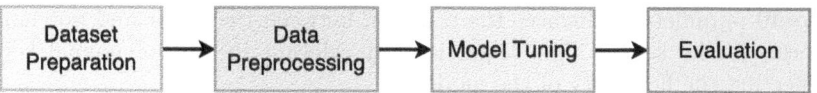

Fig. 1. Work flow of the proposed method.

Each image undergoes a series of pre-processing steps to prepare it for analysis. Initially, the images are converted to grayscale to reduce complexity, resized to a uniform dimension of 100x100 pixels, and normalized to scale pixel values between 0 and 1. An unsharp masking technique is applied to enhance image clarity, defined by (1).

$$\text{Sharpened\_Image} = I \times (1 + s) - G \times s \tag{1}$$

where I is the original image, G is the blurred image obtained through Gaussian filtering, and s is a scaling factor. Following this, features such as edges and textures are extracted, which are essential for effective classification.

Support Vector Machines are characterized by several hyperparameters that dictate their performance. The most crucial hyperparameters for SVMs include:

1. **Regularization parameter** C controls the trade-off between maximizing the margin and minimizing the classification error. The objective function for SVM can be formulated as (2).

$$\min_{\mathbf{w},b} \quad \frac{1}{2}\|\mathbf{w}\|^2 + C \sum_{i=1}^{n} \max(0, 1 - y_i(\mathbf{w}^T \mathbf{x}_i + b)) \tag{2}$$

Here, $\mathbf{w}$ represents the weight vector, b is the bias, y_i are the target labels, and $\mathbf{x}_i$ are the feature vectors. A lower value of C results in a wider margin at the cost of misclassifications, while a higher value C aims to minimize misclassifications by potentially reducing the margin.

2. **Kernel Coefficient** γ determines the influence of a single training example. The decision boundary becomes more complex with larger values of γ. The RBF kernel is given by (3).

$$K(\mathbf{x}, \mathbf{x}') = e^{-\gamma\|\mathbf{x}-\mathbf{x}'\|^2} \tag{3}$$

A low value of γ results in a smooth decision boundary, while a high value allows for more complex decision boundaries.

3. **Degree parameter** is relevant for the Polynomial kernel, determining the degree of the polynomial used in the kernel function as (4).

$$K(\mathbf{x}, \mathbf{x}') = (\mathbf{x}^T \mathbf{x}' + c)^{\text{degree}} \qquad (4)$$

Here, c is a constant that trades off the influence of higher-order terms.

4. **coef0** parameter influences the trade-off between the linear and polynomial terms in the kernel. This is particularly relevant in the polynomial kernel, affecting the flexibility of the model.

To systematically evaluate the combinations of hyperparameters for each SVM variant, we utilized the `GridSearchCV` function from the `scikit-learn` library. The process includes three steps as follows:

1. Define the parameter grids for each SVM type
   - **Linear SVM**:
     ```
     param_grid_linear = {'C': [0.01, 0.1, 1, 10, 100]}
     ```
   - **Polynomial SVM**:
     ```
     param_grid_poly = {'C': [0.01, 0.1, 1, 10, 100],
            'degree': [2, 3, 4],
            'gamma': ['scale', 'auto']
     }
     ```
   - **RBF SVM**:
     ```
     param_grid_rbf = {'C': [0.01, 0.1, 1, 10, 100],
            'gamma': ['scale', 'auto']
     }
     ```

2. Perform 5-fold cross-validation for each model to ensure robust evaluation.

$$\text{CV Score} = \frac{1}{K} \sum_{k=1}^{K} \text{Score}_k \qquad (5)$$

where K is the number of folds, and Score_k is the score obtained from the k-th fold.

3. Select the best hyperparameters based on accuracy, computed as (6)

$$\text{Accuracy} = \frac{\text{Number of Correct Predictions}}{\text{Total Predictions}} \qquad (6)$$

The results of our tuning are summarized in Table 1. Hyperparameter tuning is crucial in maximizing the performance of SVM classifiers. By employing grid search, we effectively optimized the parameters, ensuring that our models are well suited to classify cataract and normal images effectively. Performance metrics observed during the evaluation reflect the improvements achieved through this optimization process. Future work could explore automated techniques such as Bayesian optimization to further enhance performance.

Table 1. Best parameters for each SVM type

SVM Type	Best Parameters
Linear SVM	$C = 0.01$
Polynomial SVM	$C = 1$, $degree = 3$, $\gamma = $ 'scale'
RBF SVM	$C = 10$, $\gamma = $ 'scale'

4   Implementation and Evaluation

After hyperparameter tuning, we implemented a mobile application to evaluate the performance of the proposed models on the test dataset. The evaluation was based on various metrics, including accuracy, precision, recall, F1-score, and the confusion matrix.

4.1   Implementation

A mobile application for cataract detection is developed to make the model accessible to users, as shown in Fig. 2. The application is developed in Flutter and the model is deployed via Flask to create an API for communication.

The application allows users to input images from two sources. The user can take a photo directly using the mobile camera or select an image from their mobile photo gallery.

Once the image is collected, it is sent to the Flask API, where the image undergoes preprocessing (grayscale conversion, resizing, normalization, and sharpening) before being fed into the trained machine learning model. The model processes the image and returns the result, which includes:

- **Detection Status**: Whether the image shows `cataract` or `normal`.
- **Accuracy**: The confidence of the model in its classification.

The result is displayed in the application interface, providing the user with the status and average accuracy of the prediction.

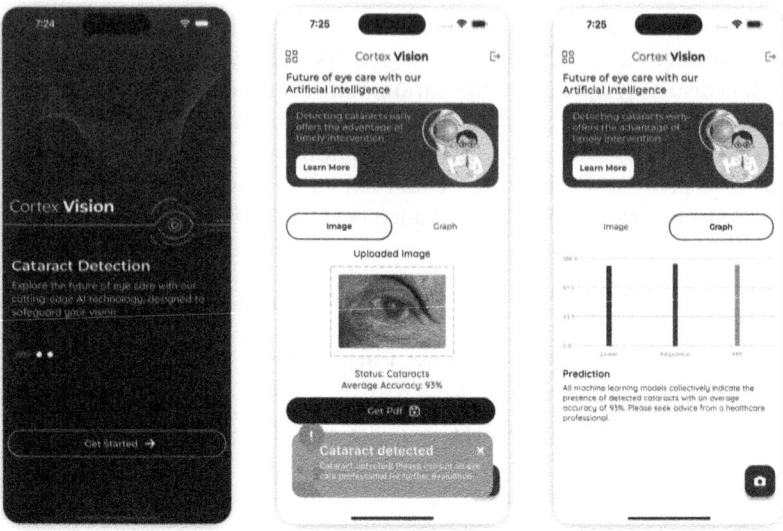

Fig. 2. Example images of the cataract detection process in the mobile application.

4.2   Performance Metrics

The key performance metrics used to evaluate the classifiers are defined below.

- **Accuracy**: The proportion of true results among the total number of cases examined.
$$\text{Accuracy} = \frac{TP + TN}{TP + TN + FP + FN} \tag{7}$$

- **Precision**: The ratio of true positives to the sum of true positives and false positives.
$$\text{Precision} = \frac{TP}{TP + FP} \tag{8}$$

- **Recall (Sensitivity)**: The ratio of true positives to the sum of true positives and false negatives.
$$\text{Recall} = \frac{TP}{TP + FN} \tag{9}$$

- **F1 Score**: The harmonic mean of precision and recall.
$$\text{F1 Score} = 2 \cdot \frac{\text{Precision} \cdot \text{Recall}}{\text{Precision} + \text{Recall}} \tag{10}$$

- **Confusion Matrix**: A table used to describe the performance of a classification model, summarizing the counts of true positive (TP), true negative (TN), false positive (FP), and false negative (FN) predictions.

4.3   Results

The experimental results in terms of various performance metrics of three SVM models are summarized in Table 2. We also provide a detailed classification report for the best performing SVM model with the RBF kernel. The results indicate that the model achieved an overall accuracy of 95% for the SVM RBF kernel. Precision and recall are closely balanced, indicating the model's ability to correctly identify both cataract and normal classes.

Table 2. Comparison of classification performance across different models

SVM Model	Accuracy	Precision	Recall	F1 Score
Linear	0.90	0.86	0.93	0.90
Polynomial	0.93	0.89	0.97	0.93
RBF	0.95	0.95	0.95	0.95

```
                  precision    recall    f1-score    support

0 (Normal)          0.95        0.95       0.95          60
1 (Cataract)        0.96        0.96       0.96          72
      accuracy                             0.95         132
     macro avg      0.95        0.95       0.95         132
  weighted avg      0.95        0.95       0.95         132
```

Table 3 displays the confusion matrix for the best-performing SVM model. The top-left cell (57) represents true positives for class 0 (normal). The bottom-right cell (69) represents true positives for class 1 (cataract). The off-diagonal cells represent misclassifications, with 3 false negatives and 3 false positives.

Table 3. Confusion matrix visualization

	0 (Normal)	1 (Cataract)
0 (Normal)	57	3
1 (Cataract)	3	69

5   Conclusion

In this study, three SVM models (Linear, Polynomial, and RBF) were evaluated for cataract detection, achieving accuracies of 90%, 93%, and 95%, respectively. The RBF SVM model demonstrated the best performance, with high precision

(95%), recall (96%), and F1 score (95%), indicating its effectiveness in accurately identifying cataract cases. The polynomial SVM followed closely, excelling in sensitivity but with slightly lower precision. Linear SVM, while effective, showed the lowest accuracy and precision. Overall, the RBF SVM model is the most suitable for clinical applications in cataract detection, providing a balance between minimizing false positives and negatives. These findings support the potential of machine learning models in improving diagnostic accuracy in ophthalmology, paving the way for timely interventions and improved patient outcomes. Future work may explore further optimization of these models and the inclusion of additional features or datasets to improve performance.

Acknowledgment. The authors acknowledge Ho Chi Minh City University of Technology (HCMUT), VNU-HCM for supporting this study.

References

1. Agarwal, V., Gupta, V., Vashisht, V.M., Sharma, K., Sharma, N.: Mobile application based cataract detection system. In: 2019 3rd International Conference on Trends in Electronics and Informatics (ICOEI). pp. 780–787 (2019). https://doi.org/10.1109/ICOEI.2019.8862774
2. Behera, M.K., Chakravarty, S., Gourav, A., Dash, S.: Detection of nuclear cataract in retinal fundus image using radialbasis functionbasedsvm. In: 2020 Sixth International Conference on Parallel, Distributed and Grid Computing (PDGC). pp. 278–281 (2020). https://doi.org/10.1109/PDGC50313.2020.9315834
3. Fuadah, Y.N., Setiawan, A.W., Mengko, T.L., Budiman: Mobile cataract detection using optimal combination of statistical texture analysis. In: 2015 4th International Conference on Instrumentation, Communications, Information Technology, and Biomedical Engineering (ICICI-BME). pp. 232–236 (2015). https://doi.org/10.1109/ICICI-BME.2015.7401368
4. Gao, W., Shao, L., Li, F., Dong, L., Zhang, C., Deng, Z., Qin, P., Wei, W., Ma, L.: Fundus photograph-based cataract evaluation network using deep learning. Frontiers in Physics **11** (2024). https://doi.org/10.3389/fphy.2023.1235856, https://www.frontiersin.org/articles/10.3389/fphy.2023.1235856
5. Jindal, I., Gupta, P., Goyal, A.: Cataract detection using digital image processing. In: 2019 Global Conference for Advancement in Technology (GCAT). pp. 1–4 (2019). https://doi.org/10.1109/GCAT47503.2019.8978316
6. Junayed, M.S., Islam, M.B., Sadeghzadeh, A., Rahman, S.: Cataractnet: An automated cataract detection system using deep learning for fundus images. IEEE Access **9**, 128799–128808 (2021). https://doi.org/10.1109/ACCESS.2021.3112938
7. Khalaf, A.T., Abdulateef, S.K.: Ophthalmic diseases classification based on yolov8. Journal of Robotics and Control (JRC) **5**(2) (2024)
8. Meegada, R.N., Lingala, A., Mamidi, V., Bharadwaj, S.A.: Efficient detection of eye diseases using ml and dl. Tech. rep, EasyChair (2024)
9. Rana, J., Galib, S.M.: Cataract detection using smartphone. In: 2017 3rd International Conference on Electrical Information and Communication Technology (EICT). pp. 1–4 (2017). https://doi.org/10.1109/EICT.2017.8275136
10. Ranjan, N., Shejul, R.H.A., Harne, K., Bhat, S.: Detection of cataract and its level based on deep learning using mobile application (2023)

11. Vasan, C.S., Gupta, S., Shekhar, M., Nagu, K., Balakrishnan, L., Ravindran, R.D., Ravilla, T., Subburaman, G.B.B.: Accuracy of an artificial intelligence-based mobile application for detecting cataracts: Results from a field study. Indian J. Ophthalmol. **71**(8), 2984–2989 (2023)
12. Yang, M., Yang, J.J., Zhang, Q., Niu, Y., Li, J.: Classification of retinal image for automatic cataract detection. In: 2013 IEEE 15th International Conference on e-Health Networking, Applications and Services (Healthcom 2013). pp. 674–679 (2013). https://doi.org/10.1109/HealthCom.2013.6720761

Real-Time Object Detection Based on Yolov8

Ngoc Dung Nguyen and Van Doan Thang[(✉)]

Industrial University of Ho Chi Minh City, Ho Chi Minh City, Vietnam
{nguyenngocdung,doanvanthang}@iuh.edu.vn

Abstract. Detecting traffic participants violating helmet regulations is a challenge. Based on that challenge, this article proposes a solution using deep learning models combined with computer vision to detect objects in real time from videos collected by surveillance cameras. In this article we focus on studying the Yolov8 model. YOLOv8, the latest version of the highly regarded real-time image segmentation and object detection model. Yolov8 was born to keep up with and respond to the development of deep learning and computer vision models, delivering outstanding performance in speed and accuracy. Finally, to evaluate the effectiveness of the proposed method, we collected data on videos of traffic participants, including people wearing helmets and not wearing helmets, on vnexpress.net. During the experiment, the results had a high detection accuracy of ≈80%, thereby showing that our method is effective.

Keywords: Deep Learning · Machine Learning · Yolov8 · R-CNN · CNN

1 Introduction

Deep Learning is a method of machine learning that utilizes deep artificial neural networks to learn and extract features from data. As a subset of artificial intelligence (AI), it plays a crucial role in Machine Learning. Deep Learning emphasizes the construction and training of neural networks with multiple layers (hidden layers) to automatically learn and represent complex data features.

Computer Vision, a branch of computer science, aims to develop computer systems that can understand and analyze information from images and videos, mimicking human vision capabilities. The close relationship between Deep Learning and Computer Vision has led to significant advancements in addressing computer vision challenges. The synergy of these two fields has driven groundbreaking progress in the field.

Benefits of Combining Deep Learning and Computer Vision:

- Learning from Data: Deep Learning enables Computer Vision systems to learn from real-world data rather than relying on pre-programmed rules. This allows the system to automatically extract important features from the data and improve accuracy over time.
- High Efficiency: Deep Learning can efficiently process large amounts of data, making the deployment of Computer Vision systems more feasible in practice.

H. X. Huynh et al. (Eds.): GOODTECHS 2024, LNICST 649, pp. 150–160, 2025.
https://doi.org/10.1007/978-3-032-01497-9_14

- Good Generalization Ability: Deep Learning allows Computer Vision systems to learn from data and apply the acquired knowledge to new scenarios, enhancing efficiency and flexibility.
- Ability to Solve Complex Problems: Deep Learning can tackle complex Computer Vision problems such as facial recognition, image classification, object tracking, etc.
- Creation of New Applications: Deep Learning has paved the way for many new applications of Computer Vision in various fields such as healthcare, security, manufacturing, transportation, etc.

The YOLO model is widely used in object detection problems and is a convolutional neural network (CNN) model. YOLO is created by combining convolutional layers and connected layers, The convolutional layers are responsible for extracting features from the input images, while the fully connected layers are tasked with predicting both the probability and the coordinates of the object. It can achieve quite high accuracy and quick speed almost in real time. Through the above reasons, The paper focuses on researching the detection of traffic participants not wearing helmets based on the Yolo8 model.

2 Related Work

To address the challenge of real-time helmet detection in traffic, numerous researchers have put forth various methodologies [3, 5, 13, 15]. Chiu et al. [5] introduced a system designed for detecting motorcyclists in surveillance videos. This system segments moving objects and tracks motorcycles along with their head regions using a probability-based algorithm to tackle occlusion issues. However, it struggles with small variations caused by noise and illumination effects. Additionally, it employs Canny edge detection within a predefined search window to identify heads.

Chiverton et al. [10] employed edge histogram-based features for motorcyclist detection. This method exhibits robust performance even under low-light conditions or poor illumination by leveraging edge histograms near the head instead of direct head feature detection. However, its reliance on circular Hough transforms for comparing and classifying helmets often leads to misclassifications, as objects resembling helmets can be wrongly categorized, and different helmet types may not be properly identified.

Silva et al. [14, 15] proposed a system aimed at mitigating the misclassification issue by tracking vehicles using Kalman filtering. One significant advantage of the Kalman tracking system is its ability to continue tracking objects even when they are partially occluded. However, it struggles when multiple motorcyclists appear in the same frame, as the Kalman filter's effectiveness diminishes due to its reliance on linear state transitions. Tracking multiple objects requires the use of non-linear functions.

Dahiya et al. [13] recently introduced a novel system that begins by employing the Gaussian mixture model to identify moving objects, offering resilience to minor background variations. This system utilizes two consecutive classifiers: one to distinguish motorcyclists from other moving objects, and another to differentiate between riders wearing helmets and those without.

YOLO serves as a CNN, a specific type of neural network renowned for its proficiency in identifying patterns, including objects, within images. Neural networks comprise layers, with CNNs predominantly composed of convolutional layers, hence the name. These layers function akin to sliding filters across images, progressively extracting increasingly complex features. YOLO implements ReLU activation. At each convolutional step, ReLU modifies the output, setting any negative values to zero while leaving positive values unchanged, effectively enhancing the model's ability to capture relevant features (Fig. 1).

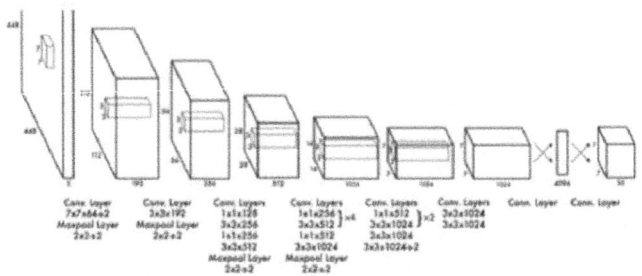

Fig. 1. Convolutional Neural Network model

Modern object detectors typically consist of two main components: a backbone, which is pretrained on ImageNet, and a head, responsible for predicting object classes and bounding boxes. On GPU platforms, common backbones include VGG, ResNet [12], ResNeXt, or DenseNet [6]. For CPU platforms, backbones such as MobileNet [1, 2], or ShuffleNet are often utilized.

Regarding the head component, it is typically classified into two types: one-stage object detectors and two-stage object detectors. The prominent two-stage object detector series is R-CNN [16], comprising variants like fast R-CNN, faster R-CNN, R-FCN [9], and Libra R-CNN. Additionally, two-stage object detectors can be adapted to anchor-free designs, such as RepPoints.

On the other hand, representative models for one-stage object detection include YOLO, SSD, and RetinaNet [17]. In recent years, anchor-free one-stage object detectors have emerged, including CenterNet [11], Corner-Net [7, 8], FCOS, among others.

3   System Architecture and YoloV8 Model

3.1   System Architecture

Object detection, a fundamental computer vision task, entails identifying and localizing objects within an image by predicting their classes and bounding boxes. YOLO stands as a cutting-edge Object Detector renowned for its ability to achieve real-time object detection with impressive accuracy.

An object detector is engineered to extract features from input images, which are subsequently processed through a prediction mechanism to delineate bounding boxes around objects and forecast their respective classes (Fig. 2).

The pioneering YOLO model introduced the groundbreaking concept of seamlessly integrating bounding box prediction with class labels within an end-to-end differentiable network architecture. Its structure comprises three fundamental components:

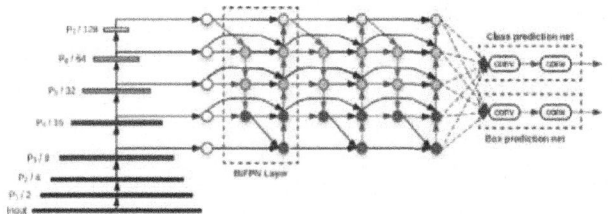

Fig. 2. The anatomy of an object detector

1. Backbone: This convolutional neural network gathers and consolidates image features across various scales and resolutions.
2. Neck: Consisting of a series of layers, the neck component is responsible for merging and refining the aggregated image features before passing them for further prediction.
3. Head: Operating downstream from the neck, the head module utilizes the refined features to execute bounding box and class prediction tasks.

3.2 Yolov8

3.2.1 Introducing YOLO

YOLO, stands out as a widely recognized object detection algorithm in computer vision. Known for its straightforward architecture and minimal training data requirements, YOLO offers ease of implementation and adaptability to diverse tasks. The YOLO algorithm processes an image input through a simple deep convolutional neural network, enabling efficient detection of objects within the image. YOLO comes in various versions, of which YOLOv8 is the latest line of YOLO-based Object Detection models from Ultralytics that offers good performance. YOLOv8 is an enhanced version offering improved speed and accuracy. Moreover, it delivers an integrated framework for training models to handle instance segmentation, object detection, and image classification.

3.2.2 Output YOLO

The YOLO model has the output as a vector which includes the following components:

$$y^T = [p_0, \underbrace{(t_x, t_y, t_w, t_y)}_{bounding\ box}, \underbrace{(p_1, p_2, ..., p_c)}_{score\ of\ classes}$$

In there:

Symbol	Explanation
p_0	probability of predicting bounding box
$\underbrace{(t_x, t_y, t_w, t_y)}_{bounding\ box}$	$t\ x, ty$ are the center coordinates tw, ty are the width and length dimensions of the bounding box. Helps define bounding box
$\underbrace{(p_1, p_2, ..., p_c)}_{score\ of\ classes}$	Prediction probability distribution vector of classes

3.2.3 Architecture of YOLOv8

YOLOv8 achieves impressive accuracy rates when evaluated against COCO and Roboflow 100 benchmarks. Its appeal extends to developers thanks to its user-friendly command-line interface (CLI) and neatly organized Python package. YOLOv8 benefits from a thriving community of both seasoned YOLO users and newcomers, ensuring robust support for individuals working in the realm of computer vision.

The YOLOv8 model is structured around a CNN, comprising two primary components: the backbone and the head. The backbone architecture, derived from a customized CSPDarknet53 design, integrates 53 convolutional layers across interconnected stages, optimizing the flow of information. The head section consists of several convolutional layers followed by fully connected layers, responsible for generating predictions related to bounding boxes, object scores, and class probabilities. YOLOv8 distinguishes itself with a unique self-attention mechanism integrated into the head, allowing the model to selectively focus on different image regions and prioritize relevant features. Moreover, YOLOv8 excels in multi-scale object detection using a feature pyramid network, enabling it to detect objects of varying sizes and scales, ensuring comprehensive coverage of both large and small objects within an image.

YOLOv8 offers models in different sizes—nano (n), small (s), medium (m), large (l), and extra-large (x)—to cater to different scenarios. Unlike previous YOLO versions, YOLOv8 substitutes the C3 structure of YOLOv5 with the C2f structure, enhancing gradient flow within the backbone and neck for improved performance. The channel numbers are adjusted for different model scales, and the two convolutional connection layers in the Neck module have been removed. The number of C2f blocks in the backbone varies between 3–6-9-3 and 3-6-6-3. Separate classification and regression branches replace the former object branch. Figure 4 illustrates the network architecture of YOLOv8.

The YOLO model's loss function utilizes three outputs from the PAN Neck to detect objects at three different scales. However, Glenn Jocher discovered that objects at each scale influence the Objectness Loss differently. Consequently, the formula for Objectness Loss was modified as follows:

$$L_{obj} = 4.0 \mathrm{x} L_{obj}^{small} + 1.0 \mathrm{x} L_{obj}^{medium} + 0.4 \mathrm{x} L_{obj}^{large}$$

This change helps YOLO focus on smaller objects and balance between bounding box prediction and object classification (Fig. 3).

3.2.4 Improvements in YOLOv8

- **Improvements in network architecture:** YOLOv8 integrates enhancements, such as the use of Transformers, which help improve the ability to learn long-term dependencies and complex relationships between objects.
- **Optimization for real-world applications:** YOLOv8 is optimized for deployment in applications such as self-driving cars, security surveillance, and other real-time systems.
- **High performance:** YOLOv8 significantly improves accuracy and speed compared to previous versions, especially when handling high-resolution images or complex environments.

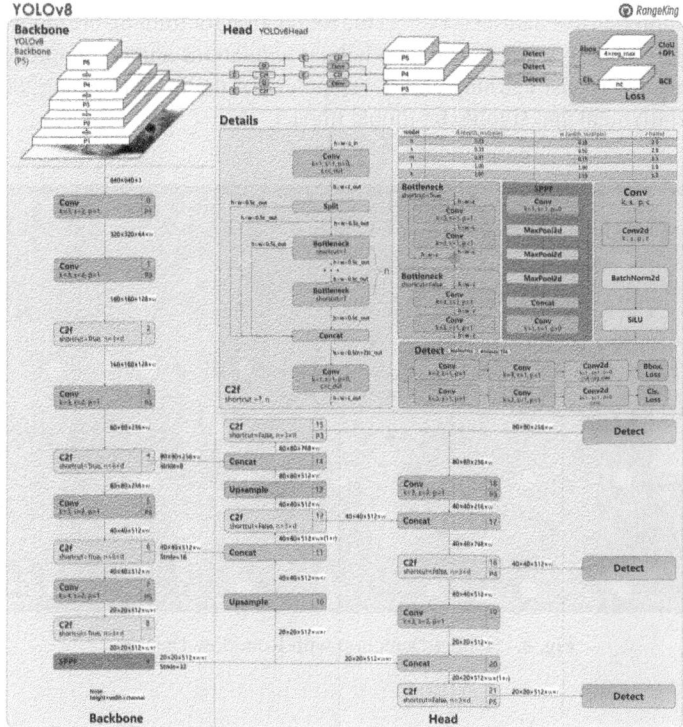

Fig. 3. YOLOv8 model architecture.

3.2.5 New Features and Usage

- **Auto-learning Augmentation:** YOLOv8 supports automatic data augmentation techniques, enhancing the model's generalization capabilities without requiring manual intervention.
- **Inference Optimization:** Prediction speed has been improved to operate efficiently on hardware-constrained devices.

3.2.6 Implementation

1. *Preparing the dataset.*

The system begins by preparing a dataset for an object detection model using the Roboflow package. This dataset consists of snapshots capturing both helmeted and unhelmeted motorcyclists, meticulously labeled to ensure clarity. The All images are resized to 416 pixels, with a focus on eliminating class ambiguity and filtering out underrepresented classes. The dataset includes 224,714 images across 805 classes.

This comprehensive dataset serves as the foundation for training the model, enabling it to accurately identify compliance with helmet regulations among motorcyclists. This approach ensures robust learning and development of the model, setting the stage for effective deployment and significant global impact.

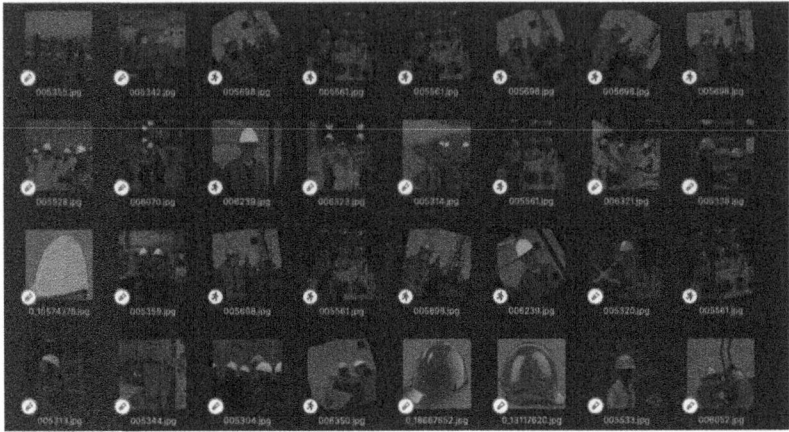

Fig. 4. Helmet Detection with Roboflow Dataset

2. *Model Train.*

To train our helmet detection model, we employed a method known as yolov8n, which offers enhanced robustness and advantages over its predecessors. The training process was conducted in Google Colaboratory. We installed ultralytics, connected to the dataset stored in Google Drive, and used specific commands to train the model with our collected dataset. Our training regimen spanned 100 epochs and completed in approximately 3 h, a notable efficiency improvement compared to other object detection algorithms. The steps are as follows:

Step 1: Configure YOLOv8 by editing the parameters, refining the number of lay-ers in the dataset, and updating the data description file.
Step 2: Update the network configuration utilizing the latest YOLOv8 model, re-nowned for its enhanced performance. Customize the parameters within the yo-lo8x.yaml file to reflect these adjustments.
Step 3: Generate a data.yml file including these parameters: 'train' for the directory containing the images, 'val' for the folder with captchas, 'nc' for the total number of classes in the dataset, and 'name' for the list of class names.
Step 4: Conduct the training process using Google Colab, which offers a conven-ient environment with high GPU availability for rapid training.
Step 5: Assess and evaluate the model's performance. Throughout the training pro-cess, metrics such as error rate, mean absolute error, and accuracy are dynamically adjusted and refined with each iteration (Fig. 5).

Fig. 5. Model Different between Helmet and Head.

4   Results

After completing the training successfully, we used the training data to detect and identify objects in the collected images. We used the data from the 1,000th iteration for comparison and updated the results of the training model accordingly (Figs. 6 and 7).

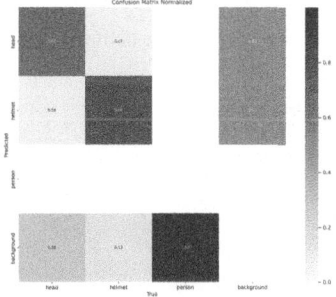

Fig. 6. Confusion matrix normalized

Based on the evaluation chart provided, it is evident that the training model performs effectively in distinguishing between individuals wearing helmets and those without. The comparison images utilized during the study underscored the model's accuracy, surpassing 80% in accurately identifying and detecting helmet usage (Figs. 8 and 9).

1. Detect images with newly trained data

2. Detect video with newly trained data

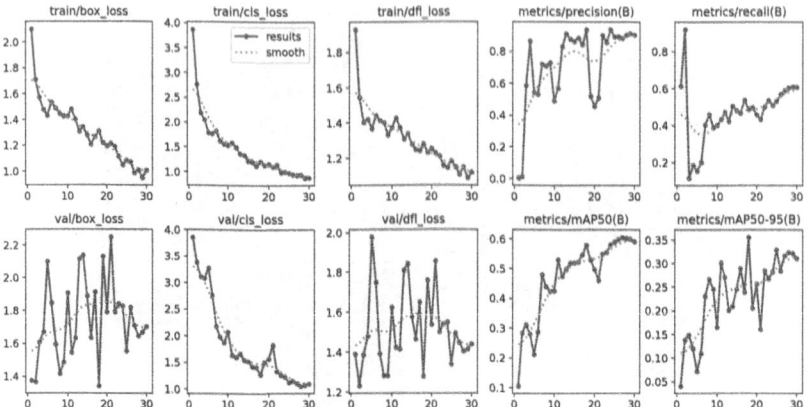

Fig. 7. Training results of the YOLOv8 model

Fig. 8. Detected images of workers wearing helmets working at a construction site

Fig. 9. Image cut from video detecting individuals participating in traffic not wearing helmets

5   Conclusion

The proposed real-time detection of motorcyclists not wearing helmets can realize diverse monitoring conditions. The article's proposal accurately identifies people who violate regulations on wearing helmets when participating in traffic. Our approach uses the YoloV8 model, YOLOv8 is the latest YOLO version of Ultralytics. YOLOv8 offers comprehensive support for various vision AI tasks, encompassing detection, segmentation, pose estimation, tracking, and classification. This flexibility allows users to leverage YOLOv8's capabilities across a variety of applications and domains. Experimental results show the effectiveness of the proposed method.

References

1. Howard, A., et al.: Searching for MobileNetV3. In: Proceedings of the IEEE International Conference on Computer Vision (ICCV) (2019)
2. Howard, A.G., et al.: MobileNets: efficient convolutional neural networks for mobile vision applications. arXiv preprint arXiv:1704.04861 (2017)
3. Vishnu, C., Singh, D., Mohan, C.K.: Detection of motorcyclists without helmet in videos using convolutional neural network. In: IJCNN, May 2017
4. Behera, C., Rautji, R., Lalwani, S., Dogra, T.D.: A comprehensive study of motorcycle fatalities in South Delhi. J. Indian Acad. Forensic Med. **31**(1), 6–10 (2009)
5. Chiu, C.-C., Ku, M.-Y., Chen, H.-T.: Motorcycle detection and tracking system with occlusion segmentation. In: International Workshop on Image Analysis for Multimedia Interactive Services, Santorini, Greece, 6–8 June 2007, pp. 32–32 (2007)
6. Huang, G., Liu, Z., Van Der Maaten, L., Weinberger, K.Q.: Densely connected convolutional networks. In: Proceedings of the IEEE Conference on Computer Vision and Pattern Recognition (CVPR), pp. 4700–4708 (2017)
7. Law, H., Deng, J.: CornerNet: detecting objects as paired keypoints. In: Proceedings of the European Conference on Computer Vision (ECCV), pp. 734–750 (2018)
8. Law, H., Teng, Y., Russakovsky, O., Deng, J.: CornerNet-Lite: efficient keypoint based object detection. arXiv preprint arXiv:1904.08900 (2019)
9. Dai, J., Li, Y., He, K., Sun, J.: R-FCN: object detection via region-based fully convolutional networks. In: Advances in Neural Information Processing Systems (NIPS), pp. 379–387 (2016)
10. Chiverton, J.: Helmet presence classification with motorcycle detection and tracking. IET Intell. Transp. Syst. (ITS) **6**(3), 259–269 (2012)
11. Duan, K., Bai, S., Xie, L., Qi, H., Huang, Q., Tian, Q.: CenterNet: keypoint triplets for object detection. In: Proceedings of the IEEE International Conference on Computer Vision (ICCV), pp. 6569–6578 (2019)
12. He, K., Zhang, X., Ren, S., Sun, J.: Deep residual learning for image recognition. In: Proceedings of the IEEE Conference on Computer Vision and Pattern Recognition (CVPR), pp. 770–778 (2016)
13. Dahiya, K., Singh, D., Mohan, C.K.: Automatic detection of bike-riders without helmet using surveillance videos in real-time. In: IJCNN, Vancouver, Canada, 24–29 July 2016, pp. 3046–3051 (2016)
14. Silva, R., Aires, K., Santos, T., Abdala, K., Veras, R., Soares, A.: Automatic detection of motorcyclists without helmet. In: Latin American Computing Conference (CLEI), Puerto Azul, Venezuela, 4–6 October 2013, pp. 1–7 (2013)
15. Silva, R.V., Aires, T., Rodrigo, V.: Helmet detection on motorcyclists using image descriptors and classifiers. In: Graphics, Patterns and Images (SIBGRAPI), Rio de Janeiro, Brazil, 27–30 August 2014, pp. 141–148 (2014)
16. Girshick, R., Donahue, J., Darrell, T., Malik, J.: Rich feature hierarchies for accurate object detection and semantic segmentation. In: Proceedings of the IEEE Conference on Computer Vision and Pattern Recognition (CVPR), pp. 580–587 (2014)

17. Lin, T.-Y., Goyal, P., Girshick, R., He, K., Dollar,. P.: Focal loss for dense object detection. In: Proceedings of the IEEE International Conference on Computer Vision (ICCV), pp. 2980–2988 (2017)
18. Rattapoom, W., Nannaphat, B., Vasan, T., Chainarong, T., Pattanawadee, P.: Machine vision techniques for motorcycle safety helmet detection. In: International Conference on Image and Vision Computing New Zealand (IVCNZ), Wellington, New Zealand, 27–29 November 2013, pp. 35–40 (2013)

Combining Accuracy and Diversity to Enhance the Quality of the Recommender System

Dinh Thi Man[1] ⓘ, Nguyen Van Long[2(✉)] ⓘ, Le Thi Vinh Thanh[3] ⓘ, and Tran Thi Van Anh[1] ⓘ

[1] Faculty of Information Technology, HCM University of Industry and Trade, Ho Chi Minh City, Vietnam
{mandt,anhttv}@huit.edu.vn
[2] University of Transport and Communications, Hanoi, Vietnam
nvlongdt@utc.edu.vn
[3] Industrial University of Ho Chi Minh City, Ho Chi Minh City, Vietnam

Abstract. In recent years, research has focused on enhancing recommendation list diversity while maintaining accuracy. Traditional methods typically use a two-stage process: first, generating a candidate list using collaborative filtering (CF) or hybrid methods to prioritize accuracy by selecting top-N items with the highest predicted ratings, and second, refining this list by re-ranking or removing similar items to improve diversity, resulting in M items (M ≤ N). However, these approaches often estimate diversity solely based on item differences, neglecting their relevance to user profiles during refinement. This paper introduces a novel approach that incorporates diversity considerations from the outset by addressing both item differences and their alignment with user profiles. Two proposed algorithms aim to enhance diversity while preserving accuracy by leveraging the distance between item content and user profiles. Experiments on the MovieLens dataset, comparing these algorithms with three baselines, demonstrate their effectiveness. The results show that emphasizing diversity from the start yields significantly more diverse recommendations than traditional two-stage methods.

Keywords: Recommender Systems · Collaborative Filtering · Diversity

1 Introduction

The rapid growth of the Internet and e-commerce has accelerated the development of recommender systems (RS), such as Amazon, MovieLens, TripAdvisor, and CiteSeer. These systems are crucial for providing personalized information based on user attributes and needs. Most RSs today use two primary methods: content-based filtering (CbF) and collaborative filtering (CF) [1].

In content-based filtering (CbF) systems, each user has a profile with personal information, preferences, and item ratings. CbF uses a vector space model to measure similarity between an item and the user's profile. However, its main limitation is the challenge

© ICST Institute for Computer Sciences, Social Informatics and Telecommunications Engineering 2025
Published by Springer Nature Switzerland AG 2025. All Rights Reserved
H. X. Huynh et al. (Eds.): GOODTECHS 2024, LNICST 649, pp. 161–172, 2025.
https://doi.org/10.1007/978-3-032-01497-9_15

of initializing user profiles, which affects new users and leads to narrow, repetitive recommendations [1, 2]. Collaborative filtering (CF), on the other hand, is more widely used. It recommends items based on ratings from similar users, bypassing the content dependency of CbF. This approach overcomes CbF's limitations, which is why many modern RSs combine both methods to maximize their strengths and address information extraction issues [3–5].

While previous studies have focused mainly on accuracy (precision), recent research has also emphasized the importance of diversity in recommendation results. Diversity improves user experience and meets the varied needs of users, prompting new research directions to enhance recommender system quality [6–8].

This paper presents two algorithms to improve recommender systems by balancing accuracy and diversity. The first uses a two-stage process: collaborative filtering for accurate recommendations, followed by refinement. However, it lacks diversity. The second algorithm integrates accuracy and diversity from the start by considering both predicted ratings and item-user profile distance. This method generates more diverse recommendations and allows fine-tuning of accuracy-diversity trade-off through a parameter, k.

The contribution of this paper is twofold: it not only enhances the diversity of recommendation lists but also provides a solution to the inherent limitations of the two-stage process, thereby improving the overall flexibility, effectiveness, and quality of modern recommender systems.

2   Foundational Theories of Recommender Systems

When faced with many unfamiliar options, seeking advice is common. For example, when organizing an event or choosing a travel tour, we share our preferences and receive recommendations based on our needs or community input [1, 9, 10]. Recently, recommender systems (RS) have become valuable in fields like e-commerce and education, using methods such as content-based and collaborative filtering. Hybrid systems combining both approaches are increasingly used to enhance performance [11].

2.1   Content-Based Filtering Meethod

Content-based filtering (CbF) recommends items similar to those a user has previously liked, purchased, or rated highly. Each user has a profile reflecting their preferences, and the system predicts interest based on this profile. The profile improves through user ratings, refining the accuracy of suggestions [12]. CbF is effective when item features are well-represented, but challenges arise in feature extraction, especially in areas like music or art. While CbF meets long-term user needs [1], it faces issues with initializing profiles, limited exploration, and a lack of diversity in recommendations, leading to potential user boredom.

2.2   Collaborative Filtering Method

Collaborative Filtering (CF) systems have become essential in modern recommender systems [5, 9, 13]. CF uses user ratings to determine "user similarity" and "item similarity." A user's rating for an item can be predicted based on ratings from similar users or items. CF's key advantage is bypassing content analysis and profile-item matching, allowing users to discover new areas through community recommendations, addressing the "narrowing" problem in personal profiles. Most systems today use pure CF or a hybrid of CF and content-based filtering [11]. However, CF still faces challenges with data sparsity. The two main CF methods are user-based, which compares users, and item-based, which compares items.

2.3 Diversity of Recommendation Lists

The quality of recommendations depends on both accuracy and diversity. In recent years, diversity has become a key factor, allowing users to explore new areas [6–8]. Two common diversity measures are:

- **Individual diversity**: Measures differences between items in a user's list, calculated as the average distance between items, with higher values indicating greater diversity [1, 14].
- **Aggregate diversity**: Measures how well the system distributes items, ensuring variety rather than just popular ones. It can struggle when focusing on best-sellers, limiting the discovery of less popular items [14].

Enhancing diversity through elimination: Removes similar items from the initial list, improving diversity by excluding those that add little to variety [15]. Enhancing diversity through ranking: Uses ranking methods, such as popularity, reverse ranking, or variance of ratings, to improve diversity in the recommendation list [16].

3 Proposed Methods

In recent years, many studies have focused on how to increase the diversity of a recommendation list while maintaining a certain level of accuracy [13, 17]. The traditional method for creating highly diverse recommendation lists involves a two-stage process as follows:

Stage 1: Create the initial candidate list. The system applies the CF method (or a hybrid method) to generate the initial recommendation list $LN(u)$ consisting of N candidate items based on accuracy.

Stage 2: Refine the result list. The system refines the initial recommendation list $LN(u)$ generated in Stage 1 by re-ranking or temporarily removing similar items, leaving a result list $LM(u)$ that only contains M items ($M \leq N$) with higher diversity than the original $LN(u)$ list.

Most current algorithms estimate diversity based on item differences within the list, neglecting the user profile. This paper proposes a new approach considering item-user profile differences, with two algorithms that enhance diversity while maintaining accuracy.

3.1 Ranking Hybrid Algorithm (RH)

The RH algorithm aims to avoid recommending items too similar to the user's profile, which would result in a monotonous experience. By suggesting items that differ significantly from the profile, the recommendation list $LM(u)$ becomes more diverse and engaging, while maintaining accuracy. Diversity is defined as the average distance between the items in $LM(u)$ and the user's profile.

$$IntraDistanceProfile(LM(u)) = \frac{1}{n} \sum_{i \in LM(u)} d(u, i) \qquad (1)$$

Where, $d(u, i)$ is the distance between the profile of user u and item i; n is the size of $LM(u)$. Measure (1) reflects how different an item is from the user's profile. If $LM(u)$ has too many similar items, its diversity is reduced. To enhance diversity, we prioritize items with content farthest from the user's profile. Therefore, the RH algorithm requires a similarity measure between items and the user's profile. Assuming that we denote $sim(u, i)$ as the similarity measure between item i and the user profile u, we can apply the cosine measure for this similarity. From this, we can calculate the distance between item i and user profile u as follows:

$$d(u, i) = 1 - sim(u, i) \qquad (2)$$

With,

$$sim(x, y) = \cos\left(\overrightarrow{x}, \overrightarrow{y}\right) = \frac{\overrightarrow{x} \cdot \overrightarrow{y}}{\|\overrightarrow{x}\|_2 \|\overrightarrow{y}\|_2} = \frac{\sum_{s \in S_{xy}} r_{x,s} r_{y,s}}{\sqrt{\sum_{s \in S_{xy}} r_{x,s}^2} \sqrt{\sum_{s \in S_{xy}} r_{y,s}^2}}$$

This paper uses formula (2) to increase diversity in the recommendation list by suggesting items that don't closely match the user's profile, helping avoid monotony. However, accuracy must also be maintained, so the RH algorithm follows a two-stage process as shown in Fig. 1.

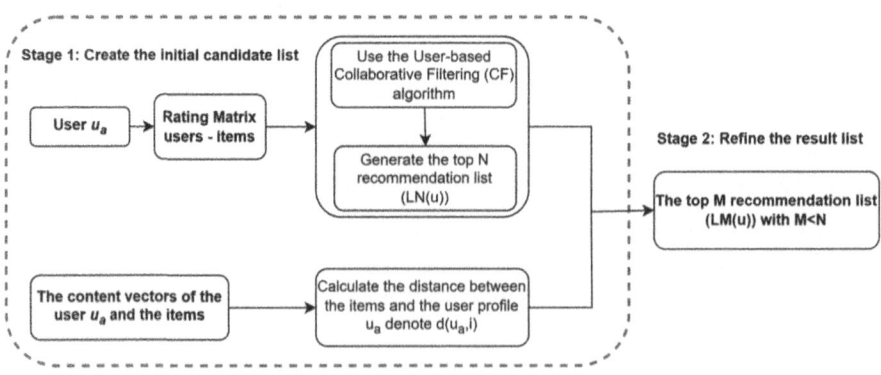

Fig. 1. Illustration of the RH algorithm.

Stage 1: Create the Initial Candidate List

The first stage aims to create the initial recommendation list $LN(u)$. The items in the $LN(u)$ set will be guaranteed for accuracy because they have been generated using one of the filtering methods. The paper proposes using the user-based Collaborative Filtering algorithm for stage 1, as is common in most recommender systems today.

This technique has two steps: a) calculating user similarity using ratings (commonly with Pearson correlation), and b) predicting rating score of user u for item i based on the ratings of their community. If the predicted rating r is below a threshold, item i is removed, and the system re-ranks to select the top N items with the highest predicted ratings for the list $LN(u)$.

Stage 2: Refine the Result List

The refinement stage aims to create the result recommendation list $LM(u)$ by removing items from $LM(u)$ that are too close to the user profile u. Thus, for each item i in the initial $LN(u)$ list, the RH algorithm calculates the value of $d(u, i)$, which is the distance between item i and the user profile u. The farther an item is from the user profile, the higher its priority for recommendation to the user. After calculating $d(u, i)$ for all items in the initial $LN(u)$ set, the RH algorithm will re-rank the items in descending order of $d(u, i)$ and select the top M items with the highest $d(u, i)$ to include in the final recommendation list $LM(u)$.

RH algorithm

Input:	Rating matrix R, user profile of user u, I = {items (content)}
Output:	Top_M recommendation list provided to user LM(u)

Begin

$\qquad$ For $(i \in I* = \{j \mid \exists\, v \in Tu : r(v, j) \neq null \wedge r(u, j) = null)$
$\qquad$ {

$\qquad\qquad$ Calculate the predicted score of user u for item i ($\hat{r}(u, i)$);
$\qquad\qquad$ $R[i] = \hat{r}(u, i)$;

$\qquad$ }

$\qquad$ $St = Sort(I*, R[i])$; // Sort function: Sort the list of items i in descending order according to R[i].

$\qquad$ $LN(u) = Filter\_TopN(St)$ // Filter_TopN function: Filter out the Top_N recommended items for the user ($LN(u)$)

$\qquad$ For $(k \in LN(u))$
$\qquad$ {

$\qquad\qquad$ Calculate the distance between the profile user u and item k, $d(u, k)$;
$\qquad\qquad$ $D[k] = d(u, k)$;

$\qquad$ }

$\qquad$ $S_{LN} = Sort(LN(u), D[k])$; // Sort function: Sort the list of items i in descending order according to $D[k]$.

$\qquad$ $LM(u) = Filter\_TopM(S_{LN})$; // Filter_TopM function: Filter out the Top_M recommended items for the user ($LM(u)$)

$\qquad$ **Return** $LM(u)$;

End

The advantage of the RH algorithm is that it can generate advisory lists that are not monotonous or boring for the user, while still maintaining a certain level of accuracy. However, since the RH algorithm also follows a two-stage process, if the advisory list $LN(u)$ in stage 1 already contains too many similar items, stage 2 cannot significantly improve the diversity. Therefore, we propose the WH algorithm to address the limitations of the RH algorithm.

3.2 Weighted Hybrid Algorithm (WH)

To overcome this limitation, the Weighted Hybrid (WH) algorithm combines two key factors: the predicted ratings (focused on accuracy) and the distance $d(u, i)$ (focused on diversity). By incorporating both accuracy and diversity in the recommendation process, the WH algorithm aims to provide a more balanced and varied set of recommendations, ensuring that the final list not only meets the user's preferences but also offers a greater variety of items to explore.

$$score(u, i) = k \times \hat{r}(u, i) + \gamma \times (1 - k) \times d(u, i); k \in [0, 1]$$

Since the predicted rating $\hat{r}(u, i)$ is in the range $[1, 5]$ and the value $d(u, i) \in [0, 1]$, we have adjusted the value of the distance $d(u, i)$ to match the same scale as $\hat{r}(u, i)$ by multiplying the distance by a scaling factor α (specifically, $\alpha = 5$).

WH algorithm

Input: user profile of user u, I ={ items (content)}, $ListR_u = \{\hat{r}(u, i), i \in I\}$
            Threshold TH , $TopM$ items to recommend
Output: $TopM$ recommendation list $L_M(u)$.
Begin

  For $(i \in I* = \{j \mid \exists\ v \in Tu: r(v, j) \neq null \wedge r(u, j) = null)$

  // T_u: is the community of user u

  {
    Calculate the predicted score of user u for item i ($\hat{r}(u, i)$);
    Calculate the distance between the profile user u and item i, $d(u, i)$;
    Compute $score(u, i) = k * \hat{r}(u, i) + (1 - k) * \gamma * d(u, i)$;
    $Sc[i] = score(u, i)$;
    }
    $SSc = SortItem(I*, Sc[i])$;
    //Function SortItem sort the items $i \in I^*$ in descending order of scores $Sc[i]$;
    $LM(u) = Filter\_TopM(SSc)$;
    // Function $Filter\_TopM$ selects the $TopM$ items $LM(u)$ recommend for user u;
    Return $L_M(u)$;
  end

Thus, after calculating $score(u, i)$ for all items, the Algorithm WH selects the $topM$ items with the highest scores for the final recommendation list $LM(u)$ for user u, without needing to generate an initial candidate list $LM(u)$.

The WH algorithm combines both predicted rating (accuracy) and distance $d(u, i)$ (diversity), overcoming the limitations of the two-stage RH algorithm and others. The use of coefficient k allows adjusting the balance between accuracy and diversity based on the application domain. However, this requires additional costs for learning the optimal value of k.

4 Experimental Procedure

The preparation process for the experiments in the paper includes: preparing the dataset, setting parameter values, selecting comparison algorithms, and choosing measures to evaluate the effectiveness of the algorithms.

4.1 Experimental Data

The experiments in this paper used the MovieLens dataset, a standard dataset in Recommender Systems, consisting of 100,000 ratings from 943 users across 1,682 movies in 19 genres. The data was split into 80% for training and 20% for testing prediction quality.

The experiments were conducted on a PC with the following specifications: CPU 13th Gen Intel(R) Core(TM) i9-13900H 2.60 GHz, RAM 32.0 GB (31.6 GB usable), 64-bit operating system, x64-based processor.

4.2 Methodology

The effectiveness of the WH algorithm is analyzed based on the coefficient k. Regarding the parameters of the algorithms, the study will select "popular" and unbiased values to ensure the objectivity of the experimental results:

To evaluate the algorithms' effectiveness, the study uses accuracy and three diversity measures. For accuracy, we apply the common measure MAE (Mean Absolute Error), as shown in the following formula:

$$MAE = \frac{1}{n} \sum_{i \in L_M(u)} \frac{|\hat{r}_{u,i} - r_{u,i}|}{l}$$

where the denominator is l, representing the rating scale, and:

- $L_M(u)$: the *Top_M* list of recommended items for user u
- n: the size of $L_M(u)$
- $\hat{r}_{u,i}$: the predicted rating of user u for item i
- $r_{u,i}$: the actual rating of user u for item i

The lower the *MAE* value, the higher the accuracy of the algorithm. Therefore, the value of $(1 - MAE)$ can be considered an indication of the algorithm's accuracy.

For diversity, three measures: *IntraDistance*, *AggDivNum*, and *IntraDistanceProfile* is used.

The diversity of the recommendation list LM(u) is considered as the degree of difference between the items in the LM(u) list. This diversity is often defined as the average distance between two items in the recommendation list LM(u) and is calculated using the following formula:

$$IntraDistance(L_M(u)) = \frac{2}{n(n-)} \sum_{i \in L_M(u)} d(i, i')$$

where, $d(i, i')$ is the energy distance between item i and item i'; n is the size of $L_M(u)$

Aggregate diversity is defined as the total number of items that the system has recommended to all users as shown in the following formula:

$$AggDivNum = \left| \bigcup_{u \in U} L_M(u) \right|$$

where, U is the set of users of the system.

The diversity of the recommendation list $L_M(u)$ is defined as the average distance of all items in the recommendation list to the user's profile.

$$IntraDistanceProfile(L_M(u)) = \frac{1}{n} \sum_{i \in L_M(u)} d(u, i)$$

where, $d(u, i)$ is the energy distance between the profile of user u and item i; n is the size of $L_M(u)$. Note that the value of $IntraDistanceProfile(L_M(u))$ is higher when the diversity of $L_M(u)$ is higher.

Since accuracy and diversity are generally opposing, the paper uses the $F\_Measure$ to balance both metrics as follows:

$$F\_Measure = \frac{2 \times (1 - MAE) \times IntraDistanceProfile}{(1 - MAE) + IntraDistanceProfile}$$

4.3 Results and Experimental Analysis

Effectiveness Based on Accuracy (MAE)

The results in Table 1 show that the CF algorithm achieves the highest accuracy with the lowest MAE, followed closely by RH, which performs similarly to CF. The PR algorithm improves accuracy compared to IPR, while WH, which incorporates diversity, shows a slight decrease in accuracy compared to the other algorithms.

Effectiveness Based on IntraDistance Diversity

Table 2 shows WH achieves the highest Intra-Distance diversity, providing varied recommendations despite slightly lower accuracy. It outperforms IPR, PR, and RH, especially in larger lists, and surpasses CF in diversity. WH is the most effective for ensuring high personal diversity.

Table 1. Accuracy of the 5 Algorithms.

Methods	Top 5	Top 10	Top 15	Top 20	Top 25	Top 30
PP IPR	0.1710	0.1708	0.1694	0.1680	0.1664	0.1627
PP PR	0.1683	0.1677	0.1664	0.1651	0.1639	0.1627
PP RH	0.1671	0.1648	0.1642	0.1640	0.1634	0.1627
PP WH	0.1714	0.1731	0.1752	0.1782	0.1794	0.1809
PP CF	0.1601	0.1618	0.1621	0.1623	0.1624	0.1627

Table 2. IntraDistance Diversity of the 5 Algorithms

Methods	Top 5	Top 10	Top 15	Top 20	Top 25	Top 30
PP IPR	0.7538	0.7098	0.6774	0.6508	0.6301	0.6113
PP PR	0.7288	0.6878	0.6544	0.6288	0.6051	0.5913
PP RH	0.7080	0.7052	0.6456	0.6449	0.6243	0.6113
PP WH	0.7578	0.7338	0.7214	0.6948	0.6741	0.6553
PP CF	0.5729	0.5893	0.5975	0.6028	0.6020	0.6023

Effectiveness Based on Overall Diversity (AggDivNum)

The results in Table 3 show that WH excels in overall diversity (AggDivNum), especially for larger groups, with a score of 834 at Top 30, outperforming other algorithms. IPR leads in smaller groups like Top 5 and Top 10 but declines as group size increases. PR and RH perform moderately, with RH improving at Top 30. CF has the lowest effectiveness, starting at 153 for Top 5 but improving in larger groups. Overall, WH is ideal for large sets, while IPR suits smaller groups. These results highlight the algorithms' flexibility based on recommendation system needs.

Table 3. AggDivNum of the 5 Algorithms

Algorithm	Top 5	Top 10	Top 15	Top 20	Top 25	Top 30
PP IPR	257	450	490	550	695	724
PP PR	230	350	461	501	645	724
PP RH	194	321	447	524	615	724
PP WH	232	408	513	625	724	834
PP CF	153	297	406	520	639	724

Effectiveness Based on IntraDistanceProfile Diversity

The results in Table 4 show that the WH algorithm excels in IntraDistanceProfile diversity across all group sizes, with scores starting at 0.7488 for Top 5 and remaining strong at 0.6103 for Top 30. IPR and RH perform moderately well, with RH slightly outperforming IPR in smaller groups, but both converge in larger groups. PR remains steady but lacks competitiveness, while CF consistently scores the lowest. Overall, WH is the most effective algorithm for optimizing IntraDistanceProfile diversity in both small and large groups.

Table 4. IntraDistanceProfile Diversity of the 5 Algorithms

Algorithm	Top 5	Top 10	Top 15	Top 20	Top 25	Top 30
PP IPR	0.6147	0.5862	0.5503	0.5349	0.5233	0.5221
PP PR	0.5714	0.5472	0.5370	0.5299	0.5223	0.5221
PP RH	0.6380	0.6152	0.5736	0.5449	0.5243	0.5221
PP WH	0.7488	0.7058	0.6744	0.6488	0.6281	0.6103
PP CF	0.4851	0.5052	0.5108	0.5149	0.5182	0.5221

Effectiveness Based on F_Measure Metric

The results in Table 5 show that WH outperforms all algorithms in balancing precision and diversity, with scores ranging from 0.8435 for Top 5 to 0.7474 for Top 30. RH ranks second, performing well in smaller groups but declining in larger ones. IPR maintains stable performance, slightly better than PR, which consistently lags. CF scores the lowest, starting at 0.6150 for Top 5. Overall, WH is the most effective algorithm for optimizing recommendation quality, particularly when both precision and diversity matter, while RH and IPR are moderate alternatives.

Table 5. F_Measure Metric of the 5 Algorithms

Algorithm	Top 5	Top 10	Top 15	Top 20	Top 25	Top 30
PP IPR	0.7512	0.7296	0.7012	0.6886	0.6790	0.6782
PP PR	0.7182	0.6987	0.6905	0.6846	0.6783	0.6782
PP RH	0.7686	0.7520	0.7201	0.6971	0.6800	0.6782
PP WH	0.8435	0.8154	0.7939	0.7757	0.7607	0.7474
PP CF	0.6150	0.6304	0.6347	0.6378	0.6402	0.6432

The experimental results show that the RH and WH algorithms consistently outperform others in diversifying recommendation lists. The WH algorithm performs competitively with IPR and PR in smaller groups (Top_M = {5, 10, 15}), but excels in larger groups (Top_M = {20, 25, 30}), making it ideal for applications requiring high diversity in larger lists. While RH maintains stable performance across all group sizes, it is less competitive than WH in larger groups. IPR and PR perform well in smaller groups but struggle with larger lists. Overall, WH is best for scenarios needing high diversity in extensive lists, while RH is a reliable alternative for moderate diversity across all group sizes.

5   Conclusion

In this paper, we have explored and proposed two enhanced algorithms to address the diversity recommendation problem in recommender systems: the Ranking Hybrid (RH) algorithm and the Weighted Hybrid (WH) algorithm. Both algorithms aim to increase the diversity of the recommendation list while maintaining a certain level of accuracy, providing an optimal user experience. The RH algorithm employs a two-stage process to combine accuracy and diversity, while the WH algorithm integrates both factors simultaneously from the initial recommendation list creation. Through experiments on the MovieLens dataset, we observed that the WH algorithm excels in increasing the diversity of the recommendation list, although its accuracy is slightly lower compared to traditional algorithms like CF. However, the trade-off between accuracy and diversity is reasonable, as the WH algorithm offers a richer set of options for users, allowing them to explore new and interesting content. The experimental results show that the WH algorithm not only performs well in improving aggregate diversity but also demonstrates its ability to offer better overall recommendation diversity for larger Top_M values. Thus, the WH algorithm effectively addresses the limitations of traditional two-stage methods and provides a more diverse and engaging recommendation experience for users.

References

1. Zangerle, E., Bauer, C.: Evaluating recommender systems: survey and framework. ACM Comput. Surv. **55**(8), 1–38 (2022)
2. Lü, L., et al.: Recommender systems. Phys. Rep. **519**(1), 1–49 (2012)
3. Burke, R.: Hybrid recommender systems: survey and experiments. User Model. User-Adap. Interact. **12**, 331–370 (2002)
4. Beel, J., et al.: Paper recommender systems: a literature survey. Int. J. Digit. Libr. **17**, 305–338 (2016)
5. Mohamed, M.H., Khafagy, M.H., Ibrahim, M.H.: Recommender systems challenges and solutions survey. In: 2019 International Conference on Innovative Trends in Computer Engineering (ITCE). IEEE (2019)
6. Kaminskas, M., Bridge, D.: Diversity, serendipity, novelty, and coverage: a survey and empirical analysis of beyond-accuracy objectives in recommender systems. ACM Trans. Interact. Intell. Syst. (TiiS) **7**(1), 1–42 (2016)
7. Duricic, T., et al.: Beyond-accuracy: a review on diversity, serendipity, and fairness in recommender systems based on graph neural networks. Front. Big Data **6**, 1251072 (2023)
8. Vrijenhoek, S., et al.: Diversity of what? On the different conceptualizations of diversity in recommender systems. In: The 2024 ACM Conference on Fairness, Accountability, and Transparency (2024)

9. Amer, A.A., Abdalla, H.I., Nguyen, L.: Enhancing recommendation systems performance using highly-effective similarity measures. Knowl. Based Syst. **217**, 106842 (2021)
10. Kim, J., Choi, I., Li, Q.: Customer satisfaction of recommender system: examining accuracy and diversity in several types of recommendation approaches. Sustainability **13**(11), 6165 (2021)
11. Çano, E., Morisio, M.: Hybrid recommender systems: a systematic literature review. Intell. Data Anal. **21**(6), 1487–1524 (2017)
12. Javed, U., et al.: A review of content-based and context-based recommendation systems. Int. J. Emerg. Technol. Learn. (iJET) **16**(3), 274–306 (2021)
13. Patel, K., Patel, H.B.: A state-of-the-art survey on recommendation system and prospective extensions. Comput. Electron. Agric. **178**, 105779 (2020)
14. Meymandpour, R., Davis, J.G.: Measuring the diversity of recommendations: a preference-aware approach for evaluating and adjusting diversity. Knowl. Inf. Syst. **62**(2), 787–811 (2020)
15. Zhang, L., et al.: Diversity balancing for two-stage collaborative filtering in recommender systems. Appl. Sci. **10**(4), 1257 (2020)
16. Anderson, A., et al.: Algorithmic effects on the diversity of consumption on spotify. In: Proceedings of the Web Conference 2020 (2020)
17. Gogna, A., Majumdar, A.: Balancing accuracy and diversity in recommendations using matrix completion framework. Knowl. Based Syst. **125**, 83–95 (2017)

Combining Lightweight Deep Learning Models with Data Augmentation for Analysis of Cervical Cells

Nga Le-Thi-Thu$^{(\boxtimes)}$ ⓘ, Phuoc Dat Doan ⓘ, An Phan-Nguyen-Thanh ⓘ,
Thanh Tran-Thi ⓘ, Dat Tran-Tuan ⓘ, and Khang Nguyen-Hoang ⓘ

Vietnam - Korea University of Information and Communication Technology, Da Nang, Vietnam
{lttnga,ddphuoc.tg,anpnt.21ad,thanhtt.21ad,dattt.22ds,
khangnh.22ds}@vku.udn.vn

Abstract. Cervical cancer is one of the most common and severe threats to women's health. Early detection of abnormal cervical cells through automated screening can improve diagnostic accuracy, allowing for timely treatment and increased survival rates. This study proposes a solution that combines lightweight deep learning models with data augmentation of microscopic cell images to detect abnormal cervical cells. Lightweight models, including MobileNetV1, MobileNetV2, MobileNetV3 (both small and large variants), and EfficientNet-B0, were tested and demonstrated promising results after data augmentation. The EfficientNet-B0 model achieved 99% accuracy with an F1 score of 98%, while the MobileNet variants also showed high performance, with F1 scores ranging from 85% to 96% and a loss as low as 0.006. These experimental results highlight the potential of lightweight deep learning models combined with data augmentation to deliver high accuracy and efficiency, making them suitable for medical datasets with limited and imbalanced data across classes.

Keywords: Lightweight deep learning · Data augmentation · MobileNet · EfficientNet · Computational efficiency · Cervical cells

1 Introduction

Developing deep learning models has led to remarkable advancements in image analysis. However, large models like ResNet and Inception require substantial hardware resources, hindering their application in resource-constrained systems [1, 2]. Lightweight models, such as EfficientNet-Lite and MobileNet, have emerged to optimize performance, reduce complexity, and meet practical needs, particularly in medical image analysis, where speed and computational efficiency are top priorities.

Unlike traditional deep learning architectures, lightweight models are designed with fewer parameters and lower computational demands. For example, MobileNet uses depthwise separable convolutions, significantly reducing the required computations. EfficientNet-Lite, a more optimized version of EfficientNet, applies compound scaling

H. X. Huynh et al. (Eds.): GOODTECHS 2024, LNICST 649, pp. 173–182, 2025.
https://doi.org/10.1007/978-3-032-01497-9_16

to adjust network depth, width, and resolution simultaneously, achieving high accuracy with minimal computational cost [3, 4, 6].

Lightweight deep learning models have become a popular research topic in image data analysis, especially for processing on resource-constrained devices. These models are typically designed to optimize computational efficiency and reduce memory requirements. Key techniques for building lightweight models include reducing the number of parameters and using simpler architectures compared to traditional models. Notable research on lightweight models includes SqueezeNet, which uses "Fire modules" to minimize the number of parameters while maintaining effectiveness in image recognition. Subsequently, architectures like MobileNet, ShuffleNet, and EfficientNet have further advanced this approach, focusing on reducing computational operations and model size through techniques like depthwise separable convolutions and scaling factors [3, 5, 9] (Table 1).

In particular, EfficientNet and its variants, such as EfficientNet-B0 to EfficientNet-B7, utilize a compound scaling method that simultaneously adjusts the model's depth, width, and resolution to maximize efficiency. These models achieve high accuracy in image classification tasks with fewer parameters and operations, making them suitable for mobile applications and embedded devices [5, 11]. Additionally, newer models like CondenseNet and GhostNet employ strategies to reduce the number of computations and resource usage by generating efficient features with fewer parameters [10].

Deep learning models often require large amounts of data to perform effectively. Data augmentation helps expand the training dataset, creating diversity without the need to collect additional data. This not only addresses issues related to data scarcity and improves the performance of deep learning models but also reduces the risk of overfitting during the training model. Proper application of augmentation techniques ensures that deep learning models achieve high accuracy and perform effectively on complex problems while maintaining stability in real-world scenarios.

However, the collected image data is often imbalanced and unevenly distributed, especially in medical datasets. For example, in cervical cell images obtained through staining, normal cells dominate the dataset, while other cell types (such as Clue Cells, Candida albicans, Actinomyces, Trichomonas vaginalis, etc.) are significantly underrepresented, particularly virus-infected and cancerous cells (e.g., Herpes, LSIL). This imbalance can negatively impact the accuracy of models. Increasing the quantity of image data and balancing the training dataset are essential steps to improve the accuracy of machine learning models, this is an important step in model development.

Cervical cancer is one of the most common and severe threats to women's health. Early detection of abnormal cervical cells through automated screening can improve diagnostic accuracy, enable timely treatment, and increase survival rates. This study proposes a solution that combines lightweight deep learning models with data augmentation of microscopic cell images to detect abnormal cervical cells. Lightweight models, including MobileNetV1, MobileNetV2, MobileNetV3 (both small and large variants), and EfficientNet-B0, were tested and demonstrated promising results after data augmentation. The EfficientNet-B0 model achieved 99% accuracy with an F1 score of 98%, while the MobileNet variants also showed high performance, with F1 scores ranging from 85% to 96% and a loss as low as 0.006. These experimental results highlight

Table 1. Comparison of Lightweight CNN Architectures on the ImageNet dataset

Model	Top-1	Top-5	Params. (M)	MACs (G)
AlexNet [110]	57.1	80.3	60.9	0.725
ResNet-50 [77]	76.0	93.0	26.0	4.100
SqueezeNet [98]	57.5	80.3	1.2	0.837
SqueezeNext [59]	59.1	82.6	0.7	0.282
ShuffleNetV1-1.5 [248]	71.5	–	3.4	0.292
ShuffleNetV2-1.5 [138]	72.6	90.6	3.5	0.299
1.0-MobileNetV1 [89]	70.6	–	4.2	0.569
MobileNetV2-1.4 [168]	74.7	–	6.9	0.585
MobileV3-S [88]	67.4	–	2.5	0.056
MobileV3-L [88]	75.2	–	5.4	0.219
MobileNeXt-1.0 [253]	74..0	–	3.4	0.300
ShiftResNet-20 [217]	68.6	–	0.2	0.046
ShiftResNet-56 [217]	72.1	–	0.6	0.102
ShiftNet-A [217]	70.1	89.7	4.1	1.400
ShiftNet-B [217]	61.2	83.6	1.1	0.371
FE-Net-1.0 [26]	72.9	–	3.7	0.301
FE-Net-1.37 [26]	75.0	–	5.9	0.563
AddressNet-20 [82]	68.7	–	0.1	0.022
AddressNet-44 [82]	73.3	–	0.2	0.053
AdderNet-Resnet18 [21]	67.0	87.6	3.6	–
AdderNet-Resnet50 [21]	74.9	91.7	7.7	–
DenseNet-169 [94]	76.2	93.2	14.0	3.500
DenseNet-264 [94]	77.9	93.9	34.0	6.000
CondenseNet [93]	71.0	90.0	2.9	0.274
CondenseV2-A [227]	64.4	84.5	2.0	0.046
CondenseV2-B [227]	71.9	90.3	3.6	0.146
EfficientNet-B1 [191]	79.2	94.5	7.8	0.700
EfficientNet-B7 [191]	84.4	97.1	66.0	37.000
EfficientNet-X-B7 [118]	84.7	–	73.0	91.000
EfficientNetV2-S [192]	83.9	–	24.0	8.800
EfficientNetV2-M [192]	85.1	–	55.0	24.000
EfficientNetV2-L [192]	85.7	–	121.0	53.000

the potential of lightweight deep learning models combined with data augmentation to deliver high accuracy and efficiency, making them suitable for medical datasets with limited and imbalanced data across classes.

The rest of this paper is organized as follows: Sect. 2 presents lightweight deep learning models including MobileNet (V1, V2, V3) and EfficientNet (B0). Data sets and non-mixup data augmentation techniques for expanding training data to the liquid-based cytology pap smear images are described in Sect. 3. Some experimental results are presented in Sect. 4. Finally, several concluding remarks are discussed, and future works are drawn in Sect. 5.

2 Lightweight Deep Learning Models

Lightweight models are neural network architectures designed to optimize model size and computational speed while maintaining high performance. These models typically have fewer parameters, reducing inference time and resource consumption, making them especially suitable for deployment on mobile devices or in resource-constrained environments. Notable models in this category include MobileNet (V1, V2, V3) and EfficientNet (B0), which incorporate advanced designs such as depthwise separable convolutions and compound scaling to balance performance with resource efficiency [10–12] (Fig. 1).

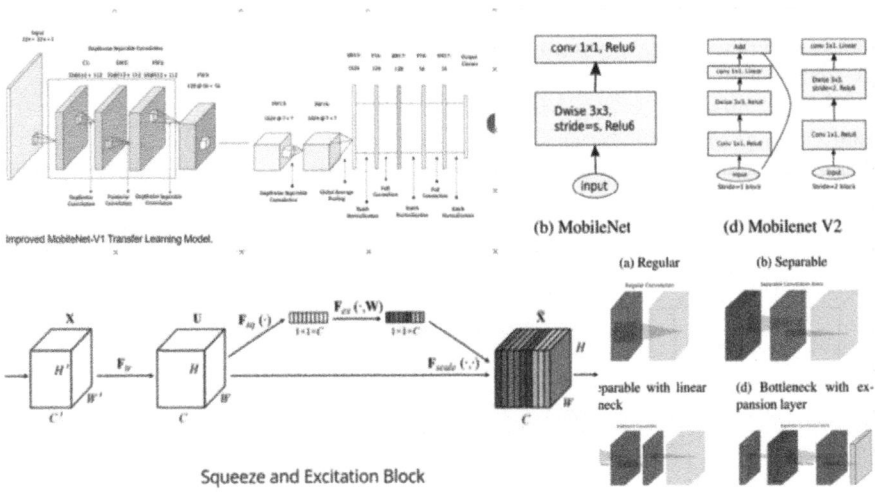

Fig. 1. MobileNet (V1, V2, V3) architecture [11]

MobileNet-V1 introduces the concept of depthwise separable convolution, significantly reducing the number of computations compared to traditional CNNs while maintaining accuracy. The model's advantages are highly efficient for computation and suitable for mobile devices with limited resources. MobileNet-V2 proposes the inverted residual block structure, combined with pointwise convolution layers, enhancing the model's representational capacity without significantly increasing computation. A notable improvement in performance over MobileNetV1, especially in handling deeper networks. MobileNet-V3 uses neural architecture search techniques to optimize both the performance and size of the model. This model strikes a good balance between accuracy and computational efficiency, with flexible model sizing to meet different requirements. All three versions of MobileNet aim to create efficient CNN models that can run on mobile devices. However, each version introduces different improvements and optimizations to achieve better performance. MobileNetV3 is the latest version and is considered to have the best overall performance among the three.

EfficientNet-B0 is built by blocks (MBConv), and the Squeeze and Excitation mechanism. EfficientNet-B0 is designed to achieve high accuracy while maintaining computational efficiency. It uses several techniques, including [12]:

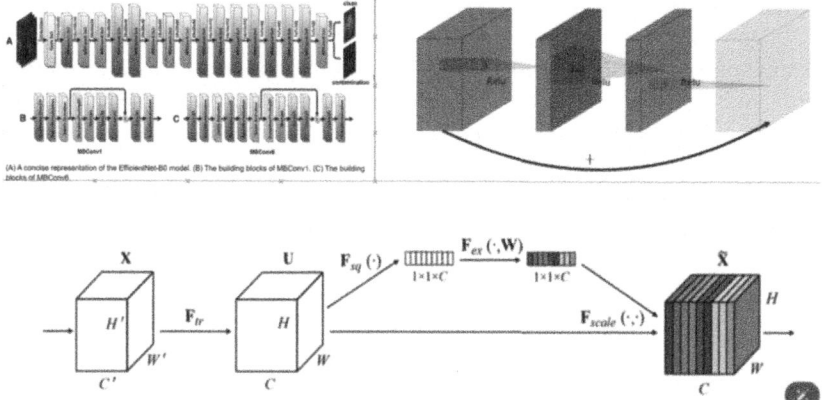

Fig. 2. EfficientNet-B0 architecture [12]

- MBConv: Combines convolution layers, activation functions, and other techniques to enhance the network's representational capacity.
- Squeeze and Excitation: Helps the network focus on the most important features of the image.

EfficientNet's design approach allows it to optimize both accuracy and efficiency, making it effective for various applications, especially in scenarios with computational constraints. Figure 2 illustrates the overall structure of EfficientNet-B0.

For the image classification task, we applied MobileNet and EfficientNet models with two main steps:

- Feature extraction: MobileNet (V1, V2, or V3) or EfficientNet-B0 are used as feature extraction models. The original architecture of the model is preserved, and its output feature vectors serve as input for subsequent classification models.
- Fine-tuning: The model architecture is modified by adding new layers at the end of MobileNet or EfficientNet. These additional layers are specifically designed to solve the target task, and the model is retrained. This process allows for optimizing the model on the new dataset while leveraging the pre-trained knowledge of MobileNet or EfficientNet. In recent benchmarks, a fine-tuning approach has demonstrated the effectiveness of these models, especially EfficientNet.

This method is especially beneficial for tasks with limited data, as it allows the model to leverage the learned features from the initial training, leading to enhanced accuracy without the need for extensive, resource-intensive training from scratch. Fine-tuning is widely used with models such as MobileNet and EfficientNet, which are designed for efficient performance on smaller datasets.

3 Data Augmentation

In this study, we used the Liquid-Based Cytology (LBC) pap smear dataset for multi-class diagnosis of cervical cancer [13]. Data were collected from a clinical setting including 963 pap smear images prepared via liquid-based cytology from 460 patients. The images were captured using a Leica ICC50 HD microscope at 40x magnification. These images are intended for research on image segmentation and classification, specifically aimed at improving decision support systems in medical diagnostics (Table 2).

Table 2. LBC Pap Smear Dataset of Cervical Cells

Class	Quantity	Quantity after data augmentation
NILM	613	6130
LSIL	163	1630
HSIL	113	1130
SCC	74	740

The dataset is divided into four distinct classes of cervical lesions based on The Bethesda System: High Squamous Intraepithelial Lesion (HSIL), Low Squamous

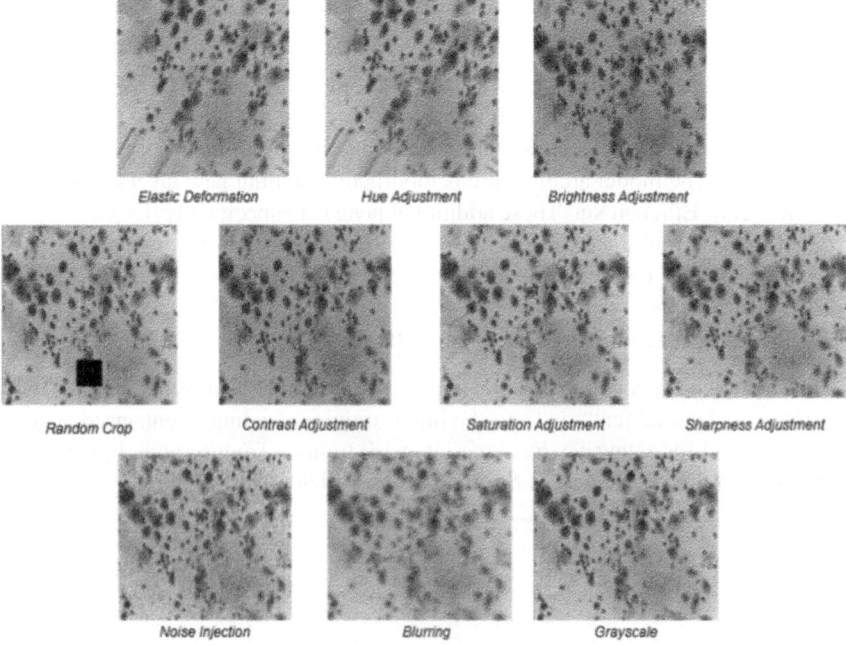

Fig. 3. Data Augmentation

Intraepithelial Lesion (LSIL), Negative for Intraepithelial Malignancy (NILM), and Squamous Cell Carcinoma (SCC) (Fig. 3).

Data augmentation is a technique for expanding training data by applying transformations, which helps reduce overfitting and improves model generalization. In this approach, to enhance model performance and generalization, we applied 10 non-mixup data augmentation techniques to the liquid-based cytology pap smear images: Random Crop, Brightness Adjustment, Contrast Adjustment, Saturation Adjustment, Hue Adjustment, Noise Injection, Blurring, Sharpness Adjustment, Elastic Deformation, and Grayscale. These methods introduce visual variability, allowing the model to train on a more diverse dataset and adapt better to real-world data complexities. These transformations included elastic deformations, brightness and contrast adjustments, noise addition, and more. Each image underwent multiple augmentations, effectively increasing the dataset size by a factor of 10. This significant expansion in image diversity allows the model to generalize better to real-world variations, improving classification accuracy for the four lesion categories: HSIL, LSIL, NILM, and SCC.

4 Experimental Results

In this research, we use three pre-trained convolutional neural network (CNN) models: MobileNetV1, MobileNetV2, and MobileNetV3, all trained on the ImageNet dataset. These models are employed for feature extraction and fine-tuning to classify cervical cancer from liquid-based cytology pap smear images.

MobileNet models are used as feature extractors by removing the top layers and passing the extracted features through a custom classifier. We apply fine-tuning to the deeper layers of these models, allowing them to adapt to our dataset. Fine-tuning is performed with a lower learning rate to avoid disrupting the pre-learned features while optimizing the model's performance for cervical cancer classification. EfficientNet B0, known for its efficiency and accuracy, is similarly used for feature extraction. We unfreeze the top layers and fine-tune the model on our dataset using a gradual learning rate to optimize its performance for cervical cancer classification.

Table 3. Experimental results on LBC pap smear dataset without data augmentation

Model	Accuracy	Loss	Precision	Recall		F1 Score
MobileNet-V1	0.83	0.42	0.89		0.67	0.70
MobileNet-V2	0.91	0.33	0.82		0.70	0.68
MobileNet-V3 Small	0.83	0.45	0.69		0.71	0.70
MobileNet-V3 Large	0.91	0.33	0.61		0.66	0.63
EfficientNet-B0	0.95	0.30	0.88		0.86	0.87

Table 3 shows a performance comparison of lightweight models without data augmentation. MobileNet (V1, V2, V3 Small, V3 Large) and EfficientNet-B0 on key criteria including Accuracy, Loss, Precision, Recall, and F1 Score. EfficientNet-B0 achieves the highest Accuracy (0.95) and F1 Score (0.87), along with the lowest Loss (0.30). MobileNet-V1 has the highest Precision (0.89), but its other metrics, such as Recall and F1 Score, are lower compared to the other models. The MobileNet-V2 and MobileNet-V3 Large versions have relatively high Accuracy (0.91) and lower Loss compared to MobileNet-V1 and MobileNet-V3 Small, indicating that these models perform better in certain aspects.

Table 4. Experimental results on LBC pap smear dataset with data augmentation

Model	Accuracy	Loss	Precision	Recall	F1 Score
MobileNet-V1	0.98	0.006	0.93	0.85	0.91
MobileNet-V2	0.98	0.031	0.87	0.90	0.85
MobileNet-V3 Small	0.95	0.013	0.95	0.97	0.96
MobileNet-V3 Large	0.99	0.006	0.86	0.83	0.85
EfficientNet-B0	0.99	0.010	0.93	0.94	0.98

Table 4 shows the results after applying data augmentation. It shows a significant improvement in the performance of all models. The EfficientNet-B0 model achieved 99% accuracy with an F1 score of 98%, while the MobileNet variants also showed high performance, with F1 scores ranging from 85% to 96% and a loss as low as 0.006.

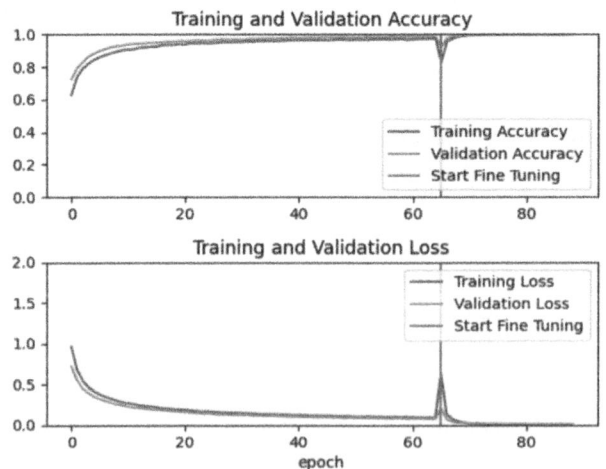

Fig. 4. Loss and Accuracy of MobileNet V1 after data augmentation

Figure 4 illustrates the loss and accuracy of the MobileNet V1 model training process after applying data augmentation. In the early phase (0–60 epochs), both training and validation accuracy increase gradually, while the loss decreases, indicating stable learning by the model. After the fine-tuning phase (starting from epoch 60), accuracy continues to improve while the loss significantly drops. The accuracy of both the training and validation sets increases with t Feature extraction: he number of epochs, eventually reaching a stable level. The loss function for both the training and validation sets decreases gradually with the number of epochs.

The comparison Table 5 provides a comprehensive view of the above models, illustrating the trade-off between model complexity and resource efficiency.

Table 5. Model performance metrics

Model	Number of Parameters	Checkpoint Size	Training Time	Memory Usage
MobileNet-V1	3,232,964 (12.33 MB)	22.8 MB	1 h 20 min	12.33 MB
MobileNet-V2	2,263,108 (8.63 MB)	16.8 MB	1 h 16 min	8.63 MB
MobileNet-V3 Small	941,428 (3.59 MB)	7.1 MB	1 h 5 min	3.59 MB
MobileNet-V3 Large	3,000,196 (11,44 MB)	22.8 MB	1 h 10 min	11.44 MB
EfficientNet-B0	4,054,695 (15.47 MB)	29.6 MB	1 h 37 min	15.47 MB

EfficientNet B0 has the highest number of parameters (4,054,695) and the largest checkpoint size (29.6 MB), resulting in the longest training time (1 h 37 min) and the highest memory usage (15.47 MB). This model is suitable for applications that require high accuracy, though it demands more resources and processing time. In contrast, MobileNet V3 Small has the fewest parameters (941,428) and the smallest checkpoint size (7.1 MB), leading to a shorter training time (1 h 5 min) and minimal memory usage (3.59 MB). MobileNet V3 Small is ideal for devices with limited resources, making it suitable for applications needing fast deployment and memory efficiency. MobileNet V1, V2, and V3 Large provide a balance between complexity and resource efficiency, with MobileNet V2 featuring fewer parameters than MobileNet V1 while significantly improving checkpoint size and memory usage.

5   Conclusion

Medical image data is often imbalanced, with the number of normal samples significantly exceeding the number of abnormal samples. Applying data augmentation to medical image datasets helps improve model accuracy. By leveraging lightweight deep learning models such as EfficientNet-B0 and variants of MobileNet trained on augmented datasets, experimental results demonstrate a notable improvement in the performance of these models.

However, this research represents an initial attempt, primarily focusing on fine-tuning the models. Future work will aim to further optimize these models to achieve higher accuracy while reducing computational resource requirements. Additionally, the research needs to be extended to larger and more diverse datasets, incorporating more advanced augmentation techniques to enhance diagnostic precision. This study contributes to the development of automated cervical cancer diagnostic systems, helping to improve the quality of healthcare services.

Acknowledgments. This paper was supported by The University of Danang, Vietnam - Korea University of Information and Communication Technology.

References

1. Szegedy, C., Ioffe, S., Vanhoucke, V., Alemi, A.A.: Inception-v4, inception-ResNet and the impact of residual connections on learning (2017)
2. Iandola, F.N., Han, S., Moskewicz, M.W, Ashraf, K., Dally, W.J., Keutzer. K.: SqueezeNet: AlexNet-level accuracy with 50x fewer parameters and <0.5 MB model size (2017)
3. Chollet, F.: Xception: deep learning with depthwise separable convolutions. In: Proceedings of the IEEE Conference on Computer Vision and Pattern Recognition (2017)
4. Xiang, Y., Sun, W., Pan, C., Yan, M., Yin, Z., Liang, Y.: A novel automation-assisted cervical cancer reading method based on convolutional neural network. Biomed. Eng. (2020)
5. Zhang, X., Zhou, X., Lin, M., Sun, J.: ShuffleNet: an extremely efficient convolutional neural network for mobile devices. In: CVPR, pp. 6848–6856 (2018)
6. Cheng, S., Liu, S., Yu, J., et al.: Robust whole slide image analysis for cervical cancer screening using deep learning. Nat. Commun. (2021)
7. Tang, H., Cai, D., Kong, Y., et al.: Cervical cytology screening facilitated by an artificial intelligence microscope: a preliminary study. Cancer Cytopathol. (2021)
8. Leila, A., et al.: Diagnosis of cervical cancer and pre-cancerous lesions by artificial intelligence: a systematic review. Diagnostics (2022)
9. He, K., Zhang, X., Ren, S., Sun, J.: Deep residual learning for image recognition. In: Proceedings of the IEEE Conference on Computer Vision and Pattern Recognition (2016)
10. Tan, M., Le, Q.: EfficientNet: rethinking model scaling for convolutional neural networks. In: International Conference on Machine Learning (2019)
11. Howard, A.G., et al.: MobileNets: efficient convolutional neural networks for mobile vision applications (2017)
12. Tan, M., Le, Q.: EfficientNetV2: smaller models and faster training. In: International Conference on Machine Learning (2021)
13. Hussain, E.: Liquid based cytology pap smear images for multi-class diagnosis of cervical cancer. V4 (2019)

Energy-Based Framework for Tag-Based Recommendation Systems

Dao Xuan Thi Nguyen[1,2(✉)] (iD) and Khoi Nguyen-Tan[1]

[1] Da Nang University of Science and Technology, Da Nang City, Vietnam
daontx@ueh.edu.vn, ntkhoi@dut.udn.vn
[2] Faculty of Information Technology, Vinh Long Campus, University of Economics, Ho Chi Minh City, Vinh Long Province, Vietnam

Abstract. Tag-based recommendation systems leverage user-generated tags to personalize content filtering, but integrating this data effectively remains challenging due to complex relationships in the user-item-tag space. Existing approaches often overlook triadic relationships among users, items, and tags, limiting the potential of tag-based recommendations. To address these issues, a novel framework incorporating energy distance measures was proposed to model interactions in tag-based RS. This framework introduces an energy-based tag model capturing non-linear relationships through an incompatibility matrix, integrating tag semantics and user behavior modeling. Evaluation on the Movielens 20M dataset showed significant improvement in recommendation accuracy compared to traditional methods, highlighting the capability of energy distance to capture complex tag-based relationships. The study emphasizes the importance of modeling energy-based relationships in utilizing tag information for more effective recommendations, offering theoretical insights and practical implications for personalized system development.

Keywords: Energy- based tag Framework · Energy Distance · Tag-based recommendation

1 Introduction

Tag-based recommender systems recommend relevant items to users based on their tag assignments and rating patterns. There are many implementations of tag-based recommender systems using different approaches, such as determining similarity scores based on tag co-occurrence (e.g., cosine) [1], using tag semantics (e.g., entropy) [2], or analyzing tag distributions (e.g., statistical implication) [3, 4].

Traditional tag-based collaborative filtering models mainly focus on linear relationships between users and items via tags. However, most tag interactions in the real world exhibit complex nonlinear patterns that are difficult to capture using conventional methods. Currently, research exploring nonlinear relationships using energy-based approaches in tag-based recommender systems is limited.

© ICST Institute for Computer Sciences, Social Informatics and Telecommunications Engineering 2025
Published by Springer Nature Switzerland AG 2025. All Rights Reserved
H. X. Huynh et al. (Eds.): GOODTECHS 2024, LNICST 649, pp. 183–190, 2025.
https://doi.org/10.1007/978-3-032-01497-9_17

In this paper, we propose a unified framework that leverages energy distance metrics to model complex interactions in the tag space. Our approach relies on identifying the relationships between users and items through their tag assignments, specifically using Newton's gravitational potential between user-item-tag triples. The relationships are captured through computing the maximum mean difference (MMD) and dissimilarity measures in the tag space.

The paper is organized as follows: Section III presents the theoretical background. Section IV describes our proposed energy-based framework. Section V details the experimental evaluation. Section VI concludes the paper.

2 Theoretical Foundation

2.1 Tag-Based Recommendation Systems

Tag-Based Recommendation Systems [5] use tags provided by the user or the system to categorize items. Tag-based recommendation allows for improved recommendation accuracy by leveraging additional context and interest information.

Tag-based recommender systems are modeled using the set $S = < U, I, T, f >$ where:

$U = \{u_1, u_2, ..., u_n\}$ is a finite set of n users

$I = \{i_1, i_2, ..., i_m\}$ is a finite set of m items

$T = \{t_1, t_2, ..., t_k\}$ is a finite set of k tags

$R = \{r_{ij}\}$ is the rating matrix where rij represents the rating of user u_i for item i_j

$f: U \times I \times T \to R$ is the decision function mapping user-item-tag triplets to ratings

2.2 Data Representation

In a tag-based recommender system the interaction between user, item, and tag is represented through three matrices:

User-Tag (UT) (1) matrix showing tag usage by users

$$UT = \begin{bmatrix} u_{11} & u_{12} & \cdots & u_{1T} \\ u_{21} & u_{22} & \dots & u_{2T} \\ \vdots & \vdots & \ddots & \vdots \\ u_{U1} & u_{U2} & \dots & u_{UT} \end{bmatrix} \tag{1}$$

where:

U_{UT} is a value representing the level of interaction or interest of user U in tag T. This value can represent the frequency, weight, or number of times the user is interested in that tag.

Item-Tag (IT)(2) matrix indicating tag assignments to items, with t_{IT} is a value that represents the degree of association or relationship between tag T and item I_j. This value can represent the frequency of use, the degree of association, or the weight between the tag and the item.

$$
IT = \begin{bmatrix} t_{11} & t_{12} & \cdots & t_{1T} \\ t_{21} & t_{22} & \ldots & t_{2T} \\ \vdots & \vdots & \ddots & \vdots \\ t_{I1} & t_{I2} & \ldots & t_{IT} \end{bmatrix} \tag{2}
$$

User-Item (UI) (3) matrix capturing rating patterns, v_{UI} user rating u_i for item i_j

$$
UI = \begin{bmatrix} v_{11} & v_{12} & \cdots & v_{1I} \\ v_{21} & v_{22} & \ldots & v_{2I} \\ \vdots & \vdots & \ddots & \vdots \\ v_{U1} & v_{U2} & \ldots & v_{UI} \end{bmatrix} \tag{3}
$$

User-Item matrix, which summarizes the relationship between users and items through tags. UI Matrix determines which items are recommended to users based on their level of interest in related tags.

2.3 Energy Distance in Tag Space

Energy distance [6, 7] in tag space is a measure of the distance between probability distributions of tag vectors. Given two tag vectors T_1 and T_2 with distributions F and G respectively, the squared energy distance is defined as:

$$
TagED^2(F, G) = 2E\|T_1 - T_2\| - E\|T_1 - T_{1'}\| - E\|T_2 - T_{2'}\| \geq 0 \tag{4}
$$

where:

- T_1, T_2 are independent random vectors from F,G
- T_1', T_2' are iid copies of T_1, T_2
- ‖.‖ denotes Euclidean norm

The tag-based energy measure measures the difference between the distributions of tag sets. Given two tag sets $T = \{t_1, \ldots, t_n\}$ and $S = \{s_1, \ldots, s_n\}$ of sizes n and m respectively, the energy measure is calculated as:

$$
TagED_{n,m}(T, S) := 2A - B - C \tag{5}
$$

where A is the average similarity between tags of two sets T and S:

$$
A = \frac{1}{(nm)} \sum \sum TagSim(t_i, s_j) \tag{6}
$$

$$
B = \frac{1}{n^2} \sum \sum TagSim(t_i, t_j), \tag{7}
$$

$$
C = \frac{1}{m^2} \sum \sum TagSim(s_i, s_j) \tag{8}
$$

TagSim() is a function to measure the similarity between tags, this measure allows to determine the level of difference between tags, the closer to 0, the more similar these two sets are. The result is used to build the TED tag energy matrix for neighbor finding and recommendation. And TagSim is calculated by the following formulas:

$$TagSim\_Jaccard(T_1, T_2) = \frac{|T_1 \cap T_2|}{|T_1 \cup T_2|} \tag{9}$$

With T_1, T_2 being two sets of tags, values in the range [0,1].

3 Energy-Based Tag Framework

3.1 Energy Tag Model

For users u and v, the tag energy distance is defined:

$$E(u, v) = \sum wt|t_1 - t_2| \tag{10}$$

In which, t_1, t_2 number of times u,v tag is used; wt in number of tags.
User-tag energy interaction between user and tag is calculated as follows:

$$E_{ut} = -\log(\frac{n}{N}) \tag{11}$$

Item tag energy interaction between item and tag is calculated as follows:

$$E_{it} = -\log(\frac{m}{M}) \tag{12}$$

With, n number of times user uses tag, N total number of user tags, m number of times item is tagged, M total number of tags of item.
Unified Energy Measure combines the above ingredients with the following formula (13) and a, b, c are adjustment coefficients:

$$\sum E = aE_{ut} + bE_{it} + cE \tag{13}$$

3.2 Incompatibility Matrix

The incompatibility matrix E represents the energy distance between users based on the tag relationship. The element e_{ij} indicates the energy distance between user i and user j, n is the number of users.

$$E = \begin{bmatrix} e_{11} & e_{12} & \cdots & e_{1n} \\ e_{21} & e_{22} & \ldots & e_{2n} \\ \vdots & \vdots & \ddots & \vdots \\ e_{n1} & e_{n2} & \ldots & e_{nn} \end{bmatrix} \tag{14}$$

The e_{ij} elements are calculated based on the user-tag based energy distance, item-tag based energy distance and the energy distance between user i and user j, according to the formula

$$e_{ij} = \alpha E_{ut} + \beta E_{it} + \gamma E(i,j) \tag{15}$$

Based on the incompatibility matrix E, the Tag-based neighborhood of a user u is determined:

$$N(u) = \{v | e_{uv} \leq \theta\} \tag{16}$$

where:
v: is any user other than u in the system
e_uv: Element in matrix E.
θ: Energy distance threshold.

3.3 Rating Prediction

Rating prediction for a user-item pair (u,i) is done using the formula:

$$\hat{r}_{ui} = \overline{r}_u + \frac{\sum_{v \in N(u)} e^{-e_{uv}} (r_{vi} - \overline{r}_v)}{\sum_{v \in N(u)} e^{-e_{uv}}} \tag{17}$$

Principal components:

- $\hat{r}_{ui}$: user u's predicted rating for item i
- $\overline{r}_u, \overline{r}_v$: Average rating of users u and v
- e_{uv} Energy gap (incompatibility) between u and v
- $-e_{uv}$: energy weight, which helps prioritize users with lower energy gap

Top-N recomendation, to suggest the N most relevant items for user u, a combined evaluation function is used:

$$score(u, i) = \alpha \widehat{r_{ui}} + (1 - \alpha) sim_{tag}(u, i) \tag{18}$$

4 Experiment

4.1 Datasets

We experiment using the Movielens 20M real-world dataset to assess the suggested framework. In December 2005, Movielens [8] implemented tagging. The suggested movie labeling behavior is described in this dataset. Over 20 million ratings and 465,000 tagging applications applied to 27,000 films by 138,000 users make up the stable benchmark dataset. It contains tag genome data on 1,100 tags with 12 million relevance ratings. April 2015 release; October 2016 update.

We sample the Movielens 20M dataset with the following conditions: objects present in both ratings and tags; users have more than 20 ratings and tags; the tags of the selected person or item remain intact; Time-segregated ratings. Users also tagged a minimum of five products. At least five individuals used tags. At least five tags were applied to each item.

With k-folds = 10, this sample dataset is separated into a training set and a test set. Ten equal-sized subsets make up the dataset; eight subsets, or 80% of the total, are used for training, and two subsets, or 20%, are utilized for testing. To make sure that all users and things are taken into account for both training and testing, the model is assessed ten times recursively, each time using a different train/test split. The final result is then calculated by averaging the results.

4.2 Baseline Methods

To evaluate the effectiveness of the energy-based framework, we compare it with the following baseline methods:

- User-Based Collaborative Filtering (User-CF) [9]: Traditional collaborative filtering method based on user similarity.
- Item-Based Collaborative Filtering (Item-CF) [10]: Based on the similarity between items.
- Tag-BF [11]: Using tag-based weights in collaborative filtering model.

4.3 Evaluation Metrics

The effectiveness of the model is evaluated through 1. RMSE (Root Mean Square Error) [12, 13] Measures the error in rating prediction; 2. Precision@N Accuracy in recommending Top-N items; 3.NDCG (Normalized Discounted Cumulative Gain) [14] Measures the relevance of the recommended item to the user's preferences.

4.4 Implementation

In the implementation process, the framework components include constructing an incompatibility matrix (E-matrix) based on the energy distance between tag vectors, utilizing energy distance to compute tag-based similarity, and making predictions for ratings while selecting the Top-N items. Parameter settings involve tuning the adjustment coefficients a, b, c through grid search and adjusting the energy distance threshold (θ) based on optimizing NDCG. The training process consists of dividing the data into training (80%) and testing (20%) sets, training both baseline models and the framework on the training set, and evaluating their performance on the testing set.

4.5 Results and Analysis

We compared RMSE, Precision, and NDCG using the Movielens dataset to assess the energy-based framework model's performance for tag-based recommendation systems. With the lowest RMSE of 0.789, the suggested model outperforms Tag-BF, User-CF, and Item-CF in terms of prediction accuracy. The suggested model outperforms item-CF and user-CF, achieving the highest Precision@10 score of 0.75, followed by Tag-BF.

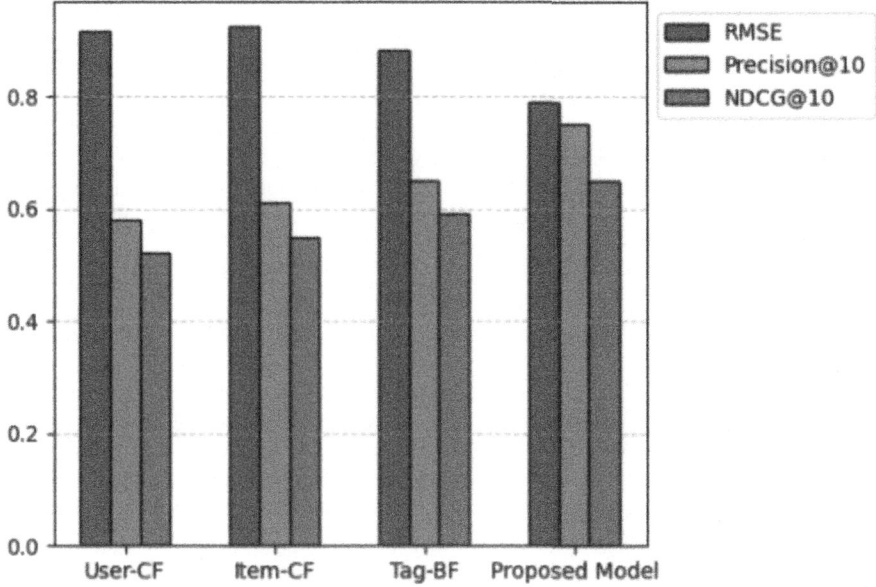

Fig. 1. Results of comparison basic methods

The greatest NDCG@10 value is 0.65 for both the suggested model and Tag-BF, 0.52 for Item-CF, and 0.55 for User-CF are shown in Fig. 1. Using the same sample dataset, the suggested model performs better across the board.

The proposed model uses energy distance to capture non-linear relationships between users, items and tags. Enhanced precision in settings with sparse data.

5   Conclusion

In this paper, we propose a unified framework based on energy distance for tag-based recommendation systems. This framework leverages energy distance metrics to capture complex nonlinear interactions in the user-item-tag space, thereby overcoming the limitations of traditional methods that rely on linear relationships or treat tags as simple metadata.

Experimental results on real-world datasets, such as Movielens 20M, show significant improvements in recommendation accuracy. The proposed method achieves up to 14% reduction in RMSE compared to baseline models, confirming the effectiveness of using energy distance in handling sparse data and modeling complex relationships between users, items, and tags.

References

1. Singh, R.H., Maurya, S., Tripathi, T., Narula, T., Srivastav, G.: Movie recommendation system using cosine similarity and KNN. Int. J. Eng. Adv. Technol. **9**(5), 556–559 (2020)

2. Chandrashekhar, H., Bhasker, B.: Personalized recommender system using entropy based collaborative filtering technique. **12**(3), 214 (2011).
3. Huynh, H.X., Phan, N.Q., Duong-Trung, N., Nguyen, H.T.T.: Collaborative filtering recommendation based on statistical implicative analysis. In: Advances in Computational Collective Intelligence: 12th International Conference, ICCCI 2020, Da Nang, Vietnam, November 30–December 3, 2020, Proceedings 12, pp. 224–235. Springer (2020)
4. Phan, L.P., Huynh, H.H., Huynh, H.X.: Hybrid recommendation based on implicative rating measures. In: Proceedings of the 2nd International Conference on Machine Learning and Soft Computing, 50–56 (2018)
5. Bogers, T. Technologies. Tag-based recommendation. 441–479 (2018)
6. Rizzo, M.L., Székely, G.J.: Energy distance. **8**(1), 27–38 (2016)
7. LeCun, Y., Chopra, S., Hadsell, R., Ranzato, M., Huang, F.J.: A tutorial on energy-based learning. **1**(0), (2006)
8. Harper, F.M., Konstan, J.A.: The movielens datasets: history and context. **5**(4), 1–19 (2015)
9. Ekstrand, M.D., Riedl, J.T., Konstan, J.A.J.F., Interaction, T.i.H.C.: Collaborative filtering recommender systems. **4**(2), 81–173 (2011)
10. Sarwar, B., Karypis, G., Konstan, J., Riedl, J.: Item-based collaborative filtering recommendation algorithms," presented at the Proceedings of the 10th international conference on World Wide Web, Hong Kong, Hong Kong (2001). Available: https://doi.org/10.1145/371 920.372071
11. Liang, H., Xu, Y., Li, Y., Nayak, R.: Tag based collaborative filtering for recommender systems. In: Rough Sets and Knowledge Technology: 4th International Conference, RSKT 2009, Gold Coast, Australia, July 14–16, 2009. Proceedings 4, pp. 666–673. Springer (2009)
12. Herlocker, J.L., Konstan, J.A., Terveen, L.G., Riedl, J.T.: Evaluating collaborative filtering recommender systems. **22**(1), 5–53 (2004)
13. Schafer, J.B., Frankowski, D., Herlocker, J., Sen, S.: Collaborative filtering recommender systems. In: The adaptive web: methods and strategies of web personalization, pp. 291–324. Springer (2007)
14. Naidu, G., Zuva, T., Sibanda, E.M.: a review of evaluation metrics in machine learning algorithms. In: Computer Science On-line Conference, pp. 15–25. Springer (2023)

Enhancing Water Level Forecasting Models Based on Ensemble Learning

Duong Thi Kim Chi[✉]

Institute of Information Technology and Digital Transformation Training, Thu Dau Mot University No. 06 Tran Van On, Phu Hoa Ward, Thu Dau Mot City, Binh Duong Binh Duong Province, Viet Nam
chidtk@tdmu.edu.vn

Abstract. Water shortages and concerns about water supply are prevalent in many parts of the world. Analyzing the factors that affect water reserves over time is crucial. This study developed a machine learning model for groundwater level forecasting based on various factors influencing water storage. The manuscript proposes a new method for automatically handling missing data and calculating temporal variables before including them in the training dataset. Subsequently, an ensemble learning approach was applied to build the water level forecasting model. The results demonstrate that the proposed model can accurately predict the trend of water level changes in storage areas such as aquifers and lakes. In particular, the forecasting performance of the proposed model, measured by R2 and MSE, shows outstanding results with an R2 score of 0.99 and an MSE of 0.004. This suggests significant potential for implementing water level forecasting models in real-world applications.

Keywords: Ensembles Learning · Light Gradient-Boosting Machine · XGBoost · Water level forecasting

1 Introduction

Climate change is happening globally, water shortages and floods are becom-ing more and more common around the world. Concerns about water resources are always present. Forecasting and assessing water levels are always of concern. Wa-ter level forecasting using modern techniques can be summarized as follows: ARIMA (Autoregressive Integrated Moving Average), SARIMA (Seasonal Auto-regressive Integrated Moving Average). Forecasting water levels in rivers, streams, and reservoirs is a crucial aspect of environmental management, and ARIMA and SARIMA models provide the tools to effectively model and predict any time series. However, both models can struggle with unusual data or outliers. Additional-ly, the forecast accuracy of SARIMA often degrades over time, especially in long-term forecasts [1–4].

Machine learning and deep learning methods can significantly enhance the efficiency of developing water level forecasting models for rivers and groundwater. In these studies,

H. X. Huynh et al. (Eds.): GOODTECHS 2024, LNICST 649, pp. 191–201, 2025.
https://doi.org/10.1007/978-3-032-01497-9_18

historical hydrological and weather factors are commonly utilized as input datasets for the forecasting models [10]. In this study, a novel water level forecasting model was developed based on a multivariate dataset including both hydrological and weather factors. In this study, a new water level forecasting model was built on a multivariate dataset including hydrological and weather factors. The proposed model incorporates time factors into the input features for the training data and utilizes an advanced ensemble learning algorithm, enabling accurate predictions for short-term datasets spanning a week [11]. The design solutions of the proposed model will be detailed in Sect. 2. The experimental process of the model will be specifically illustrated in Sect. 3. Section 4 will pro-vide an analysis and comparison of results with other studies on the same topic. Finally, Sect. 5 will summarize the achieved results.

In all experiments, machine learning models consistently outperform traditional statistical methods in terms of prediction accuracy and robustness. This is particularly evident in water level forecasting, where many deep learning methods have achieved outstanding results, including Artificial Neural Networks (ANN), Multilayer Percep-trons (MLP), Convolutional Neural Networks (CNN) [5], and Long Short-Term Memory networks (LSTM) [6–8]. Among these, LSTM stands out as a prominent solution. For instance, Anh Duy Nguyen (2022) [1] utilized LSTM to predict reservoir water levels based on a single factor. Even more impressive results were reported by D. Martinho et al. (2023) [9], employed modern machine learning models such as Extreme Learning Machine (ELM), Ex-treme Gradient Boosting (XGBoot), and Support Vector Regression (SVR) for forecasting. This study used a dataset comprising four factors: streamflow, precipi-tation, evaporation, and relative humidity, alongside water level. The forecasting results achieved an R2 accuracy of 0.97 with the XGB algorithm.

2   Methodology

2.1   Machine Learning Solutions Used to Build Forecasting Models.

2.1.1   Extreme Gradient Boosting (XGBoost):

XGBoost is a machine learning method based on the Gradient Boosting Ma-chine model developed by Jerome H. Friedman. However, XGBoost has under-gone significant development and improvement to enhance the efficiency and ac-curacy of the model [12]The core idea of XGBoost is its approach to building sequential decision trees. Each tree is constructed to minimize the loss function for data points that were misclassified by the previous trees. This sequential building of regression trees allows the model to learn from its mistakes, progressively im-proving its predictions. One of the notable strengths of XGBoost is the incorpora-tion of the Split Finding algorithm, which contributes to its speed in computation. This capability enables XGBoost to handle large datasets effectively while main-taining high accuracy, particularly when working with sparse data. Overall, XGBoost's enhancements make it a powerful tool in the realm of machine learn-ing, particularly for tasks involving regression and classification.

2.1.2 Light Gradient Boosting Machine (LightGBM):

LightGBM [13] is a machine learning method created by Microsoft Research Asia in 2017. LightGBM uses *some* special optimization techniques such as Gra-dient-based One-Side Sampling (GOSS) and Exclusive Feature Bundling (EFB) to speed up computation and reduce memory usage during model training. GOSS is an optimization technique used to sample data points and reduce the number of data points used during model training. EFB is an optimization technique used to group similar features together to reduce memory usage during model training. EFB stands for Exclusive Feature Bundling/Mutually Exclusive Feature Bundling. For data with high-dimensional sparse features, many mutually exclusive features (i.e., at most one feature out of many features has a non-zero value), EFB forms a "big feature" by merging many mutually exclusive features, thereby significantly reducing the number of features equivalent to the data dimensionality reduction method. This is very suitable for the feature set of the proposed dataset including lag features, and rolling features.

2.2 Time Series Indicators

The dataset used for the proposed model was collected and published by Acea Group. It pertains to unconfined aquifers, which can be considered a type of groundwater table that is also fed by the Chiascio River [14]. The groundwater level here is influenced by the following factors: rainfall, depth of the groundwater, temperature, drainage volume, and river hydrometry the water level of the Chiascio River.

2.2.1 Simple Moving Average (SMA)

The SMA is a crucial technique in time series forecasting analysis. It is particularly effective for smoothing data, making it easier to identify trends in datasets that contain discrete variables. The SMA was applied to two parameters: rainfall and drainage volume. Calculating and adding the 3 day; 5 day; 7 day. The SMA is typically stable and easy to track on a chart, offering quick and reliable overview of price trends, calculation formula shown in the in Eq. (1). [15]

$$SMA = \frac{A_1 + A_2 + ... + A_n}{n} \qquad (1)$$

In which: n = time period; Ai: the rainfall;drainage volume at each period.

2.2.2 Lag Technique

Lag features involve creating variables that represent previous values in a time series. These features are crucial for capturing temporal dependencies, al-lowing models to leverage historical data to improve forecasting accuracy. These features were considered as input data for machine learning models for water level forecasting models for rivers, lakes, and groundwater [16]. In this proposal, the lag technique is applied to the parameters: groundwater depth, temperature, and river hydrology. These parameters are calculated with lags of 1 day, 3 days, 5 days, and 7 days. This means that the values of these parame-ters are shifted forward by 1 day, 3 days, 5 days, and 7 days to create new fea-tures.

2.3 Proposed Model

To build a water level fluctuation prediction model, machine learning algorithms such as XGBoost, LightGBM are used. The detailed steps are as follows in Fig. 1.

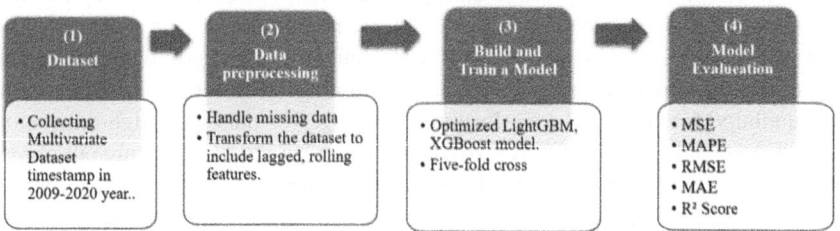

Fig. 1. General procedure used to Prediction of water levels

The detailed steps are as follows:

(1) Dataset: The dataset used in the experiment pertains to the Petrignano aquifer [14]. The dataset consists of 5,223 rows and includes five attributes: temperature, rainfall, groundwater depth, drainage volume, water level of the Chiascio River. The dataset used in experiment spans from January 1, 2009, to June 30, 2020.

(2) Data Preprocessing
Handling Missing Data:
     In this study, the missing data includes two main types: discrete data, such as rainfall, and continuous data, such as groundwater depth, temperature, drainage volume, and river hydrology. To address missing data, this manuscript proposes two different techniques: (i) For discrete data, missing values are imputed to zero; (ii) For continuous data, a linear interpolation technique is applied to estimate missing values.

Building Time series features for training data
     The input training dataset consists of five parameters: *depth groundwater, temperature, drainage volumes river hydrometry, and rainfall* In this framework, *depth to groundwater* serves as the output variable, while the other variables act as input variables. In this proposal, the lagged variables are combined into the set of input variables. The determination of the number of lags or SMA to forecast groundwater levels over four time intervals (1 day, 3 days, 5 days, 7 days) is carried out in two ways:

- Calculating the SMA for the variables rainfall (R) and drainage_volumes (V).
- Calculating the lag values for the remaining three variables: *depth to groundwater* (D), *temperature* (T), and *river hydrometry* (H).

     Figure 2 ilustrates the SMA values of rainfall in D1_Data. Additionally, slope values were generated for the attributes to improve the recognition and stability of the model. Figure 3 illustrates the slope SMA values.
     Figure 4 illustrates the MA_Lag values for *depth_to_groundwater, temperature, and river_hydrometry* in the dataset referred to as D1_Data.

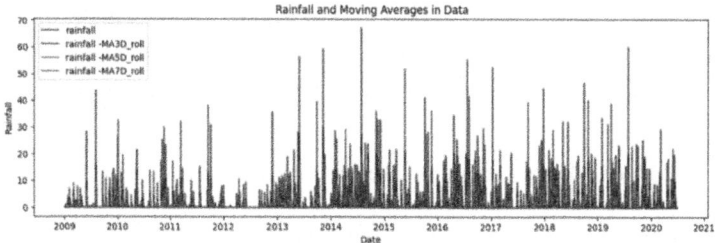

Fig. 2. Illustrates the relationship between SMA values for rainfall in the D1_Data

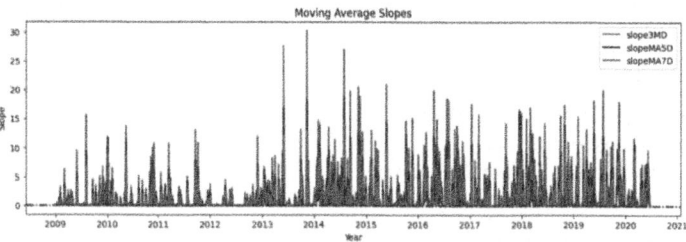

Fig. 3. Illustration of slope values in Dataset

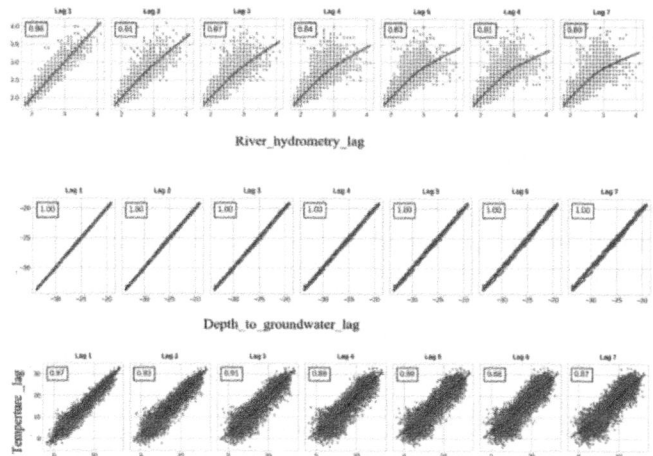

Fig. 4. Illustration of lag features in D1_Data: temperature_lag, river_hydrometry_lag, and depth_to_groundwater_lag

(3) Building the Proposed Model: The steps involved in building the proposed model during this phase include:

(i) Training model; (ii)Tuning the hyperparameters to optimize model performance; (iii) Building and evaluating models to predict water level fluctuations using the XGBoost and LightGBM algorithms; (iv) Comparing the performance of the models to select the best one for forecasting water levels over a 7-day period.

(4) Model evaluation: To assess and measure the performance of the water level fluctuation forecasting model, this study employs several commonly used metrics. These metrics provide insights into the accuracy and effectiveness of the model in Table 1 [15]:

Table 1. Metrics to evaluate the performance of proposed models

Performance metrics	Equation
Mean absolute percentage error (MAPE): MAPE calculates the average absolute percentage error of predicted values compared to actual values, providing an intuitive view of forecast accuracy	$MAPE = \frac{1}{n} \sum_{i=1}^{n} \frac{|Y_i - \hat{Y}_i|}{|Y_i|} \cdot 100\%$ where: Y_i is the actual value, i is the predicted value, n is the number of observations
Mean squared error (MSE): The MSE is measures the average of the squares of the errors. It penalizes larger errors more than MAE, making it sensitive to outliers	$MSE = \frac{1}{n} \sum_{i=1}^{n} |Y_i - \hat{Y}_i|^2$
Root mean squared error (RMSE): The RMSE is a widely used metric for assessing the accuracy of a predictive model	$RMSE = \sqrt{\frac{1}{n} \sum_{i=1}^{n} (Y_i - \hat{Y}_i)^2}$
R-squared (R^2): The R^2 represents the proportion of the variance in the dependent variable (e.g., currency prices) that can be explained by the independent variables (predictors) in the model	$R^2 = 1 - \frac{\sum_{i=1}^{n} (Y_i - \hat{Y}_i)^2}{\sum_{i=1}^{n} (Y_i - \overline{Y}_i)^2}$
Mean absolute error (MAE): The MAE is measures the average absolute difference between predicted and actual values. It provides a straightforward interpretation of prediction accuracy	$MAE = \frac{1}{n} \sum_{i=1}^{n} |Y_i - \hat{Y}_i|$

3   Model Forecast Results and Discussion

3.1   Model Forecast Results

This D1_Data consists of 5,223 rows and 20 attributes. The two algorithms, XGBoost and LightGBM, were utilized to build the water level forecasting model. The results of both models are summarized in Table 2.

Both models provide the same water level forecast for the following day. However, when comparing performance, the model developed using the LightGBM algorithm demonstrates superior results compared to the one built with XGBoost. Figure 5 clearly illustrates the overall forecasting results of the model developed using LightGBM, showcasing its effectiveness in predicting water levels.

Table 2. Performance comparison results of the two proposed models

Metrics/models	XGBoost	LightGBM
MAPE	0.002139	0.00201
MSE	0.005	0.00445
RMSE	0.069	0.0667
MAE	0.0538	0.05
R-squared	0.999	0.999
Explained variance	0.999	0.999
Next day predicted level water	− 25.227	− 25.227

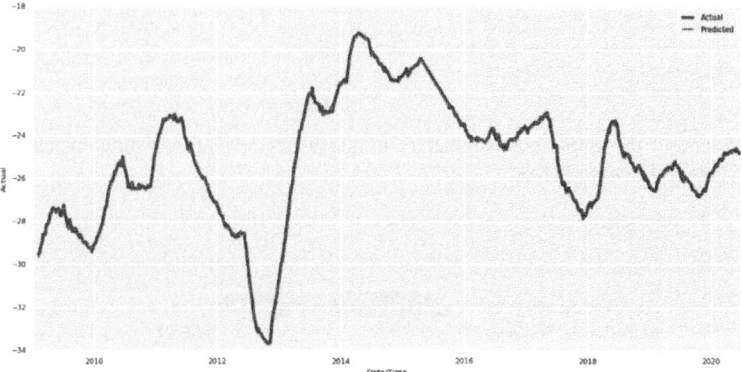

Fig. 5. The data trend with the D1 dataset using LightGBM

In the proposed study, SHAP (SHapley Additive exPlanations) [17] is utilized as a powerful tool to explain the influence of input variables on the model output. The mean absolute values of SHAP for the water level forecasting model in the D1_Data dataset are shown in Figs. 6, 7. An analysis of the input factors yielded the following results:

Depth to Groundwater: Exhibits very high SHAP values, indicating it is the most significant predictor of groundwater levels. Minor changes in this variable can greatly affect forecasts.

3-Day Depth to groundwater Moving Average (MA3D): While its SHAP value is lower than the current depth, it still plays an important role in smoothing short-term fluctuations and contributes to predictions.

5-Day Depth to groundwater Moving Average (MA5D): Provides insights into medium-term trends, but its impact is lesser compared to the 3-day moving average.

Temperature: Generally has a minimal direct impact on groundwater levels.

7-Day Moving Average (MA7D): Shows a negligible influence, suggesting that long-term temperature trends are not particularly informative for groundwater predictions.

Drainage *Volume:* The current drainage volume is crucial, with both the current value and short-term averages showing significant predictive power.

5-Day (MA5D) and 7-Day (MA7D): Both moving averages provide useful, albeit smaller, insights into drainage trends.

Other Features: The combined influence of 11 other features is minimal, indicating these factors are less critical for model performance.

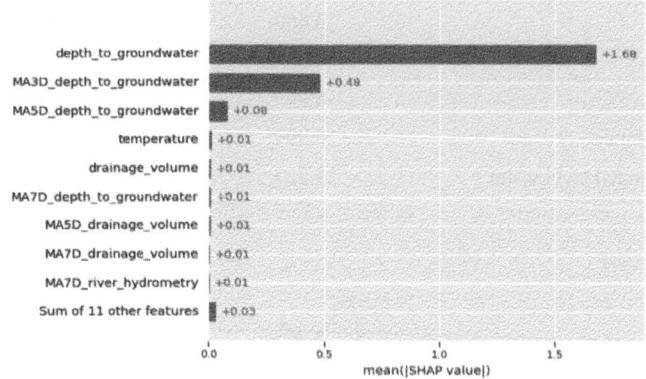

Fig. 6. Presenting the important parameters of the water level forecasting model using the LightGBM algorithm with SHAP

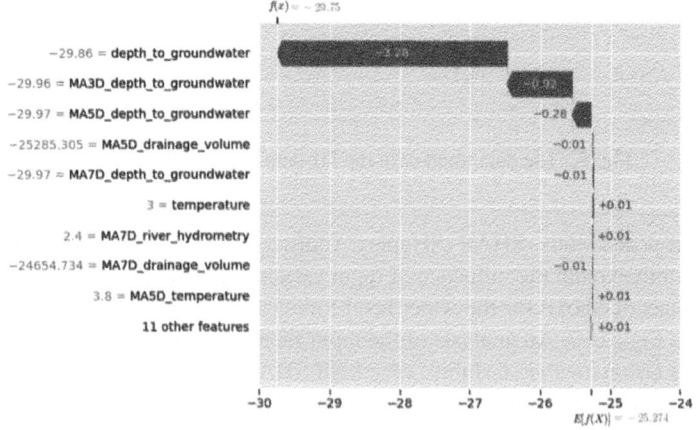

Fig. 7. Results of parameter analysis of the water level forecasting model using the LightGBM algorithm with waterfall SHAP

The water level forecasting model in this study employs ensemble learning algorithms such as LightGBM and XGBoost to compare its performance with other studies that share the same research goal of water level forecasting. The manuscript benchmarks two studies: one focusing on univariate datasets and the other on multivariate datasets.

For the first comparison, the study by Nguyen (2022) [1] represents an application of machine learning solutions to forecast univariate datasets, achieving results of NSE

$= 0.918$ and MSE $= 85.62$. In contrast, the proposed model delivers equivalent results with $R^2 = 0.997$ and MAE $= 0.05$.

The second benchmark is the advanced study by Alfeu D. Martinho (2023) [9], which has implemented cutting-edge machine learning methods for multivariate datasets. This author created a new feature set using the lag technique, adding 28 features to the machine learning model training dataset. The results from Alfeu D. Martinho's proposal are impressive, with an R^2 value of 0.979.

Overall, the results of the proposed model in this study demonstrate stronger performance than both the univariate and multivariate water level prediction models mentioned above. Table 3 summarized the performance metrics of the proposed model alongside other relevant studies, facilitating a clear comparison of efficacy in water level forecasting.

Table 3. Performance Comparison of the proposed forecasting model with other models

Ref	Dataset (Features, Rows)	Method	MAPE	MSE	RMSE	MAE	R^2	Explained variance	Next day predicted level water
Present	**(5, 5223)**	XGBoost	0.0021	0.005	0.069	0.0538	0.999	0.999	− 25.227
		LightGBM	**0.0020**	**0.0044**	**0.066**	**0.0500**	**0.999**	**0.999**	**− 25.227**
Anh Duy Nguyen, 2022 [1]	(1, 13140)	LSTM/ensemble-learning with genetic	0.0258	85.62	0.053	7.17	–	–	–
Alfeu D. Martinho, 2023 [9]	(4, 5844)_D1	XGBoost	5.64	–	0.131	0.094	0.979	0.994	0.994
	(4, 834)_D7	XGBoost	10,95	–	0.261	0.186	0.923	–	–

4 Conclusions

This study presents a tree ensemble learning model designed to predict fluctuations in underground water levels, showing strong potential for real-world applications in environmental assessment and resource management. The model's accuracy improved significantly with the inclusion of rolling averages and lagged values. Ensemble Learning techniques like XGBoost and LightGBM were employed to effectively manage the trade-offs between bias and variance, reducing overfitting and enhancing generalization.The analysis emphasized important parameters, including the 3-day moving average of drainage volumes and the 7-day moving average of rainfall, which significantly influence groundwater level predictions.The model demonstrated the ability to perform well with varying dataset sizes, making it adaptable for different applications in water resource management where data quality and availability fluctuate.While the model showed strong performance, there is room for improvement in parameter tuning for each ensemble learning model.The proposed model offers a robust tool for forecasting groundwater levels, with significant implications for environmental management and planning. Its combination of multiple ensemble learning models and comprehensive parameterization enables it to manage complex datasets effectively, supporting informed decision-making and resource management.

References

1. Nguyen, A.D., Le Nguyen, P., Vu, V.H., Pham, Q.V., Nguyen, V.H., Nguyen, M.H., Nguyen, K.: Accurate discharge and water level forecasting using ensemble learning with genetic algorithm and singular spectrum analysis-based denoising. Sci. Rep. **12**(1), 19870 (2022)
2. Ahmadi, A., et al.: Groundwater level modeling with machine learning: a systematic review and meta-analysis. Water **14**(6), 949 (2022)
3. Rahman, A.S., Hosono, T., Quilty, J.M., Das, J., Basak, A.: Multiscale groundwater level forecasting: coupling new machine learning approaches with wavelet transforms. Adv. Water Resour. **141**, 103595 (2020)
4. Pham, Q.B., Kumar, M., Di Nunno, F., Elbeltagi, A., Granata, F., Islam, A.R.M.T., Anh, D.T.: Groundwater level prediction using machine learning algorithms in a drought-prone area. Neural Comput. Appl. **34**(13), 10751–10773 (2022)
5. Sudriani, Y., Ridwansyah, I., Rustini, H.A.: Long short term memory (LSTM) recurrent neural network (RNN) for discharge level prediction and forecast in cimandiri river, indonesia, *(2019)*. In: IOP Conf. Ser. Earth Environ, (2019)
6. Le, X.-H., Ho, H.V., Lee, G., Jung, S.: Application of long short-term memory (lstm) neural network for flood forecasting. Water, (2022)
7. Lin, H., Gharehbaghi, A., Zhang, Q., Band, S.S., Pai, H.T., Chau, K.W., Mosavi, A.: Time series-based groundwater level forecasting using gated recurrent unit deep neural networks. Eng. Appl. Comput. Fluid Mech. **16**(1), 1655–1672 (2022)
8. Shen, C., Lawson, K.: Applications of deep learning in hydrology. In: Deep Learning for the Earth Sciences: A Comprehensive Approach to Remote Sensing, Climate Science, and Geosciences, pp. 283-297 (2021).
9. Martinho, A.D., Hippert, H.S., Goliatt, L.: Short-term streamflow modeling using data-intelligence evolutionary machine learning models. Sci. Rep. **13**(1), 13824 (2023)
10. Kochhar, A., Singh, H., Sahoo, S., Litoria, P.K., Pateriya, B.: Prediction and forecast of pre-monsoon and post-monsoon groundwater level: using deep learning and statistical modelling. Model. Earth Syst. Environ. **8**(2), 2317–2329 (2022)
11. Khan, J., Lee, E., Balobaid, A.S., Kim, K.: A comprehensive review of conventional, machine leaning, and deep learning models for groundwater level (GWL) forecasting. Appl. Sci. **13**(4), 2743 (2023)
12. Chen, T., Guestrin, C.: XGBoost: a scalable tree boosting system. In: KDD '16: Proceedings of the 22nd ACM SIGKDD International Conference on Knowledge Discovery and Data Mining, Association for Computing Machinery, New York, NY, United States, (2016)
13. Ke, G.: LightGBM: a highly efficient gradient boosting decision tree. Adv. Neural Inf. Process. Syst. 3147–3155 (2017)
14. "https://www.kaggle.com/c/acea-water-prediction/data," Acea Group, 13 4 2024. [Online]. Available: https://www.kaggle.com/c/acea-water-prediction/data
15. Islam, M.S., Hossain, E.: Foreign exchange currency rate prediction using a GRU-LSTM hybrid network. Soft Comput. Lett. **3**, 100009 (2021)

16. Tongal, H., Booij, M.J.: Simulation and forecasting of streamflows using machine learning models coupled with base flow separation. J. Hydrol. **564**, 266–282 (2018)
17. Mangalathu, S., Hwang, S.-H., Jeon, J.-S.: Failure mode and effects analysis of RC members based on machine-learning-based SHapley Additive exPlanations (SHAP) approach. Eng. Struct. **219**, 110927 (2020)

Advanced Predictive Modeling of Forex Market Fluctuations Using Ensembles Learning

Duong Thi Kim Chi[1]([✉]), Luong Thi Hong Lan[2], and Nguyen Le Minh Hoa[1]

[1] Institute of Information Technology and Digital Transformation Training, Thu Dau Mot University No. 06 Tran Van On, Phu Hoa Ward, Thu Dau Mot City, Binh Duong Binh Duong Province, Vietnam
chidtk@tdmu.edu.vn

[2] Faculty of Information Technology, Hanoi Industry University, 6th Floor, A1 Building - No. 298 Cau Dien Street, Bac Tu Liem District, Hanoi, Vietnam

Abstract. In this study, the authors proposed a new method for constructing an developing an effective model aimed at assessing and predicting fluctuations in the foreign exchange (Forex) market using the Ensemble learning method. Accurately forecasting the trends in Forex trading offers investors more suitable options for their trading decisions. The model is equipped with the capability to automatically process trading parameters from online information sources, allowing it to predict market trends with high accuracy. It integrates time-related features and intelligently optimizes parameters for training, which contributes to its clear stability and high performance. Specifically, the model achieved impressive performance metrics, with an R-squared value of 0.999 and a root mean squared error (RMSE) of 0.00357. This proposal not only offers an effective method for predicting fluctuations in the Forex market but also highlights significant potential for future developments in assessment and prediction models within the currency field.

Keywords: Forex market trends · Random Forest · XGBoost · Trading indicators · Currency market forecasting

1 Introduction

Economic trends in countries around the world are indeed constantly changing, and the ability to forecast and evaluate stock and currency market patterns has become increasingly important. To effectively analyze the factors influencing the foreign exchange market, it is essential to utilize reliable and continuously updated data sources from the online market. In this context, machine learning and deep learning algorithms have emerged as powerful tools for developing predictive and classification models for the currency market. Here are some of the popular models used for forecasting:

- **Autoregressive (AR):** The AR model utilizes past values of a time series to forecast future values, making it particularly suitable for continuous data over time. This model is effective in capturing trends and patterns inherent in historical data.

© ICST Institute for Computer Sciences, Social Informatics and Telecommunications Engineering 2025
Published by Springer Nature Switzerland AG 2025. All Rights Reserved
H. X. Huynh et al. (Eds.): GOODTECHS 2024, LNICST 649, pp. 202–211, 2025.
https://doi.org/10.1007/978-3-032-01497-9_19

- **Support Vector Machine (SVM):** SVM is a robust algorithm used for classification and regression tasks. It helps in determining the separating boundaries between different classes of data, making it useful for identifying trends and patterns in the currency market.
- **Bayesian Additive Regression Trees (BART):** BART is a flexible regression model that can handle nonlinear relationships and interactions within the data. Its probabilistic framework allows for uncertainty quantification in predictions, which is beneficial for understanding the variability in market behavior.
- **Random Forest (RF):** As an ensemble learning method, RF combines multiple decision trees to enhance accuracy and mitigate the risk of overfitting. This approach is particularly effective in handling large datasets with complex interactions among variables.

These models have shown significant promise in improving forecasting accuracy and providing insights into market dynamics. Table 1 in your document likely illustrates the effectiveness of these algorithms and their specific performance metrics in forecasting tasks.

Table 1. Illustrates the effectiveness of these algorithm for forecasting tasks

Ref	Methods	Performance metrics			
		MAPE	MSE	RMSE	R-squared
Petropoulos, 2017 [1]	SVM, RF, BART, NN, and AR	–	–	0.0074, 0.0073, 0.0075, 0.008, 0.0084	–
Das SR, 2020 [2]	ELM-TLBO	0.13599	0.0000877	0,00500	
Islam, Md Saiful, 2021 [3]	GRU-LSTM hybrid network	0.00261	0.00001	0.00362	0.99205
P Escudero, 2021 [4]	Recurrent neural networks and ARIMA	–	0.00001615	0.004	–
M. A. Junior, 2022 [5]	LSTM	–	0.00001807	0.004251	–

From our literature review, we observed that many researchers have employed machine learning methods to predict exchange rates. However, there are few studies that automatically incorporate time-varying attributes into the training dataset, despite the fact that these features have a proven direct impact on forecasting models. Our proposed method aims to enhance the accuracy and reliability of exchange rate predictions, ultimately benefiting investors and practitioners in the financial market. The motivation behind this study is to improve the capability of time series models in predicting exchange rate prices through a suitable machine learning approach. By integrating time-varying attributes, we seek to develop a more robust predictive framework that can better adapt to the dynamic nature of exchange rate movements.

2 Methodology

2.1 Machine Learning Solutions Used to Build Forecasting Models

Random Forest (RF) [6]: RF algorithm is a powerful tool in the realm of ensemble learning, known for its ability to enhance predictive accuracy by leveraging multiple decision trees. The process of building a tree: The process of building a tree T from the training data set X involves:

(i). Randomly sampling subsets from the training set T;

(ii). Building Independent Trees: Construct regression trees for each subset $(T_1, T_2,..T_K)$, with the characteristic that the trees are completely independent of each other;

(iii). Finally, combining all the trees to create a forecasting model (by averaging or majority voting the forecast results from the aforementioned regression trees). Each subsequent tree is built using results from previous trees. The regression function obtained from the regression tree is:

$$\hat{f}(x) = b_1 f_1(x) + b_2 f_2(x) + \cdots + b_T f_T(x), \tag{1}$$

with the general regression function:

$$Y = \beta_1 + \beta_2 X_{2i} + \beta_3 X_{3i} + \ldots + \beta_k X_{ki} + \varepsilon_i, \tag{2}$$

where Y is a measure of the model's predictive performance,

$X_1, X_2,..X_p$ are the dependent variables, and $\beta_1, \beta_2,.. \beta_p$: are the regression coefficients. The residual error is given by $\varepsilon = Y - \hat{f}(x)$.

XGBoost (Extreme Gradient Boosting) [7]: XGBoost is an ensemble learning method in machine learning. It combines multiple regression trees to create a more powerful predictive model. It employs a gradient boosting technique to build each regression tree sequentially, with each tree aiming to improve the difference between the current predictions and the actual values. XGBoost is a form of ensemble learning that can efficiently handle large datasets and can run on multiple processors in parallel. Additionally, XGBoost can be used for both classification and regression tasks and can be tuned to fit various types of data.

2.2 Dataset

Forex trading indicators are specialized analytical tools that traders use to assess market trends, evaluate price volatility, and determine trading direction. These mathematical calculations, based on price, volume, or other market data, provide traders with visual representations to interpret market conditions and identify potential opportunities. Each indicator serves a unique function in trading analysis [8]. Some are considered leading indicators, attempting to predict future price changes, while others are lagging indicators that confirm current trends. Technical indicators can be categorized into several main types. Traders can optimize their entry and exit points using trend indicators such as the

Relative Strength Index (RSI), Average True Range (ATR), and Simple Moving Average (SMA), which are essential features for forecasting in financial trading.

Relative Strength Index (RSI): The RSI can signal to investors when a trend may be on the verge of changing. The RSI index is calculated according to the following Eq. (3) [9, 10]:

$$RSI = 100 - \left[\frac{100}{1 + \frac{\text{Average increase}}{\text{Average loss}}} \right] \quad (3)$$

Average True Range (ATR): The ATR is a vital tool in technical analysis used to measure price volatility. It determines the average level of volatility of an asset over a specific period, making it particularly useful for assessing market fluctuations. The ATR is calculated according to Eq. (4) [11, 12]

$$ATR = \frac{ATR_i.(n-1) + TR}{n} \quad (4)$$

In which: n = time period, TR = true range. The true range is calculated as follows: (i) The highest price of today minus the lowest price of today; (ii) The absolute value of the highest price of today minus the closing price of yesterday.

Simple Moving Average (SMA): The SMA is calculated by summing the closing prices of an asset over a specified period and then dividing that sum by the number of trading sessions within that period. The SMA is typically stable and easy to track on a chart, offering investors a quick and reliable overview of price trends, as shown in Eq. (5). [13, 14]

$$SMA = \frac{A_1 + A_2 + ... + A_n}{n} \quad (5)$$

In which: n = time period; A_i: the closing price at each period.

2.3 Methods

This article will utilize online currency trading data from Yahoo Finance (https://finance.yahoo.com/recent-quotes (2023)) [15], and combine trend indicators like RSI, ATR, and SMA to build a dataset for the proposed model. The process for the Forex trend forecasting model using ensemble learning solutions is illustrated in Fig. 1.

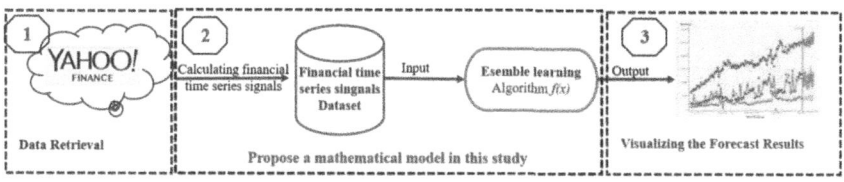

Fig. 1. Forex trend forecasting model using ensemble learning solutions

(1). Data Retrieval: Download currency trading data from Yahoo Finance, including the Open, High, Low, Close, Adjusted Close, and Volume metrics.

(2.1). Database Construction: Create a database for the forecasting model by calculating values such as ATR, RSI, Average, MA40, MA80, and TargetNextClose from the Yahoo Finance dataset;

(2.2). Model Development: Build the forecasting model using machine learning algorithms like Decision Tree and XGBoost to predict cash flow trends.

(3). Visualizing the Forecast Results: visualize the forecast results of the currency market for the next day.

Table 2. Metrics to evaluate the performance of proposed models

Performance metrics	Equation
Mean Absolute Percentage Error (MAPE): Measures the average absolute difference between predicted and actual values	$MAPE = \frac{1}{n} \sum_{i=1}^{n} \frac{|Y_i - \hat{Y}_i|}{|Y_i|} . 100\%$ Where Y_i represents the actual value, i represents the predicted value, and n is the number of observed values.
Mean squared error (MSE): The MSE is measures the average of the squares of the errors. It penalizes larger errors more than MAE, making it sensitive to outliers	$MSE = \frac{1}{n} \sum_{i=1}^{n} |Y_i - \hat{Y}_i|^2$
Root Mean **Squared Error (RMSE):** The RMSE is a widely used metric for assessing the accuracy of a predictive model	$RMSE = \sqrt{\frac{1}{n} \sum_{i=1}^{n} (Y_i - \hat{Y}_i)^2}$
R-squared (R^2): The R^2 represents the proportion of the variance in the dependent variable (e.g., currency prices) that can be explained by the independent variables (predictors) in the model	$R^2 = 1 - \frac{\sum_{i=1}^{n} (Y_i - \hat{Y}_i)^2}{\sum_{i=1}^{n} (Y_i - \overline{Y}_i)^2}$
Mean Absolute Error (MAE): The MAE is measures the average absolute difference between predicted and actual values. It provides a straightforward interpretation of prediction accuracy	$MAE = \frac{1}{n} \sum_{i=1}^{n} |Y_i - \hat{Y}_i|$
Explained Variance: Explained variance is a metric that quantifies how much of the total variance in the dependent variable (e.g., currency prices) is accounted for by the model's predictions	$Explained Variance = 1 - \frac{Var(Y - \hat{Y})}{Var(Y)}$

3   Performance Metrics

Evaluating the performance of currency forecasting models is crucial for un-derstanding their effectiveness and reliability. Here are some common methods and metrics used for this evaluation in Table 2 [3]:

Table 3. Forecast performance of the model.

Algorithm	MAPE	MSE	RMSE	MAE	R-squared	Explained variance	Next day predicted close
Random forest	**0.002567**	**0.0000127**	**0.00357**	**0.00263**	**0.998**	**0.998**	**1.0835**
Xgboost	0.002812	0.0000165	0.004	0.0030	0.998	0.998	1.0806
Gradient Boosting Machines	0.002734	0.0000211	0.00045	0.0031	0.997	0.997	1.0926
P Escudero, 2021 [4]	-	0.00001615	0.004	0,0031	-	-	-
M. A. Junior, 2022 [5]	-	0.00001807	0.004251	0.003365	-	-	-
Das SR, 2020 [2]	0.13599	0.00008771	0,00500	0.045	-	-	-

4   Implementation Prediction Model Results

4.1   Repair Dataset

Using the currency trading dataset sourced from Yahoo Finance, which includes Open, High, Low, and Close prices, we constructed a training database that incorporates these four values along with additional indicators: ATR, RSI, Average, MA40, MA80, MA160, and TargetNextClose. Figure 2 illustrates the directional pulses of each value downloaded from Yahoo Finance.

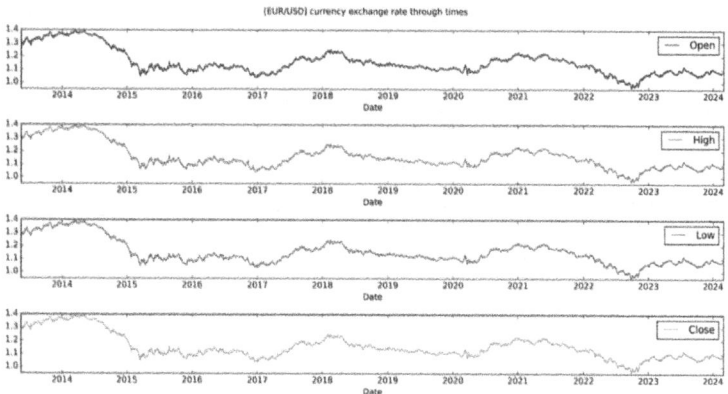

Fig. 2. Four attributes form the foundation of the dataset

Then The additional indicators are described as followsWith the currency trading dataset sourced from Yahoo Finance, which includes Open, High, Low, and Close prices, we constructed a training database that incorporates these four values alongside additional indicators: ATR, RSI, Average, MA40, MA80, MA160, and TargetNextClose. Figure 2 illustrates the directional pulses of each value downloaded from Yahoo Finance. Then we constructed a training database that incorporates these four values alongside additional indicators: ATR, RSI, Average, MA40, MA80, MA160, and TargetNextClose. The additional indicators are described as follows:

Moving Average: The average price of the currency pair has been calculated and added to the dataset. This moving average reflects the average of the bid and ask prices, serving as a simple indicator of market sentiment.

MA40 (40-Day Moving Average): The Simple Moving Average (SMA) of the closing price over a 40-day period has been computed and included. The SMA is a trend-following indicator that smooths price fluctuations, aiding in the identification of trends.

MA80 (80-Day Moving Average): An 80-day SMA has been calculated and added to the dataset, providing insights into longer-term market trends.

MA160 (160-Day Moving Average): A 160-day SMA has also been computed and included in the dataset, enhancing the analysis of longer-term price trends.mentioned models including moving averages (MA40, MA80, and MA160).

Therefore, with the initial six attributes as in including: Open, High, Low, Close, Adj Close, Volume, the study has added 15 additional attributes represented including: ATR, RSI, Average, MA40, MA80, MA160, slopeMA40, slopeMA80, slopeMA160, AverageSlope, RSISlope, Target, TargetNextClose. Figure 3 illustrates the relationship between the 40-day (MA40), 80-day (MA80), and 160-day (MA160) moving averages. Figure 4 illustrates the relationship between slopeMA40, slopeMA80, slopeMA160 moving averages slops. This visualization allows traders to observe how the different moving averages interact with each other and how they respond to price movements over varying time frames.

Fig. 3. Illustrates the relationship between the 40-day

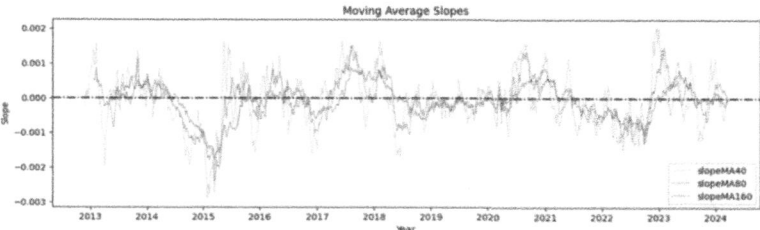

Fig. 4. Illustrates the relationship between different moving average slopes.

4.2 Summary of Forecast Performance and Comparison with Other Models

Implementation of the methodology often utilizes programming language such as Python and tools like Pandas, NumPy, Matplotlib, and SHAP. We also explored machine learning tools like Scikit-learn. These tools facilitate efficient data handling, model training, and evaluation, supporting reproducibility and scalability in time series analysis workflows. We evaluated several ensemble learning models, including bagging methods like Random Forest and gradient boosting machines like XGBoost. Quantitatively, the comparison revealed significant improvements in forecasting accuracy metrics such as: MAPE, MSE, RMSE, MAE, R-squared for ensemble learning models.

The forecasting model employing the Random Forest algorithm has demonstrated notable performance in predicting currency prices and evaluating currency flows. Below is a summary of its forecast performance, along with a comparison to other models, The results are summarized in Table 3.

The forecasting model employed in this study utilizes the Random Forest algorithm, which has shown favorable results across various scenarios compared to other models, as highlighted in multiple studies [2, 4, 5]. This positions Random Forest as a robust machine learning approach, integrating multiple decision trees within an ensemble framework.

A significant advantage of this proposed model is its ability to autonomously identify important variables within the dataset, thereby enhancing prediction accuracy. Additionally, it mitigates the risk of overfitting through the use of multiple decision trees and bootstrap aggregation techniques, as illustrated in Figs. 5, 6.

The SHAP waterfall chart illustrates the effects of features transformed into probabilities, as shown in Fig. 6. In this context, $E[f(x)]$ represents the baseline prediction of the Random Forest model, while $f(x)$ denotes the actual prediction for the specific case being analyzed. All SHAP values are converted to probabilities, providing a clear understanding of each feature's contribution to the final prediction. In Fig. 6, the model identifies nine important factors that directly influence the prediction outcome. This clarifies the roles of the baseline and actual predictions and emphasizes the importance of the features identified in the waterfall chart.

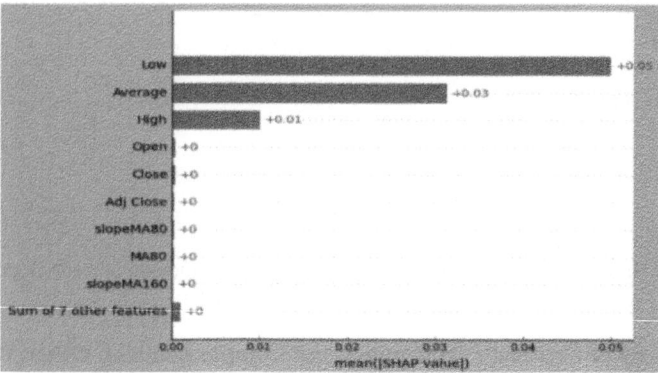

Fig. 5. Feature Importance;

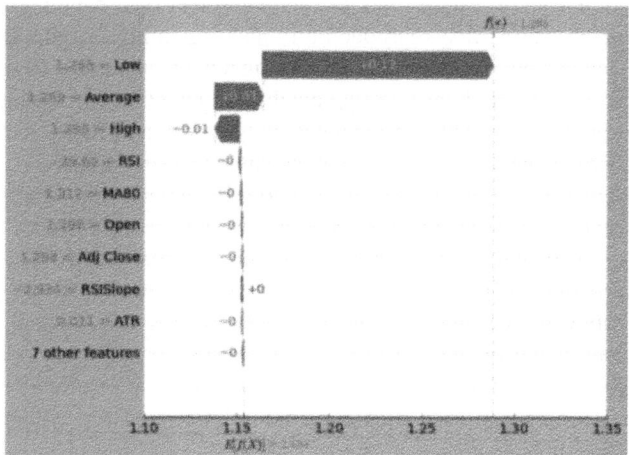

Fig. 6. Important features in random forest model with SHAP waterfall

5   Conclusions

In this study, the author proposed a novel method for building a forecasting model to predict volatility in the foreign exchange market (Forex). By integrating essential features for forecasting in financial trading: such as the Relative Strength Index (RSI), Average True Range (ATR), and Simple Moving Average (SMA). The training dataset was enhanced, enabling the proposed model to outperform existing machine learning methods. The model's ability to provide more accurate forecasts of market volatility empowers investors to make timely and informed decisions, which leads to better risk management, improved portfolio performance, and increased investment returns. Overall, this research aims to equip investors with powerful tools to identify growth patterns based on buying and selling prices in the market. The findings of this study contribute not only to the field of currency trading but also to the broader domain of machine learning applications in finance.

References

1. Petropoulos, A., Chatzis, S.P., Siakoulis, V., Vlachogiannakis, N.: A stacked generalization system for automated FOREX portfolio trading. Expert Syst. Appl. **90**, 290–302 (2017)
2. Das, S.R., Mishra, D., Rout, M.: A hybridized ELM-Jaya forecasting model for currency exchange prediction. J. King Saud Univ. Comput. Inf. Sci. **32**(3), 345–366 (2020)
3. Islam, M.S., Hossain, E.: Foreign exchange currency rate prediction using a GRU-LSTM hybrid network. Soft Comput. Lett. **3**, 100009 (2021)
4. Escudero, P., Alcocer, W., Paredes, J.: Recurrent neural networks and ARIMA models for euro/dollar exchange rate forecasting. Appl. Sci. **11**(12), 5658 (2021)
5. Ayitey Junior, M., Appiahene, P., Appiah, O.: Forex market forecasting with two-layer stacked long short-term memory neural network (LSTM) and correlation analysis. J. Electr. Syst. Inf. Technol.s **9**(1), 14 (2022)
6. Chen, T., Guestrin, C.: Xgboost: a scalable tree boosting system. In: Proceedings of the 22nd ACM SIGKDD International Conference on Knowledge Discovery and Data Mining, pp. 785–794. (2016)
7. Sagi, O., Rokach, L.: Ensemble learning: a survey. Wiley Interdiscip. Rev. Data Min. Knowl. Discov. **8**(4), e1249 (2018)
8. Shynkevich, Y., McGinnity, T.M., Coleman, S.A., Belatreche, A., Li, Y.: Forecasting price movements using technical indicators: investigating the impact of varying input window length. Neurocomputing **264**, 71–88 (2017)
9. Pramudya, R.: Technical analysis to determine buying and selling signal in stock trade. Int. J. Financ. Bank. Stud. **2147–4486**(9), 58–67 (2020)
10. Pramudya, R., Ichsani, S.: Efficiency of technical analysis for the stock trading. Int. J. Financ. Bank. Stud. **9**(1), 58–67 (2020)
11. Aslam, F., Mughal, K.S., Ali, A., Mohmand, Y.T.: Forecasting Islamic securities index using artificial neural networks: performance evaluation of technical indicators. J. Econ. Admin. Sci. **37**(2), 253–271 (2021)
12. Ntakaris, A., Kanniainen, J., Gabbouj, M., Iosifidis, A.: Mid-price prediction based on machine learning methods with technical and quantitative indicators. PLoS ONE **15**(6), e0234107 (2020)
13. Dongrey, S.: Study of market indicators used for technical analysis. Int. J. Eng. Manag. Res. **12**(2), 64–83 (2022)
14. Kardile, R., Ugale, T., Mohanty, S.N.: Stock price predictions using crossover SMA. In: 2021 9th International Conference on Reliability, Infocom Technologies and Optimization (Trends and Future Directions)(ICRITO), pp. 1–5. IEEE (2021)
15. Jagwani, J., Gupta, M., Sachdeva, H., Singhal, A. (2018). Stock price forecasting using data from yahoo finance and analysing seasonal and nonseasonal trend. In: 2018 Second International Conference on Intelligent Computing and Control Systems (ICICCS), pp. 462–467. IEEE.

Data Analysis and Classification of the News

Tran Ngoc Viet$^{(\boxtimes)}$, Doan Ngoc Do, Nguyen Tuyen Linh, and Tran Kim My Van

Faculty of Information Technology, Van Lang University, Ho Chi Minh City, Vietnam
{viet.tn,linh.nt,van.tkm}@vlu.edu.vn,
do.207ct68625@vanlanguni.vn

Abstract. In the Fourth Industrial Revolution Era with the fast-growing of multiple types of massive data, digitalized content as well as text-based information, which is increased through social media like Youtube, Facebook,... Many scientists worldwide are deeply interested in data analysis. Many researchers have applied various text classification techniques to improve the Naive Bayes algorithm, particularly due to its tendency for attribute dependence. Resolving this interdependence is key to enhancing the model's accuracy. The Multinomial Naïve Bayes model is widely used in text classification, where each document is represented by a feature vector of length d, corresponding to the number of words in the dictionary. The manual process of selecting articles is to filter and extract them into lists of documents. But as relevant information is getting more complicated day by day and bulky, together with it is the increasing of fake news, wrong information. That's why the ability to be able to precisely filter out these online articles is highly important. To ensure whether the readers receive the reliable information or not. That is why we need to develop a precise news selecting system and also get our hands on the predict and filter system to sort out online articles using the strong and well-known Naïve Bayes Algorithm to do the work since it is simple, fast and accurate.

Keywords: Data analytics · Machine learning · Artificial intelligence · Naïve Bayes · Computational

1 Introduction

In the Fourth Industrial Revolution Era with the fast-growing of multiple types of massive data, digitalized content as well as text-based information, which is increased through social media like Youtube, Facebook,...

The manual process of selecting articles is to filter and extract them into lists of documents. But as relevant information is getting more complicated day by day and bulky, together with it is the increasing of fake news [1, 4], wrong information. That's why the ability to be able to precisely filter out these online articles is highly important. In this article, we define classification of the news by using the Multinomial Naïve Bayes model is widely used in text classification, where each document is represented by a feature vector of length d, corresponding to the number of words in the dictionary. In

© ICST Institute for Computer Sciences, Social Informatics and Telecommunications Engineering 2025
Published by Springer Nature Switzerland AG 2025. All Rights Reserved
H. X. Huynh et al. (Eds.): GOODTECHS 2024, LNICST 649, pp. 212–221, 2025.
https://doi.org/10.1007/978-3-032-01497-9_20

which the value of the i component in each vector represents the number of times the i appears in the text [5, 7].

To ensure whether the readers receive the reliable information or not. That is why we need to develop a precise news selecting system and also get our hands on the predict and filter system to sort out online articles using the strong and well-known Naïve Bayes Algorithm to do the work since it is simple, fast and accurate [8, 10].

We use the Naive Bayes model which can process extremely fast compared to other categorical data analysis algorithms. Algorithm works based on Bayes theorem of probability to train data and predict classify of unknown set of data. The purpose of this paper is to provide a brief overview of data analysis and classification of the news.

2 Naïve Bayes Classifier

Naive Bayes is a classification algorithm for multiclass classification problems. It is called Naive Bayes because the calculations of the probabilities for each class are simplified to make their calculations tractable.

Naive Bayes classifiers are built on Bayesian classification methods [2, 10]. These rely on Bayes's theorem, equation describing the relationship of conditional probabilities of statistical quantities. In Bayesian classification, we're interested in finding the probability of a label given some observed features.

We can write as $P(S/T)$, tells us how to express this in tern of quantities we can compute more directly

$$P(S/T) = \frac{P(T/S).P(S)}{P(T)} \tag{1}$$

The Naïve Bayes classifier assigns to each instance the class value having the highest conditional probability.

$T = (t_1, t_2, ..., t_n)$ and a class variable S_k

Bayes theorem states that

$$P(S_k/T) = \frac{P(T/S_k).P(S_k)}{P(T)}, for\ k = 1,2,..,K \tag{2}$$

$P(^{S_k}/_T)$ the conditinal probability that even S_k occurs, given that T has occurred.

$P(^{T}/_{S_k})$ the conditinal probability that even T occurs, given that S_k has occurre.

Multinomial Naive Bayes

$$P(^{T}/_{S_k}) = P(^{t_1, \ldots, t_n}/_{S_k}) =$$
$$P(^{t_1}/_{t_2, \ldots, t_n}, S_k) . P(^{t_2}/_{t_3, \ldots, t_n}, S_k) \ldots P(^{t_{n-1}}/_{t_n}, S_k) . P(^{t_n}/_{S_k}) \qquad (3)$$

$P(t|w_1 .. w_n) \propto P(t)P(w_1 .. w_n|t)$

$P(w_1 .. w_n|t) = \prod_i P(w_i|t)$

Parameters: $P(w|t)$ for each document category t and wordtype w

$P(t)$ prior distribution over document categories t

Learning: Estimate parameters as frequency ratios

$$P(w|t, \alpha) = \frac{(w \text{ occurrences in docs with label } t) + \alpha}{(tokens \text{ total ocross docs with label } t) + T\alpha}$$

Predictions: Predict class

$$\operatorname*{argmax}_p P(= (t|w_1 \ldots w_n)) \qquad (4)$$

3   Naïve Bayes Classifier Algorithm

Deploying the Naive Bayes algorithm model is quite simple and mainly involves estimating parameters from training data, which is described as 4 simple steps.

*Input: Training data file.csv.

*Output: New data with forecast results and accuracy assessment.

Step 1: Collect data file/ Build data set framework.

Collect data by extracting from existing data archives such as kagge.com, online article websites... Manage and organize data, including data processing, data cleaning or data deletion for unnecessary ones.

Step 2: Create a Naïve Bayes algorithm model.

Exploit and process data, present issues that need in-depth analysis and research from the proposed problem.

Step 3: Training and test data.

Analyze and train in-depth data from the Naïve Bayes multi-class probability model and check unlabeled data, predicting which network the articles and results will belong to.

Step 4: Predict with new data set and evaluate accuracy.

Forecast, warn according to new data results and store the results.

3.1 The Complexity of the Algorithm

Let n is number of training examples, l^* is dimensionality of the features and m is number of classes. All it needs to do is computing the frequency of every feature value l^* for each class, but space complexity of training is $O(m.l^*.n)$ since you need to store the data which also takes time [10].

The computational complexity efficiency of Naive Bayes lies in the fact that the runtime complexity of Naive Bayes classifier is $O(m.l^*.n)$.

3.2 Data Analysis Problem

Get data from existing data archives such as kagge.com, online article websites.

The scope of the research is limited to the 10 categories with the largest number of 238,643 articles in total and each category is divided equally into 1000 records (Table 1).

Table 1. Dataset_articles_NoID.csv

Data extraction includes 10 records corresponding to 10 different articles in 3 categories: business (3 vectors), education (3 vectors) and sports (4 vectors).

The word vocabulary list includes vector e1 – vector e10 with words and number of words extracted based on words that appear in online articles (Fig. 1).

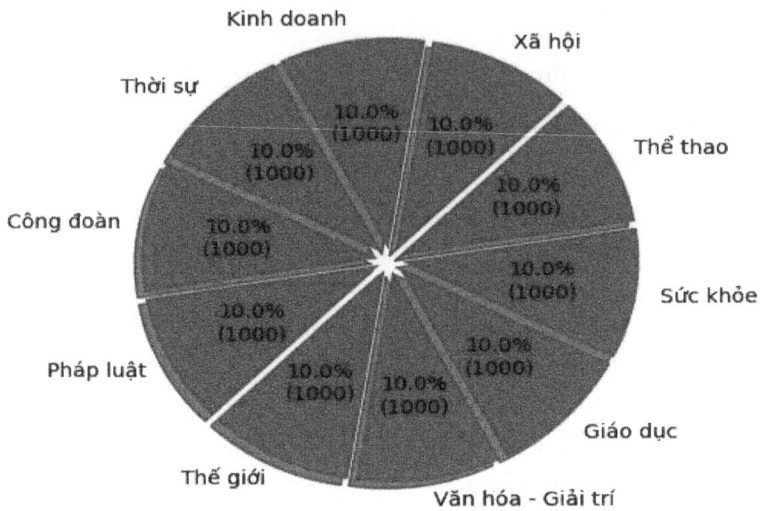

Fig. 1. Limited to the 10 categories

A. Training Data

The word vocabulary list includes vector e1 – vector e10 with words and number of words extracted based on words that appear in online articles (Fig. 2).

		giá	vàng	đồng	giao_dịch	bhtg	thực_hiện	thí_sinh	thí	toán	giải	rubik	khoa_học	luận_án	cầu_thủ	huấn_luyện_viên	trận	milan	sân	thắng	đội
	e1	2	2	1	0	0	0	0	0	0	0	0	0	0	0	0	0	0	0	0	0
	e2	0	2	1	1	0	0	0	0	0	0	0	0	0	0	0	0	0	0	0	0
Kinh doanh	e3	0	0	0	0	2	2	0	0	0	0	0	0	0	0	0	0	0	0	0	0
	Total	2	4	2	1	2	2	0	0	0	0	0	0	0	0	0	0	0	0	0	0
	A	3/33	5/33	3/33	2/33	3/33	3/33	1/33	1/33	1/33	1/33	1/33	1/33	1/33	1/33	1/33	1/33	1/33	1/33	1/33	1/33
	e4	0	0	0	0	0	0	0	2	1	1	0	0	0	0	0	0	0	0	0	0
	e5	0	0	0	0	0	0	1	2	0	1	1	0	0	0	0	0	0	0	0	0
Giáo dục	e6	0	0	0	0	0	1	0	0	0	0	0	2	2	0	0	0	0	0	0	0
	Total	0	0	0	0	0	1	3	3	1	1	1	2	2	0	0	0	0	0	0	0
	A	1/34	1/34	1/34	1/34	1/34	2/34	4/34	4/34	2/34	2/34	2/34	3/34	3/34	1/34	1/34	1/34	1/34	1/34	1/34	1/34
	e7	0	0	0	0	0	0	0	0	0	0	0	0	0	0	1	2	1	1	0	0
	e8	0	0	0	0	0	0	0	0	0	0	0	0	0	1	0	0	2	1	0	0
Thể thao	e9	0	0	0	0	0	0	0	0	0	0	0	0	0	0	0	2	0	0	1	1
	e10	0	0	0	0	0	0	0	0	0	0	0	0	0	2	1	0	0	0	1	1
	Total	0	0	0	0	0	0	0	0	0	0	0	0	0	5	2	3	2	1	2	3
	A	1/38	1/38	1/38	1/38	1/38	1/38	1/38	1/38	1/38	1/38	1/38	1/38	1/38	6/38	3/38	4/38	3/38	2/38	3/38	4/38
e_test		0	1	0	0	0	1	0	0	0	0	0	0	0	0	1	0	1	1	0	2	1

Fig. 2. Training data – from vector e1 to vector e10 and e_test

B. Test Data

e1 = ['giá','giá','vàng','vàng','đồng']
e2 = ['vàng','vàng','đồng','giao_dịch']
e3 = ['bhtg','bhtg','thực_hiện','thực_hiện']
e4 = ['thí_sinh','thí_sinh','thi','toán']
e5 = ['thi','thi','thí_sinh','giải','rubik']
e6 = ['khoa_học','khoa_học','luận_án','luận_án', 'thực_hiện']
e7 = ['cầu_thủ','cầu_thủ','huấn_luyện_viên','trận']
e8 = ['cầu_thủ','milan','milan','sân']
e9 = ['trận','trận','thắng','đội','đội']
e10 = ['cầu_thủ','cầu_thủ','đội','huấn_luyện_viên','thắng']

D = ['giá', 'vàng', 'đồng', 'giao_dịch', 'bhtg', 'thực_hiện', 'thí_sinh', 'thi', 'toán', 'giải', 'rubik', 'khoa_học', 'luận_án', 'cầu_thủ', 'huấn_luyện_viên', 'trận', 'milan', 'sân', 'thắng', 'đội']

The test set includes online article data that is not included in the original model training data.

Test set 1: 100 sports news.

Test set 2: 50 education news + 50 sports news.

Test set 3: 30 business news + 30 education news + 40 sports news.

$d = |V| = 20; N_{KD} = 13; N_{KD} + d = 33$

$d = |V| = 20; N_{GD} = 14; N_{GD} + d = 34$

$d = |V| = 20; N_{TT} = 18; N_{TT} + d = 38$

$$p(KD|e\_test) \propto p(KD)\prod_{i=1}^{d} p(x_i|KD) = \frac{3}{10}\frac{5}{33}\frac{3}{33}\frac{1}{33}\frac{1}{33}\frac{1}{33}(\frac{1}{33})^2\frac{1}{33}$$

$$\approx 3.2 \times 10^{-12}$$

$$p(GD|e_{test}) \propto p(GD)\prod_{i=1}^{d} p(x_i|GD) = \frac{3}{10}\frac{1}{34}\frac{2}{34}\frac{1}{34}\frac{1}{34}\frac{1}{34}(\frac{1}{34})^2\frac{1}{34}$$

$$\approx 3.36 \times 10^{-13}$$

$$p(TT|e_{test}) \propto p(TT)\prod_{i=1}^{d} p(x_i|TT) = \frac{4}{10}\frac{1}{38}\frac{1}{38}\frac{6}{38}\frac{4}{38}\frac{3}{38}(\frac{3}{38})^2\frac{4}{38}$$

$$\approx 2.38 \times 10^{-10}$$

$$\Rightarrow p(x_i|TT) > p(x_i|KD) > p(x_i|GD)$$

$$p(TT|e\_test) = \frac{2.38 \times 10^{-10}}{3.2 \times 10^{-12} + 3.36 \times 10^{-13} + 2.38 \times 10^{-10}} = 0.9854$$

$$p(KD|e\_test) = \frac{3.2 \times 10^{-12}}{3.2 \times 10^{-12} + 3.36 \times 10^{-13} + 2.38 \times 10^{-10}} = 0.0132$$

$$p(GD|e\_test) = \frac{3.36 \times 10^{-13}}{3.2 \times 10^{-12} + 3.36 \times 10^{-13} + 2.38 \times 10^{-10}} = 0.0014$$

$$\Rightarrow e\_test \in \text{lớp thể thao.}$$

C. Model Evaluation

Observing the confusion matrix, the number of correct predictions in each class ranges from 200–300, sport class and culture-entertainment class had the greatest number of correct predictions (Fig. 3).

On the contrary, current affairs and society are the two areas with the least predictions.

For the current affairs class, chart that shows the number of wrong predictions in this class is frequently mistakenly predicted in other courses such as society, law, and trade unions.

For the social class, "confusion" cases fall into a variety of topics with relatively similar numbers.

For 23 samples of the class, "Society" was misinterpreted for "Law". This is the group with the most misunderstanding (Table 2).

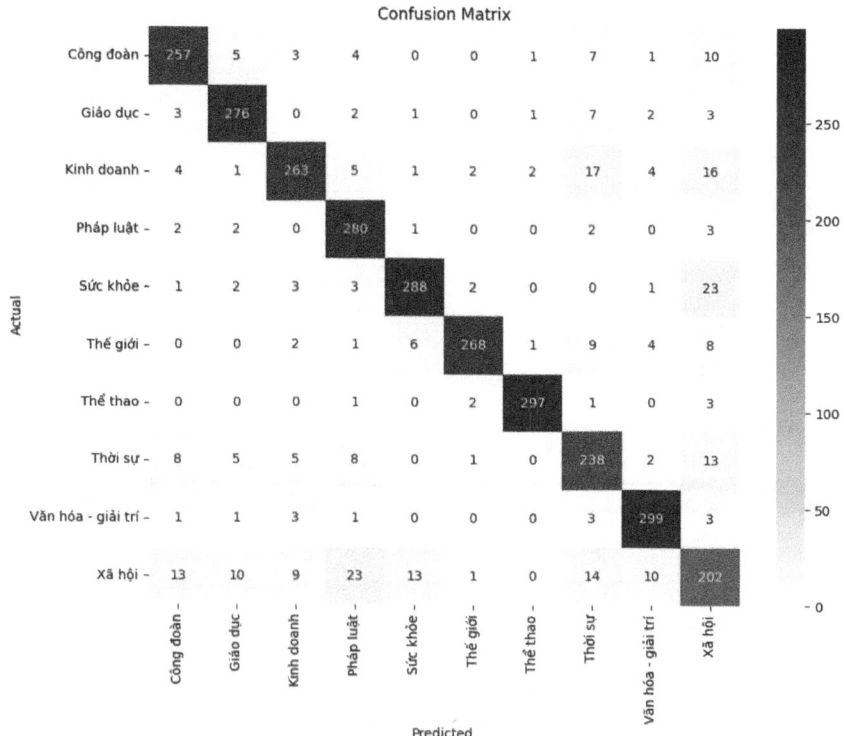

Fig. 3. Confusion matrix

Table 2. Evaluate the Accuracy of the test sets

	Test set 1	Test set 2	Test set 3
Accuracy	97%	94%	89%

Article classification is only one part of the text classification problem. Results of building a simple test program to implement news classification (Fig. 4).

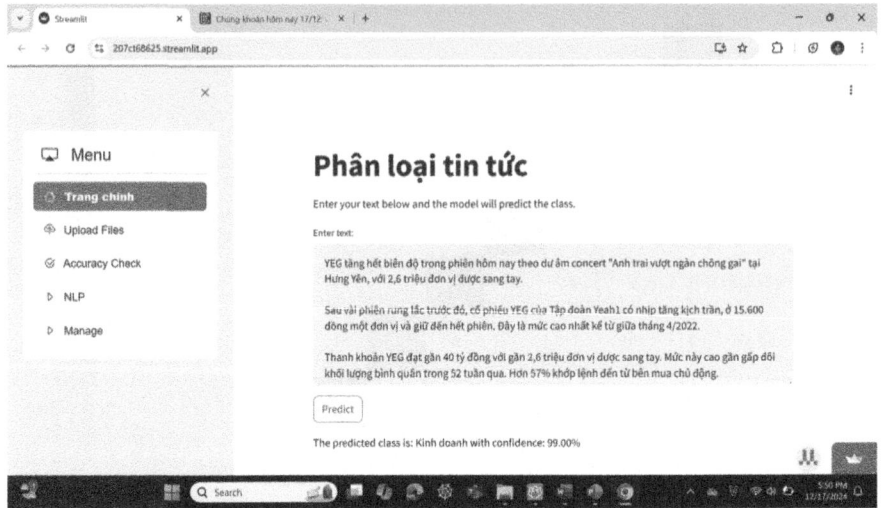

Fig. 4. Results Classification of the news

4 Conclusion

In this article, we build a data analysis model by applying the Naïve Bayes probability formula with the purpose of modeling real problems that can be applied accurately and effectively. Following that, it is proposed to build a data analysis model and data classification results to achieve high accuracy. Finally, a detailed computational illustration is presented as well as its complexity calculation.

Acknowledgements. The authors would like to thank Van Lang University, Vietnam for funding this work.

References

1. Nishadi, A.T.: Text analysis: Naïve Bayes algorithm using Python JupyterLab. Int. J. Sci. Res. **9**(11), 126–135 (2019)
2. Prasetiyowati, S.S., Sibaroni, Y.: Analytics that inform the university: using data you already have. J. Big Data, 7–8 (2024)
3. Al-Sultan, T., Abduljabar, A.Q.: A new approach to develop biometric fingerprint using human right thumb fingernail. J. Electr. Eng. Comput. Sci., 100–101 (2023)
4. VanderPlas, J.: Frequentism and Bayesianism: a Python-driven primer (2014)
5. Webb, G.I., Boughton, J., Wang, Z.: Not so naive Bayes: aggregating one-dependence estimators. Mach. Learn. **58**(1), 5–24 (2005)
6. Witten, I.H., Frank, E.: Data Mining: Practical Machine Learning Tools and Techniques with Java Implementations. Morgan Kaufmann, San Francisco, CA (2000)
7. Abdous, M.H., Wu, H., Yen, C.J.: Using data mining for predicting relationships between online question theme and final grade. J. Educ. Technol. Soc. **15**(3), 77–88 (2012)

8. Campbell, J.P., DeBlois, P.B., Oblinger, D.G.: Academic analytics: a new tool for a new era. EDUCAUSE Rev. **42**(4), 40–57 (2007)

9. Dietz-Uhler, B., Hurn, J.E., Hurn, Making use of data in an LMS to predict student performance: a learning analytics investigation. Unpublished manuscript (2012)

10. Viet, T., Le Minh, H.: The Naïve Bayes algorithm for learning data analytics. J. Comput. Sci. Eng. **12**(4), 1039–1040 (2021)

11. Dringus, L.P.: Learning analytics considered harmful. J. Asynchronous Learn. Netw. **16**(3), 87–100 (2012)

12. Dyckhoff, A.L., Zielke, D., Bultmann, M., Chatti, M.A., Schroeder, U.: Design and implementation of a learning analytics toolkit for teachers. J. Educ. Technol. Soc. **15**(3), 58–76 (2012)

13. Brain, D., Webb, G.I.: The need for low bias algorithms in classification learning from large data sets. In: Proceedings of the 16th European Conference on Principles of Data Mining and Knowledge Discovery (PKDD2002), pp. 62–73 Springer, Berlin, Verlag (2002)

14. Dziuban, C., Moskal, P., Cavanaugh, T., Watts, A.: Analytics that inform the university: using data you already have. J. Asynchronous Learn. Netw. **16**(3), 21–38 (2012)

15. Greller, W.: Drachslrer, Translating learning into numbers: A generic framework for learning analytics. J. Educ. Technol. Soc. **15**(3), 42–57 (2012)

16. Jones, S.J.: Technology review: The possibilities of learning analytics to improve learner centered decision making. Commun. Coll. Enterp. **18**(1), 89–92 (2012)

17. Zheng, Z., Webb, G.I.: Lazy learning of Bayesian rules. J. Mach. Learn. **41**(1), 53–84 (2000)

18. Koller, D., Friedman, N.: Probabilistic Graphical Models: Principals and Techniques. MIT Press (2009)

Building an Automatic Traffic Monitoring System Based on WEBGIS 3D

Ho Minh Hoang and Nguyen Tan Khoi[✉]

Faculty of Information Technology, University of Science and Technology, University of Da Nang, Da Nang, Vietnam
ntkhoi@dut.udn.vn

Abstract. This paper presents a machine learning-based methodology for the classification and real-time statistical analysis of vehicular traffic to facilitate the assessment of traffic flow on important routes. We propose a system architecture model to integrate monitoring devices, data processing capabilities, and user interaction through interfaces, including a 3D WebGIS system utilized for the simulation of traffic system. Moreover, this study conducts experimental scenarios to evaluate the system's performance in the context of traffic management and monitoring in Da Nang. The results of this research not only provide valuable insights for planners in monitoring and coordinating traffic flow but also contribute to the construction of a Digital Twin system, thereby supporting the future development of smart city.

Keywords: WebGIS · Digital Twins · machine learning · traffic flow · yolo · object detection

1 Introduction

Traffic flow is a critical factor in the management and establishment of urban infrastructure, particularly in the context of smart city development [1]. Effective management of traffic flow presents a significant challenge for urban planners and administrators. According to data from the Vietnam General Register, as of March 2023, there are 5,014,243 registered vehicles in circulation nationwide. Consequently, the integration of technology for monitoring road traffic has become increasingly imperative, as it facilitates the provision of accurate, real-time information regarding traffic flow and conditions.

The integration of sensors and big data sources in the development of a Digital Twin system facilitates the real-time representation of the status and activities of physical objects or systems within the digital space. This approach enhances traffic management and improves safety for individuals engaging in transportation activities. The application of advanced technologies not only augments the effectiveness of monitoring but also supports data-driven decision-making, thereby fostering a more intelligent traffic environment.

H. X. Huynh et al. (Eds.): GOODTECHS 2024, LNICST 649, pp. 222–239, 2025.
https://doi.org/10.1007/978-3-032-01497-9_21

Moreover, the positioning of objects in the creation of Geographic Information System (GIS) maps plays a vital role in the advancement of smart city systems. To effectively analyze data from surveillance cameras, it is essential to employ modern machine learning techniques for the identification of traffic participants, thus generating valuable insights into traffic flow. Subsequently, data retrieval will be conducted through Application Programming Interfaces (APIs) that access the database, enabling the simulation of traffic conditions on a WebGIS map to enhance the visualization of the traffic monitoring system.

Based on the potential advantages associated with the development of a traffic flow identification and simulation system utilizing city camera infrastructure, and with the aim of enhancing smart city management capabilities, this paper proposes the establishment of a smart traffic flow monitoring system. The primary contributions of this study include the following: 1) Proposing an architectural model of an intelligent traffic monitoring system, which that leverages public traffic camera networks, private camera systems, and their integration into 3D WebGIS platforms; 2) Proposing enhancements to the YOLOv8 model to improve the accuracy and efficiency of traffic object identification; 3) Representing a solution for traffic monitoring and statistics on the 3D WebGIS platform, facilitating effective analysis and visualization of traffic data.

1.1 Related Studies

Currently, Viet Nam is exploring the implementation of advanced technologies such as traffic monitoring systems utilizing camera networks, including the Wiki Traffic system, which aims to provide traffic flow data; however, its effectiveness remains limited. In Ho Chi Minh City, efforts have been made to deploy a comprehensive smart traffic system, particularly focusing on road monitoring. This system incorporates a range of complex technological components, from peripheral devices to sophisticated software solutions. The primary emphasis has been on employing image processing technologies through urban cameras, with data synchronized via a central control center [1].

Globally, numerous cities have successfully adopted smart traffic monitoring systems, reflecting a growing trend in urban traffic management. Over the years, research has concentrated on developing recognition systems that integrate machine learning techniques with traffic planning to extract pertinent traffic information. This information is crucial for traffic image analysis and control, encompassing various factors such as vehicle counts, travel trajectories, vehicle tracking [12], traffic classification [13], density, and velocity [14], as well as lane changes [17] and license plate recognition. Vehicle identification systems are particularly relevant for detecting traffic lanes and classifying different vehicle types on the road.

Current object recognition methodologies can be categorized into two primary types: feature-based methods and deep learning-based methods.

Feature-based methods commonly utilize machine learning algorithms such as Support Vector Machines (SVM) and Random Forests (RF), in conjunction with classical deep learning techniques such as Histogram of Oriented Gradients (HOG) [2], Scale-Invariant Feature Transform (SIFT) [3], and Haar-like features. These approaches offer advantages in non-linear data processing and demonstrate efficiency in object recognition across varying conditions. For instance, the paper [11] presents a rapid vehicle classification method grounded in contour features. Furthermore, the findings reported in [14] introduce a straightforward and effective camera calibration technique that enables precise calculation of vehicle speed. These methodologies are characterized by their straightforward implementation, which relies on specific characteristic datasets, resulting in high effectiveness for image analysis and object recognition tasks. However, the generalizability of these models may be constrained when applied to new datasets. Additionally, the performance of many machine learning models based on fundamental algorithms tends to be sensitive to noise and variations in images and data sources, particularly in response to changes in lighting conditions or image noise.

The deep learning-based approach is increasingly employed in object recognition tasks. Prominent architectures such as YOLO (You Only Look Once) [4], SSD (Single Shot MultiBox Detector) [5], and Faster R-CNN (Region Convolutional Neural Network) [6] have demonstrated significant advantages over traditional feature-based object recognition methods [10]. These deep learning models automatically extract features from images through multiple layers, enabling simultaneous recognition of objects without the need for pre-classification of specific regions. One of the key advantages of these methods is their efficient processing of image data, which facilitates highly accurate object recognition. Moreover, they exhibit superior generalization capabilities, allowing for effective performance across varied conditions, largely due to their ability to learn from extensive and diverse datasets. Additionally, these architectures can adjust weights and enhance their performance through dense training layers, rendering them particularly suitable for complex object recognition applications in practical settings.

1.2   WebGIS 3D Platform Modeling

Simulating identification results and delivering information to users is crucial for the effective implementation of intelligent transportation systems. WebGIS represents a technology that facilitates the management, display, and interaction with geographic information systems on a web platform.

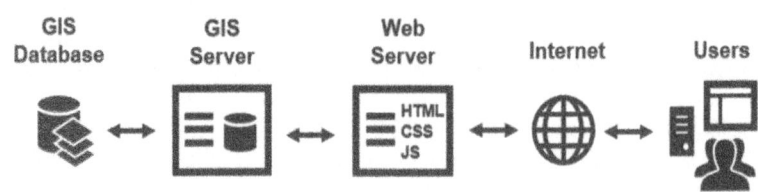

Fig. 1. WebGIS System

A WebGIS system will usually have the following 4 components: Database, Web Server, Application Server, and Client. Figure 1 shows the WebGIS system including components:

- Database: This component is responsible for storing geographic data and is managed by database management systems. Data may also be organized in file formats such as Shapefile or GeoPackage..

- Application Server (Business Layer): The application server processes requests from clients, retrieves relevant data from the database, and presents information in accordance with user specifications.
- Web Server: This server handlesrequests from clients, returns data and resources, and optimizes page load speed and load capacity.
- Client: The client is either a web browser or a desktop application that enables users to search, analyze, and visually display geographic data.

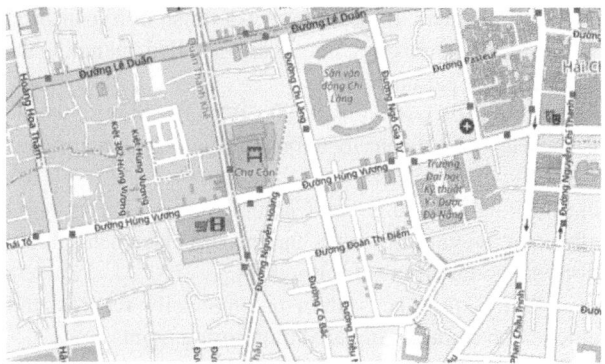

Fig. 2. GIS map of Da Nang city

A 3D GIS map facilitates the representation of objects associated with geographic information in a three-dimensional spatial context (Fig. 2). One of the primary objectives of 3D modeling is to accurately recreate urban environments, encompassing elements such as roads, bridges, traffic signs, and various infrastructure components. Information obtained from city camera sources and sensors contributes to the assessment of geographic topographic factors, as well as the positioning of simulated blocks based on a specified 2D map (Fig. 3).

Fig. 3. 3D Map simulation

In this paper, we combine the optimization of modern object detection models and WebGIS 3D applications to simulate traffic flows and objects in the construction of intelligent transportation systems.

2 Building a Traffic Monitoring System

The proposed intelligent traffic monitoring system encompasses the following key functions:

- Management of City Camera Information: Administrators can input and manage camera data for locations where city cameras are installed, including the configuration of coordinates and image parameters.
- Viewing and Searching for Locations on the WebGIS Map: Users are able to easily search for and view significant locations on the digital map, thereby enhancing accessibility to traffic information.
- Detailed Route Information and Urban Camera Access: The system provides comprehensive information regarding routes and camera placements, including real-time traffic conditions and simulations of traffic flow.
- Vehicle Count Monitoring: The system automatically records and analyzes the number of vehicles traversing designated monitoring points.
- Traffic Alerts: The system issues notifications on the map application screen when vehicle density exceeds a predefined safe threshold, providing information on the number of vehicles in the affected area.
- 3D WebGIS Map Modeling: The system integrates 3D technology to simulate two-dimensional maps within urban environments.

2.1 System Architecture Construction

Based on the analyzed functions, the developed system must fulfill the requirements for connecting a diverse range of hardware and IoT devices [19], facilitating communication and data exchange among various software modules, and operating across multiple network domains. In this section, we propose an architectural model for an intelligent traffic monitoring system that incorporates YOLO and WebGIS technologies, as illustrated in Fig. 4.

1. Physical layer: This layer includes physical devices such as access points, wireless routers, and 4G/5G technology, as well as peripherals for traffic monitoring, including traffic cameras.
2. Connectivity layer: This layer specifies the protocols that facilitate connections through various network methods, such as Wi-Fi and Low Power Wide Area Network (LPWAN).
3. Service layer: This layer comprises API services that support business processing, integration with machine learning models, and management and security operations.
4. Presentation layer: This layer includes a web application that enables users to interact with the WebGIS system.

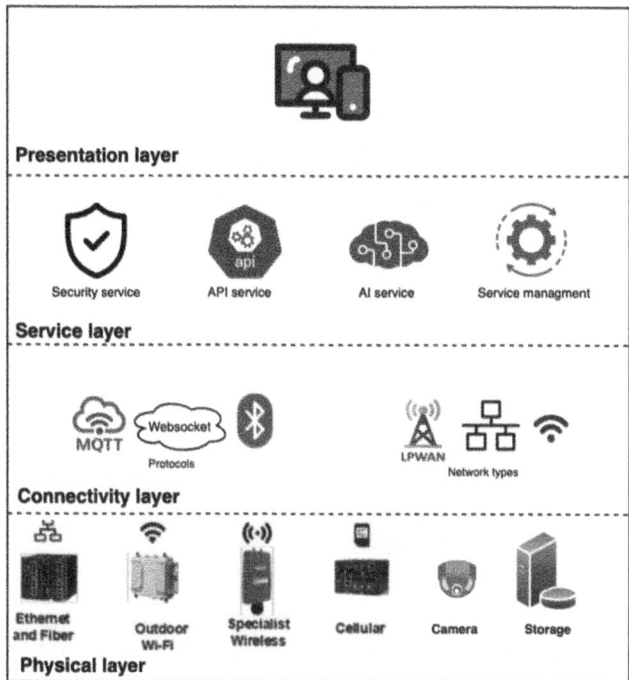

Fig. 4. Architectural model of system layers

Information about traffic conditions on the routes will be collected from city surveillance cameras through a streaming camera platform. This data will be transmitted through a machine learning model to analyze and extract the necessary information, subsequently stored in a relational database and cache for further analytical operations (Fig. 5).

The results of the identification process, along with the vehicle count, will be presented on the end-user's screen, thereby facilitating effective monitoring and management of traffic conditions.

2.2 Data Flow and System Flow

Building upon the object recognition results derived from machine learning models, an integrated management system has been developed and implemented on the WebGIS platform. This system visualizes the identified objects and maps them onto a city map, as illustrated in the following block diagram (Fig. 6).

According to the diagram presented above, the intelligent traffic monitoring system comprises the following key components:

- Video recording: The system utilizes surveillance cameras to continuously record traffic footage. This camera infrastructure is sourced from the city's existing camera network, enabling effective operation under diverse lighting conditions.
- Identification: The video data is transmitted to the server for processing, undergoing several stages:

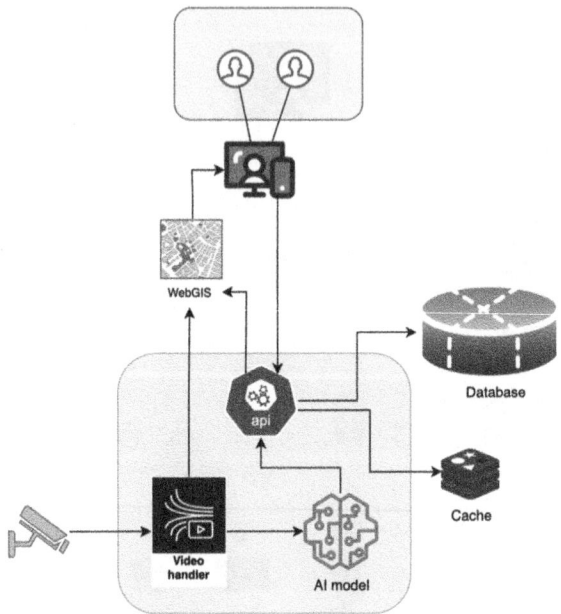

Fig. 5. Diagram of the exchange flow between components in the system

- Pre-processing: Video frames are resized, color-adjusted, and filtered for noise to enhance image quality.
- Feature extraction: The YOLO model analyzes the frames to extract significant features that facilitate the identification process.
- Vehicle detection: The system identifies the types of vehicles present (including cars, motorcycles, buses, etc.) along with their locations within each frame.

- Streaming: The processed video is broadcast live via a web interface, providing real-time traffic information, including vehicle counts and traffic density on the roadway.
- Data storage: The system archives information regarding vehicles and traffic conditions for subsequent analysis.

To perform the mapping from the image obtained from the camera onto the 2D projection (BEV - Bird Eye View) of the map, the Homography matrix is calculated to perform the coordinate projection (Fig. 7).

Let $P(x_p, y_p)$ denote the point on the image. The conversion homography matrix can be expressed as follows:

$$H_p = \begin{bmatrix} h_{11} & h_{12} & h_{13} \\ h_{21} & h_{22} & h_{23} \\ h_{31} & h_{32} & h_{33} \end{bmatrix}$$

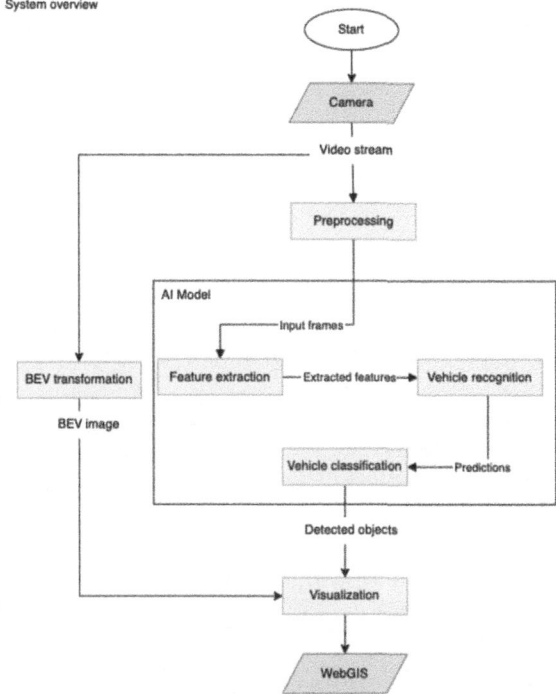

Fig. 6. System flow overview

Homogeneous coordinates on a vertical projection will be calculated as:

$$P_{homo} = \begin{bmatrix} x_{homo} \\ y_{homo} \\ w \end{bmatrix} = H_p \bullet \begin{bmatrix} x_p \\ y_p \\ 1 \end{bmatrix}$$

To determine the Cartesian coordinates on the vertical projection plane, it is necessary to perform uniform coordinates normalization on the weighted w

$$P_{BEV} = (\frac{x_{homo}}{w}, \frac{y_{homo}}{w})$$

Homography matrix allows the conversion of points in 3D space into points in 2D dimension [9], thereby creating an accurate projection to simulate objects on the road.

2.3 Improved YOLOv8 Model with Pruning of Convolutional Layers Weights

In practice, the selection of the YOLO model must be carefully considered in relation to specific needs and available development resources. The objective is to ensure that the model not only achieves high accuracy in vehicle identification but also operates efficiently under conditions of limited resources.

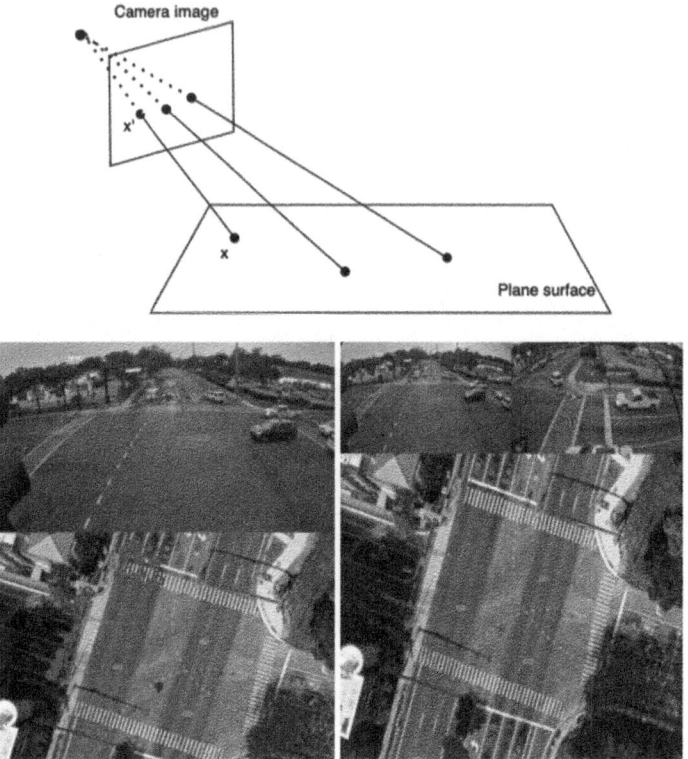

Fig. 7. Projections using the Homography matrix [8]

We collect dataset from surveillance cameras in Da Nang City to train various versions of the YOLO model. The experimental results indicate that the YOLO11 model demonstrates high accuracy; however, it necessitates substantial system resources. In contrast, the YOLOv8 model [15, 18] also maintains a high level of accuracy while requiring fewer system resources. Consequently, we have opted to utilize the YOLOv8 model architecture for training on the data collected from the cameras for the purposes of vehicle identification and classification (Fig. 8).

The architecture of YOLOv8 consists of three main components: the backbone, the neck, and the head layer.

Small Object Detection In order to detect small objects (Fig. 9), we propose to combine the YOLOv8 model with the SAHI enhanced sliding window method [16].

In this method, the input image is partitioned into fixed-size slices, enabling focused analysis of areas likely to contain small objects. Each segment is processed independently using the YOLO model to identify objects within the subregions. Furthermore, the SAHI approach extends beyond the individual processing of each slice; it utilizes hierarchical information across slices to enhance the identification of objects within the broader context of the entire image.

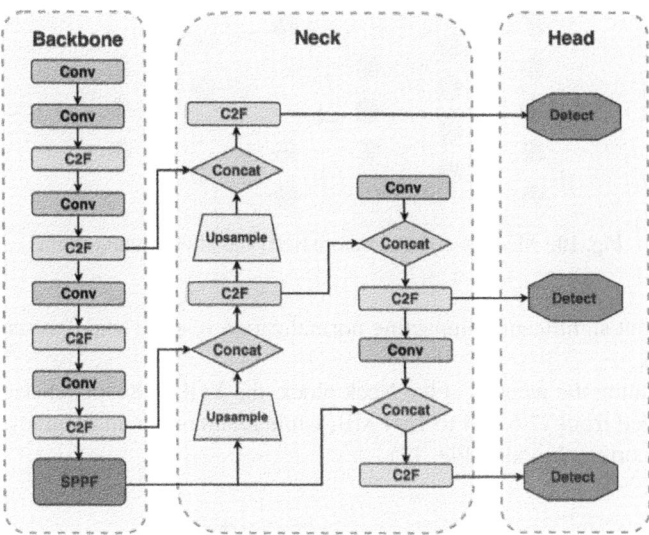

Fig. 8. YOLOv8 model overview

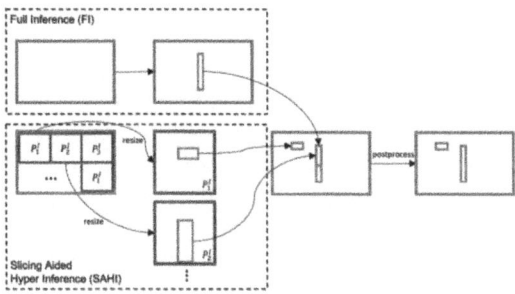

Fig. 9. SAHI implementation [16]

Optimize Inference Speed: The number of parameters of the YOLO model is generally large (more than 5 million parameters for the YOLOv8s model). Therefore, during the retraining process on the actual set, some parameters with small weights can be omitted, which helps to speed up the training process on the new dataset and increase the efficiency of the recognition process later (Fig. 10).

We propose a solution to prune the neck block of the YOLOv8 model during training with the collected dataset. The neck block encompasses weights associated with convolutional layers, batch normalization, and upsampling layers. In the Neck block, the convolution layers in the C2f block have the ability to connect features from different stages, which makes C2f have a high weighting density and contain weights that contain unnecessary distant contexts. Therefore, we propose to prune the weights of the convolution layers. Additionally, the batch normalization and upsampling layers play essential roles in data normalization and geometric transformation. Therefore, these layers can be

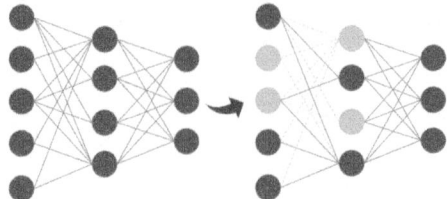

Fig. 10. Model weighting before (left) and after pruning (right)

pruned without significantly impacting normalization results, while preserving overall performance.

After pruning the weights at the Neck block, the YOLOv8s model size was significantly reduced from 22.6 MB to 15.4 MB, while maintaining an accuracy comparable to that of the original model (Fig. 11).

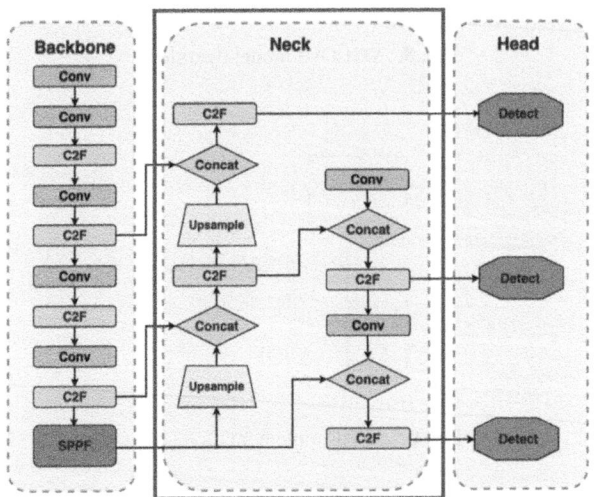

Fig. 11. Pruning the Neck block of the YOLOv8 model

Furthermore, in practical applications, the management of latency associated with the recognition performance of YOLO models presents certain limitations. A primary factor contributing to this issue is the emphasis on achieving high accuracy in the development of recognition models, which necessitates the frequent utilization of operations involving floating-point data types, such as float32 or float64. This reliance on floating-point operations can result in increased response times during both the training and detection phases of the model (Fig. 12).

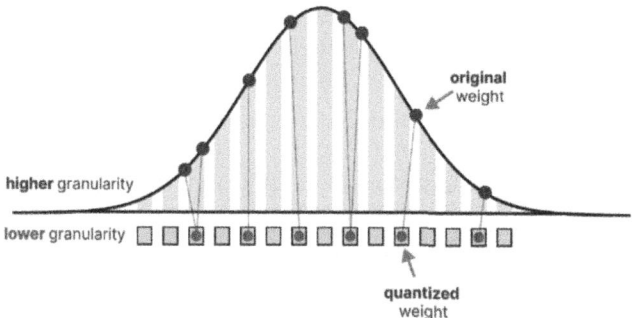

Fig. 12. Model weights after quantization [7]

We propose a solution to speed up the YOLO model through the application of the quantization method. Specifically, this method involves converting weights from a floating-point representation (32-bit) to an integer representation (8-bit). The objective of this approach is to optimize the processing time of the model. By utilizing tensor computations and storage with data types that require fewer bits than floating-point representations, this method significantly reduces both computational speed and resource consumption.

3 Experiment and Evaluation

The system is deployed on a dedicated server, with the database and API system hosted on a server configured with 64 GB of RAM and 40 core/80 threads, RTX 3090. Comprehensive data and program details can be found on https://github.com/minhhoangho/camera_detection.

Below is a list of configurable cameras within the system (Fig. 13).

ID	Tên địa điểm	Mô tả	Vĩ độ	Kinh độ	Thời gian tạo	Thao tác
1	Cổng trường Nguyễn Huệ	Camera cổng trường Nguyễn Huệ Đà Nẵng	16.074091	108.216351	11/05/2024 15:50	✎ 🗑
2	Cổng sau Bệnh viện C	Camera cổng sau bệnh viện C	16.073769	108.215290	16/04/2024 23:30	✎ 🗑
3	Nút tây Cầu Rồng	Camera nút giao thông tây Cầu Rồng Đà ...	16.061124	108.223578	16/04/2024 23:28	✎ 🗑
4	Cổng sau bệnh viện Đa Khoa	Cổng sau bệnh viện Đa Khoa Đà Nẵng	16.073750	108.214813	16/04/2024 22:35	✎ 🗑

Fig. 13. List of camera configuration locations

3.1 Prediction Results Under Different Conditions

In practice, traffic monitoring systems that utilize city cameras must operate effectively under varying weather and lighting conditions. We conducted experiments to evaluate the identification results of the proposed model across multiple locations, each characterized by different environmental conditions (Table 1).

Table 1. Identification results under different conditions

	Gate of Nguyen Hue School		Hospital C Gate		Dragon Bridge Area (wide view)	
	Predict	Actual	Predict	Actual	Predict	Actual
Normal Conditions	10	11	10	10	19	21
Dark weather conditions	13	14	8	9	19	25
Rainy weather conditions	7	9	6	7	6	12

According to the results presented in the table above, the proposed model demonstrates strong performance under normal conditions, achieving high accuracy across all three surveyed locations. However, the model's recognition performance significantly declines when environmental conditions change, particularly in dark and rainy settings.

The results presented below compare the detections of small-sized objects using the SAHI method with that of the YOLO model in isolation. It is evident that, relative to the latest YOLO model (YOLOv11), the number of detected objects is considerably low in relation to the total number of objects. However, the incorporation of the SAHI enhancement model has led to a significant increase in recognition counts. Despite this improvement, the number of identified objects remains limited compared to the overall volume of vehicles participating in traffic, highlighting a notable limitation of object identification methods concerning small-sized objects (Figs. 14 and 15).

Fig. 14. Identification results using the YOLO11 model

3.2 Application Results

The main user interface is represented by a map image that provides comprehensive information regarding the geographic layout of the city. This system not only displays

Fig. 15. Detection results using the proposed YOLO model

the locations of installed cameras but also facilitates user-friendly searches for specific places (Fig. 16).

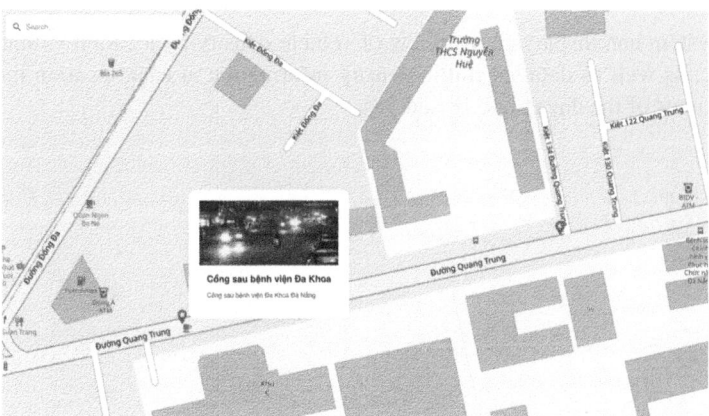

Fig. 16. Maps and camera information

The place details management system allows administrators to perform various operations, including the specification of camera locations and coordinates on the map. Furthermore, administrator can upload corresponding vertical projection images to enhance the accuracy and efficiency of object location (Fig. 17).

Cổng trường Nguyễn Huệ

Fig. 17. Location detail with camera information

The system can display an overview of vehicle density by location within a 5-min timeframe, as well as detailed traffic density information at each location throughout different times of the day (Figs. 18 and 19).

Fig. 18. Traffic statistics on routes

WebGIS 3D maps offer a visually engaging representation of the area, modeling buildings and sites to assist users in identifying and analyzing their surroundings (Fig. 20).

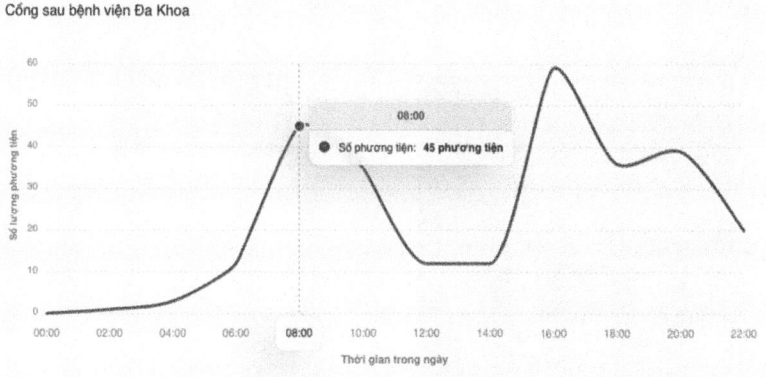

Fig. 19. Traffic flow statistics at the location by time range

Fig. 20. WebGIS 3D map

The detailed interface for camera and traffic flow management allows for the identification of vehicles on the roadway and simulates their movement directions on the map. This functionality provides visual insights into traffic conditions and supports users in monitoring and analyzing vehicle movement trends, thereby enhancing the efficiency of traffic management (Fig. 21).

Fig. 21. Cameras and traffic flow at one location

4 Conclusion and Further Work

This paper proposes methodologies for constructing intelligent traffic monitoring systems. The primary contributions of this research are as follows: 1) the proposal of an architectural model for a traffic flow monitoring system applicable to urban environments, with potential for extension to other regions; 2) the enhancement of the YOLO model through weight pruning methods in specific layers and quantization techniques to improve the efficiency of the object recognition process; and 3) the deployment of the system on a WebGIS 3D platform, which facilitates the real-time visual representation of traffic flow.

The system aggregates data from existing public cameras in the city and possesses the capability to integrate with private cameras and other sensors. This integration not only enriches the data sources but also enhances the effectiveness of traffic monitoring. The WebGIS 3D system is employed to simulate traffic flow and generate traffic statistics for critical routes within the city. Consequently, the system not only improves traffic monitoring but also establishes a Digital Twin model for Da Nang City, enabling the simulation and analysis of various road traffic scenarios.

By incorporating real-time data from sensors and cameras, the model offers a comprehensive overview of traffic conditions, thereby assisting managers in planning and optimizing transportation infrastructure. Furthermore, the system's potential can be augmented by integrating technologies such as IoT and artificial intelligence, thereby enhancing predictive capabilities and providing intelligent solutions that improve responsiveness to emergency traffic situations. Ultimately, this contributes to the development of a more sustainable and intelligent traffic environment.

References

1. Hung, N.V.: Research and development of solutions for traffic monitoring and vehicle management through surveillance cameras. Hanoi, (2020)
2. Dalal, N., Triggs, B.: Histograms of oriented gradients for human detection, San Diego, CA. IEEE, USA (2005)
3. Martinez-Gil, J.: SIFT: An Algorithm for Extracting Structural Information From Taxonomies, (2016)
4. Redmon, J., Divvala, S., Girshick, R., AFarhadi, A.: You only look once: unified, real-time object detection. Facebook AI Research, (2015)
5. Liu, W., Anguelov, D., Erhan, D., Szegedy, C., Reed, S., Fu, C.-Y., Berg, A.C.: SSD: single shot MultiBox detector. In: Computer Vision – ECCV 2016, pp. 21–37. Springer International Publishing, (2016).
6. Reis, D., Kupec, J., Hong, J., Daoudi, A.: Real-time flying object detection with YOLOv8. arXiv, (2023)
7. M. Grootendorst. A Visual guide to quantization. Exploring Language Models, (2024)
8. Anon. OpenCV: Basic concepts of the homography. OpenCV, Online. Available: https://docs.opencv.org
9. Zhao, J., Shi, J., Zhuo, L.: BEV perception for autonomous driving: state of the art and future perspectives. Expert Syst. Appl. **258**, 125103 (2024)
10. Nguyen, N.D., Do, T., Ngo, T.D., Le, D.D.: An evaluation of deep learning methods for small object detection. J. Electr. Comput. Eng. **2020**(1), 3189691 (2020)
11. Can, N.V., Hung, N.T., Thuan, D.P., Tien, N.D.: Rapid classification method of vehicles based on contours. In: Proceedings of the VIII National Conference on Applied Research in Information Technology (FAIR)
12. Zhenyu Wang, W.: Detecting Everything in the Open World: Towards Universal Object Detection, CVPR, (2023)
13. Psyllos, A., Anagnostopoulos, C.N., Kayafas, E.: Vehicle model recognition from frontal view image measurements. Comput. Stand. & Interfaces **33**, 142–151 (2011)
14. Do, V.-H., Nghiem, L.H., Thi, N.P., Ngoc, N.P.: A simple camera calibration method for vehicle velocity estimation. In: International Conference on Electrical Engineering/Electronics, Computer, Telecommunications and Information Technology, ECTI-CON, Thailand, (2015)
15. Varghese, R., Sambath, M.: YOLOv8: A Novel Object Detection Algorithm with Enhanced Performance and Robustness, Chennai, India: IEEE (2024)
16. Akyon, F.C., Altinuc, S.O., Temizel, A.: Slicing aided hyper inference and fine-tuning for small object detection. In: IEEE International Conference on Image Processing (ICIP), Bordeaux, France, (2022)
17. Ghahremannezhad, H., Shi, H., Liu, C.: Real-time accident detection in traffic surveillance using deep learning. arXiv, (2022)
18. Shaqib, S., Alo, A.P., Sultan, R.S., Haque, U., Khan, S.S., Rahman, M.S.: Vehicle speed detection system utilizing YOLOv8: enhancing road safety and traffic management for metropolitan areas. arXiv, (2024)
19. Guerrero-Ibáñez, J., Zeadally, S., Contreras-Castillo, J.: Sensor Technologies for Intelligent Transportation Systems. Sensors **18**(4), 1212 (2018)

Detecting Abnormal Cervical Cells Based on Segmentation of Overlapping Cells

Hao Nguyen-Duc⑩, Lien Nguyen-Thi-Ngoc⑩, Phuoc Dat Doan⑩,
and Nga Le-Thi-Thu$^{(\boxtimes)}$ ⑩

Vietnam - Korea University of Information and Communication Technology, Da Nang, Vietnam
{haond.21ad,lienntn.21it,ddphuoc.tg,lttnga}@vku.udn.vn

Abstract. Segmentation of overlapping cells in biological images remains a challenging task due to the complexity introduced by occlusion and overlap, which often leads to decreased accuracy in automated medical diagnostics systems. This research focuses on improving the segmentation of overlapping cells using an advanced deep learning approach. The model is trained on the ISBI2014 dataset of cervical cytology cells, a collection of images with noisy and overlapping cells. Experimental results demonstrate that the proposed model achieves higher accuracy, even with limited labeled data. By calculating the nucleus-to-cytoplasm (N/C) ratio from the segmentation results, the proposed method determines whether a cell is normal or exhibits pathological characteristics. The proposed method provides an efficient and scalable solution for the classification and segmentation of overlapping cells, offering new opportunities for advancements in automated image analysis and contributing to the development of more accurate and reliable systems for cell-based medical diagnosis.

Keywords: Cervical cells · Overlapping cell · Classification · Segmentation · Deep learning

1 Introduction

With the rapid development of information technology and artificial intelligence (AI) in particular, the healthcare sector has seen transformative advancements in recent years. One significant challenge in biomedical image analysis is the accurate classification and segmentation of overlapping cells. Overlapping cells complicate automated analysis by reducing the precision of classification and segmentation, especially when cells partially obscure one another or when images contain noise. This issue is crucial in medical diagnostics, where precise cell analysis ensures accurate diagnosis and treatment planning [4–6].

Recent advancements in deep learning and artificial intelligence have made a significant impact in improving biomedical image analysis, especially for tasks like cell classification. Methods that combine large datasets, including both labeled and unlabeled data, have shown substantial improvements in classification tasks, particularly when applied

© ICST Institute for Computer Sciences, Social Informatics and Telecommunications Engineering 2025
Published by Springer Nature Switzerland AG 2025. All Rights Reserved
H. X. Huynh et al. (Eds.): GOODTECHS 2024, LNICST 649, pp. 240–249, 2025.
https://doi.org/10.1007/978-3-032-01497-9_22

to complex and noisy biomedical image data [10]. These techniques enhance model robustness and accuracy, offering promising solutions for overlapping cell classification. Although AI techniques in biomedical image analysis are well-studied worldwide, the field remains emerging in Vietnam. However, the potential for growth in this area is considerable, as demand for precise and automated cell classification methods continues to rise. Some Vietnamese research institutions and universities are gradually investing in AI and machine learning for biomedical image analysis, signaling a promising opportunity for future research in cell segmentation and classification [7, 8].

The increasing volume of cell image data generated in biomedical research and diagnostics highlights the need for accurate and efficient cell classification and segmentation methods. Overlapping cells, which are obscured or clustered in images, pose significant challenges for automated classification systems and reduce system accuracy. Addressing this issue with AI techniques can help improve the accuracy of automated classification systems [11]. Cell overlapping presents a significant challenge in cytology image analysis, particularly in tasks such as cell instance segmentation. Overlapping cells in cytology images often form translucent clusters, making it difficult to clearly define the boundaries of individual cells, which is especially challenging in cervical cell images. The semi-transparency of the cytoplasm in these clusters distinguishes the problem in computer vision. Despite overlapping cells, the affected regions still retain valuable shape information [14, 15].

This research focuses on improving the segmentation of overlapping cells using an advanced deep learning approach. The model is trained on the ISBI2014 dataset of cervical cytology cells, a collection of images with noisy and overlapping cells. Experimental results demonstrate that the proposed model achieves higher accuracy, even with limited labeled data. By calculating the nucleus-to-cytoplasm (N/C) ratio from the segmentation results, the proposed method determines whether a cell is normal or exhibits pathological characteristics. The proposed method provides an efficient and scalable solution for the classification and segmentation of overlapping cells, offering new opportunities for advancements in automated image analysis and contributing to the development of more accurate and reliable systems for cell-based medical diagnosis.

The structure of this paper is organized as follows: Sect. 2 provides an overview of the segmentation method using Deep De-overlapping Network, which serves as the foundation for developing our proposed model. Section 3 presents the ISBI2014 dataset used for training and evaluation, along with the architecture of the proposed model and evaluation metrics. Section 4 offers a comprehensive analysis of the experimental results, demonstrating the model's improved performance metrics for cell segmentation and cell classification based on the nuclear-to-cytoplasmic (N/C) ratio. Finally, conclusions are presented in Sect. 5 highlighting further enhancements for cell classification and segmentation in biomedical imaging.

2 Deep De-overlapping Network

Deep De-overlapping Network (DoNet) is a complex deep learning model developed to address the specific challenges of segmenting overlapping cells in cytology images, where traditional segmentation models often struggle due to translucent, clustered cell boundaries.

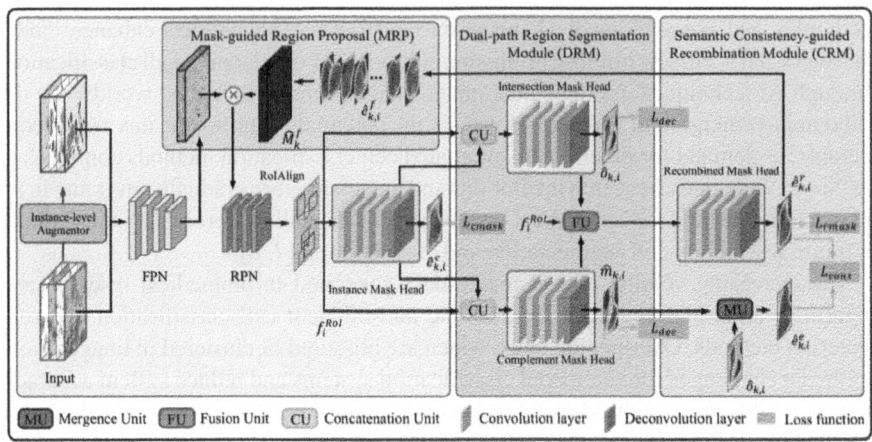

Fig. 1. DoNet architecture with four main parts [1]: (1) Segmentation with Mask R-CNN; (2) DRM; (3) CRM; (4) MRP

The DoNet introduces a unique decompose-and-recombine strategy that enhances boundary accuracy and relationship modeling within overlapping cell regions. DoNet architecture with four main parts including Segmentation with Mask R-CNN, Dual-path Region Segmentation Module (drm), Semantic Consistency-guided Recombination Module (CRM), and Mask-guided Region Proposal (MRP).

2.1 Initial Segmentation with Mask R-CNN

DoNet begins by generating initial coarse masks for cell clusters using Mask R-CNN. While effective for general instance segmentation, Mask R-CNN alone cannot accurately delineate the ambiguous boundaries between overlapping, translucent cells [8].

Prior research on Mask R-CNN has shown performance in instance segmentation [9, 11, 13], and this capability has been integrated into DoNet for coarse mask segmentation. Following the standard losses used in [11], a multi-task loss Lcoarse for coarse mask segmentation is as follows:

$$Lcoarse = Lreg + Lcls + Lcmask \tag{1}$$

where Lreg is the smooth-L1 loss for bounding box regression, Lcls is the cross-entropy (CE) loss for classification, and Lcmask is the pixel-wise CE loss for segmentation. Each component's loss will contribute to future deployments of the model's capabilities [1].

2.2 Dual-Path Region Segmentation Module (DRM)

In Fig. 1, DRM is designed with the same architecture by an Intersection Mask Head Ho and a Complement Mask Head. To refine these coarse masks, DRM decomposes each cell cluster into two distinct sub-regions:

- Intersection Regions, which capture areas of overlap between cells.

– Complement Regions, representing the non-overlapping parts of each cell. This decomposition enables the model to distinguish overlapping from non-overlapping areas, allowing for more precise boundary identification.

2.3 Semantic Consistency-Guided Recombination Module (CRM)

After decomposition, CRM recombines the separated intersection and complement regions, creating refined segmentation masks that maintain semantic consistency. This module leverages instance features from both DRM and Mask R-CNN's RoIAlign layer, ensuring that the final segmentation respects the structural relationships between cell regions.

For improving the perception capability for overlapping instances, CRM is designed to encourage DoNet to perceive integral instances. This combination facilitates CRM to leverage contextual information of overlapping instances, leading to the improvement of perception capability. The refined mask from CRM is optimized by segmentation loss Lrmask.

2.4 Mask-Guided Region Proposal (MRP)

To further enhance accuracy, particularly in detecting cell nuclei, MRP uses attention maps from the cytoplasm to guide segmentation, reducing false positives caused by debris and other artifacts that resemble nuclei.

A mask guided to encourage the model to generate nuclei proposals in intra-cellular regions. The raw predictions are first mapped back and then summed up according to their bounding box predictions in the detection head, followed by a Sigmoid function to normalize them into probabilities. The decompose-and-recombined strategy is also applied to empower the perception capability of the model for overlapping translucent regions.

3   Segmentation of Overlapping Cells

In this paper, we fine-tune the DoNet model for cell segmentation due to its proven effectiveness in handling overlapping cells in cytology images. DoNet employs a decomposition-and-recombination strategy making it well-suited for handling translucent, overlapping cell clusters in cervical images. The model initially generates coarse masks using Mask R-CNN, and then refines these masks through the Dual-path Region Segmentation Module (DRM) and the Semantic Consistency-guided Recombination Module (CRM). This approach ensures precise and consistent segmentation of individual cell instances. Furthermore, the Mask-guided Region Proposal (MRP) module reduces the impact of hard mimics, crucial for accurately distinguishing cell boundaries from other similar-looking structures. With its state-of-the-art performance on datasets such as ISBI2014 and CPS, DoNet has demonstrated a superior ability to segment overlapping cells, making it an ideal foundation for our proposed approach.

3.1 The Dataset

The dataset ISBI2014, used in this study, consists of 16 real Extended Depth of Field (EDF) cervical cytology images and 945 synthetic images [2]. The dataset facilitates two types of evaluation: qualitative and quantitative. Qualitative assessment is performed using the 16 real EDF cervical cytology images, while quantitative evaluation is conducted using the 945 synthetic images, allowing participants to evaluate their algorithms' performance. It contains high-quality pixel-level annotations for both nuclei and cytoplasm with a resolution of 512 × 512.

This dataset enables a comprehensive evaluation of segmentation algorithms by combining qualitative analysis based on real images and quantitative analysis based on synthetic images, thereby fostering the development of robust algorithms for overlapping cell segmentation.

3.2 Model Architecture

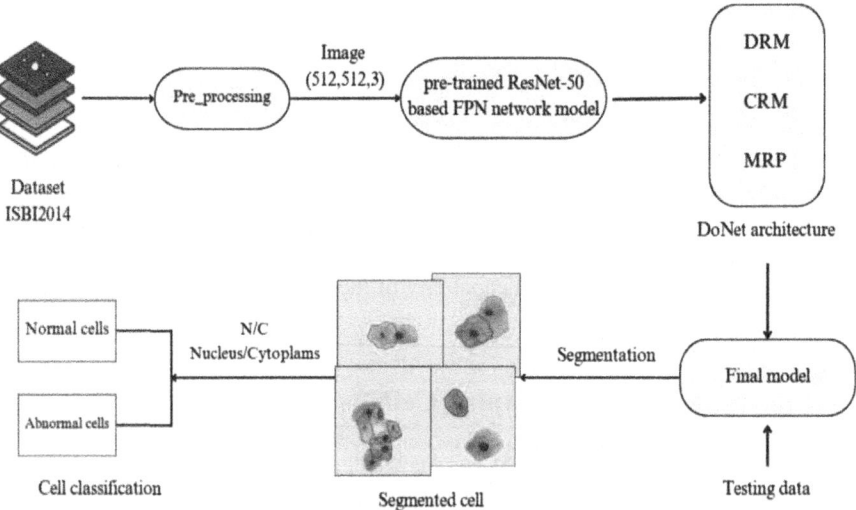

Fig. 2. Proposed model architecture

The proposed model is illustrated with specific components in Fig. 2. Firstly, we explored and analyzed the ISBI2014 dataset. Then, a pre-trained ResNet-50 base FPN network with pre-processed cell image 512 × 512 × 3 was used in all the experiments. DoNet architecture was also used to train our model as a segmentation stage and de-overlapping cell stage for applying classification techniques afterward. Finally, the output consists of two classes, normal and abnormal cervical cells, classified based on the N/C ratio.

3.3   Evaluation Metrics

We assess the overall performance of the proposed model using four commonly used evaluation metrics in instance segmentation:

- AP (Average Precision): Measures overall model performance across multiple IoU thresholds, and calculates the area under the precision-recall curve.
- AP50, AP75: Measure performance at IoU thresholds of 50% and 75%, respectively, by averaging precision at recall for IoU $\geq$ 0.5 and IoU $\geq$ 0.75.
- APs, APm, APl: Evaluate performance for small (APs), medium (APm), and large (APl) objects. It is calculated similarly to AP with specific size categories.
- AP per category: Measures performance for each object category individually, and calculate the average precision at various recall levels for each category.

4   Experimental Results

4.1   Experimental Results for Segmentation

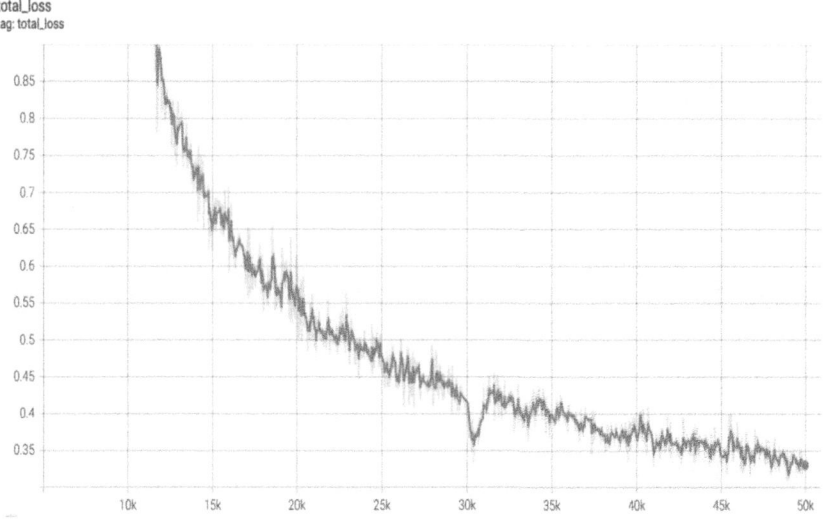

Fig. 3. Total_loss for 50,000 iter

Figure 3 illustrates the total loss during the training process of the model. The loss steadily decreases after 50,000 iterations. The detailed results in Table 1 show that our proposed approach does better in the majority of the evaluation metrics. AP, AP50, and AP75 of the proposed model show slight increases, while APm shows a minor drop for medium objects. The evaluation metrics APs and APl improve for both small and large objects.

Table 1. Evaluation Metrics

Metric	Baseline (%)	Proposed model (%)
AP (Average Precision)	57.949	58.148
AP50	89.262	89.775
AP75	68.978	69.544
APs (Small)	63.017	63.581
APm (Medium)	50.680	49.908
APl (Large)	64.679	65.150

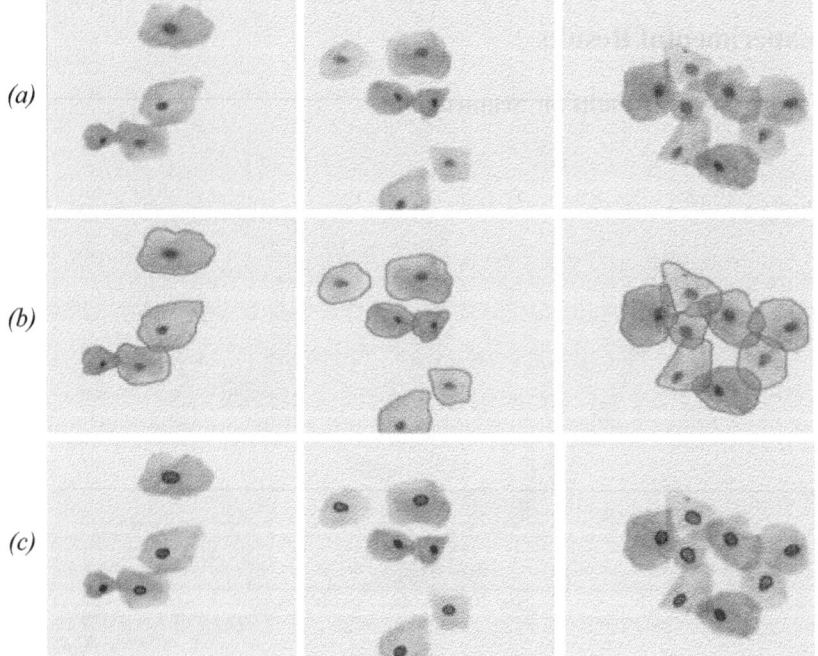

Fig. 4. Segmentation results: (a) input image, (b) cell segmentation, (c) nuclei segmentation.

Figure 4 illustrates the segmentation results of overlapping cells from the proposed model. The top row shows input images of cervical cells. The second row depicts segmentation results for overlapping cells, with nuclei and cytoplasm outlined in red. The bottom row highlights the segmented nuclei as dark blue regions.

Table 2 describes the Average Precision (AP) per specific category for segmentation, including cells and nuclei. The metric in the table shows that the proposed model is now better, with a small increase in accuracy for both cell and nuclei segmentation.

Table 2. Average Precision per specific category

Category	Baseline (%)	Proposed model (%)
Cell	52.904	53.374
Nuclei	62.994	63.296

4.2 Experimental Results for Classification

To perform the cell classification process, we investigated and found that the nuclear-to-cytoplasmic (N/C) ratio significantly influences the determination of whether a cell exhibits malignancy. Analysis in [3, 4] shows that variations in the N/C ratio can effectively differentiate between benign and malignant cells, with an increase in this ratio corresponding to higher-grade lesions. By comparing the N/C ratio across various diagnostic groups, these researchers show a clear trend where the N/C ratio progressively increased from benign to malignant conditions. This trend underscores the N/C ratio as a reliable parameter in cytological analysis for classifying lesion severity. It is essential for accurate diagnosis and informed treatment planning in cervical cancer screening (Fig. 5).

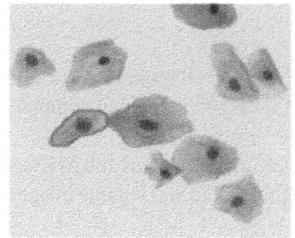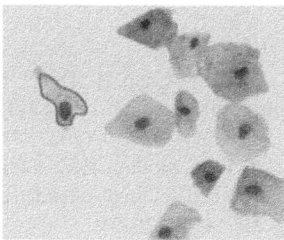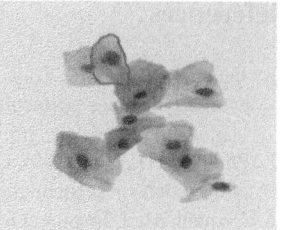

Fig. 5. Demonstration of abnormal cells with enlarged nuclei (N/C > 15%)

After implementing de-overlapping cell state classification on the ISBI2014 dataset test set, we achieved promising results by calculating the nuclear-to-cytoplasmic (N/C) ratio with a threshold of 15%, identifying 3983 normal cells and 38 cells potentially exhibiting pathological characteristics.

Based on these studies, after segmentation of overlapping cells on the ISBI 2014 test dataset, we calculated the cell area and nucleus area, thereby determining the nucleus-to-cytoplasm (N/C) ratio. With a 15% threshold, we classified cervical cells as normal or abnormal. For the test dataset, we identified 3,983 normal cells and 38 cells potentially exhibiting pathological characteristics.

5   Conclusion

Overlapping cells pose a significant challenge in automatic classification systems, as they reduce the accuracy of current analytical methods. This study proposes a model based on fine-tuning the parameters of the DoNet model to segment overlapping cells.

Experimental results demonstrate that the proposed approach outperforms the baseline model. Using the segmentation results and evaluation metrics, we calculated the nucleus-to-cytoplasm (N/C) ratio to detect abnormal cervical cells.

This research, conducted on the ISBI2014 dataset and compared only to the baseline model, limits the generality and objectivity of the evaluation. In the future, we plan to experiment with additional medical datasets, further improve the model, and establish abnormality thresholds based on multiple metrics. We also plan to incorporate semi-supervised learning techniques for the segmentation and classification of overlapping cells.

Research into solutions for segmenting and classifying overlapping cells not only enhances the quality of biological data analysis but also opens new opportunities for applying artificial intelligence in this field. Notably, improving methods for cell segmentation and classification could lead to significant advancements in medical diagnosis and biomedical research, ultimately contributing to better healthcare and promoting scientific progress.

Acknowledgments. This paper was supported by The University of Danang, Vietnam - Korea University of Information and Communication Technology.

References

1. Jiang, H., Zhang, R., Zhou, Y., Wang, Y., Chen, H.: Donet: Deep de-overlapping network for cytology instance segmentation. In: Proceedings of the IEEE/CVF conference on computer vision and pattern recognition, pp. 15641–15650, (2023).
2. Phoulady, H.A., Goldgof, D., Hall, L.O., Mouton, P.R.: A framework for nucleus and overlapping cytoplasm segmentation in cervical cytology extended depth of field and volume images. Comput. Med. Imaging Graph. **59**, 38–49 (2017)
3. Mishra, S., Khurana, U., Kapoor, N., Joshi, A., Joshi, D.: Evaluation of the cytonucleomorphometric parameters for cases diagnosed as squamous cell abnormality on conventional cervico-vaginal pap smears. J. Cytol. **40**(1), 5–11 (2023)
4. Kamal, M., Topiwala, F.: Nonneoplastic cervical cytology. Cytojournal, **19** (2022).
5. Hörst, F., et al.: Cellvit: vision transformers for precise cell segmentation and classification. Med. Image Anal. **94**, 103143 (2024)
6. Zhou, Y., Chen, H., Lin, H., Heng, P.A.: Deep semi-supervised knowledge distillation for overlapping cervical cell instance segmentation. In: Medical Image Computing and Computer Assisted Intervention–MICCAI 2020: 23rd International Conference, Lima, Peru, October 4–8, 2020, Proceedings, Part I 23, pp. 521–531. Springer International Publishing (2020).
7. Chen, J., Zhang, B.: Segmentation of overlapping cervical cells with mask region convolutional neural network. Comput. Math. Methods Med. **2021**(1), 3890988 (2021)
8. Ramakrishnan, V., et al.: Nuclei detection and segmentation of histopathological images using a feature pyramidal network variant of a mask R-CNN. Bioengineering **11**(10), 994 (2024)
9. Zhang, W., Fan, H., Xie, X., Wang, Q., Tang, Y.: Mask guidance pyramid network for overlapping cervical cell edge detection. Appl. Sci. **13**(13), 7526 (2023)
10. Tareef, A.: Adaptive shape prediction model (ASPM) for touched and overlapping cell segmentation in cytology images. Softw. Impacts **17** (2023).
11. Lu, Z., et al.: Evaluation of three algorithms for the segmentation of overlapping cervical cells. IEEE J. Biomed. Health Inform. **21**(2), 441–450 (2016)

12. Naruenatthanaset, K., Chalidabhongse, T.H., Palasuwan, D., Anantrasirichai, N., Palasuwan, A.: Red blood cell segmentation with overlapping cell separation and classification on imbalanced dataset (2020). arXiv preprint arXiv:2012.01321

13. Kiu, S.M., Wang, Y.C.: Geometric feature extraction for identification and classification of overlapping cells for Leukaemia. BioMedInformatics **2**(2), 234–243 (2022)

14. Win, K.Y., Choomchuay, S., Hamamoto, K., Raveesunthornkiat, M.: Detection and classification of overlapping cell nuclei in cytology effusion images using a double-strategy random forest. Appl. Sci., **8**(9) (2018).

15. Paulauskaite-Taraseviciene, A., Sutiene, K., Valotka, J., Raudonis, V., Iesmantas, T.: Deep learning-based detection of overlapping cells. In: Proceedings of the 3rd International Conference on Advances in Artificial Intelligence, pp. 217–220 (2019).

A Multi-model Testcase Recommendation System for Teaching Programming in Higher Education

Tien Vu-Van[1,2], Huy Tran[1,2], Hoang-Anh Pham[1,2(✉)], and Nguyen Huynh-Tuong[3]

[1] Ho Chi Minh City University of Technology (HCMUT), Ho Chi Minh City, Vietnam
{vvtien,tranhuy,anhpham}@hcmut.edu.vn
[2] Vietnam National University Ho Chi Minh City (VNU-HCM), Ho Chi Minh City, Vietnam
[3] Industrial University of Ho Chi Minh City (IUH), Ho Chi Minh City, Vietnam
htnguyen@iuh.edu.vn

Abstract. In educational programming courses, students are tasked with solving large-scale programming projects to apply and reinforce their understanding of key concepts and skills. Testcase Recommendation Systems (TRS) offer personalized support by suggesting curated testcases tailored to the skill levels of individual learners. However, existing approaches, such as those based on Regularized Singular Value Decomposition (RSVD), struggle to effectively incorporate students' submission histories, limiting the personalization and diversity of recommendations. To address these challenges, this paper presents a novel Multi-model Testcase Recommendation System (MTRS) that integrates multiple recommendation models, including the enhanced TimeSVD model, which leverages temporal data to improve accuracy and adaptability. The proposed MTRS evaluates user satisfaction through two metrics: Rating and Usage, while assessing recommendation efficacy with Coverage and Novelty. It has also been successfully implemented in university-level programming courses, with feedback collected through detailed surveys. The results show that TimeSVD excels in generating testcases with high Novelty, whereas RSVD performs better in other metrics, demonstrating the complementary strengths of these models.

Keywords: Testcase Recommendation System · Learning Management System · Time-based Singular Value Decomposition · Regularized Singular Value Decomposition

1 Introduction

Recommender systems (RS) have found an increasingly prominent role in education, transforming how learners access content and resources. In traditional

H. X. Huynh et al. (Eds.): GOODTECHS 2024, LNICST 649, pp. 250–262, 2025.
https://doi.org/10.1007/978-3-032-01497-9_23

education systems, learners often face challenges in navigating a large amount of learning material to identify the resources that best fit their needs. RS in education addresses these challenges by personalizing learning experiences and adapting content recommendations to individual learners' preferences, abilities, and goals. For instance, the authors in [18] developed a system that recommends textbooks and supplementary materials based on a learner's academic performance and areas of improvement. Similarly, [8] proposed an adaptive learning system that dynamically adjusts recommendations based on real-time learning engagement metrics, such as time spent on topics or quiz performance. These systems significantly enhance the learning process by reducing cognitive overload and promoting efficient self-paced study.

Learning Management Systems (LMS) have become indispensable in higher education, facilitating connections and strong interactions between teachers and learners [1]. LMS platforms provide numerous management tools and learning support utilities tailored to managers, lecturers, and learners, focused on tracking the progress of the learner and evaluating performance [21]. Depending on their scale and functionality, LMSs include modules such as lecture videos, social media integration, and learning management tools [14]. Furthermore, LMS platforms support data-driven educational research by enabling automated evaluation of learning achievements, analyzing learning styles, and assessing learner satisfaction [6].

E-learning platforms have particularly benefited from recommender systems, enabling personalized pathways through diverse course offerings. In [7], a system was developed to recommend suitable courses based on the previous learning history and the skills gaps of the student. Another notable example is the work of [12], which combined sentiment analysis with collaborative filtering to recommend discussion threads and peer interactions that aligned with learners' emotional states and academic objectives. Furthermore, [15] demonstrated the potential of RS to improve academic advising by suggesting personalized career paths and course schedules. By leveraging advanced algorithms such as collaborative filtering and content-based methods, educational RS fosters a tailored learning environment, increasing motivation and success rates while reducing dropout rates.

One significant challenge in programming education is the evaluation of learning outcomes. Assignments, a key assessment method, are often complex and require learners to deeply understand lectures and conduct self-research. In programming assignments, evaluation typically involves running student-submitted code against predefined test cases of input-output pairs designed to verify program correctness. Scores are assigned based on the percentage of test cases passed, which directly correlates with the achievement of learning outcomes. However, programming assignments, which often span several weeks, are challenging for learners, who may struggle to debug and test their code efficiently. Given the large class sizes in programming courses, Automatic Grading Systems (AGS) are widely used to grade code submissions. Although AGS tools significantly reduce grading time, they fail to assist learners in improving their code or address specific weaknesses [9,17].

To address these limitations, a Testcase Recommendation System (TRS) has been proposed, aiming to guide students in debugging their code by recommending specific test cases tailored to their learning progress [13]. Unlike AGS, TRS focuses on improving the learner by selecting test cases that are both challenging and achievable [3]. However, traditional TRS methods, such as those leveraging Regularized Singular Value Decomposition (RSVD), fail to consider temporal dynamics, such as how students' performance evolves over iterative feedback cycles [4,19].

Incorporating time-sensitive models, such as TimeSVD, can bridge this gap by accounting for temporal progression. Students typically submit multiple iterations of code over time, and each submission reflects their evolving knowledge and skills. In addition, submission patterns often indicate learner characteristics, such as diligence or difficulty in mastering concepts. Time-sensitive models can adapt recommendations to each student's changing abilities and behaviors, offering a personalized learning experience [4,5,20].

In this study, we propose a multi-model test case recommendation system (MTRS) that integrates TimeSVD to address the limitations of existing TRS approaches. Using temporal dynamics, the MTRS adapts the recommendations to the progress of each learner, enhancing their ability to debug code effectively. Furthermore, we evaluate the system using both quantitative metrics and qualitative surveys in two programming courses at our university. The findings establish a foundation for future integration of advanced models and provide insights into the evolving landscape of personalized learning in programming education.

The remainder of this paper is organized as follows. Section 2 discusses the proposed methodology, Sect. 3 details the implementation and evaluation of the MTRS, and Sect. 4 concludes with insight and future directions.

2   Proposed Approach

2.1   The TRS Integrated with Multiple Recommendation Models

The previous approach, known as the Testcase Recommendation System (TRS) [11], focused on a single model framework. This system comprised two main processes: the training process and the recommendation process. In the training process, learners interact with the system by submitting their source code assignments through the **Learner Submissions** component. These submissions were then forwarded to the Assessment Grading Service (**AGS**) for evaluation, with the results stored in the **Submission Result Data** component. Each night during the assignment timeline, the **Training Scheduler** component would utilize the accumulated submission result data up to that point to automatically train a new model for the next day. The output of this process was a set of saved models intended for testcase recommendations.

Our proposed Multi-model Testcase Recommendation System (MTRS) enhances the previous Testcase Recommendation System (TRS) by integrating multiple models and continuously evaluating their effectiveness. The MTRS, illustrated in Fig. 1, focuses on two main components:

(a) **Training Scheduler.** Instead of relying on a single model trained once per day, the *Training Scheduler* continuously analyzes data from the *Learner Sampling* component, which groups learners based on their initial proficiency levels. Each night, as new submissions are received, the *Training Scheduler* trains multiple recommendation models, each tailored to a specific learner group. This process produces optimized models designed to provide targeted recommendations to each group.

(b) **Learner Sampling.** This component segments the learner population into small groups assigned to specific recommendation models. Each learner group is matched with a single model, ensuring consistency in recommendations throughout the assignment process. The *Learner Sampling* component groups learners according to their initial proficiency, which is determined by scores on an initial set of testcases provided through Moodle. Learners are divided into three categories: high proficiency (scores over 8), moderate proficiency (scores between 5 and 8), and low proficiency or non-submission (scores below 5). These groups are then distributed across recommendation models, such as RSVD, TimeSVD, and others, within the Training Scheduler.

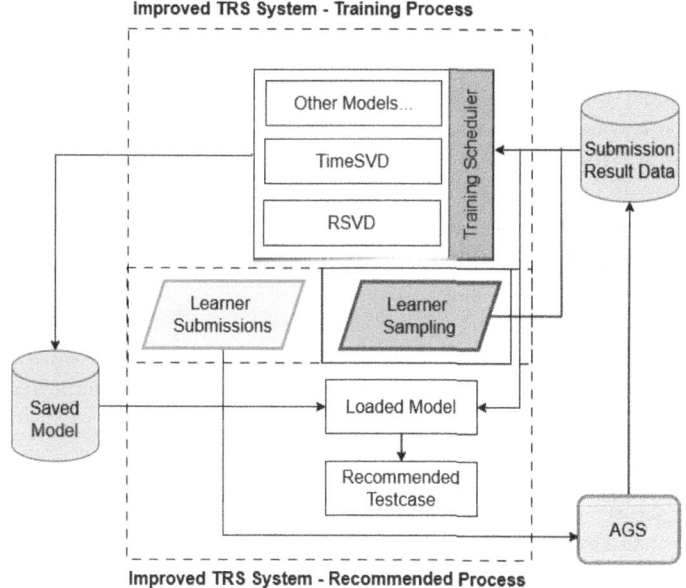

Fig. 1. Overview about the MTRS and the AGS.

The MTRS workflow consists of several interconnected components designed to optimize testcase recommendations. First, the *Learner Submissions* component collects initial submissions from learners. Based on these submissions, the **Learner Sampling** component groups learners by proficiency level. This grouped data is then used by the **Training Scheduler**, which trains multiple recommendation models. These trained models are stored in the **Saved Model** database.

As learners submit their assignments to the **Automated Grading System** (AGS), the AGS evaluates each submission and stores the results in the **Submission Result Data** database. The **Submission Result Data** serves two main purposes. First, it is used by the **Loaded Model** to provide each learner with personalized **Recommended Testcases** tailored to their current skill level. Second, each night, these data are fed into the **Training Scheduler** to retrain and optimize the recommendation models, ensuring continuous improvement for future recommendations.

Building on the implementation described above, we evaluate the feasibility of the RSVD and TimeSVD models within the MTRS. Notably, this marks the first application of the TimeSVD model to the testcase recommendation problem. Looking ahead, the system will be extended to incorporate additional deep learning models in the future.

2.2 Evaluation Metrics

To evaluate the performance of the Testcase Recommendation System (TRS), we utilize two established metrics, **Coverage** [2] and **Novelty** [10].

Furthermore, the authors in [16] defined **Utility** as the value obtained by the system or user from a recommendation. The evaluation of utility can be straightforward from the point of view of the recommendation engine or the owner of the recommendation system. However, evaluating the utility of recommendations is tricky because it involves capturing individual user preferences and figuring out how to combine these preferences to calculate a score for the recommender. Therefore, we propose two new metrics, **Usage** and **Rating** to assess the **Utility** metric explicitly.

Coverage. Coverage measures the system's ability to recommend a wide range of test cases, ensuring fairness and effective utilization of the repository. A higher Coverage indicates that learners access diverse test cases, reducing redundancy. It is calculated as:

$$CC = \frac{|\bigcup_{l=1}^{m} T_l|}{n}, \tag{1}$$

where T_l is the set of test cases recommended to learner l, n is the total number of test cases, and m is the number of learners.

Novelty. Novelty quantifies how unique and unfamiliar the test cases recommended are to learners, promoting engagement and exploration of new challenges. A higher score indicates that learners encounter diverse and previously unseen test cases. Novelty is computed as:

$$novelty(L_l, N) = \frac{|L_l \backslash A_t|}{N}, \tag{2}$$

where L_l is the recommended set for learner l, A_t is the set of all test cases recommended before time t, and N is the total number of test cases.

Usage. Usage reflects the proportion of test cases recommended actively used by learners, with higher values indicating better engagement and utility. It is defined as:

$$U = \frac{\sum_{l=1}^{m} U_l}{m}, \tag{3}$$

where U_l is the number of test cases used by learner l.

Rating. Rating measures learner satisfaction with the difficulty of the recommended test cases, gauging their suitability to foster skill development. A higher score suggests alignment with learner proficiency. Rating is calculated as:

$$R = \frac{\sum_{l=1}^{m} R_l}{m}, \tag{4}$$

where R_l is the satisfaction score given by learner l.

Unlike **Coverage** and **Novelty**, which rely on system-generated logs, **Usage** and **Rating** are based on user feedback collected via questionnaires, providing qualitative insights into the TRS's effectiveness.

2.3   User Feedback Collection Questionnaire

While **Coverage** and **Novelty** metrics rely on system-generated logs, **Usage** and **Rating** require direct user feedback. To gather this information, a survey form (Fig. 2) was distributed after learners completed a set of test cases.

Usage reflects the number of recommended test cases learners actively used. Learners were asked, *"What test cases did you actually use?"*, allowing us to quantify the engagement by counting the utilized test cases.

Rating measures satisfaction with the difficulty of recommended test cases. Learners responded to *"Are you satisfied with the difficulty of the recommended test cases?"* on a 5-point scale (1 = very dissatisfied, 5 = very satisfied). This simple scale ensured clarity and standardized feedback.

Additional questions explored learner perceptions, such as arranging test cases by time spent. However, this data is excluded from the current analysis for future study due to complexity and unrelated factors (e.g., testcase design vs. difficulty). Learners also had the opportunity to provide open-ended feedback, aiding system refinement but less relevant to this research.

3   Implementation and Results

3.1   Implementation

We developed and deployed a Testcase Recommendation System (TRS) to support learners in submitting their code, receiving feedback, and obtaining recommended test cases to improve their programming skills. This system was

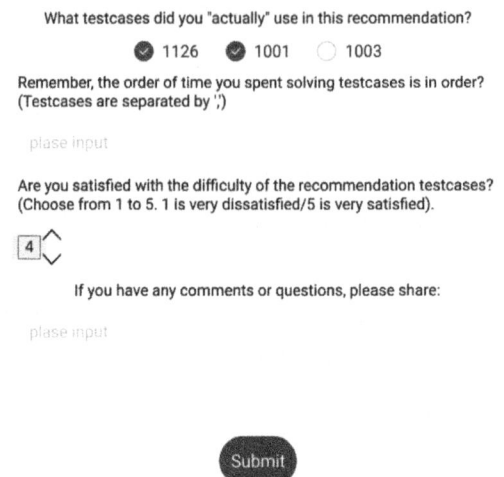

Fig. 2. Survey Form.

implemented on a Linux server configured with Ubuntu 22.04.2 LTS, a 4-core CPU, 8 GB of RAM, and SSD storage with approximately 160 GB capacity.

To evaluate the system, the dataset was split in a way that respects the chronological order of submissions. For each learner, the first submission date was excluded from the training process to avoid any potential bias. Data from all submission dates prior to the current evaluation date were aggregated to form the training set, while submissions on the evaluation date were used as the test set.

The models used in the evaluation included TimeSVD and RSVD. The TimeSVD model was configured with a regularization parameter of 0.05 and a learning rate of 0.001. For comparison, the RSVD model was set up with the same regularization parameter but used a higher learning rate of 0.05.

In the MTRS workflow, learners begin by uploading their code and tracking the submission status through the interface. Once submitted, they are directed to the recommendation module, where testcases tailored to their code are provided, along with detailed input and output information to assist in debugging and achieving the correct result. To access the next set of recommendations, learners must first resolve any errors in their code and ensure mastery of the current set.

After completing the recommended testcases, learners participate in the feedback loop by filling out an evaluation form (Fig. 2). This form asks learners to select the testcases used in their code improvement process, report the time spent on each, and rank them from longest to shortest. They are also asked to rate their satisfaction with the testcases and suggest improvements for the system. Upon completion of the survey, learners are provided with new recommended testcases.

3.2 Results

The proposed MTRS is deployed for university-level students in two courses: Programming Fundamentals (PF) and Data Structures and Algorithms (DSA). Table 1 summarises the statistical results that offer valuable insights into the engagement and performance of learners in two distinct subjects. In the PF course, out of 1576 learners, a significant proportion of 978 actively participated by submitting code over five days. This resulted in 3887 submissions and 1137 recommendations, indicating an average of approximately 3.97 submissions per learner. Besides, in the DSA course, out of 537 learners, 295 were actively engaged, with submissions occurring over seven days totaling 4788. Notably, the recommendation count stands at 937, highlighting a robust engagement within this subject area. Notably, the average number of submissions per learner in DSA is substantially higher, indicating a deeper level of involvement and potentially heightened interest, with an average of approximately 16.23 submissions per learner.

Table 1. Statistical results after assignment implementation

Course	Programming Fundamentals	Data Structures and Algorithms
Total learners	1576	537
Learners used TRS	978	295
Days with submissions	5	7
Submissions	3887	4788
Recommendations	1137	937
Average submissions per learner	3.97	16.23

Table 2a presents evaluation metrics for the RSVD and TimeSVD models when deploying the proposed MTRS within the PF course. Both models demonstrated competitive performance across the evaluation metrics. RSVD model achieved a Rating of 3.48 and a Usage score of 2.63, with a Coverage metric of 0.71 and a Novelty score of 0.65. In comparison, TimeSVD attained a Rating of 3.26 and a slightly lower Usage score of 2.4. TimeSVD outperformed RSVD in terms of Novelty, scoring 0.93, albeit with a lower Coverage metric of 0.61. Overall, RSVD outperformed TimeSVD in terms of Rating, Usage, and Coverage metrics. Conversely, TimeSVD exhibited higher Novelty compared to RSVD.

Meanwhile, Table 2b reports evaluation metrics for the RSVD and TimeSVD models for the DSA course. Both models exhibit robust performance, with slight variations in specific metrics. RSVD achieved a Rating of 3.3 and a Usage metric of 2.61, alongside a notably high Coverage score of 0.83, albeit with a relatively lower Novelty score of 0.33. In contrast, TimeSVD outperformed RSVD marginally in terms of Rating and Novelty, attaining a Rating of 3.35 and a Novelty score of 0.36. Additionally, TimeSVD demonstrated a higher Usage score of 2.75, although its Coverage metric remained similar to RSVD at 0.84. In the metrics considered for the DSA course, all four metrics indicate that TimeSVD performs better than RSVD, although there is not much improvement. This result is similar to the findings from MovieLens [20], where TimeSVD is better than RSVD but not significantly.

Table 2. Average Evaluation Metrrics

(a) Programming Fundamentals

Model	Rating	Usage	Coverage	Novelty
RSVD	3.48	2.63	0.71	0.65
TimeSVD	3.26	2.40	0.61	0.93

(b) Data Structures and Algorithms

Model	Rating	Usage	Coverage	Novelty
RSVD	3.3	2.61	0.83	0.33
TimeSVD	3.35	2.75	0.84	0.36

From both Tables 2a and 2b, we can see that for each assignment, the metric values within each model can be close together, as seen in the DSA course, or they can vary considerably, as observed in the PF course. The proposed MTRS, as a multi-model system, helps assess the effectiveness of each model and compare them to each other. This benefit can be utilized to select the best recommendation model or combine multiple models to provide recommendations that compromise numerous metrics simultaneously.

3.3   Additional Analysis

We analyzed the metric trends for two courses, Programming Fundamentals (PF) and Data Structures and Algorithms (DSA), to evaluate the stability and performance of the RSVD and TimeSVD models. The results reveal clear differences in how each model performs across various metrics, offering insights into their suitability for different learning contexts.

Figures 3 and 4 illustrate these trends. In PF, RSVD excelled in Usage, Coverage, and Rating (Figs. 3b, 3c, and 3a), while Novelty trends (Fig. 3d) showed a linear decline for RSVD and a concave pattern for TimeSVD. In DSA, TimeSVD led in Usage and late-stage Rating (Figs. 4b and 4a), whereas RSVD demonstrated stronger performance in Coverage and Novelty toward the assignment's end (Figs. 4c and 4d).

In the PF course, RSVD consistently outperformed TimeSVD in Rating, Usage, and Coverage across all assignment days. Specifically, Rating scores were relatively stable from the second day onward, with RSVD maintaining a slight

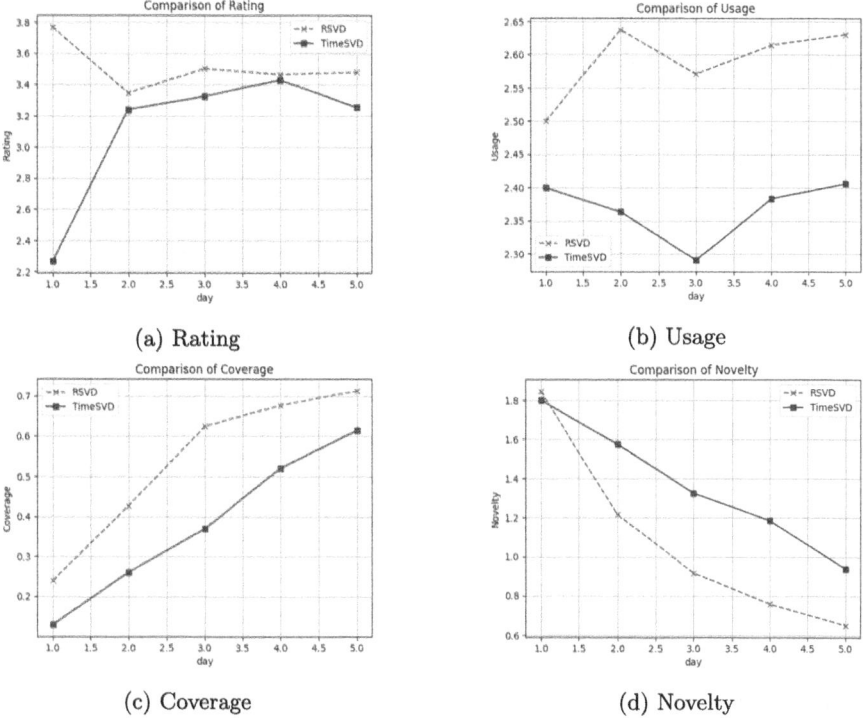

Fig. 3. MTRS's evaluation per day for the Programming Fundamentals course.

advantage except on day three, where TimeSVD momentarily improved. The Usage metric demonstrated significant differences, with RSVD consistently scoring higher by an average of 12%, reflecting better student engagement and utility. Similarly, in Coverage, RSVD exhibited superior performance, averaging a 14% advantage, indicating its ability to present a broader range of test cases. In contrast, Novelty scores showed TimeSVD performing better on most days, reflecting its steadier approach to introducing new test cases. RSVD followed a linear decline in novelty, suggesting it challenges advanced learners early on, while TimeSVD's concave novelty curve may benefit average learners by providing a gradual increase in new content.

For the DSA course, the results showed distinct patterns in model performance. Rating scores stabilized from the third day onward, with TimeSVD outperforming RSVD by the end of the assignment. In Usage, TimeSVD consistently scored higher across all days, with an average advantage of 9%. However, in Coverage, RSVD generally outperformed TimeSVD, except on the final day when TimeSVD exhibited a brief improvement. The average difference in Coverage was smaller in DSA (7%) compared to PF. Regarding Novelty, RSVD tended to perform better on most days toward the end, with smaller average differences (5%) than observed in the PF course.

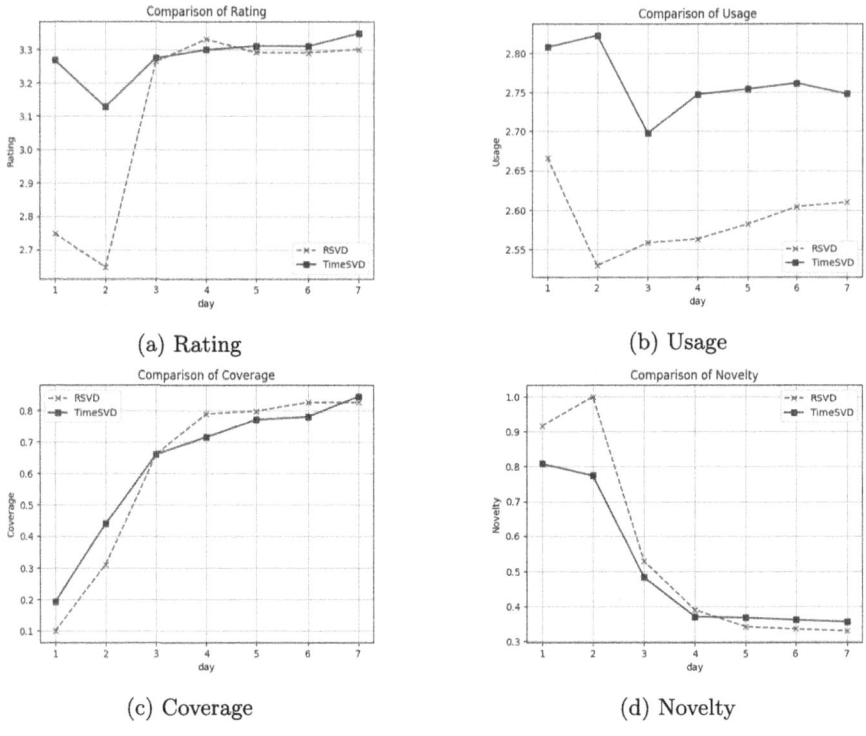

(a) Rating

(b) Usage

(c) Coverage

(d) Novelty

Fig. 4. MTRS's evaluation per day for the Data Structures and Algorithm course.

Overall, the results of the PF course suggest that the emphasis on early novelty and broader test coverage of RSVD is particularly beneficial for dynamic and advanced learners, while TimeSVD's steady novelty curve may suit learners who require a more gradual introduction to diverse content. In the DSA course, TimeSVD's higher Usage scores indicate greater accessibility and practical application, while RSVD's strengths in Coverage and Novelty favor students who benefit from more comprehensive test cases and diverse knowledge.

In conclusion, RSVD demonstrated superior performance across most metrics in the PF course, while in DSA, its effectiveness depended on specific learning goals. The steadier novelty of TimeSVD and the higher usage scores make it suitable for general learners in DSA. However, RSVD remains advantageous for scenarios that require broad test coverage or greater diversity in test cases. These findings highlight the importance of aligning model selection with course objectives, particularly to balance novelty, coverage, and usage.

4   Conclusion

This study presents MTRS, a multi-model testcase recommendation system designed to enhance programming education by integrating multiple recommendation models. The system introduces adjusted metrics (Coverage and Novelty) and proposes new metrics, Rating and Usage, to evaluate recommendations comprehensively. Deployed in introductory programming courses during the 2023-2024 academic year, MTRS enabled a comparative analysis of TimeSVD, optimized for temporal dynamics, and RSVD, the previously used model. The findings reveal significant differences in model performance, particularly in Usage and Ratings, underscoring the value of a multi-model approach in adapting to students' evolving needs.

Although the results are promising, the study has limitations. The dataset was relatively small due to the short deployment period, limiting the generalizability of the findings. Additionally, the focus on classical machine learning models leaves room for exploring advanced techniques such as deep learning. The study also did not investigate extensively how model performance varies across different assignments or courses, which could further enhance personalization.

Future work will address these limitations by deploying MTRS over multiple semesters to gather larger datasets and test its adaptability in diverse contexts. Incorporating deep learning and methods for dynamically selecting or integrating models will further enhance recommendation accuracy and personalization. These developments aim to create a more robust and learner-centric system that effectively supports programming education.

Acknowledgment. This research is funded by Vietnam National University Ho Chi Minh City (VNU-HCM) under grant number DS2022-20-07. The authors also acknowledge Ho Chi Minh City University of Technology (HCMUT), VNU-HCM for supporting this study.

References

1. Adzharuddin, N.: Learning management system (LMS) among university students: does it work?. Int. J. e-Educ. e-Bus. e-Manag. e-Learn. **3**(233) (2013)
2. Aggarwal, C.C.: An Introduction to Recommender Systems. The Textbook, Recommender Systems (2016)
3. Azizi, M., Do, H.: A collaborative filtering recommender system for test case prioritization in web applications. In: Proceedings of the 33rd Annual ACM Symposium on Applied Computing. Association for Computing Machinery, pp. 1560–1567 (2018)
4. Bell, Y.K.C.V.R.: The Bellkor 2008 solution to the Netflix prize. Technical Report if applicable, AT&T Labs (2008)
5. Ding, Y., Li, X.: Time weight collaborative filtering. In: Proceedings of a Conference (if applicable), pp. 485–492 (2005)
6. Graf, S., Kinshuk, D.: Analysing the behaviour of students in learning management systems with respect to learning styles. Proc. Europ. Conf. Technol. Enhanc. Learn. (2008). https://doi.org/10.1007/978-3-540-76361_3
7. Hofmann, T.: Latent semantic models for collaborative filtering. ACM Trans. Info. Syst. **22**(1), 89–115 (2004)

8. Hofmann, T., Puzicha, J.: Latent class models for collaborative filtering. In: Proceedings of the Sixteenth International Joint Conference on Artificial Intelligence (IJCAI '99), pp. 688–693 (1999)

9. John, S.B., Gaur, D., Siddiqui, A.: Test case recommendation for regression with named entity recognition for test step prediction. In: Proceedings of the 4th Biennial International Conference on Nascent Technologies in Engineering, pp. 1–6 (2021)

10. Lathia, N., Hailes, S., Capra, L., Amatriain, X.: Temporal diversity in recommendersystems. In: Proceeding of the 33rd International ACM SIGIR Conference on Research and Development in Information Retrieval, pp. 210—-217 (2010)

11. Lee, J., Sun, M., Lebanon, G.: A comparative study of collaborative filtering algorithms. CoRR **abs/1205.3193** (2012). http://arxiv.org/abs/1205.3193

12. Mehta, B., Hofmann, T., Nejdl, W.: Robust collaborative filtering. In: Proceedings of the 2007 ACM Conference on Recommender Systems (RecSys '07), pp. 49–56 (2007)

13. Nandan, S.: Test case recommendation system. Int. J. Adv. Res. Ideas Innov. Technol. **52** (2019)

14. Otchie, W., Pedaste, M.: Social media as a learning management system: is it a tool for achieving the goal of "education for all"?. US-China Educ. Rev. A **9**, 79–90 (2019). https://doi.org/10.17265/2161-623X/2019.02.003

15. Rennie, J.D.M., Srebro, N.: Fast maximum margin matrix factorization for collaborative prediction. In: Proceedings of the 22nd International Conference on Machine Learning (ICML '05), pp. 713–719 (2005)

16. Shani, G., Gunawardana, A.: Evaluating recommendation systems, vol. 8, pp. 257–294 (2011). https://doi.org/10.1007/978-0-387-85820-3

17. Shimmi, S., Rahimi, M.: Leveraging code-test co-evolution patterns for automated test case recommendation. In: Proceedings of the 3rd ACM/IEEE International Conference on Automation of Software Test (AST), pp. 65–76 (2022)

18. Strainu, R.M.P., Georgescu, M.: SOA: the link between modern educational technologies and mobile learning in the higher education landscape. Timisoara J. Econ. Bus. **10**(1), 120–133 (2017)

19. Töscher, A., Jahrer, M.: The Bigchaos Solution to the Netflix Prize 2008 (2008). technical report

20. Xiang, L., Yang, Q.: Time-dependent models in collaborative filtering based recommender system. In: 2009 IEEE/WIC/ACM International Conference on Web Intelligence and Intelligent Agent Technology - Workshops, pp. 450–457 (2009)

21. Yildirim, S., Temur, N., Kocaman, A., Goktas, Y.: What makes a good LMS: an analytical approach to assessment of LMSS. In: Proceedings of the 8th International Conference on Information Technology Based Higher Education and Training, pp. 125–130 (2004). https://doi.org/10.1109/ITHET.2004.1358150

Energy-Based Bounding Box Generation for Object Detection

Dung Thi Dang$^{(\boxtimes)}$ ⓘ

Can Tho University of Technology, Can Tho City, Vietnam
dtdung@ctuet.edu.vn

Abstract. In this study, we apply the energy model to improve accuracy and performance in object detection. The research uses popular datasets such as PASCAL VOC 2012 to train and evaluate the model. The results show that by integrating energy models instead of relying solely on regression methods to predict the bounding box coordinates, as in traditional approaches, this energy-based framework combines visual, geometric, and spatial factors to optimize object detection more comprehensively and accurately.

Keywords: Deep Learning · Object Detection · Energy Basic Model · Bounding Box Detection · Image Processing

1 Introduction

Although regression-based methods are fundamental in object detection, they face three critical challenges: visual consistency issues where IoU-focused optimization leads to poorly fitted bounding boxes, geometric constraint limitations in handling object-specific aspect ratios and deformations, and inadequate modeling of spatial relationships between objects [1, 2]. To address these limitations, we propose a novel approach that moves beyond traditional coordinate prediction to integrate visual characteristics assessment, geometric constraint modeling, and spatial relationship analysis for more comprehensive and accurate object detection [3, 4]. This method demonstrates significant improvements over conventional regression-based approaches by considering the holistic context of object detection rather than treating each component in isolation. The proposed framework integrates three key components to improve object detection accuracy: visual consistency assessment using deep CNN features to ensure that the bounding boxes match the characteristics of the objects (color, texture, shape) [5, 6] geometric constraint assessment that leverages prior knowledge about object properties (e.g., aspect ratios, size constraints) to generate more reasonable predictions [5, 7]; and spatial relationship modeling that handles complex scenarios with multiple overlapping objects considering their relative positions and interactions [4, 8]. This comprehensive approach aims to overcome the limitations of traditional regression-based methods by incorporating visual, geometric, and contextual information in a unified detection framework.

© ICST Institute for Computer Sciences, Social Informatics and Telecommunications Engineering 2025
Published by Springer Nature Switzerland AG 2025. All Rights Reserved
H. X. Huynh et al. (Eds.): GOODTECHS 2024, LNICST 649, pp. 263–272, 2025.
https://doi.org/10.1007/978-3-032-01497-9_24

In summary, instead of relying solely on regression methods to predict bounding box coordinates as in traditional approaches, this energy-based framework combines visual, geometric, and spatial factors to optimize object detection more comprehensive and accurate manner. The article is organized into 5 parts. Part 1 introduces the research context and proposes the EBM_BOX approach for effective bounding-box detection. Part 2 presents an overview of related research, highlighting limitations in current studies. Part 3 describes in detail the visual consistency, geometric constraints, and spatial relationships between bounding boxes. Part 4 presents the experimental results with different scenarios. Part 5 is the conclusion.

2 Related Research

Many object detection methods have been developed, including

2.1 Traditional Methods Based on Anchor Boxes

Traditional object detection methods are mostly based on using anchor boxes as the basis for bounding box detection. In one-stage object detection, [9] proposed YOLO (You Only Look Once), a breakthrough model that uses a grid system to predict bounding boxes and confidence. The development of YOLO through versions with many important improvements has been summarized and analyzed in detail by [10]. In parallel, [11] developed SSD (Single Shot Detector), an advanced method that uses multi-scale feature maps to detect objects, then [12] improved SSD by optimizing the default box mechanism and feature extraction to increase the accuracy for small objects. In a two-stage architecture, [13] proposed Faster R-CNN with Region Proposal Network (RPN), a major step forward in generating potential bounding box proposals based on anchor boxes. [14] further improved the performance through redesigning the architecture and improving the learning mechanism.

2.2 Anchor-Free Trends

The trend of eliminating the need for predefined anchor boxes has been strongly developed recently. [3] proposed FCOS, an anchor-free object detection method with a simple design but high efficiency. This method eliminates the use of anchor boxes, instead directly predicting bounding boxes from feature points on the feature map. [15] introduced RepPoints, a new method that uses point sets instead of traditional anchor boxes. RepPoints not only eliminates the need for predefined anchor boxes, but also provides a more flexible representation of objects. This method automatically learns to place representative points at important locations of the object, which helps to better capture the shape and structure of the object. In particular, FCOS developed by Tian et al. demonstrated that anchor-free methods can achieve performance on par with or even outperform anchor-based methods [3]. FCOS uses a fully convolutional network to directly predict the bounding box and score for each location on the map, eliminating the need to design and tune anchor boxes.

These methods show that anchor-free can achieve comparable or superior performance to anchor-based, reducing the need to design and tune anchor boxes.

2.3 Energy-Based Models (EBMs)

Traditional models in machine learning usually focus on two main tasks: classification and regression. These tasks include tasks such as image classification, text or object recognition in classification and continuous value prediction such as house prices or sales in regression. However, EBMs [16, 17] open up a new direction with the ability to estimate probability over the entire data space, not just limited to classification and regression. As a result, the energy model brings high flexibility and applicability, can model complex distributions of data and generate highly realistic patterns. LeCun [18] pointed out that avoiding the costly normalization process is an important advantage of EBMs, especially in classification and object detection problems.

Recent studies by LeCun and Huang [18] have highlighted the flexibility of EBMs in integrating with neural network architectures, while Du and Mordatch [19] have shown the ability to accept approximate results when searching for the lowest energy. Grathwohl et al. [20] proposed the Energy Discrepancy method, which allows for more efficient model training without the need for complex sampling. Duvenaud et al. [21] further improved the traditional MCMC-free training method. EBMs have proven effective in many practical applications from face recognition to language processing. Suhail et al. [5] applied EBMs in modeling scene graphs from images, while Wu et al. [22] developed Conjugate Energy-Based Models (CEBMs) to extend the capabilities in computer vision.

3 Proposed Method

3.1 Proposed Algorithm

Input image $I \in R^{(HxWx3)}$, the goal is to determine the set of optimal bounding boxes B $= \{b_1, b_2, ..., b_n\}$, in which each box $b_1 = (x_i, y_i, w_i, h_i)$ exactly surrounds the object in the image where x_i, y_i upper left corner coordinates; w_i, h_i width and height; n: number of objects to be detected. The optimization model is based on three components.

3.1.1 Evaluate Image Conformity (Visual Energy)

Based on the image energy $E_{visual}(b_i)$, reflecting the confidence $P(c_i \mid I, b_i)$ provided by the object detection model, by the formula.

$$E_{visual}(b_i) = -\log(P(c_i \mid I, b_i)) \tag{1}$$

where:

- b_i: Bounding box corresponding to object i.
- I: Input image.
- c_i: Object class of b_i
- $P(c_i \mid I, b_i)$: Confidence score, value from 0 to 1.
- The $-\log$ function ensures that E_{visual} is always positive and lower energy.

    corresponds to higher confidence.

Algorithm 1: VisualEnergy Procedure

Input: Bounding box b_i
Output: Visual energy E_{visual} (b_i)
   Confidence score: $P(c_i \mid I, b_i)$
   Visual energy: E_{visual} $(b_i) \leftarrow -\log(P(c_i \mid I, b_i))$
return E_{visual} (b_i)

3.1.2 Geometric Energy Egeometric (Geometric Energy)

$E_{\text{geometric}}(b_i)$ ensures appropriate box ratio and size.

$$E_{\text{geometric}}(b_i) \leftarrow \lambda_1 \left(ar - ar^*\right)^2 + \lambda_2(s - s^*)^2 \qquad (2)$$

where:

- (ar^*) ideal aspect ratio and (s^*) ideal size.
- $ar = \text{height}(b_i) / \text{width}(b_i)$: Actual aspect ratio.
- $s = \text{width}(b_i) \times \text{height}(b_i)$: Actual size.
- λ_1, λ_2: Priority weight between ratio and size.

The smaller the $E_{\text{geometric}}$ result, the closer the b_i block is to the ideal parameter.

Algorithm 2 GeometricEnergy Procedure

Input: Bounding box b_i
Output: Geometric energy $E_{geometric}$ (b_i)
   Aspect ratio: $ar \leftarrow \text{height}(b_i) / \text{width}(b_i)$
   Size: $s \leftarrow \text{width}(b_i) \times \text{height}(b_i)$
Geometric energy:
   $E_{geometric}$ $(b_i) \leftarrow \lambda_1 (ar - ar^*)^2 + \lambda_2 (s - s^*)^2$
return $E_{geometric}$ (b_i)

3.1.3 Evaluate Spatial Relationship (Context Energy)

E_{context} (b_i, b_j) calculates the relationship between boxes.

$$E_{\text{context}}(b_i, b_j) = w(b_i, b_j) \times \text{IoU}(b_i, b_j) \qquad (3)$$

where:

- $w(b_i, b_j)$: Spatial weight between b_i and b_j
- $\text{IoU}(b_i, b_j)$: Ratio of the intersection area of two bounding boxes.

Algorithm 3 ContextEnergy Procedure

Input: Bounding box b_i, b_j
   Output: Contextual energy $E_{\text{context}}(b_i, b_j)$
   Compute spatial weight: $w(b_i, b_j)$
   Compute IoU: $\text{IoU}(b_i, b_j)$
   Contextual energy: $E_{\text{context}}(b_i, b_j) \leftarrow w(b_i, b_j) \times \text{IoU}(b_i, b_j)$
   return $E_{\text{context}}(b_i, b_j)$

The total energy function E(B|I) combines three components.

$$E(B|I) = \Sigma E_{\text{visual}}(b_i) + \Sigma E_{\text{geometric}}(b_i) + \Sigma_{\text{context}}(b_i) \tag{4}$$

The goal is to optimize B^* to determine the most appropriate bounding box set, ensuring high reliability, correct geometry and reflecting spatial relationships.

3.2 Proposed Method

The general architecture of the bounding box detection model with the energy modeling approach is modeled as shown in Fig. 1:

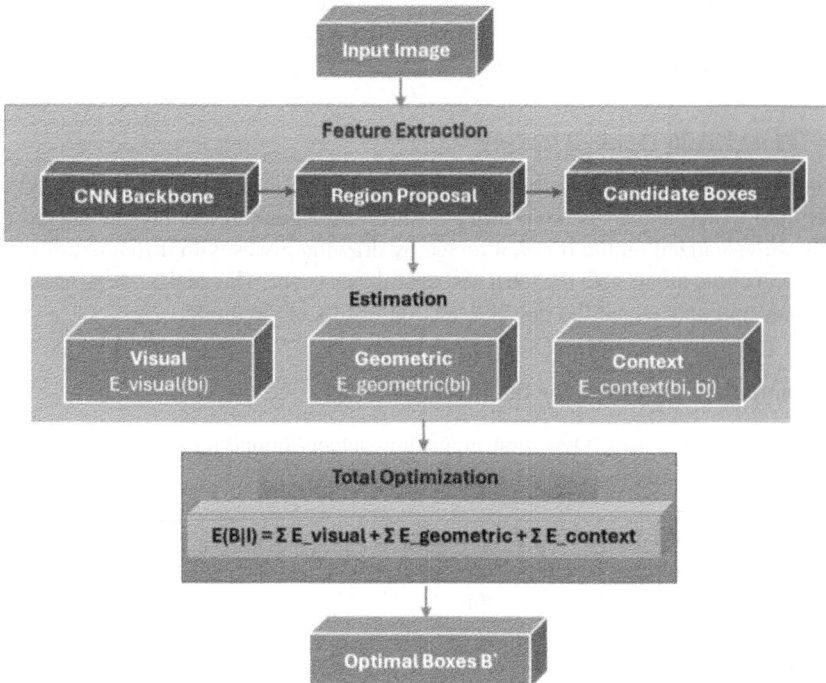

Fig. 1. General architecture of the bounding box detection model.

3.2.1 Feature Extraction

The process begins with an input RGB image of size H × W × 3, which is passed through a CNN backbone such as VGG, ResNet to extract important features. Feature maps are generated at different layers, capturing both local and global information of the image. Next, the Region Proposal Network (RPN) will propose regions that are likely to contain objects, thereby generating a set of initial Candidate Boxes. This stage forms the basis for evaluating and optimizing the boxes in the following steps.

3.2.2 Estimation

After obtaining the set of candidate boxes, the model calculates three main components. Visual Energy (E_{visual}) evaluates the confidence of each box through the probability of containing an object, using the formula (1). Geometric Energy ($E_{geometric}$) considers the geometric suitability of boxes through their proportions and sizes, using the formula (2). Context Energy ($E_{context}$) evaluates the spatial relationship between boxes through the formula (3).

3.2.3 Total Optimization

The total optimization is combined into a total function (4). The optimization process will try to minimize this energy function to determine the optimal box set B^*. The minimization also considers the confidence of the detection, the geometric suitability, and the relationship between the boxes.

3.2.4 Final Result Optimal Boxes B^*

The output consists of a set of refined optimal boxes B^*, , each labeled with a specific object class (such as car, person) along with a corresponding confidence score. The results are visualized on the original image by drawing boxes with different colors for each object class, along with the label and confidence score. This makes it easy for users to evaluate and understand the object detection results of the model.

3.3 Simulation Algorithm for the Problem

The EBM-Bounding Box Detection algorithm detects bounding boxes based on the energy calculated from the visual image features shown.

Algorithm 4 EBM-Bounding Box Detection Procedure

Input: Set of bounding box $B = \{b_1, b_2, ..., b_n\}$
Output: Optimized total energy value
$E_{total} \leftarrow 0$
for $b_i \in B$ **do**
   $E_{total} \leftarrow E_{total} + \text{VisualEnergy}(b_i) + \text{GeometricEnergy}(b_i)$
   for $i = 1$ to $n - 1$ **do**
   for $j = i + 1$ to n **do**
   $E_{total} \leftarrow E_{total} + \text{ContextEnergy}(b_i, b_j)$
   return $MinimizeEnergy(B, E_{total})$

Input: B = $\{b_1, b_2, ..., b_n\}$: Set of bounding boxes to be optimized.

Output: Optimal energy value Etotal.

Initialization: $E_{total} \leftarrow 0$: Initially, the total energy is initialized to 0.

Calculate energy for each bounding box $b^i \in$ B:

• **Visual energy:** Use the VisualEnergy(b_i) function to calculate the visual energy for bounding box b_i.

• **Geometric energy:** Use the GeometricEnergy(b_i) function to calculate the geometric energy.

• **Addition:**

$$E_{total} \leftarrow E_{total} + \text{VisualEnergy}(b_i) + \text{GeometricEnergy}(b_i) \qquad (5)$$

Calculate the context energy for each pair of bounding boxes:

• For each pair $b_i, b_j \in$ B (i $\neq$ j).

Use the ContextEnergy(b_i, b_j) function to calculate the context energy between the two bounding boxes.

• **Addition:**

$$E_{total} \leftarrow E_{total} + \text{ContextEnergy}(b_i, b_j) \qquad (6)$$

Optimize the total Etotal energy:

• Call the MinimizeEnergy(B, E_{total}) function to find the bounding box B configuration so that the total E_{total} energy is the smallest.

Return:

• The optimal E_{total} energy value after optimization.

4 Experiment

4.1 Data

In this study, we use the PASCAL VOC 2012 dataset [23] consisting of 20 object classes with 11,540 images and 27,450 objects to evaluate the performance of the EBM_BOX model.

4.2 Environment Setup

We train the model on Google Colab Pro; the code is sent to Google's server, which will execute and return the results. We choose the Tesla K80 GPU environment with about 12 GB of RAM and V100 GPU, the Python programming language and the necessary libraries, including NumPy, Torch, Pickle, Cv2, Argparse, TorchVision, operating system, Python image library (PIL). The first round of training and testing is performed with a relatively small dataset from the Database. The first round of training and testing was performed with a relatively small image dataset from the Database.

The analysis results in Fig. 2 show that In terms of overall improvement, the system achieved the most significant progress in the Visual aspect with an average increase of 10.7%. Meanwhile, the improvement in the Geometric aspect was only 0.7% and the

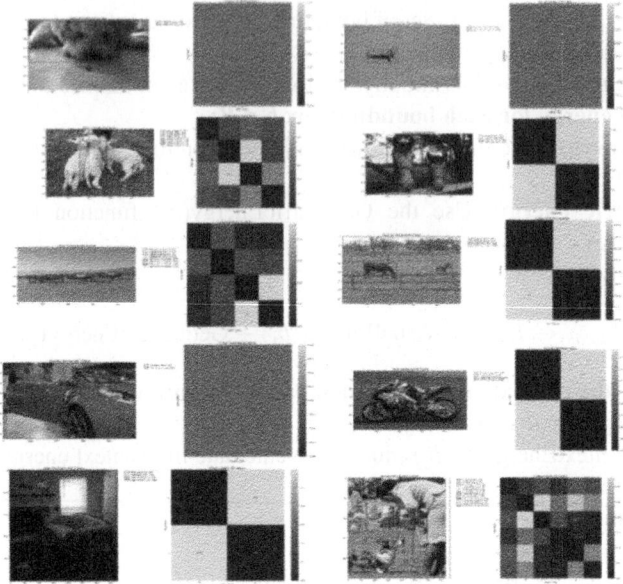

Fig. 2. Test results Energy-based Bounding Box Generation for Object Detection.

Context aspect was even more modest at 0.1%. This shows that the system has made significant progress in image recognition, but still needs further improvement in the geometric and contextual aspects.

A detailed analysis of each object class shows the unevenness in the improvement level. The most prominent is the "car" class with a Visual improvement of up to 23.2%, followed by "dog" with 20.63% and "horse" with 16.68%. In particular, the "motorbike" class shows an unusual result with a negative Visual index (− 0.5%) but the highest Geometric improvement (1.9%).

In terms of Geometric, in addition to "motorbike", the classes "person" (1.52%) and "car" (1.1%) also showed significant improvements. This shows that the system has made progress in determining the location and shape of these objects. However, the class "sofa" did not record any improvement in all three aspects, which needs to be considered and adjusted in future versions.

As for the Context improvement, although generally limited, some classes such as "sheep" (0.17%) and "aeroplane" (0.16%) showed small improvements. This suggests that the system has begun to be able to understand the relationships between objects in the environment, albeit at a modest level.

5 Conclusion

EBM_BOX is a potential method for object detection, combining visual, geometric and spatial elements. These three components are integrated through the energy function $E(B|I)$, which is optimized to determine the optimal bounding box set B^*.

We propose a new method based on the energy model with a solid theoretical foundation. This method uses a convolutional neural network architecture, thanks to its ability to handle geometric variations, visual matching and spatial relationships. As a result, the method brings high flexibility and significantly improves the accuracy of bounding box detection. This method opens up the potential for wide application in many fields such as medicine (tumor detection), remote sensing (terrain change detection) and industry (product quality inspection).

References

1. Zheng, Z., Wang, P., Liu, W., Li, J., Ye, R., Ren, D.: Distance-IoU loss: faster and better learning for bounding box regression. Proc. AAAI Conf. Artif. Intell. **34**(07), 12993–13000 (2020). https://doi.org/10.1609/aaai.v34i07.6999
2. Rezatofighi, H., Tsoi, N., Gwak, J., Sadeghian, A., Reid, I., Savarese, S.: Generalized intersection over union: a metric and a loss for bounding box regression. In: Proceedings of the IEEE/CVF Conference on Computer Vision and Pattern Recognition, pp. 658–666 (2019)
3. Tian, Z., Shen, C., Chen, H., He, T.: FCOS: a simple and strong anchor-free object detector. Proc. IEEE Trans. Pattern Anal. Mach. Intell. (2020). https://doi.org/10.1109/TPAMI.2020.3032166
4. Zhu, X., Su, W., Lu, L., Li, B., Wang, X., Dai, J.: Deformable DETR: Deformable transformers for end-to-end object detection. In: Proceedings of the (2020) arXiv:2010.04159
5. Suhail, M., Mittal, A., Siddiquie, B., Broaddus, C., Eledath, J., Medioni, G.: Energy-based learning for scene graph generation. In: Proceedings of the IEEE/CVF Conference on Computer Vision and Pattern Recognition, pp. 13936–13945 (2021)
6. Wu, H., Esmaeili, B., Wick, M., Tristan, J.B., Van De Meent, J.W.: Conjugate energy-based models. In: Proceedings of the International Conference on Machine Learning. PMLR., pp. 11228–11239 (2021)
7. Li, X., Wang, W., Wu, L., Chen, S., Hu, X., Li, J., et al.: Generalized focal loss: learning qualified and distributed bounding boxes for dense object detection. Proc. Neural Inf. Process. Syst. **33**, 21002–21012 (2020)
8. Divvala, S.K., Hoiem, D., Hays, J.H., Efros, A.A., Hebert, M.: An empirical study of context in object detection. In: Proceedings of the IEEE Conference on Computer Vision and Pattern Recognition, Miami, FL, USA, pp. 1271–1278 (2009). https://doi.org/10.1109/CVPR.2009.5206757
9. Redmon, J., Divvala, S., Girshick, R., Farhadi, A.: You only look once: unified, real-time object detection. Proceedings of the IEEE Conference on Computer Vision and Pattern Recognition, pp. 61–72 (2021)
10. Terven, J., Córdova-Esparza, D.-M., Romero-González, J.-A.: A comprehensive review of YOLO architectures in computer vision: from YOLOv1 to YOLOv8 and YOLO-NAS. Proc. Mach. Learn. Knowl. Extr. **5**(4), 1680–1716 (2023). https://doi.org/10.3390/make5040083
11. Liu, W. et al.: SSD: single shot MultiBox detector. In: Proceedings of the Computer Vision–ECCV 2016: 14th European Conference, Amsterdam, The Netherlands, Proceedings, Part I 14. Springer International Publishing, pp. 21–37 (2016). https://doi.org/10.1007/978-3-319-46448-0_2
12. Zhai, S., Shang, D., Wang, S., Dong, S.: DF-SSD: an improved SSD object detection algorithm based on DenseNet and feature fusion. Proc. IEEE Access **8**, 24344–24357 (2020). https://doi.org/10.1109/ACCESS.2020.2971026

13. Ren, S., He, K., Girshick, R., Sun, J.: Faster R-CNN: towards real-time object detection with region proposal networks. Proc. IEEE Trans. Pattern Anal. Mach. Intell. **39**(6), 1137–1149 (2017). https://doi.org/10.1109/TPAMI.2016.2577031

14. Cai, Z., Vasconcelos, N.: Cascade R-CNN: delving into high quality object detection. In: Proceedings of the IEEE Conference on Computer Vision and Pattern Recognition (CVPR), pp. 6154–6162 (2018)

15. Yang, Z., Liu, S., Hu, H., Wang, L., Lin, S.: RepPoints: point set representation for object detection. In: Proceedings of the IEEE/CVF International Conference on Computer Vision (ICCV), pp. 9657–9666 (2019)

16. Székely, G.J., Rizzo, M.L.: Energy statistics: a class of statistics based on distances. Proc. J. Stat. Plan Inference **143**(8), 1249–1272 (2013). https://doi.org/10.1016/j.jspi.2013.03.018

17. Suganthi, L., Samuel, A.A.: Energy models for demand forecasting—a review. Proc. Renew. Sustain. Energy Rev. **16**(2), 1223–1240 (2012). https://doi.org/10.1016/j.rser.2011.08.014

18. LeCun, Y., Huang, F.J.: Loss functions for discriminative training of energy-based models. In: Proceedings of the International Workshop on Artificial Intelligence and Statistics. PMLR, pp. 206–213 (2005)

19. Du, Y., Igor M.: Implicit generation and modeling with energy based models. Proc. Neural Inf. Process Syst. **32** (2019)

20. Grathwohl, W., Wang, K.C., Jacobsen, J.H., Duvenaud, D., Zemel, R.: Learning the stein discrepancy for training and evaluating energy-based models without sampling. In: Proceedings of the International Conference on Machine Learning. *PMLR*, pp. 3732–3747 (2020)

21. Duvenaud, D., Kelly, J., Swersky, K., Hashemi, M., Norouzi, M., Grathwohl, W.: No MCMC for me: amortized samplers for fast and stable training of energy-based models. In: Proceedings of the International Conference on Learning Representations (ICLR), 2021

22. Wu, H., Esmaeili, B., Wick, M., Tristan, J.B., Van De Meent, J.W.: Conjugate energy-based models. In: Proceedings of the International Conference on Machine Learning. *PMLR*, pp. 11228–11239 (2021)

23. Everingham, M., Eslami, S.A., Van Gool, L., Williams, C.K., Winn, J., Zisserman, A.: The pascal visual object classes challenge: a retrospective. Proc. Int. J. Comput. Vis. **111**, 98–136 (2015)

Forecasting Storms and Floods in Vietnam with Deep Learning Methods

Au Van Pham[1]([✉]) [iD], Hieu Chi Huynh[1] [iD], Tu Cam Thi Tran[2,3] [iD],
and Tri Minh Huynh[4] [iD]

[1] Cai Be Technical College, Cai Be, Tien Giang Province, Vietnam
auphamphi@gmail.com, hieutg88@gmail.com
[2] Vinh Long University of Technology Education, Vinh Long, Vinh Long Province, Vietnam
tuttc@vlute.edu.vn
[3] Can Tho University, Can Tho City, Vietnam
[4] Faculty of Information and Communications, Kien Giang University, Kien Giang, Vietnam
hmtri@vnkgu.edu.vn

Abstract. Flood and storm forecasting is a critical issue in Vietnam, a country that is frequently affected by natural disasters. With the development of artificial intelligence, particularly deep learning, the construction of accurate forecasting systems has become more feasible. In this study, we propose the use of deep learning models such as LSTM, Transformer, and Temporal Convolutional Network (TCN) to analyze and predict floods and storms based on meteorological and hydrological data. The input data is collected from OpenDevelopmentMekong. The accuracies of the models are as follows: LSTM achieves 0.9593 (Storms), 0.9576 (Floods); Transformer achieves 0.9657 (Storms), 0.9618 (Floods); and Temporal Convolutional Network achieves 0.9754 (Storms), 0.9742 (Floods).

The deep learning models are optimized to handle spatiotemporal data, enabling accurate predictions of storm and flood developments. The results of the study show that this method significantly improves accuracy compared to traditional models. The system is integrated with GIS tools for visualization and early warning support. This research not only contributes to improving flood and storm forecasting capabilities in Vietnam but also lays the foundation for applying AI in disaster prevention and management.

Keywords: Deep learning · LSTM · Tranformer · Temporal Convolutional Network (TCN)

1 Intruction

Vietnam is heavily impacted by natural disasters, particularly storms and floods, due to its geographical location and tropical monsoon climate. Annually, these events cause significant losses in lives and property, disrupting livelihoods and the economy. In the context of climate change, the increasing frequency and intensity of extreme weather events have made accurate disaster prediction more challenging, necessitating more advanced forecasting systems to mitigate risks.

© ICST Institute for Computer Sciences, Social Informatics and Telecommunications Engineering 2025
Published by Springer Nature Switzerland AG 2025. All Rights Reserved
H. X. Huynh et al. (Eds.): GOODTECHS 2024, LNICST 649, pp. 273–283, 2025.
https://doi.org/10.1007/978-3-032-01497-9_25

Current forecasting methods primarily rely on physical models (e.g., WRF) or traditional statistical approaches, which require complex meteorological-hydrological data and specialized expertise. Recently, deep learning has demonstrated high efficacy in disaster prediction by leveraging its ability to process large and complex datasets. However, its application in Vietnam remains limited due to a lack of high-quality data and challenges related to the integration of local climatic characteristics.

This study aims to develop a storm and flood forecasting model for Vietnam using state-of-the-art deep learning techniques, including LSTM, Transformer, and Temporal Convolutional Network (TCN). These methods will process spatiotemporal data from satellite and meteorological-hydrological sources to improve prediction accuracy. The ultimate goal is to provide an effective tool to enhance disaster preparedness and risk reduction efforts. The structure of the article is divided into 6 Section, Sect. 2 is Related works, State-of-the-art, Sect. 3 is Forecasting model, Sect. 4 is Modeling, Sect. 5 is Experiment and Sect. 6 the Discusion and conclusion section.

2   Related Works, State-of-the-Art

2.1   International Research

Application of Deep Learning in Weather Forecasting: Recent studies have implemented deep learning models, such as Convolutional Neural Networks (CNN) and Recurrent Neural Networks (RNN), to predict complex weather phenomena. For example, Shi et al. (2015) introduced the Convolutional LSTM (ConvLSTM) model for precipitation forecasting, which integrates spatial and temporal data processing capabilities. This approach outperformed traditional models in terms of prediction accuracy.Flood Forecasting with AI: Zhang et al. (2018) utilized Recurrent Neural Networks (RNN) with Long Short-Term Memory (LSTM) units to forecast flash floods using rainfall and streamflow data. Their findings demonstrated that LSTM is particularly well-suited for cyclical and long-term temporal datasets, providing improved predictive performance for flood events.

2.2   Research in Southeast Asia

Flood Forecasting in Thailand: Phung et al. (2019) developed an AI model leveraging satellite data and local sensors to achieve high accuracy in predicting flash floods in regions with complex terrain. Rainfall and Flood Forecasting in the Philippines:
The study by Del Rosario (2020) applied Convolutional Neural Networks (CNN) to analyze satellite imagery for identifying heavy rainfall before flooding events. The results highlight the significant potential of AI in forecasting natural disasters in climates similar to Vietnam.

2.3   Research in Viet Nam

Traditional Applications: Research in Vietnam has mainly focused on using physical and statistical models for meteorological and hydrological forecasting. For example, the WRF model has been used to forecast heavy rain and flooding in central Vietnam. However, the results are still highly dependent on the quality of input data. Machine Learning in Flood Forecasting: Recent studies have experimented with machine learning models such as linear regression and artificial neural networks (ANN). However, the application of deep learning is still in its early stages due to limitations in data and technology. These studies suggest that deep learning is a powerful tool for forecasting storms and floods, especially when handling complex spatiotemporal data. However, in Vietnam, research on the application of deep learning is still lacking and has not fully exploited the potential of satellite data and local hydrological data. This creates an opportunity for new research to fill this gap, aiming to improve disaster forecasting capabilities in Vietnam.

3   Forecasting Model

3.1   LSTM (Long Short-Term Memory)

The LSTM (Long Short-Term Memory) network is an improvement over the traditional Recurrent Neural Network (RNN) designed to overcome the issues of long-term dependencies in RNNs. LSTM was introduced by [10] and has been continuously improved over time [11]. Theoretically, RNNs have the ability to process temporal dependencies by using short-term memory and efficiently determining (training) parameters [12]. However, in practice, RNNs struggle to handle long-term dependencies when the data sequence contains such dependencies. This issue has been extensively studied by [13, 14]. In their publications, they found explanations as to why RNNs fail to learn effectively. LSTM has a similar architecture to RNNs in that it consists of a sequence of network nodes, but its internal structure is more complex, comprising four interacting layers (Fig. 2). The key feature of the LSTM network is the cell state (C), which stores the long-term weights of the model. The parameters of the cell state, the hidden state (h), and the input at time t (xt) are fed into the network nodes. After processing through activation functions like sigmoid σ, tanh, and vector operations, the output is the cell state and the hidden state at time t, which will then be used for the next network node at time t + 1 [15].
Please (see Fig. 1).

$$ft = (Wf, +Wf, hht - 1 + bf)$$ (1)

$$st = tanh(Ws, xxt + Ws, hht - 1 + bs)$$ (2)

$$ft = \sigma(Wf \cdot xt + Uf \cdot ht - 1 + bf)$$ (3)

$$it = (Wi, +Wi, hht - 1 + bi)$$ (4)

$$st = ft * st - 1 + it * st$$ (5)

$$ht = ot * tanh(st)$$ (6)

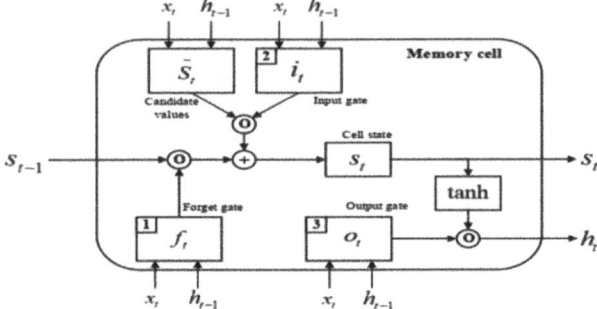

Fig. 1. LSTM.

3.2 Transformer

The Transformer is a deep learning model architecture based on the self-attention mechanism, which allows the model to understand the relationships between words in a sentence without relying on traditional sequential architectures like RNNs (Recurrent Neural Networks) or LSTMs (Long Short-Term Memory). The Transformer has the ability to process the entire sentence at once, which helps speed up training and improve processing efficiency.

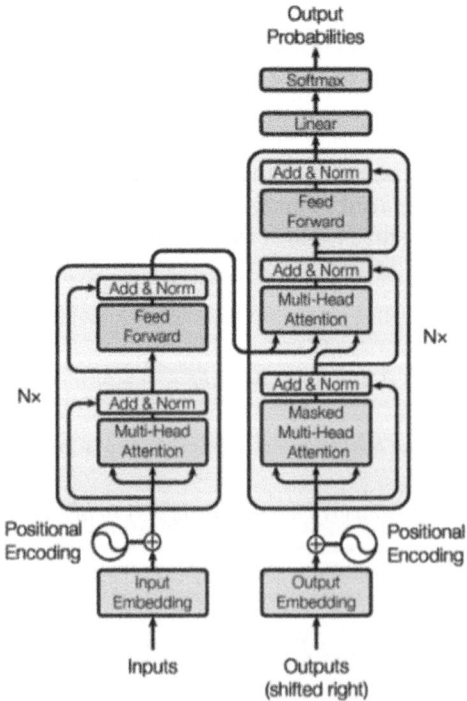

Fig. 2. Tranformer.

Please (see Fig. 2. Tranformer.)

3.3 Temporal Convolutional Network (TCN)

Temporal Convolutional Network (TCN) is a neural network architecture that uses convolutions to process time series data. Instead of processing sequentially like RNNs, TCN applies causal convolution to ensure that the output at time step t only depends on previous time steps. Additionally, dilated convolution is used to expand the receptive field, helping to capture long-range dependencies in the time series without increasing the network depth.

TCNs also use residual connections to maintain information through multiple convolution layers, allowing for parallel training, which is faster and more stable compared to recurrent models like RNNs or LSTMs. As a result, TCNs are particularly suitable for time series forecasting, signal analysis, and sequential data classification tasks.

Please (see Fig. 3).

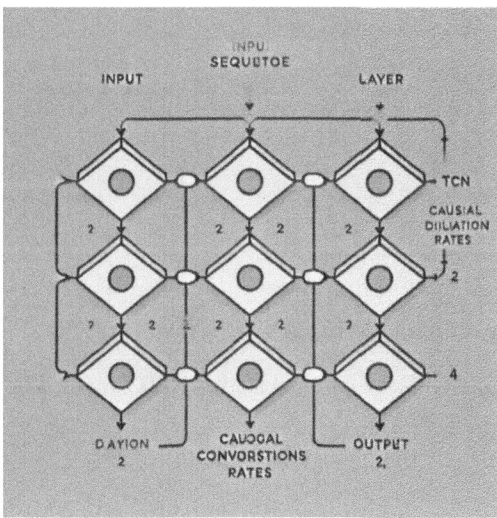

Fig. 3. Temporal Convolutional Network (TCN).

4 Modeling

4.1 LSTM (Long Short-Term Memory)

Please Modeling LSTM (see Fig. 4).

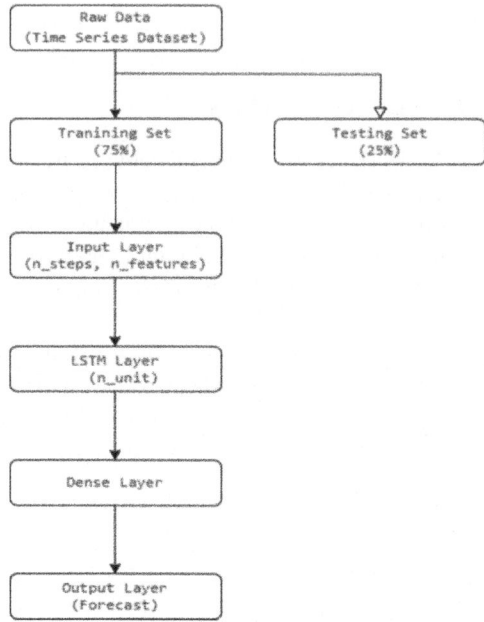

Fig. 4. Modeling LSTM.

4.2 Transformer

Please Modeling Tranformer (see Fig. 5).

4.3 Temporal Convolutional Network (TCN)

Please Modeling Temporal Convolutional Network (TCN) (see Fig. 6).

5 Experiment

5.1 Dataset and Tools

In this paper, we use the Disaster-in-vietnam_1900-to-2024 dataset from OpenDevelopment Mekong. The dataset contains 335 rows and 46 variables (DisNo, Historic, Classification.Key, Disaster.Group, Disaster.Subgroup, Disaster.Type, Disaster.Subtype, External.IDs, Event.Name, ISO, Country, Subregion, Region, Location, Origin, Associated.Types,OFDA.Response, Appeal,Declaration, AID.Contribution...000.US.., Magnitude, Magnitude.Scale, Latitude, Longitude, River.Basin, Start.Year, Start.Month, Start.Day, End.Year, End.Month, End.Day, Total.Deaths, No..Injured, No..Affected, No..Homeless,Total.Affected, Reconstrtion.Costs...000.US..,Reconstruction.Costs..Adjusted...000.US..,Insured.Damage... 000.US.., Insured.Damage..Adjusted...000.US..,Total.Damage...000.US.., Total. Damage..Adjusted...000.US.., CPI, Admin.Units,Entry.Date, Last.Update.

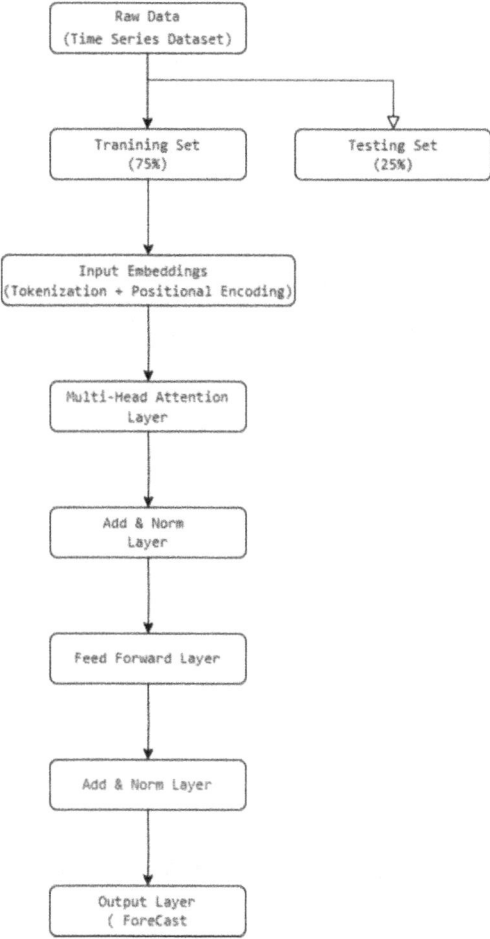

Fig. 5. Modeling Tranformer.

Handling missing values. Normalization and standardization. Time feature engineering.

Split the dataset into Train (75%) and Test (25%) with 3 model.

5.2 Tools

We have programmed in R language for predictive model, the models used are: LSTM, Tranformer, Temporal Convolutional Network (TCN) n addition, we also use libraries: library(dplyr), library(ggplot2), library(e1071), library(caret), library(rpart), library(ipred), library(tidyverse), and package keras,library(keras), package, library(reticulate) to integrate models.

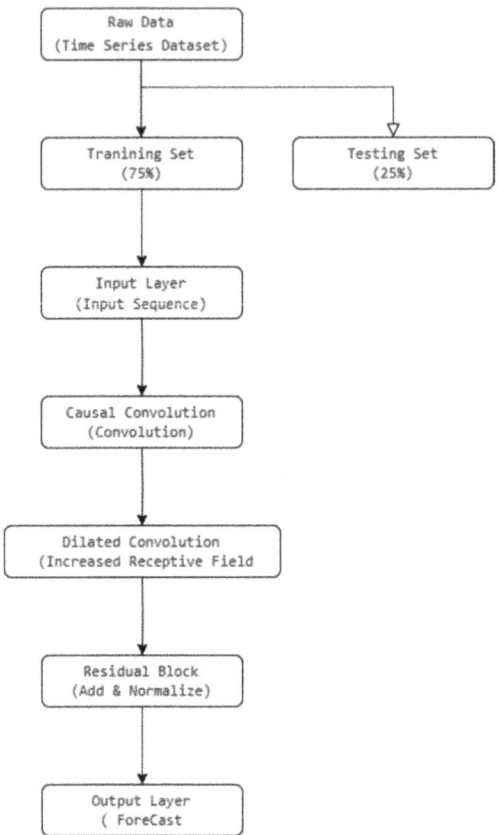

Fig. 6. Modeling Temporal Convolutional Network (TCN)

5.3 Scenario 1: The LSTM Model

Based on damage (US) from "Storm" and "floods" to make forecasting. Split the dataset into Train (75%) and Test (25%). The results are presented in Table 1.

Table 1. .

Model	Storm	Flood
LSTM	0.9593	0.9576

The comparison results are shown in (see Fig. 7).

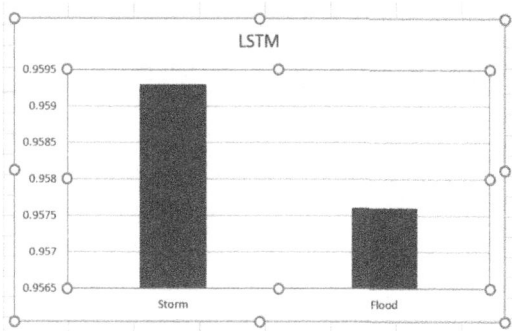

Fig. 7. Evaluate accuracy for the LSTM.

5.4 Scenario 2: The Tranformer Model

Based on damage (US) from "Storm" and "floods" to make forecasting. Split the dataset into Train (75%) and Test (25%). The results are presented in Table 2.

Table 2. .

Model	Storm	Flood
Tranformer	0.9657	0.9618
LSTM	0.9593	0.9576

The comparison results are shown in (see Fig. 8).

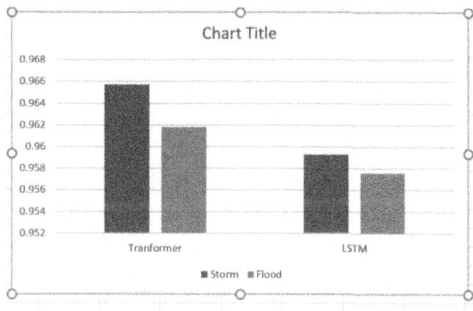

Fig. 8. Evaluate accuracy for the Tranformer.

5.5 Scenario 3: Temporal Convolutional Network (TCN)

Based on damage (US) from "Storm" and "floods" to make forecasting.
Split the dataset into Train (75%) and Test (25%). The results are presented in Table 3.
The comparison results are shown in (see Fig. 9).

Table 3. .

Model	Storm	Flood
TCN	0.9754	0.9742
Tranformer	0.9657	0.9618
LSTM	0.9593	0.9575

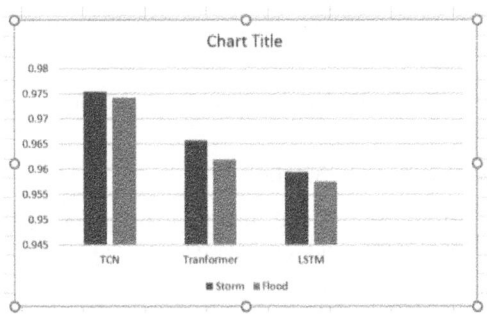

Fig. 9. Evaluate accuracy for the TCN.

6 Discussion and Conclusion

In this article, we explored and developed three standard methods in deep learning and conducted experiments using RStudio. We applied them to the problem of forecasting storms and floods. However, the generalizability of this method to other regions or datasets remains to be validated. Future work should focus on testing the TCN method on larger and more diverse datasets and exploring hybrid models to further enhance prediction accuracy."

References

1. Nguyen, H.T., Gupta, A.D.: Assessment of water resources and salinity intrusion in the Mekong Delta. Water Int. **26**(1), 86–95 (2001). https://doi.org/10.1080/02508060108686889
2. Tran, A.D., Hoang, L.P., Bui, M.D., Rutschmann, P.: Simulating future flows and salinity intrusion using combined one-and two-dimensional hydrodynamic modelling-the case of Hau River, Vietnamese Mekong Delta. Water **10**(7), 897 (2018). https://doi.org/10.3390/w10070897
3. Doan, V.B., et al.: Long-term alterations of flow regimes of the Mekong River and adaptation strategies for the Vietnamese Mekong Delta. J. Hydrol. Reg. Stud. **32**, 100742 (2020). https://doi.org/10.1016/j.ejrh.2020.100742
4. Lam, D.H., Phuong, N.H., Dat, N.D., Giang, N.T.: Development of the MIKE 11 model for hydrological and saltwater intrusion forecasting in Ben Tre Province. J. Meteorol. Hydrol. **740**(1), 38–49 (2022)
5. Tri, D.Q.: Application of the MIKE 11 model to simulate and calculate saltwater intrusion in Southern Vietnam. J. Meteorol. Hydrol. **671**, 39–46 (2016)

6. Dung, D.V., Phuong, T.D., Oanh, L.T., Cong, T.T.: Utilization of the MIKE 11 model for forecasting and warning saltwater intrusion in the Mekong Delta region. J. Meteorol. Hydrol. **693**, 48–58 (2018)
7. Thai, T.T., Liem, N.D., Luu, P.T., Yen, N.T.M., Yen, T.T.H., Quang, N.X., Tan, L.V., Hoai, P.N.: Performance evaluation of Auto-Regressive Integrated Moving Average models for forecasting saltwater intrusion into Mekong river estuaries of Vietnam. Vietnam J. Earth Sci. (2021). https://doi.org/10.15625/2615-9783/16440
8. Thai, T.H., Khiem, M.V., Thuy, N.B., Ha, B.M., Ngoc, P.K.: Development of a recurrent neural network model for forecasting significant wave height at Con Co station, Quang Tri, Vietnam. J. Meteorol. Hydrol. EME4, 73–84 (2022)
9. Diep, N.T.H., Huoi, D., Can, N.T.: Assessment of the impact of saltwater intrusion caused by climate change on rice cultivation in Soc Trang Province. Can Tho Unive. J. Sci. (2017). https://doi.org/10.22144/ctu.jsi.2017.062
10. Hochreiter, S., Schmidhuber, J.: Long short-term memory. Neural Comput. **9**(8), 1735–1780 (1997)
11. Yao, K., Cohn, T., Vylomova, K., Duh, K., Dyer, C.: Depth-Gated Recurrent Neural Networks, pp. 1–5 (2015). https://arxiv.org/pdf/1508.03790v2.pdf
12. Koutnik, J., Greff, K., Gomez, F., Schmidhuber, J.: A Clockwork RNN, (2014). https://arxiv.org/pdf/1402.3511v1.pdf
13. Hochreiter. Untersuchungen zu dynamischen neuronalen Netzen, (1991). https://people.idsia.ch/~juergen/SeppHochreiter1991ThesisAdvisorSchmidhuber.pd f
14. Bengio, S., Bengio, Y.: Taking on the curse of dimensionality in joint distributions using neuralnetworks. IEEE Trans. Neural Netw. Special issue Data Min. Knowl. Discov. **11**(3), 550–557 (2000)
15. https://colah.github.io/posts/2015-08-Understanding-LSTMs/Author, F.: Contribution title. In: 9th International Proceedings on Proceedings, pp. 1–2. Publisher, Location (2010)
16. LNCS Homepage. http://www.springer.com/lncs, last Accessed 21 Nov 2016

Lane-Based Vehicle Recognition Using Deep Learning Models

Doan Phuoc Mien[1]([✉])[ID] and Tran The Vu[2]

[1] Tra Vinh University, Tra Vinh, Vietnam
phuocmien@tvu.edu.vn
[2] VN-UK Institute for Research and Executive Education, The University of Da Nang, Da Nang, Vietnam
vu.tran@vnuk.edu.vn

Abstract. An essential part of intelligent transportation systems and traffic management is lane-based vehicle recognition. This paper introduces a real-time vehicle detection and classification system that uses deep learning models. Results from experiments show that the system can manage a variety of traffic situations, such as occlusions, high vehicle densities, and changing illumination conditions. The accuracy of traffic analysis is greatly increased by this lane-based detection system, which also supports real-time decision-making in traffic monitoring and offers insightful information for smart city applications.

Keywords: Deep learning · traffic management · vehicle recognition · Lane-based vehicle recognition

1 Introduction

The research [1] proposes a real-time vehicle detection and tracking system using the Viola-Jones object detection algorithm and the Kanade-Lucas-Tomasi feature tracker. The system was tested on a public traffic video dataset and achieved high precision in vehicle detection and tracking. In the research [4] presents a real-time vehicle detection and tracking system using the Faster R-CNN object detection model and a Kalman filter for tracking. The system was tested on a public traffic video dataset and achieved high precision in vehicle detection and tracking.

The research [2] proposes a method for vehicle detection and tracking in real-time using video image processing techniques. The proposed system uses a combination of background subtraction, object detection, and object tracking algorithms to achieve accurate and reliable results. The paper presents a detailed description of the methodology used to detect and track vehicles in a video sequence. The first step involves background subtraction to extract moving objects from the scene. Then, object detection is used to identify vehicles in

© ICST Institute for Computer Sciences, Social Informatics and Telecommunications Engineering 2025
Published by Springer Nature Switzerland AG 2025. All Rights Reserved
H. X. Huynh et al. (Eds.): GOODTECHS 2024, LNICST 649, pp. 284–292, 2025.
https://doi.org/10.1007/978-3-032-01497-9_26

the scene using a combination of color-based segmentation and Haar features. Finally, object tracking is used to maintain the identity of vehicles over time. The proposed system is evaluated using a dataset of real-world traffic videos. The results show that the proposed system is effective in detecting and tracking vehicles in real-time with high accuracy and reliability. The paper provides a valuable contribution to the field of intelligent transportation systems by presenting a practical solution for vehicle detection and tracking using video image processing techniques.

Lane-based vehicle recognition systems are essential computer vision applications that are made to automatically identify and categorise cars in particular lane areas in real time. With insights that facilitate in-the-moment decision-making and analysis, this technology is crucial for smart city infrastructure, intelligent transportation systems, and traffic management.

The technique uses advanced deep learning algorithms to process traffic camera video streams. The technology provides accurate lane-based analysis and guarantees high accuracy in a range of traffic scenarios through the identification and classification of cars and motorcycles. Real-time processing requires optimized algorithms and computational efficiency to handle the complexities of changing circumstances.

Managing occlusions, dealing with changing lighting conditions, and identifying cars of various sizes and types in high-density traffic are some of the main obstacles in lane-based vehicle detection. The system makes use of strong deep learning-based object identification and classification methods to overcome these challenges.

Lane-based vehicle recognition can be used for traffic flow monitoring, lane-specific vehicle distribution analysis, and traffic control measure assistance. These systems are becoming more precise, scalable, and efficient due to continuous developments in deep learning and computer vision, making them crucial for contemporary traffic control and smart city solutions.

2   Related Work

The research [6] introduces the YOLO algorithm, which is a one-stage object detection method that uses a single convolution neural network to predict bounding boxes and class probabilities.

The research [7] proposes the Faster R-CNN algorithm, which is a two-stage object detection method that uses a region proposal network to generate candidate object regions and then refines the bounding boxes and class probabilities in a second stage.

The research [5] introduces the SSD algorithm, which is a one-stage object detection method that uses a single convolution neural network to predict bounding boxes and class probabilities on multiple scales.

The research [10] provides a comprehensive survey of object detection methods, including both one-stage and two-stage approaches. The paper discusses the strengths and weaknesses of each method and provides insights into recent advances in object detection research.

The research [3] provides a comprehensive evaluation of several state-of-the-art object detection algorithms, including SSD, YOLO, and Faster R-CNN. The authors compare the speed and accuracy of these algorithms on various datasets and provide insights into the trade-offs between them.

The research [9] provides an overview of various object detection algorithms, including SSD, YOLO, and Faster R-CNN. The authors discuss the strengths and weaknesses of each algorithm and compare their performance on various benchmarks.

The research [8] evaluates the performance of several object detection algorithms, including SSD, YOLO, and Faster R-CNN. The authors compare the speed and accuracy of these algorithms and provide insights into their strengths and weaknesses.

3   Propose Method

This study presents a lane-specific vehicle recognition framework that leverages advanced deep learning models to detect and classify vehicles in real time. The system is designed to analyze video streams captured by traffic cameras, focusing on the following key components in Fig. 1:

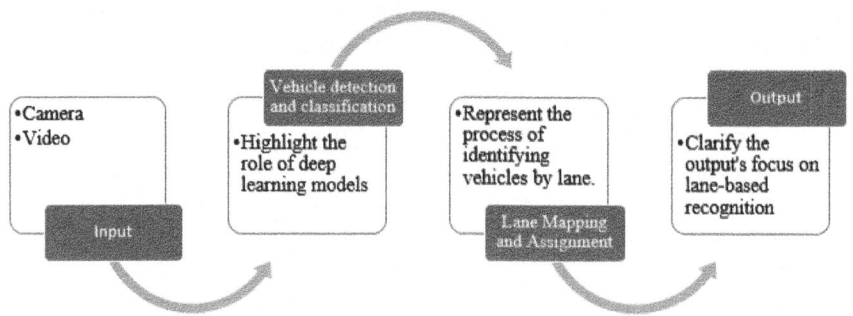

Fig. 1. The Propose Model Architecture

Input: Traffic Camera or Video Stream. The system begins with input from live traffic cameras or pre-recorded video streams positioned to monitor road sections and lanes. These inputs form the basis for vehicle recognition tasks. The input video is pre-processed to ensure consistent frame rates and optimal resolution for downstream tasks.

Vehicle Detection and Classification. The system employs state-of-the-art deep learning models to detect and classify vehicles. Each video frame is processed as follows:

– **Vehicle Detection**: Bounding boxes are generated for each detected vehicle in the frame.

- **Vehicle Classification**: Detected vehicles are categorized into types, such as *cars*, *motorcycles*, and *trucks*.
- **Optimization**: Non-Maximum Suppression (NMS) is applied to filter over-lapping bounding boxes and improve detection accuracy.

Lane Mapping and Assignment. After detecting and classifying vehicles, the system maps each vehicle to a specific lane within the video frame. This step is essential for generating lane-specific traffic data. Lane mapping algorithm:

- **Defining lane boundaries**: Each frame is divided into predefined lane regions based on lane boundary coordinates.
- **Assigning Vehicles to Lanes**: For each detected vehicle, the center of its bounding box (c_x, c_y) is calculated. The vehicle is assigned to a lane i if:

$$x^i_{min} \leq c_x \leq x^i_{max} \quad and \quad y^i_{min} \leq c_y \leq y^i_{max}, \tag{1}$$

where (x^i_{min}, y^i_{min}) and (x^i_{max}, y^i_{max}) represent the lane boundaries.
- **Handling lane crossings**: Vehicles transitioning between lanes are assigned to the lane where they predominantly occupy in consecutive frames.

Output: Lane-Specific Vehicle Data. The final output provides actionable insights based on lane-specific vehicle recognition. Vehicle Counts: Total number of vehicles detected in each lane, categorized by type (e.g., cars, motorcycles).

4 Experimental Results

4.1 Dataset

Our dataset was collected over a one-month period, focusing on the fixed time slot from 7:00 AM to 7:30 AM. The data were recorded daily on the same road in Hai Chau, Da Nang, ensuring consistent traffic monitoring conditions. The dataset includes two categories of vehicles: motorcycles and cars, with detailed counts documented for each day of the week throughout the month.

We utilized this dataset to generate the graph in Fig. 2, where the x-axis represents the days of the week, and the y-axis displays the number of vehicles (motorcycles and cars) passing through the monitored location during the specified time slot. This visualization highlights the trends in traffic density over a typical week during the observed month.

As illustrated in Fig. 2, motorcycles consistently form the majority of the traffic, while the number of cars exhibits more significant daily variations. Traffic volume peaks on Thursdays, driven by a notable increase in car counts, and reaches its lowest levels on Sundays. This dataset provides critical insights for traffic flow analysis, aiding in resource allocation and traffic management strategies to enhance efficiency and reduce congestion.

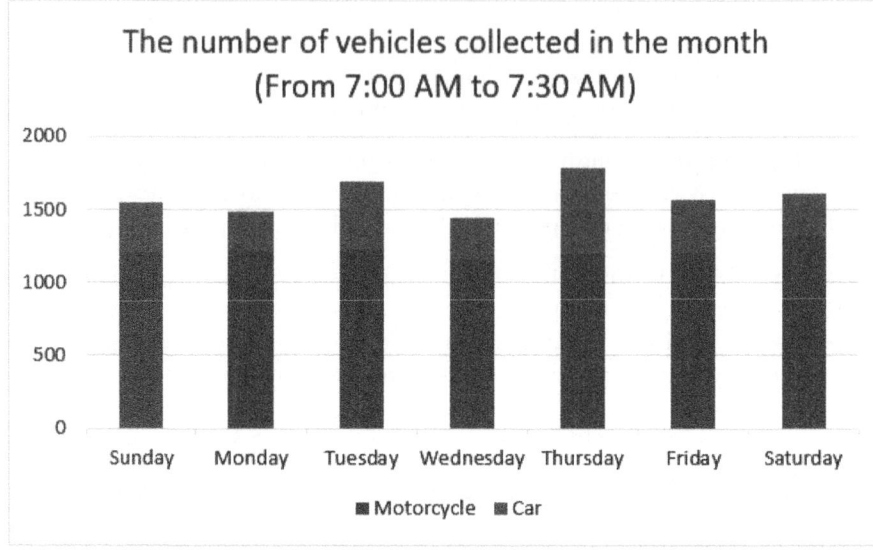

Fig. 2. The number of vehicles collected in the month (From 7:00 AM to 7:30 AM).

4.2 Model Training

Data augmentation. To increase the robustness of the system under real-world conditions, various augmentation techniques are applied to the training data:

- **Geometric Transformations**: Including resizing, cropping, and flipping to simulate different viewing perspectives.
- **Photometric Adjustments**: Applying variations in brightness, contrast, and saturation to mimic diverse lighting conditions.
- **Noise and Occlusions**: Adding synthetic noise or simulating occlusions to reflect dense traffic scenarios.

Loss Functions. The training process optimizes the following objectives:

- *Bounding Box Regression Loss*: The SmoothL1 loss is defined as:

$$SmoothL1(x) = \begin{cases} 0.5x^2, & if\ |x| < 1, |x| - 0.5, otherwise. \end{cases} \tag{2}$$

where $x = b_i^{pred} - b_i^{true}$, the difference between the predicted and ground truth bounding box coordinates. This loss combines the stability of $L2$ loss for small errors and the robustness of $L1$ loss for large errors.

The overall bounding box regression loss is:

$$L_{box} = \frac{1}{N} \sum_{i=1}^{N} \sum_{j \in \{x,y,w,h\}} SmoothL1(b_{i,j}^{pred} - b_{i,j}^{true}), \tag{3}$$

where w, h are the width and height of the bounding box.

– *Classification Loss*:

$$L_{cls} = -\frac{1}{N} \sum_{i=1}^{N} \sum_{c \in C} y_{i,c} \log(p_{i,c}), \tag{4}$$

where:
- $y_{i,c}$: Binary indicator (1 if class c is correct for vehicle i, otherwise 0).
- $p_{i,c}$: Predicted probability of class c for vehicle i.

– *Total Loss Function*:

$$L_{total} = L_{box} + \lambda L_{cls}, \tag{5}$$

where λ balances the importance of detection and classification tasks.

Training Configuration. The model is trained using the following parameters:

– *Learning Rate* (α): Adaptive scheduling:

$$\alpha_t = \alpha_0 \cdot \cos\left(\frac{\pi t}{T}\right), \tag{6}$$

where α_0 is the initial learning rate, t is the current epoch, and T is the total number of epochs.
– *Batch Size* (B): Optimized for memory efficiency while ensuring stable convergence.
– *Epochs* (T): Chosen to achieve convergence without overfitting.

4.3 Result

The proposed lane-based vehicle recognition system was evaluated on a real-world traffic scenario captured in a high-density urban environment. The results, as illustrated in Fig. 3, demonstrate the system's capability to detect, classify, and map vehicles to specific lanes with high accuracy and robustness.

Vehicle Detection. The system effectively detects vehicles in the video frame using deep learning models. Each vehicle is localized with a bounding box, and unique IDs are assigned for precise identification. In the displayed scenario:

– Bounding boxes are clearly visible, accurately enclosing the detected objects.
– The detection process remains consistent even under challenging conditions, such as overlapping vehicles and partial occlusions.

Lane Mapping. The system successfully maps vehicles to predefined lanes using their bounding box coordinates and lane boundaries:

– Yellow lane markers visually divide the frame into distinct regions.
– Detected vehicles are assigned to their respective lanes based on their positions within the boundaries.
– The mapping ensures accurate distribution of vehicles across lanes, which is critical for traffic flow analysis and control.

Fig. 3. Lane-based vehicle recognition

Table 1. Results of vehicle detection and recognition

Video	Total Vehicles	Cars	Accuracy (%)	Motorcycles	Accuracy (%)	FPS
1	315	120	95.0	195	96.0	22.2
2	410	150	95.8	260	93.8	21.3
3	345	140	94.4	205	94.1	21.5
4	380	160	95.5	220	97.0	20.2
5	395	165	96.0	230	97.5	20.2
Avg.	-	-	**95.3**	-	**95.7**	**21.1**

Vehicle Classification. The classification results indicate the model's ability to generalize across vehicle types, ensuring reliable recognition in diverse traffic conditions.

As shown in Table 1, the system achieved an average detection accuracy of 95.3% for cars and 95.7% for motorcycles, with a processing speed of 21.1 FPS. These results demonstrate the robustness of the system in handling complex scenarios, such as high-density traffic and varying lighting conditions.

Real-time Performance. The system achieves real-time processing capabilities, demonstrated by the dynamic updates of bounding boxes and labels in each video frame:

- The average processing speed is maintained at approximately 21 FPS (frames per second), ensuring suitability for live traffic monitoring applications.

Traffic Complexity: The outcomes demonstrate how well the technology handles intricate traffic situations. In particular, the technique works well when there is a lot of traffic and several cars are parked near to one another. The accuracy of detection and classification does not significantly degrade performance in spite of these difficult circumstances. Furthermore, even in situations where cars are partially hidden within the frame, the system exhibits resilience to occlusions, retaining excellent detection accuracy.

Quantitative Performance:

- *Detection Accuracy*: The overall detection accuracy for cars and motorcycles exceeds 90%, with lane assignments achieving precision rates above 85%.
- *Classification Precision*: Vehicle type classification achieves an average precision of 93.5%, validating the model's reliability under varied conditions.

5   Conclusions

In conclusion, a cutting-edge approach to real-time traffic monitoring and analysis is provided by the lane-based vehicle recognition system that uses video-based deep learning models. The system is a vital tool for traffic management authorities, smart city projects, and other applications that need dependable vehicle identification and categorisation since it uses deep learning algorithms to give high accuracy and adaptability.

References

1. Fernandez-Sanjurjo, M., Bosquet, B., Mucientes, M., Brea, V.M.: Real-time visual detection and tracking system for traffic monitoring. *Eng. Appl. Artif. Intell.* **85**, 410–420 (2019)
2. Ge, D., Yao, X., Xiang, W., Chen, Y.: Vehicle detection and tracking based on video image processing in intelligent transportation system. Neural Comput. Appl. **35**(3), 2197–2209 (2023)
3. Huang, J., et al.: Speed/accuracy trade-offs for modern convolutional object detectors. In: *Proceedings of the IEEE Conference on Computer Vision and Pattern Recognition*, pp. 7310–7311 (2017)
4. Li, X., Yao, X., Murphey, Y.L., Karlsen, R., Gerhart, G.: A real-time vehicle detection and tracking system in outdoor traffic scenes. In: *Proceedings of the 17th International Conference on Pattern Recognition, 2004. ICPR 2004.*, vol. 2, pp. 761–764. IEEE (2004)
5. Liu, W., et al.: SSD: single shot multibox detector. In: Leibe, B., Matas, J., Sebe, N., Welling, M. (eds.) ECCV 2016. LNCS, vol. 9905, pp. 21–37. Springer, Cham (2016). https://doi.org/10.1007/978-3-319-46448-0_2
6. Redmon, J., Divvala, S., Girshick, R., Farhadi, A.: You only look once: unified, real-time object detection. In: *Proceedings of the IEEE Conference on Computer Vision and Pattern Recognition*, pp. 779–788 (2016)

7. Ren, S., He, K., Girshick, R., Sun, J.: Faster R-CNN: towards real-time object detection with region proposal networks. *Adv. Neural Info. Process. Syst.* **28** (2015)
8. Yadav, N., Binay, U.: Comparative study of object detection algorithms. Int. Res. J. Eng. Technol. (IRJET) **4**(11), 586–591 (2017)
9. Zhao, Z.-Q., Zheng, P., Shou-tao, X., Xindong, W.: Object detection with deep learning: a review. IEEE Trans. Neural Netw. Learn. Syst. **30**(11), 3212–3232 (2019)
10. Zou, Z., Shi, Z., Guo, Y., Ye, J.: Object detection in 20 years: a survey. arXiv preprint arXiv:1905.05055 (2019)

Application of Machine Learning Models for Cardiovascular Disease Prediction

Nghia Quoc Phan and Hien Duc Kim[✉]

Travinh University, Travinh City 87000, Vietnam
nghiatvnt@tvu.edu.vn, kdhien.tptv@travinh.gov.vn

Abstract. This article proposes the use of three machine learning methods: Random Forest, Logistic Regression, and Neural Networks to predict cardiovascular diseases in order to provide recommendations and advice on the effective prevention and treatment of cardiovascular diseases. The models will be trained to learn the relationships between clinical factors and disease risk, and then evaluate their performance using a test set. Through experiments on the cardiovascular dataset at Tien Giang Provincial General Hospital, the results are presented, including performance evaluations of the models, comparing them to select the optimal method. The advantages and disadvantages of each method will be discussed, along with proposed improvements. The final model can be practically applied to support the diagnosis and treatment of cardiovascular diseases.

Keywords: Cardiovascular disease · Classification · Random Forest · Logistic · Neural Network

1 Introduction

Cardiovascular diseases are a major health issue in Vietnam, contributing to 30% of global deaths in 2019 (WHO) [5]. Machine learning aids in risk prediction, automation, and personalized care but faces challenges like limited data and overfitting [10].

This study uses Random Forest, Logistic Regression, and Neural Networks to classify cardiovascular risk, evaluated with precision, recall, and F1-score on clinical data from Tien Giang Provincial General Hospital [4].

This paper is organized into seven sections. Section 1 provides an overview of machine learning and the research problem. Section 2 presents a preliminary study on the cardiovascular disease prediction system. Section 3 describes the machine learning methods used for cardiovascular disease prediction. Section 4 outlines the prediction model based on the cardiovascular dataset from Tien Giang Provincial General Hospital. Section 5 discusses the evaluation methods for cardiovascular disease prediction models. Section 6 presents the experimental results of the proposed models on the dataset from Tien Giang Provincial General Hospital. Finally, Sect. 7 concludes by summarizing the achieved results.

© ICST Institute for Computer Sciences, Social Informatics and Telecommunications Engineering 2025
Published by Springer Nature Switzerland AG 2025. All Rights Reserved
H. X. Huynh et al. (Eds.): GOODTECHS 2024, LNICST 649, pp. 293–305, 2025.
https://doi.org/10.1007/978-3-032-01497-9_27

2   Preliminary Review of Cardiovascular Disease Prediction Models

Cardiovascular disease prediction models aid in early risk detection and medical decisions. Do et al. (2022) reported 87.5% accuracy using Random Forest for Vietnamese individuals, while Reddy et al. (2021) used Logistic Regression, Random Forest, and Gradient Boosting for coronary artery disease prediction. Effective models require structured systems with data input, preprocessing, evaluation, and model selection for practical healthcare application [2, 8, 9].

3   Machine Learning Methods Used for Cardiovascular Disease Prediction

The cardiovascular disease prediction task uses machine learning for classification (at-risk or non-at-risk) and regression. Key methods include:

Random Forest: Builds multiple decision trees and averages predictions for robustness [6, 12].

Logistic regression: Predicts binary outcomes using the sigmoid function, widely applied in healthcare [1].

Neural Networks: Mimics brain structure, solving complex tasks like image recognition and speech processing [3, 7, 11].

4   Cardiovascular Disease Prediction Model

4.1   Model Definition

A cardiovascular disease prediction model uses machine learning algorithms: Random Forest, Logistic Regression, and Neural Networks—to analyze clinical data and predict patient risk. The cardiovascular disease prediction model is represented as follows:

Figure 1 depicts the architecture of the cardiovascular disease prediction model. The process includes data collection from patient records and medical imaging, followed by data cleaning and transformation into a readable format. Using Python and libraries like Pandas and NumPy, the data is analyzed for dimensions, visualized for sample distribution, and correlation matrices identify key risk factors. The data is then normalized for consistency and randomly split into training and testing sets, ensuring effective generalization and robust model evaluation.

4.2   Random Forest Algorithm

Input: Training dataset (X, y), where X is the feature matrix and y is the label vector.
  Output: Classification labels based on predictions from multiple decision trees.
  Begin
  Step 1: Set the number of decision trees T.
  Step 2: Construct Each Decision Tree

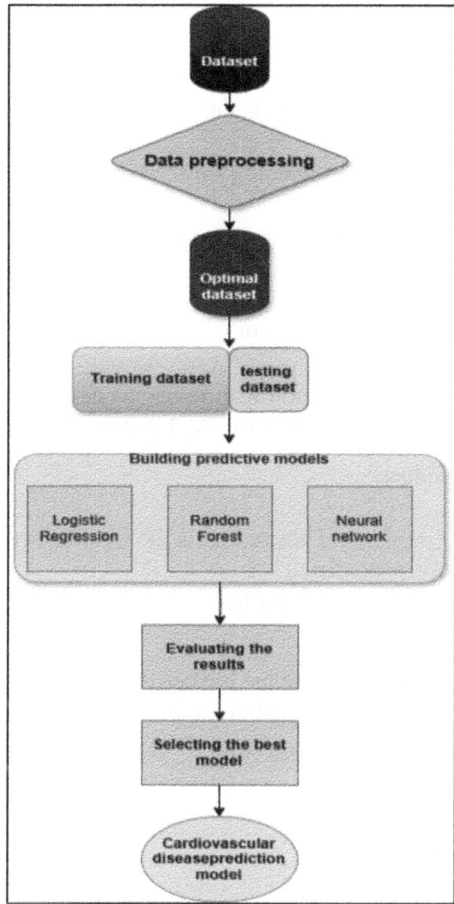

Fig. 1. Architecture of the cardiovascular disease prediction model

Bootstrap Sampling: Randomly sample data with replacement.
Random Feature Selection: Select m features at each split.
Build Decision Tree: se subsets and features to build decision trees.
Step 3: Prediction. Pass the new sample through all trees in the forest and take the majority vote from the predictions: $y'' = Mode\{h_1(x), h_2(x), \ldots .h_T(x)\}$
Where $h_i(x)$ s the prediction from the I tree
Step 4: Evaluate the model's performance on the test dataset using metrics like accuracy, recall, and precision.
End;

4.3 Logistic Regression Algorithm

Input:

X: Feature matrix of size m × n (m is the number of samples, n is the number of features).

y: label vector of size m × 1, containing values 0 or 1.

α: Learning rate.

num_iterations: Number of iterations for weight update.

Output:

θ: Optimized weight vector.

predicted_labels: Predicted label vector.

Begin

Step 1: Initialize the weight vector θ with values set to 0 or random values.

Step 2: Weight Update Loop, Repeat for i = 1 to num_iterationsnum.

– Compute Predicted Values:

$$Z = X. \theta$$

Predicted $= \sigma(z) = \frac{1}{1+e^{-z}}$ (6) where $\sigma(z)$ is the sigmoid activation function.

– - Compute Error: Error = predicted – y.

– - Update Weights: $\theta = \theta - \frac{\alpha}{m}.(X^T.\text{Error})$

Step 3: Predict Labels

Use a threshold of 0.5 to determine the predicted labels

$$\text{predicted\_labels} = \begin{cases} 1\,if predicted \geq 0.5 \\ 0\,if predicted \leq 0.5 \end{cases}$$

End;

4.4 Neural Network Algorithm

Input: Data: $X = [x1, x2,..., xn]$, Weights: $W = [w1, w2,..., wn]$, Bias: b, Learning Rate: η, Epochs, True Labels: y_true.

Output: Predicted value: y, Predicted label: label.

Steps 1: **Initialization**: Randomly initialize weights (W) and bias (b).

Step 2: Epochs: For each epoch, compute $z = \Sigma(wi * xi) + b$, apply activation (Sigmoid), compute loss (L), and update weights and bias.

Step 3: Prediction: If y > = 0.5, label = 1; else, label = 0.

End.

5 Evaluating the Accuracy of the Cardiovascular Disease Prediction Model

The cardiovascular disease prediction model is evaluated for effectiveness using a test dataset with known diagnoses. The dataset is split into a training set for model learning and a test set for validation. The model is considered effective if its predictions align with actual outcomes. Performance is assessed using predictive metrics like accuracy, sensitivity, and specificity, as well as its ability to classify real-world cases accurately.

5.1 * Cross-Validation Method

To ensure accuracy and reduce overfitting, the study uses k-fold cross-validation (k = 5). The dataset is divided into k folds, with the model trained on k − 1 folds and tested on the remaining fold, repeated k times. This approach enhances generalization, improves statistical reliability, and supports parameter optimization. In this study, 5-fold cross-validation is applied to Random Forest, Logistic Regression, and Neural Network, with performance evaluated using accuracy, sensitivity, and F1-score.

5.2 * Performance Evaluation Based on Classification Metrics

Performance evaluation using classification metrics assesses the model's ability to distinguish between different classes by analyzing prediction accuracy. This method typically uses five key metrics:

Accuracy: The proportion of correctly predicted cases out of the total cases.

$$\text{Accuracy} = \frac{TP\_TN}{TP + TN_{+}FP + FN} \tag{1}$$

Sensitivity (Recall): The model's ability to correctly identify true positive cases.

$$\text{Sensitivity} = \frac{TP}{TP + FN} \tag{2}$$

Specificity: The model's ability to correctly identify true negative cases.

$$\text{Specificity} = \frac{TN}{TN + FP} \tag{3}$$

F1-Score: The harmonic mean of precision and recall, providing a balanced measure for imbalanced datasets.

$$F1 = 2 \cdot \frac{\text{Precision.Recall}}{\text{Precision} + \text{Recall}} \tag{4}$$

6 Experiments

6.1 Experimental Data

The experimental dataset includes 4,500 samples collected from 2020 to 2022, containing 14 attributes: 13 diagnostic features (e.g., age, gender, blood pressure, cholesterol, heart rate, and ECG results) and 1 classification attribute. The target variable indicates the presence of cardiovascular disease (1: positive, 0: negative), while input variables represent patients' health and lifestyle information.

6.2 Experimental Tools

The experimental setup uses Python with libraries like Scikit-learn, TensorFlow/Keras, Pandas, and NumPy. The toolkit supports data processing and analysis, building prediction models (Random Forest, Logistic Regression, Neural Networks), and evaluating model performance.

6.3 Data Processing

6.3.1 * Data Preprocessing Ensures Accuracy and Model Performance, Involving:

Data Cleaning: Handling missing values (mean/median replacement or removal), addressing outliers (IQR or Z-score), and correcting data entry errors.

Data Processing: Clinical indicators like blood pressure, cholesterol, and blood sugar were cleaned and prepared for model input.

6.3.2 *Data Normalization:

Min-Max Scaling normalizes values to the range [0,1].

Z-score normalization standardizes data using: $z = \frac{(x-mean)}{std}$ reducing the impact of large deviations.

6.3.3 *Feature Extraction:

Python tools like Pandas are used to extract key features.

A correlation matrix identifies features strongly associated with cardiovascular disease risk.

6.3.4 *Data Splitting:

The dataset is split into training (70%) and testing (30%) sets using train test split from Scikit-learn, ensuring randomness.

6.3.5 *Cross-Validation:

5-fold cross-validation ensures model generalization, reduces overfitting, and evaluates performance across multiple subsets of data for reliable results.

The preprocessed data is split into training and testing sets to evaluate model performance. Cross-validation is applied to optimize accuracy and prevent overfitting. Model performance is assessed using precision, recall, and F1-score to compare and select the best model for cardiovascular disease prediction.

6.4 Experimental Results

6.4.1 Logistic Regression Model

The effectiveness of the Logistic Regression model in predicting cardiovascular disease was evaluated using the target variable "target." A correlation matrix identified key features associated with "target," including 'sex,' 'cp,' 'fbs,' 'restecg,' 'exang,' 'slope,' 'ca,' and 'thal.' The dataset was split into 70% training and 30% testing. The model was trained with up to 1000 iterations to ensure convergence, and its performance was assessed using Precision, Recall, and F1-score to measure prediction accuracy.

To address overfitting, the study applied L1 and L2 regularization, reducing model complexity and preventing overfitting to unnecessary data details.

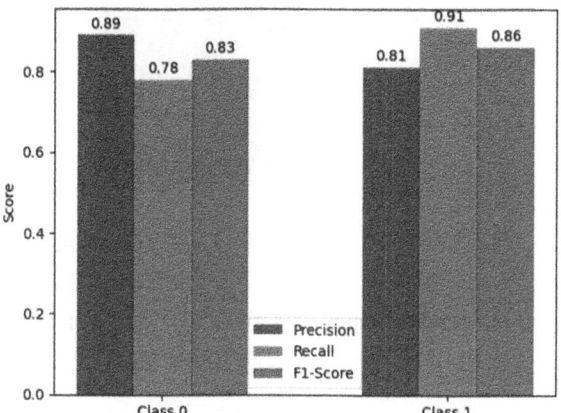

Fig. 2. Logistic Regression Model Results

Figure 2 demonstrates the performance of the Logistic Regression model, evaluated using Precision, Recall, and F1-score. The model shows strong accuracy, particularly for class 1 (at-risk), with a precision of 81% and recall of 91%. For class 0 (not at-risk), precision is 89% and recall is 78%. The F1scores for class 0 and class 1 are 0.83 and 0.86, respectively. Overall, the model performs well with minor imbalances between classes.

Figure 3 shows that Logistic Regression performs well in classification, achieving an 89% detection rate for class 0 (not at risk) and an overall accuracy of 86%. However, the model is better suited for linear problems and struggles to capture complex relationships in nonlinear features, such as ST slope or maximum heart rate.

6.4.2 Neural Network Model

Cardiovascular disease prediction is built with 7 layers, including 1 Sequential layer, 3 Dense layers, 2 Dropout layers, and 1 output layer. The model uses 13 features as input with a ReLU activation function and is trained using Keras over 50 epochs with a batch size of 10. The dataset is split into 80% training and 20% testing using Scikit-learn.

To address overfitting, the following techniques were applied:

Dropout: Randomly drops 25% of neurons in hidden layers to improve generalization.L2 *Regularization:* Limits large weight values using a kernel regularizer (0.001) to reduce model complexity.

Early Stopping: Monitors validation loss and halts training if no improvement occurs.

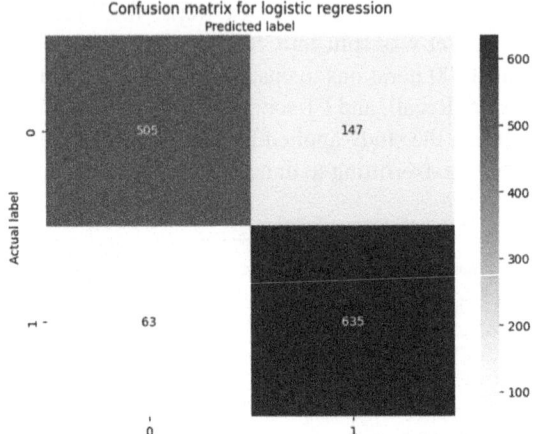

Fig. 3. Confusion Matrix of Logistic Regression

Cross-Validation: Ensures reliable performance evaluation across multiple data subsets.

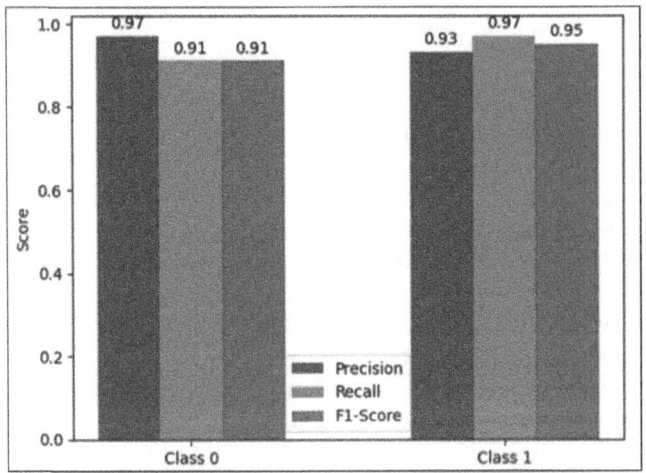

Fig. 4. Results of the Neural Network Model

Figure 4 illustrates the performance of the Neural Network model, emphasizing its high classification accuracy. The results highlight the impact of optimization techniques such as Dropout and Regularization in reducing overfitting and enhancing overall performance.

On the test dataset, the model achieves strong classification results:

Precision: 0.97 for class 0 (97% of predictions for this class are correct) and 0.93 for class 1.

Recall: 0.91 for class 0 and 0.97 for class 1 (indicating excellent detection rates).

F1-Score: 0.91 for class 0 and 0.97 for class 1, demonstrating overall high effectiveness with slight performance imbalance between classes.

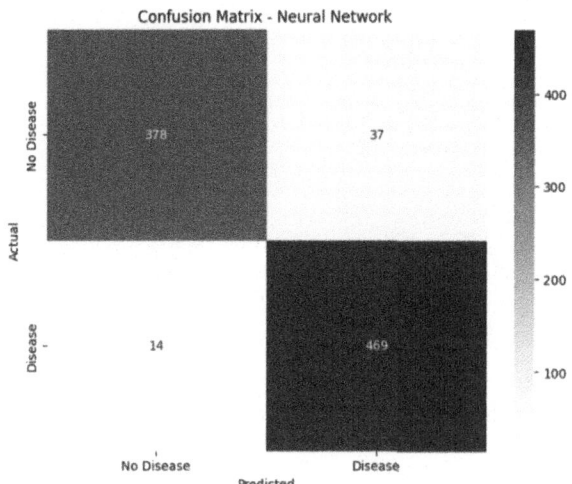

Fig. 5. Confusion Matrix of the Neural Network Model

Figure 5 shows that the Neural Network achieves 95% accuracy, attributed to its multi-layer architecture with a Dropout rate of 0.25 and L2 Regularization to reduce overfitting.

6.4.3 Random Forest Model

The Random Forest model was trained with 70% training and 30% testing data, testing n_estimators from 100 to 1000. To prevent overfitting, cross-validation optimized parameters (e.g., max_depth = 6, max_features $\approx$ 3), and bootstrap sampling improved generalization.

Figure 6 provides information on the performance of the Random Forest model, particularly its high classification accuracy.

The Random Forest model demonstrates excellent performance on the test dataset, achieving high accuracy. For class 0, precision is 99% and recall is 95%, while for class 1, precision is 96% and recall is 99%. Both classes achieve an F1-score of 0.97, reflecting the model's overall strong performance.

Figure 7 illustrates the Random Forest model's classification performance, achieving 97% accuracy by combining multiple decision trees. Techniques like bootstrap sampling enhanced tree diversity, while parameter optimization for n_estimators and max_depth improved results. Key features such as maximum heart rate (thalach), ST slope (slope), and cholesterol (chol) significantly contributed to the model's outstanding performance.

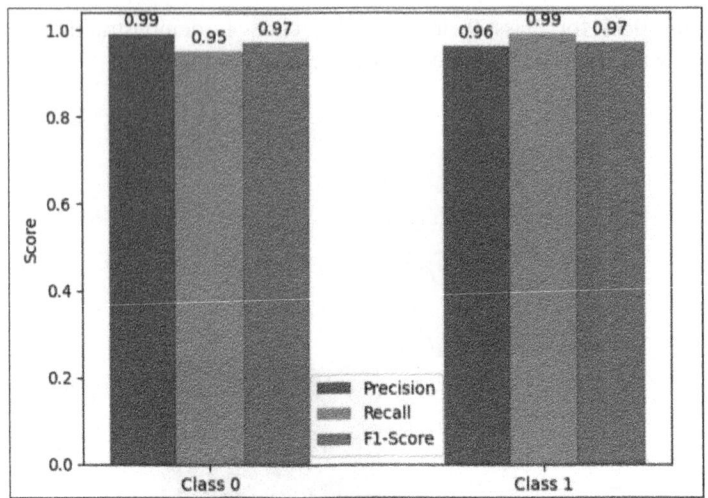

Fig. 6. Results of the Random Forest Model

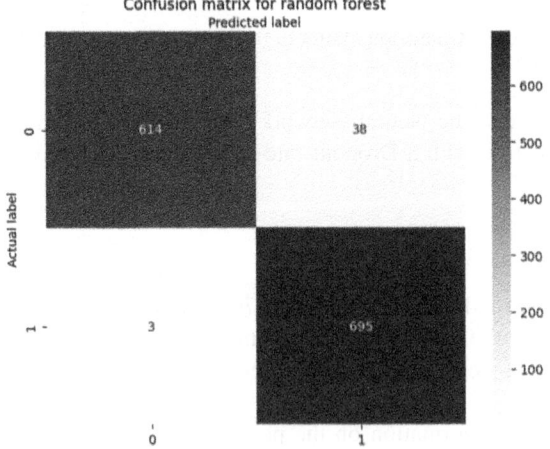

Fig. 7. Confusion Matrix of the Random Forest Model

6.5 Evaluation, Model Selection

6.5.1 Cardiovascular Disease Prediction Models

Logistic Regression, Random Forest, and Neural Networks show distinct performance differences. Logistic Regression achieves good accuracy (precision: 0.89 for class 0, 0.81 for class 1) but has a lower recall for class 0 (0.78). Random Forest outperforms with high precision (0.99 for class 0, 0.96 for class 1) and recall (0.95 for class 0, 0.99 for class 1), making it more effective at detection. Neural Networks also perform well but are not as strong as Random Forest.

6.5.2   Comparison with Previous Studies

This study's Random Forest model outperforms previous research by Nguyen et al. (2022), which achieved 87.5% accuracy, and Reddy et al. (2021), where Random Forest showed strong results with optimized parameters. Random Forest consistently performs better than Logistic Regression and Neural Networks due to its ability to combine decision trees, reducing prediction error. The study highlights the importance of data preprocessing and cross-validation in improving model performance.

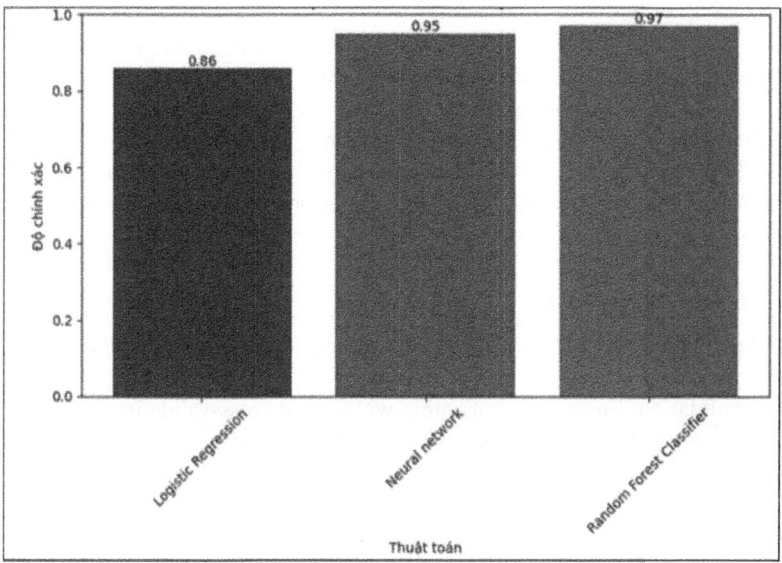

Fig. 8. Comparison of Results from the Experiments.

Figure 8 compares three models, with Random Forest performing the best due to its use of multiple decision trees. It achieves high accuracy in predicting cardiovascular disease using clinical data, with key features like maximum heart rate, ST slope, and cholesterol. Bootstrap sampling improves accuracy and reduces bias.

6.5.3   *Dataset Limitations*:

– *Sample Bias:* The data is limited to a specific region, affecting its generalizability.
– *Data Collection Period:* The 3-year timeframe may not capture long-term trends.

6.5.4   *Improvements*:

Future studies should collect data from diverse regions and extend the collection period to better capture long-term trends. The dataset's size and quality make Random Forest the ideal model for predicting cardiovascular disease.

6.6 Optimization of Methods

6.6.1 * Random Forest:

– Hyperparameter Optimization: Use grid or random search for values like n_estimators (100–1000), max_depth (to prevent overfitting), and max_features (e.g., square root of total features).
– Bootstrap Sampling: Improve generalization and reduce overfitting.
– Feature Selection: Remove irrelevant features to reduce noise.

6.6.2 * Neural Networks:

– Dropout Layers: Prevent overfitting by randomly dropping units.
– Early Stopping: Stop training when validation loss stops improving.
– Learning Rate Scheduling: Decrease learning rate as the model converges.
– Batch Normalization: Speed up convergence and improve generalization.
– Data Augmentation: Generate new data variations (e.g., adding noise or rotating images).

6.6.3 * *Logistic Regression:*

– Regularization: Use L1 (Lasso) to remove irrelevant features and L2 (Ridge) to reduce complexity.
– Cross-Validation: Ensure generalization with k-fold cross-validation.
– Feature Scaling: Normalize data (e.g., Min-Max or Z-score) for faster convergence.

7 Conclusion

This paper proposes a machine learning-based approach to predict cardiovascular disease using Random Forest, Logistic Regression, and Neural Networks, improving prediction accuracy over traditional methods. Results from clinical data at Tien Giang Provincial General Hospital show higher accuracy, demonstrating that machine learning can enhance cardiovascular diagnosis and improve healthcare quality. Additionally, techniques like Gradient Boosting and Support Vector Machines (SVM) have shown effectiveness, but they can be computationally expensive or less efficient with large datasets. The methods used in this study provide a good balance between interpretability and performance, particularly for the dataset in question.

References

1. Abubaker, MB., & Babayiğit, B.: Detection of cardiovascular diseases in ECG images using machine learning and deep learning methods. IEEE Trans. Artif. Intell. 373–382 (2023).
2. Ambrish, G., Ganesh, B., Ganesh, A., Srinivas, C., Dhanraj, Mensinkal, K.: Logistic regression technique for prediction of cardiovascular disease (2022)
3. Grandchamp des Raux, H., Ghilardi, T., Ossmy, O.: The effects of rewards on trial-and-error learning in school-aged children (2020)

4. Kruppa, J., Ziegler, A., Kongig, I.R.: Risk estimation and risk prediction using machine-learning methods (2012)
5. McGurnaghan, S., et al.: Cardiovascular disease prevalence and risk factor prevalence in Type 2 diabetes: a contemporary analysis. Diabet. Med. **36**(6), 718–725 (2019)
6. Nguyễn Thị Thu Hương và Đỗ Thị Hồng (2022) sử dụng phương pháp học máy Random Forest để dự đoán nguy cơ bệnh tim mạch ở người dân Việt Nam
7. Pham Dinh Khanh (2021) Neural network definition
8. Rajamhoana, S., Devi, C.A., Umamaheswari, K., Kiruba, R., Karunya, K., Deepika, R.: Analysis of neural networks based heart disease prediction system. 2018 11th International Conference on Human System Interaction (HSI) (2018).
9. Reddy, K.V.V., Elamvazuthi, I., Aziz, A.A., Paramasivam, S., Chua, H.N., Pranavanand, S.: Prediction of heart disease risk using machine learning with correlation-based feature selection and optimization techniques. In: 2021 7th International Conference on Signal Processing and Communication (ICSC), 228–233 (2021).
10. Samuel, A.L.: Some studies in machine learning using the game of checkers. IBM J. Res. Dev. **3**, 210–229 (1959)
11. Nandy, S., Adhikari, M., Balasubramanian, V., Menon, V.G., Li, X., Zakarya, M.: An intelligent heart disease prediction system based on swarm-artificial neural network (2021)
12. Su, X., Xu, Y., Tan, Z., Wang, X., Yang, P., Su, Y., Shang, L.: Prediction for cardiovascular diseases based on laboratory data: an analysis of random forest model (2020)

Author Index

© ICST Institute for Computer Sciences, Social Informatics and Telecommunications Engineering 2025
Published by Springer Nature Switzerland AG 2025. All Rights Reserved
H. X. Huynh et al. (Eds.): GOODTECHS 2024, LNICST 649, pp. 307–308, 2025.
https://doi.org/10.1007/978-3-032-01497-9

The manufacturer's authorised representative in the EU is Springer
Nature Customer Service Centre GmbH, Europaplatz 3, 69115 Heidelberg,
Germany. If you have any concerns regarding our products, please
contact ProductSafety@springernature.com

Printed and bound by CPI Group (UK) Ltd, Croydon, CR0 4YY

28/04/2026

02098515-0004